A LIFE IN
SERVICE

STORIES & TEACHINGS FROM
MALA SPOTTED EAGLE

HERMINE SCHURING

A Life in Service
© 2019 by Hermine Schuring

ISBN (Print): 978-1-54398-078-3
ISBN (eBook): 978-1-54398-079-0

The wounded healer is the person who has gone through suffering, sometimes great, and as a result of that process has become a source of great wisdom, healing power and inspiration for others. They can transcend it and successfully lead themselves into a path of service.

Carl Jung: the archetype of Chiron, The Wounded Healer

"*Mala showed me by his teachings and by his example how to find a deep connection to Mother Earth and within my own being, which builds the foundation for a good life. He showed me the essence of it all. I feel I am returning to a place that has always been there, but I have now shed light upon it and can finally feel it in myself. It's like a homecoming.*

Mala is the connector per se. Deeply connected within himself and to his culture, the Earth, and Creation, he connects others through his example and teaches about the importance of this reconnection."

A comment from one of Mala's workshops,
recorded in Graz, Austria

CHAPTER 3: THE NORTH   177

PREFACE

S hortly after having started our book project, Mala had a powerful dream, which he knew was important to share with me. The message of the dream told him it would take at least four years to accomplish the book. He was a little hesitant how I would take this information, since he assumed I'd be upset about the length of time it was prophesying. As a matter of fact, I was immediately relieved. What initially had started out as an idea embraced naively on my end had already grown into something far bigger than I had ever imagined. Far from what I expected to be doing, namely just writing down and formulating Mala's recorded words in book form, something else had emerged: a journey Mala and I were embarking on that would eventually be reflected and expressed in a book.

After the first recordings were made in autumn of 2012, I started with some attempts in written form. I saw myself as the channel to configure Mala's spoken words into written words. My goal was that -- while reading -- one would hear Mala speak. I was to become a kind of in-between adapter from audio into visual and vice versa. Usually when people listen to Mala, they are captured by the way he speaks, not only by the content, but also by the tone of his voice, using simple words and phrasing simple sentences, yet going to the heart of things.

As an indigenous person being brought up around traditional Native American elders, thus coming from an oral tradition, his power lies in passing on knowledge by speaking from the heart, reaching people by telling compelling stories. This is emphasized by the energy of his presence and amplified by the use of his drum and his singing voice. Listening to him stirs something inside of you, awakening old memories of sitting around the fire during long winter nights, listening to stories being told over and over again. Or sitting quietly in nature waiting for the rain to pass and sharing insights with each other, or being taught as a youngster by an elder how to deal with a problem in life. You can call it memories or you can call it a sense of longing for something lost and forgotten. It has a magical quality to it that touches your heart and spirit.

It happened to me when I first met him in 1995 and heard him speak while he was sitting under a tree with a group of people gathered around him. He had come to Europe to be part of the Discover Life Festival, celebrating for two weeks on the Danube Island in the capital of Austria, Vienna, and I have witnessed it time and time again with other people who came to his talks and workshops. Mala embodies this link to times gone by but affirms that we all have an indigenous part in us that is connected to every bit of the Universe, to the Mother Earth, to Life and to Nature. He awakens our spirits and opens our hearts when he speaks and sings but is never intrusive, waiting till the time is right, only speaking when you are willing and ready to listen.

The decision to finally write down his teachings and stories came after a long process of knowing how difficult it would be to match the effect his spoken words and voice have on people with plain written words black ink on white paper. Was it possible to grasp that energy and transform it? Could we capture that frequency and reach people at a heart-level, get across that feeling of being stirred, being touched within? It was a huge undertaking with high stakes! Mala had been asked many times to write down what he was saying, was being urged to do so because his message was important to share. Mala himself always emphasized that he was only speaking from the heart and he didn't consider himself anyone special, no better or less than others. He did say he realized his purpose in life was to go out and reach people from all walks of life. Besides going on speaking tours, a book could become a part of it and add an extra layer. He never felt comfortable with writing it on his own nor with anybody else offering to do the writing for him.

That I became the person to do the writing was a process of its own. But somehow we were both guided to this point: Mala was ready to finally take that step to direct what he was sharing into a book, and I felt I was able to make a commitment to give my best to be the intermediary.

So we started recording, gathering topics and stories. It soon dawned on me how much work this task would mean, how much time it would consume to listen to the tape over and over again, write his words down in his style, grasp the content, and yet make it into a smooth reading experience as if the reader was listening to him speaking. I came to the understanding that I had unknowingly taken on a huge task and it needed my commitment on a higher level.

I have known Mala for many years and heard him speak on countless occasions, I have accompanied him and translated for him many times, witnessed him in ceremonies, taken part in sweat lodges, seen him solve difficult situations in a very special way – which I would later come to identify as a "typical Native" way. I have visited him on his homeland, met his family over there and traveled with him. Through all that he became a catalyst for major changes in my life, which were somehow meant to be.

Taking on the task of writing Mala's life stories down was an honor but also a promise to give it my very best, in order to create something that would not only merge his spoken words, stories, and teachings, but do justice to the traditional Native people at the same time. That would please his family, be received with joy by those that have met and been around him on his many travels and trips, and also go beyond that and reach people hopefully who have never met him and heard him speak. The ultimate goal was to write a book that could be a source of inspiration for any reader.

Now that was a big undertaking, and how on earth would I be able to accomplish that?!

I went back and forth between: "You are out of your mind. You have no writing experience at all. This is enormous!" and "Go ahead and try, do the best you can. You will be guided along the way!"

Mala had been very reluctant about ever wanting to have his stories written down. Coming from a verbal tradition, he was aware that in today's society the use of written information is widely used and also useful, but he recognized the danger in it at the same time. He wanted to prevent any abuse and wanted to be connected both to the writer and the book all the way.

On my end, I became aware of how much weight words actually carry. I felt the need to stay as close as possible to Mala's own vocabulary. Yet I couldn't deny I had a personal impact on the book as well. Not only by choosing certain topics and interviewing him, but also in adding some of my own experiences along the way.

Mala's own life vision has been to build a bridge between the Native perspective and Western culture, and for people to learn from each other along the way. I was now part of that bridge.

When he shared his dream of the book as a process of four years, my sense of relief was that I could take my time. Even more so: those four years totally made sense! They symbolized the four directions, which are at the core of the Native American belief system and Way of Life. We both understood that the four directions represented four different energies that needed to be incorporated in this book, making it into a circular creative project and yet at the same time to have an ultimate linear goal in the form of a book.

Those four energies of the East, North, West and South were to be reflected in the making of the book, in the process itself and in its content. Where and how we did not know and it wasn't important. All we knew was that it felt right in our hearts. How obvious and beautiful to write under the guidance of those energies and to create it as a circle! We needed to internalize the cycle of the four directions and live through it in the journey of creating this book.

This leaves me to express my hope that the words in this book may carry good energy and spark a positive change towards thinking, speaking, and living from the heart. Enjoy reading and make your own journey of it.

Hermine Anne Petra Schuring, 2015, Vienna, Austria

EDITOR'S NOTE

I met Mala back in 1995 when he first came to Austria. His teachings spoke to me, and I also enjoyed his Talking Circles and drumming. When Hermine asked me to edit this book (her mother tongue being Dutch, coloring her English somewhat) my whole body responded with a strong flow of energy. I love language and linguistics, and have been self-employed since 2002 with energy work, translation, correction, and editing, later also Human Design. I am completely bilingual in English/German, with a Master's degree in translation. The challenge here was finding a synthesis: the native tradition of oral stories meeting the written word. Hermine and I decided that keeping Mala's rhythm and flow was more important than rendering totally "perfect" sentence structure and grammar to honor and deliver as closely as possible Mala's characteristic way of speaking. I also sought to keep Hermine's unique style as much as possible.

Thus, dear reader, I now invite you to enjoy an acoustic journey through time, letting your imagination take flight on the wings of Mala Spotted Eagle's stories...

Christina Müller, July 2019, Vienna, Austria

INTRODUCTION

In traditional Native American culture one learns through the examples one lives with, in other words from your elders and the community you are a part of. The indigenous Way of Life is embedded in the culture, the ceremonies, the daily life, and work. We didn't learn through books and writing things down. We shared stories and repeated them over and over again.

I was lucky to grow up around a lot of people still living according to the traditional Native Way of Life and my life task has been to share the ways of my people, largely through talks and giving workshops while traveling around in the United States and several countries in Europe.

At one point I decided to go ahead with the writing of a book, because it is an opportunity to reach more people without meeting them personally. Hopefully, people will, after reading the book, be touched by it and are able to look at life from a different perspective and maybe find a different approach towards spirituality.

This book is about sharing what was passed on to me, and is shared from my heart. It is not about me personally, although a lot of the teachings mentioned in the book are explained through my examples and the lessons I have experienced throughout life. I am far from flawless, as all of us are, but I hope that the reader is able to look beyond personal aspects in my life and resonate with some of these teachings and ways.

My vision for this book is, as it has also been in my talks and workshops, to raise awareness about how all life is connected, and to demonstrate that you are not separate from your surroundings. By taking responsibility for your thoughts, words, and actions, and by sharing your gifts with the world, you are part of Creation. When you accept Nature as it is, Spirit as it is, and yourself as a spiritual human being, you become whole, and you add something valuable to the bigger whole, to the greater circle of life. It interacts and you are part of a bigger picture, even though you can't possibly see and know it all. That is where you have faith and just do your part. No more and no less.

Often I have seen myself building bridges between the indigenous way of approaching life and the western way of perceiving and living, and I envision this book contributing to that bridge.

Mala Spotted Eagle Pope

THE MEDICINE WHEEL

From here on, it is Mala who speaks and therefore "I" refers to him. Whenever this is not the case, it is mentioned clearly and for Hermine the italic form is used.

The essence of the Medicine Wheel is that it never stops and functions without a beginning or an end. It is creating and recreating over and over again. You have to bear in mind that the circle is not one-dimensional. It is not flat but it is like a multidimensional round ball. You as a person are interacting with that Wheel and you are influenced by it and at the same time you also influence it by your presence. Native People also like to look at it as a round spider web that has many layers and connections and cross points: a multidimensional grid, a huge network of energy.

Cultures that live further away from the equator are faced with the repetition of the four seasons, and their daily lives are influenced by the patterns of weather, temperature, and amounts of daylight and darkness shifting through the course of a year. So naturally over time a cyclic system was refined with four major directions.

The Medicine Wheel and the four directions in essence hold every aspect of life.

Native Americans consider the four directions a symbolical representation of life upon Mother Earth. It relates to the rising of the sun, night and day, the four seasons and the four colors of people. The Medicine Wheel encompasses everything as we know it and in each of the directions you'll find different elements of nature or emotional and psychological aspects that are connected to that particular direction.

The purpose is symbolical for us humans: a sense of direction unfolds, and some sort of order to live by. It gives a point of reference in human life from where your own spirit can grow and evolve together with everything around you. You cannot separate these matters.

Through spiritual practices like prayer, consciousness in your way of thinking and ceremonies you raise your awareness and become more in balance within yourself and with everything around you. When we make our prayers in the morning at sunrise, we address the four directions by using simple wordings. I took over the prayer of my father, who came from the Cherokee tribe: "To the East where the sun rises, to the North where the cold and the winter come from, to the South where the heat and the light come from, to the West where the sun sets…"

But the four directions represent much more than that. When the sun rises, it naturally means the starting of a new day but can also refer to anything that begins and is created fresh and anew. When the sun sets, it also means the end of the day and the beginning of the darkness and the night, which you could also explain as the closing of your life, the crossing over to the other side at the end of your days. So the East implies much more than just the rising of the sun and the West refers to a lot more than the place where the sun sets.

Most tribes have different colorings of the four directions. Often black and blue are swapped or there are different directions for yellow, white or red. Also the order and structure of the directions are filled in differently. The Western Shoshone, which is my maternal tribe, associate the West with death; for the Cherokee the South represents the place where the ancestors and spirits live. The Western Shoshone also connect the West to water. The further away the tribes live from each other geographically, the bigger the changes are within the Medicine Wheel naturally, because it is influenced by nature and cultural differences. Sometimes it is confusing, also for me, but I try to flow with the energy of the moment and what the people involved in the ceremony are connected to.

When I was young my elders told me that the original people of an area carry the energy of that place, not only through physical adaptation, but also through the emotional, mental and spiritual energy that is taken in. There is a reason for that, they said.

If you look at a certain geographical area this has a certain unique spiritual energy. The physical outlook of an area, which shows in the presence of mountains or hills, rivers or lakes, dry desert or humid climate, determines which trees grow, which plants flourish, which animals are attracted and survive, which insects are present. Each has its own specific energy, whether it's the trees, the birds, the stones, the water. Naturally the terrain, the climate and creatures that live there also affect the people that inhabit that area. The people feed on those specific plants and animal life and adapt to their surroundings. All these aspects show in their physiognomies: in the desert where I grew up, the people are dark-skinned and shorter and heavier; in the hilly forest area where my father grew up, the people's skin is lighter and they are much taller and slimmer. This comes naturally. But like I mentioned before, there is more to it than just genetically adapting to a place. The people also take in the energy of that place by living there for many generations. People are influenced by the air they breathe, the vibrations of the earth they step on, the spirits that live in the area and the communication between all those existing energies. The spiritual energy of the area in the end also shows in the physical looks. The people become literally part of the energy of the area. It is fascinating to observe!

Not that many places exist anymore where you can still witness people having lived undisturbed for hundreds of years. Throughout history, people have been moving around; they practiced intermarriage and mixed their genes. That is just the course of things and is meant to be. But if I stumble upon an area where people haven't intermarried, it's thrilling to find out certain characteristics that all the inhabitants seem to have.

With these developments and adaptations, the different ceremonies came into being, just as did the Medicine Wheel with the four directions, the colors and other allocations. They were distilled perfectly from the area. Overall there is consensus: four directions and the circle of life in general are found everywhere. But the colors and the different meanings that went along with it were a mirror of the energy of that specific area.

Every direction has a physical quality to it but is also tied to the person who thinks of the East in a certain direction from where he or she stands and of the West in a certain direction. Directions are truly points of reference, depending on where your physical body is present in geographical terms. For me living in the West of the United States, the states on the Atlantic coast are the eastern states, but Europe is even more East for me. Of course, when I am in Europe this point of reference changes and Austria is then considered a country in the eastern part of Europe, and the Netherlands for instance lie on the west coast.

Just as our personal physical point of view changes depending on where we are on the planet, the symbols change and vary depending on tribal and cultural differences.

All those different circles however, contain all the many aspects and help you throughout your life by offering a point of reference and giving your life a sense of direction and connection to the greater picture: the Circle of Life.

Basically, the message of the Medicine Wheel is simple yet profound: everything around us carries spirit, has energy. We are all related; everything is connected and happens for a reason and we all have a purpose in the sacred Circle of Life.

CHAPTER 1

THE EAST

Hermine:

The initial idea of the book sparked in the fall of 2012 in Vienna, Austria - representing the East. Here the first attempts of recording and having an outline for its content took place.

I would like to share my thoughts on my understanding and personal interpretation of the East in reference to the book. The sun rises in the East, and at dawn a new day begins. When you widen this perspective you can see it as the start of a project or a plan that unfolds itself. When I started out for Europe the very first time, I traveled not only literally to the East, but also in the sense that I embarked on a journey that built the bridge which ultimately led to the creation of this book.

It started with my opening up to the people from Europe, whom I had up to that point in my life considered as the cause for a lot of hurt and wrongdoing performed against the Native peoples over in the Americas. I carried prejudice inside and had closed my heart and mind to them.

The East to me not only represents the start of something new, but also the phase of introspection within and then seeing the whole picture and getting a wider view. This happened when I came over to Europe and met people face to face while traveling to different countries.

I realized that I had been very wrong in my judgment and imagination and I met many people of good hearts whom I felt comfortable with. It created a big shift inside of me and helped me to open up my narrow-mindedness and put me on a whole different journey than I had ever expected. The Eagle, which to my people is the bird connected to the East and which I carry in my name, finally had matured enough and flew up higher to have the wide-angled perspective. My purpose in life unfolded itself and let me experience new habits, people, and cultures, which changed my way of thinking.

When I look back, I also realize that through meeting Hermine in Austria on my first trip to Europe, a relationship began that was much more than a deep personal connection but was meant to result in this book. We started the journey already back then, we just weren't aware of it yet. I knew inside when I saw Hermine for the first time that she would be very important in my life: Spirit told and showed me this clearly. So in that sense, the East is the opening of a pathway for me to become a speaker and for Hermine and me to come together in the writing of this book.

Certainly inspiration comes to mind while thinking of the East and in relation to the book. Originally I was inspired because my children asked me to share with them about my life: "Why don't you write it down, Dad?"

Later on others encouraged me to follow up on that wish. My personal inspiration became more than just the sharing of what happened to me in my life, but much more the sharing and passing on of the knowledge of the elders and the Old Ways, since I had been brought up around those older generations. I thought it was of great importance to pass on this source of information considering what we as humans are struggling with nowadays and the consequences our behavior has on the Mother Earth as a whole.

I hope this book can inspire people to look at things differently, change their way of thinking and can help people in their lives. It might be just

one little story that sticks in somebody's mind or touches a person within
-- that would already make me happy.

Hermine:

*Mala spoke these words on my trip to the US in September
2017 while I was visiting him in Eugene, Oregon in the Senior
Living Community where he lived. We were about to finish the
manuscript of the book and again I felt Spirit carrying the project
in a strong way. On the day before my departure, we stood on the
little balcony of his small apartment at sunrise, overlooking a
parking lot. There were some trees in front of us and we could see
the rising sun only around the corner of the block. It was not how
we used to do the sunrise ceremony, going out on the land, making
a fire sometimes, drumming and singing out loud. We didn't
want to wake the elderly neighbors, so we said our prayers quietly
and sang softly, but this didn't lessen the focus of our intent. The
smell of sage was in the air and it felt good. A few minutes later
a flock of wild turkeys arrived at the scene. For Native people,
Wild Turkey has been associated with honoring Nature and the
Earth, and encourages us to value our sources of nourishment
and be in a harmonious relationship with the earth: a symbol
of abundance and at the same time of contentment, satisfaction
and having enough. Turkeys were often used as giveaways to
other tribes. In modern American times the turkey has become
an important part of Thanksgiving Day, which commemorates
the pilgrim's first harvest. Although this celebration is in its heart
also about sharing food in the community with gratitude and
still carries the same message of Turkey, a lot of the honoring
and being respectful to the resources of Nature and the Earth has
dwindled. I can't stop myself from wondering about what price
the indigenous tribes had to pay for the taking of their land by*

the European invaders: the loss of their culture, their languages, the genocide of many of their tribes. What a paradox that the invaders used the Native giveaway symbol for giving thanks, although they took almost everything from the indigenous people and gave so little in return.

What a beautiful teacher Mother Earth is! By reflecting on what the turkey stands for, I gain another layer of understanding. It never ceases to amaze me, and I am deeply grateful for all the lessons I have learned and the incredible experiences I have lived through while on this journey.

Mala carries the Eagle Spirit in his name, and both the ability to focus as well as having the gift of overview are part of that Medicine. Eagle can fly the highest of all birds, comes closest to the Creator and carries vision. It scans everything below while it spans its wings, then tunes its focus to an aspect or detail which it can see very clearly at the same time. The way Mala described the creation of the book shows that wider view from above, where all the different streams coming from many directions flowed together and became a larger pool of information. Sometimes we know these things in advance, are maybe shown them in a vision, and sometimes all of a sudden, the veil lifts and you get a clear insight into that woven tapestry. Native people might say: Sunlight shines on Grandmother Spider's Web.

The East gives a spark of light, a golden ray of the sun and the possibility of embracing a new beginning every day, while at the same time the wheel continues as certain things come to an end or a life ends.

Where I come from

My full name is Mala Spotted Eagle Pope.

When Native people introduce themselves to other people, it is common to explain your family heritage and which area of the country you come from. It is important to put yourself in reference to your relations. Then it is considered okay to speak about yourself.

My mother was a Western Shoshone, native to the Nevada desert and was named Helen Spotted Fawn. My father was called John Rolling Thunder Pope: he was from the Cherokee Nation and was brought up in the Oklahoma area. Since a lot of the Native American people are organized in a matriarchal way, my father moved, after he had married my mother, into the Western Shoshone tribe.

When my mother was young, she worked in a restaurant as a waitress. My father was a wandering man; he traveled all over the country, working on and off jobs all over the place. One day he stopped to get something to drink and eat and that is where he saw my mother the first time. I guess he decided to stay. He got a job at the railroad and married my mother. Being an Indian, he was actually very lucky to get that job. You see, my father being Cherokee had very light skin. The people from that area, my people, the Shoshones of Nevada, are very dark skinned. So they never figured my father was Native, they assumed he was mostly white. He registered under John Pope, leaving his Native middle name "Rolling Thunder" out. After some years he was offered a promotion and had to sign a paper stating that he had 100 % white blood heritage. I have seen the paper with my own eyes. My father couldn't sign it since he would have to deny his Native heritage. So he never got the promotion and stayed in the same job for all those years.

I was born and raised in the high mountain desert of Nevada next to a town called Carlin, which originally was called Fort Carlin, since it had been a military base for a long time. We lived together with some other

Indian families on the edge of the town, which was not reservation land. We only had gravel roads, in contrast to the town where there were paved streets and where the white people lived. There is no exact record of my time of birth, but I was registered in the hospital as being born on the 8th of December 1952.

Our home was a traditional Native American household. We lived according the traditional spiritual Way of Life. Over the years my mother became considered a so-called Clan Mother and my father was a well-known healer and Medicine Man. Our house was open to people from all walks of life, and apart from our direct family we usually had many visitors from all over sharing meals with us.

Remembering the rest of my family, there aren't many relatives that I can think of. I had some cousins from my mother's side. And there was one uncle, my mother's brother that I recall we visited from time to time. I think she had three brothers and two sisters in total, but I only met Uncle Leo; he died when I was about eight or nine. All the others had passed on. You have to remember that in those days there wasn't a high survival rate amongst Indians. There were so-called accidents; things the cops or cowboys would do to them. I don't know any family members on my father's side. I know a lot of them had been killed off. I never met any of my grandparents from either side. My father grew up with one of his grandmothers up in the hills. All I know about her is that she was very strict. I don't have any stories to share about the rest of my family. We never spoke about them much and I never asked about them either. I guess, because you could feel it: there wasn't a happy history to be told.

We intentionally didn't live on reservation land since it would mean we needed to follow special Indian reservation laws and not the usual US laws that apply everywhere else. Life on reservations, especially in those days back then, was extremely desolate and people lived under poor conditions with no respect for their culture and traditions and with no positive perspective for the future. It was a very hard place to be.

All together we were six siblings. I had a brother and sister that were from my father's previous marriage. My mother already had a son too before my parents got together. Those siblings were all a lot older than me. Then I have two sisters who are younger than me. One of them was adopted into our family and one is from my mother and father. Today only myself, one brother and two sisters remain.

The name I am called by is Mala: it is a Cherokee word and means the "Strong One". Spotted Eagle is the Shoshone part of my name, which is "Beaguina" in the Shoshone language.

My mother was fluent in Shoshone, but wasn't allowed to speak her language while she was in Boarding School. When she came out of that system, she pretty soon got to know my dad and spoke mostly English from then on. Due to the fact that my father was from another tribe, they couldn't speak their Native languages when they were together, so they used English instead. She did speak Shoshone when she was with her friends, but to us, her children, she didn't use her own mother tongue much. Even when I was little I cannot recall my mother speaking in Shoshone to me. This is the reason why I refer to myself as Mala Spotted Eagle and never speak of Mala Beaguina. I was simply never called this way.

At some point our mother did offer to teach us some Shoshone, but in those days I wasn't so interested in learning the old language. As a young person, I didn't realize how important a language is for one's culture.

I learned a few words, but really not much. When I grew up, there was a huge pressure to not speak the Native language. Although it wasn't forbidden any more, you would be looked down upon when you spoke any Indian language. Being an American Indian was by far the lowest on the scale of all the different cultures and colors in the United States at that time. At the top of the list were the white people, and then came the black people, then the Mexicans, and finally the Indians. As an Indian you really weren't treated very nicely in those days; a lot of hurtful things happened, so you didn't want to draw extra attention to yourself, you know, not stick out. It was about trying to blend in with the dominant culture.

Like I said before, my mother did offer to teach us sometimes, but both my parents believed that it was our free choice to learn and they didn't want to push it on us. Although we lived together with some other Shoshone families, even as kids amongst each other we all spoke English. None of our peers spoke in their Native tongue. It was somehow not the time to speak your Native language. Compared to nowadays, where young people take pride again in speaking the old languages. Times have fortunately changed a lot.

Name-giving

In the Native tradition, in the way I was taught, our name reflects our connection to nature and spirit. We say we are all born with a special and personal connection in nature. Sometimes we also refer to it as our spirit totem or animal totem. The connection I am talking about takes it even further than just something in nature that has meaning to you and you feel good about. It exists on a much deeper level within you, as much physically and emotionally as well as spiritually. It can be anything, like water or fire or an animal, a tree, clouds, anything in nature. It is there to help you and to teach you, it gives you strength and it supports you. It can make you feel happy and strong - it can make you feel calm and centered. As you learn more about it and learn how to work with it, it helps you in your life. You can connect with it to get guidance, for protection, for many different things. As everything has two sides, strong points but also weaknesses, you also learn about duality. So by acknowledging those weak areas in nature, it teaches you something about your own weak parts and your own struggles in life too.

When a child is born, a spiritual or Medicine person who has understanding of how nature works is usually present outside where the birth is taking place. You see, they say that at the time of birth, something in nature will show itself in a striking way. So it is necessary that the observing person is someone who knows how nature normally works and can recognize the difference by being aware of any changes at the time of birth. There is a strong pull between the two, the child and that part in nature, and it will reveal itself by acting out of the normal order. In this way the connection the child has to nature and spirit will become clear and results in how you name it. We believe every person has a spiritual connection to something in nature and it will have meaning for the rest of your life.

There are different ways of naming a baby amongst the different tribes, but this is how I was taught and it basically comes down to that special connection to nature that gives you your name.

My name came to me a little differently though. When my mom was about six months pregnant, she was in the bedroom of our house. She had opened a window to let fresh air in, which was the kind you could open up halfway from the top to the bottom downward. It was a pretty big opening. My mom was lying on the bed while resting a bit and my father was sitting close by her. They were talking to each other about the new baby that was coming. They were startled when they heard a loud flapping sound and when they looked up, they saw a big eagle had landed on the windowsill in the opening of that window. It was sitting there looking right at them. They knew right away that something special was about to happen, because this is not what eagles normally do. They got all quiet and they both heard a voice coming from the eagle, speaking to them in their heads. My mother was told to open her hand and look at it: she had some white sperm in her hand, which represented me as the baby inside of her. The eagle told my parents what my name was supposed to be. He also spoke of my life's journey, how my life would unfold, with all the challenges and struggles, what I was supposed to do and the ways I was to be brought up. When the eagle finally finished speaking, it turned around and flew away. My parents checked with each other about what the eagle had said to them both and they each had gotten the same message.

When I was seven years old, they shared this prophecy with me and to be honest, as I grew up I had mixed feelings about it. My life was all laid out for me and it didn't leave me with a lot of choices. I was told: this is your path and the spirits are going to make sure you follow it. I would have rather had a life where everything was open. On the one hand the eagle spoke of many good things that were going to happen; on the other hand though, it spoke of the many challenges, strong struggles and hardships I would encounter through life. I have often tried to resist this path that I was told I should walk, trying to avoid it or to get around it, but it has been the foundation of my life and has made me to who I am. Basically when you live a spiritual life, you have no choice and I had to follow that path, whether I liked it or not. I have learned to accept it, but I also did things in my own way, as you will get to understand while reading this book.

Mala, "the Strong One", is the Cherokee part of my name and my father chose it for me. He told me he prayed over it for some time and this was the name that came to him. He didn't explain it any further.

My parents never told me specifically if it really was a spotted eagle that came to sit in that window. They are extremely rare or maybe even extinct. I was told that the white people had killed off the spotted eagles long ago. I looked it up once in an old book and found a picture of a North American spotted eagle. It's a species of its own, it is not a young eagle; it is a full-size white eagle covered with black spots.

Once in my life I saw a spotted eagle at Meta Tantay, the Indian Camp in Nevada I lived at for 10 years. I was the first person coming out of a sweat lodge, which was held in the middle of the desert with a lot of sagebrush all around it. Right in front of me on one of those sagebrush bushes sat a spotted eagle, looking at me and watching me. A few other people came out of the lodge and saw the eagle there. But then when more people came to join us, it flew away. But I knew it came especially for me - it wanted to share something with me. It was the only time I have seen the bird I am named after in nature.

Memories from Early Childhood

When I was little, we would sometimes go to a small Indian reservation, actually a so-called Indian colony[1], next to Battle Mountain, a town 50 miles away from where we lived. It's called this because there once was fought a huge battle between the Shoshone and the white people. On the reservation there were still a lot of traditional buildings, wickiups and teepees and so on. You know, we would visit some Shoshone families, bring some groceries, just to help out. My father, already in the position of spokesman for the tribe, was often asked to work on a legal issue or do some healing work on somebody.

I remember one time we went there. I must have been pretty little since I remember reaching up to hold my father's hand. My parents called us kids together and said: "We are going to have a lot of people, especially elders, coming to live with us. There has been another violation of the treaties." They explained: the white people from town, especially the ranchers, wanted the reservation land for their own use. The Indians, who had lived there for many generations, had managed to create some green pasture, which was an exception in Nevada, being mostly a desert state. Although Native

---

1   Indian Colony is basically an Indian reservation but only on a smaller parcel of land and mostly closer to a town. About 30 to 60 families usually live there; in Nevada you had Battle Mountain, Elko, Washoe, Las Vegas, Love Lock. Reno, Werington, Wells, and Winnemucca. A reservation is a much bigger piece of land. In total there are 32 Indian reservations and colonies in Nevada.
Both colonies and reservations are under BIA, both on Indian Land

people were running the Bureau of Indian Affairs, the so-called BIA, which was in charge of the reservations, white people were basically -- unofficially -- controlling the Bureau. With the help of the State government they had come up with a plan to put a highway that was going to be built right through the reservation, leading up to the town of Battle Mountain. Now, that was really a strange thing to do, because the existing highway came from another direction and they had to make like an extra half circle, miles away, just to make sure it would hit the reservation territory. So sure enough, this is what happened and you can still see it today, the highway makes a big loop before entering Battle Mountain. The ranchers got what they had been after, you know, their green grazing land. The reservation was moved to the other side of town, much smaller than what it was before, and basically on just barren soil where there was no room for pasture and green areas at all.

My parents offered their house to those who were forced off the old reservation land and about eight or nine people chose to come back and live with us. I remember as a child I would walk outside and see the women tanning hides, using cottonwood tree poles which they had stripped clean of the bark and made into thin, slick poles. The hides of the animals were thrown over the poles and the women worked really hard with special kinds of knives called "drawknives" to get the membranes of the hides. Then they flipped it over and would take off the fur. I also watched the older men when they were chipping arrowheads and spearheads using deer-antlers and buckskin. I loved to sit with them and listen and just be around them. A lot of times the women were also busy with basketmaking. My mom was well known for the making of buckskin moccasin gloves. People from all over would come and buy them from her, even ranchers, because they were very soft and warm and you could easily pick things up and still use your hands with them on. Nowadays hardly anybody can make those any more. I remember all these things very well growing up as a young child around the elders. There were times that all the older people would gather either in the house or somewhere outside and talk together. For some reason I was drawn to listen in on them. So I would hide some place close to hear what they were talking about. Years later of course, I found out that they always knew I was doing that and were actually happy about it. A lot of it was about issues they had to deal with, and also about what the white man was doing to them, about all the hardship and so on. But they also shared stories sometimes or talked about the old days and how things used to be. I just wanted to hear it all. Even if I didn't understand everything, it was important for me to be part of it, and I did that for years.

Yeah, those are good memories. There were also things that weren't so nice and easy in my childhood. As children we always had to do work around the house and some of it was pretty heavy and not so much fun.

I remember when I was about eight years old, my brothers and I had to dig out a hole underneath the house which would be turned into a root cellar for my father to use. The house didn't have a basement, so we had to build it from scratch. My two older brothers had to dig all the dirt out. We first made a ramp of dirt and I, being the youngest, had to haul all that dirt out with a little red wagon I had and dump it somewhere else on the property. We worked on it for a year, summer and winter, no matter what kind of weather.

When I was a young child, my father and other adults would take me out in the desert and show me things, talk about the animals, the herbs, where to find them, how to approach them, what they were for. They showed me where the springs were and how to look for them. They would explain how every part of the desert is alive and that it all has spirit. They taught me how you should treat every part of nature with respect. Sometimes they took me along when they were hunting and gathering herbs. At that time I didn't know about the prophecy of my path yet, but later on I understood that it was all part of the training already.

The desert was literally deserted of humans: you could walk, as they'd say, for a 100 miles in each direction and not meet a single person. At some point -- I must have been about seven years old -- I went out alone in the desert, sort of my backyard, so to speak. My plan was to take a different route each time to explore and get to know the whole area. I took my 22-caliber rifle with me, which is actually the smallest rifle with small bullets, good for hunting rabbits and ground squirrels, and suitable for a young kid like me. I wandered around for half a day and on my way back I started hunting so I would only have to carry my catch on the way back. We depended on the food from the desert for a large bit, so it was always welcomed to bring some food for everybody to share.

It made me feel at peace when I was out there, and I was never afraid. You know, I was brought up with Nature and Spirit and to me there was nothing strange about spirits talking to me or giving me signs. To me, going to town was dangerous and I didn't feel safe there. You had to be careful not to be shot at or hurt in some other way or be called all kinds of bad names. So I preferred to be out in the desert by myself where I wasn't bothered and I felt peaceful and welcomed.

My brothers and sisters had a different attitude towards our traditional Native way of living. They didn't like it and didn't follow this path like I did. Because I was taken out into the desert and got special treatment, they were resentful and jealous of me. I always tried to be extra nice to them so they would accept me. Their nickname for me was "Goody Two-shoes."

There is a little story that illustrates why. My parents had bought an abandoned "cat house". This name refers to the prostitutes, called "cats", who used to live and work in these houses. Prostitution was legal in Nevada in those days. It had four bedrooms to the side, a big living room, and in the back a kitchen and a bathroom. Because of its history the whole yard was littered with the broken glass of old liquor bottles. You could hardly walk around freely; it was just everywhere. My dad gave us the option to help clean the yard. He offered us five cents for each gallon of broken glass. Of course five cents isn't much, but as a kid you could buy some candy for it, which made it attractive. I thought: "Oh cool, I'll go for that! " So I started out picking up the glass pieces and filled the gallon can, got my nickel and went to the grocery store in town that wasn't too far away from home. It was enough to buy one package of juicy fruit gum, which had five sticks in it. At that time, there were six of us living in the house. So I came back proudly with my well-earned gum and by coincidence everyone was at home. I went around with my gum and offered everyone a piece of it, which didn't leave one for me anymore. But I didn't show it and I didn't care. It just felt nice to share and give away. When my siblings found out, they pointed to their heads and gave me my nickname "Goody-Two-Shoes".

My siblings were just normal teenagers and didn't think twice about certain things they did or didn't do. I was different in that sense and stood out. I was always trying to find balance in everything and be good. I gave everything away I had. My behavior sometimes irritated my brothers and sisters. They felt I was being phony, that I was trying to be too good and it wasn't for real. They couldn't understand why I was like that and thought I was doing it deliberately; they couldn't relate to it. It was the little things, you know. Like I refused to cuss or go along with some of the games they played. They thought I was trying to be better than them. But I did it because it made me feel good inside to share and it just made me happy. It had nothing to do with them at all. They compared my behavior to theirs and drew their conclusions from that. To give always felt good to me and my mother was very proud of me, because she always emphasized how important it is to give: it is the key to a traditional, spiritual Way of Life.

I was different from my brothers and sisters in other ways too, although I didn't realize it at the time. Already when I was little, I had dreams that told me something or that foresaw things. One of my gifts was having dream power. I would go and tell my parents about it and mostly in a day or two these premonitions would come true. I also had special experiences with animals and eagles. Or spirits just came and talked to me to tell certain things, you know, I didn't think much of it; I thought everybody was experiencing this and had no idea that it was something uncommon.

When I got to be seven years old, my parents told me how my name had come to me and what path I was supposed to walk. Pretty soon my siblings also knew and realized that was why I had a special position within the family and why the elders took me out on walks and explained things to me. It did create jealousies, and I was made fun of. When I grew older and I more openly chose to grow my hair long and be proud of being an Indian, the difference became even bigger between us. And yet I wanted desperately to belong and be accepted as one of them, so in turn I went out of my way to be accepted by them. They could tease me or even physically harass me, and I would never tell on any of them. Nevertheless I have always felt very connected to them, they meant a lot to me and still do.

One of the dreams I had had to do with my oldest sister. She was quite some years older than me and didn't live at our house anymore. I was about 12 or 13 and shared a room with my brother, sleeping in a bunk bed. He was staying over at a friend's house so I was by myself. In the middle of the night something woke me and I sat straight up in bed wide-awake. I felt there was a presence in the room and I saw a misty figure in front of me. I realized it was my sister and she started speaking to me: "Mala, I want you to know I have just crossed over but you don't need to be sad because I am doing fine. I am much happier now. You have to let mom and dad know that I'm not alive anymore but am doing okay. I will leave a sign for you to see." It was like a dream and very real at the same time and I fell asleep again. The next morning after I woke up, I was looking for the sign. I told you I was in a bunk bed. The two parts are usually attached together, top to bottom with bolts, but since these were long lost, we used thick nails that my dad had brought home from work, so the bed wouldn't fall apart. The nails were made out of very strong steel and were thick, normally used for trains on the rail-road-tracks, so no way you could move or bend them. They were hanging out of the holes on each side. My sister's spirit had bent each and every one of those metal spikes into a full circle, which for a human is impossible to do. She had visited me to pass on the message and leave a sign to prove it so that we were warned and somewhat prepared for what had happened.

I went to tell my parents that my sister had come to say she had passed away. At first they didn't want to believe me, but I told them: "No, she left a sign!" When I showed them, my parents, both very strong in their belief of spiritual ways, took this message for real and my mother started to cry, my father got really quiet. They knew it was true. A few hours later, we got a phone call from the police that she had died a tragic and violent death. My sister had gone away on a trip to Yosemite where she would stay for a few days. She was still very young, in her early twenties.

This is not a pleasant story to share, but it shows that when you are open to Nature and Spirit you can get really clear messages; you are connected to the other side, as well as to other levels of consciousness. When your own spirit and heart are open and receptive, this is a major source for knowledge, truth and connection. I was gifted in this way and was used to having dreams and premonitions. My parents have always supported this and never mocked me. On the contrary, they have guided me with the information I sometimes got and helped me to understand and accept it as a part of life.

Another time, I remember clearly what happened when we were going on a trip to a spring way out in the desert. We had fixed that spring up, dug it out more deeply and made it all nice with rocks around it. We went there every two weeks with a bunch of kids, 13 and 14 years old, to fetch water. This was considered much cleaner and purer water than the water that came out of the tap. My dad always said that this was good water to do medicine with. The night before I got a premonition as a warning. You know, it was that kind of a dream where you know it is a special dream, a dream where things are much clearer and somehow different from an ordinary dream. I saw our old army pickup truck with some of the kids in the back and the dirt road we were always taking. A huge boulder, which apparently had fallen onto the road, appeared just around the corner where you couldn't see it when you were coming from that direction. I saw how we crashed our car into that big rock and that people got badly hurt, some even killed, because the car tumbled over. So I told my dad about this dream before we left and we took off. When we came to that specific spot - I knew exactly where the curve in the road was - we slowed down and sure enough, around the corner there was the boulder. We were able to move it a little off the road and drive safely around it. That was a good day!

I had a number of dreams that foretold things. To me, that wasn't very special; you just grow up with these things. The elders and my parents always encouraged me to tell them about it, never to hide them. They helped me to understand them. I also had journeys that took me to other, far-away spiritual places, some heavy journeys, not always lighthearted. But some were extremely beautiful too. I remember a very powerful dream, when I was about ten years old that took me to the so-called Tree of Life[2]. The Tree of Life is the subject of many Native legends: it is said that as long as this tree stands, there is hope for the human beings, the two-legged ones. As soon as the Tree of Life dies, humans will not be able to survive and exist anymore. In my vision I took a long walk and came to this magnificent, enormous willow tree, which had rainbow-colored leaves, all of it vibrating with light and of extreme beauty. I recognized the Tree of Life immediately. It was telling me many things, and I stood under it for a long time. Then

---

2   In the movie Avatar by James Cameron (2009) the Tree of Life that plays such an important holistic role in the movie comes from this legend.

finally I came back. That vision has stayed with me until today and I will always carry it inside of me. I was so very happy there.

Teaching on Weather

When I was a young kid, around nine or ten, I loved the snow. I would sit in front of the window, just watching how the snowflakes fell down in winter. Nevada in the summer is extremely hot, but in winter we do get a lot of snow and it is quite the opposite, with extreme cold weather too. I loved the freshness and the quiet falling down of snowflakes layer upon layer on the earth. My parents observed my fascination for it and started to teach me things about the snow and wintertime. In our area the cold temperatures and snow are important and beneficial because it helps to crack open certain kinds of nuts which would otherwise not bring new seeds again the next season. The earth can rest beneath that white, cold layer and replenish. The mountain snow is essential for the creeks and rivers to fill up again in spring. The cold that comes along in winter helps to kill germs and bacteria that otherwise would explode in numbers. It brings balance in this way. It keeps the ecosystem healthy and strong. They told me also: "It is good that you like the snow but you should at the same time respect it. Getting to know the snow can really help you become stronger and healthier too." I asked how I could do that because I felt an urge to understand more. They said: "The most important thing is that you should learn to approach it without fighting it. Usually, when you look outside and it snows, your first reaction is to bundle up in a lot of clothes to go outside. But you shouldn't do that. You signal that you feel a need to protect yourself against the snow and that you can only confront yourself with the snowy conditions by putting on a lot of clothes. In that sense, you are already starting to fight the snow. You are actually signaling: "I'm in battle with you. I fear you and resist you."

But snow is part of nature, and if you want to be close to nature you have to allow it to be close to you. You should give it a chance to get to know you too. The only thing is though that you always need to be aware of its power and strength. If you don't respect the power of the cold, the fire, the water, whatever it is, you will end up getting hurt. You need to respect and honor it. As long as you do that, all those things from nature, like cold, fire and water will work with you. You need to learn to flow with it and not fight it."

Then my parents suggested that I should go sit outside and see how it would work for me, taking that information in account. So they pointed to a little chair, which had a thin cushion on it and told me to go outside, just as I was dressed now, in a pair of jeans and a t-shirt. I was actually excited about this prospect and went out immediately. They also pointed out to me not to dwell on feeling cold but only to honor and respect it. As soon as you dwell on something you give it more power: it gains strength and becomes more in your perception then it really is.

When I went out, I noticed the snow coming down slowly covering the grass and twigs on the earth. There was a dogwood bush close by, and I saw how it was being covered too. Then I thought: "This is what I'm going to do. I'm going to watch how the flakes fall down, as they cover up everything." When I took my place on the chair, I thanked the snow for being there and asked if there was anything it could teach me to be in a good way with it, if the snow could teach me to understand its ways. Then I just let it go and focused on the snowflakes. The first time I still had my tennis shoes on and I didn't stay out for very long. But I really enjoyed doing it, and every time it snowed I took the opportunity and sat with the snowflakes, watching them, observing them, enjoying their beauty. During that winter I used to sit for hours in a row, wearing no shoes at all anymore, not bothered by the cold. My parents were getting a little concerned about this new habit, but I was actually feeling comfortable doing this. Only upon coming back in the house, I would feel the cold, funny enough. While I was out there, I wouldn't feel it as much. I didn't feel warm either, but it was neutral.

As I was so much into it, my parents taught me more ways how to be with the cold, and I would like to share those ways with you here. When you feel the cold coming to you, you can perceive it as a coat you put on, like an extra layer that covers you. It just sits there and in a way protects you. You actively visualize how the cold is like a blanket on top of your skin and - very importantly - you give it thanks for what it does for the Mother Earth and welcome its beauty in. It is only on the outside of your skin and doesn't go deeper inside. Embrace it and observe your own body intensely; open your senses to how it affects you. Watch your own fear and physical reactions, they might not be as strong as you originally thought they would be. They change as you change your attitude towards it. In this way, you can actually become warm.

Then there is also the possibility to work with the heat within the Mother Earth. Deep down in her, she stores all that heat, that fireball at the core of her being. If you ask her if she is willing to send that heat up through to your feet, you will start to feel warm. First your feet get warm and then the warmth spreads through your whole body. Another way that they shared with me is to remember that as soon as you start to feel cold, you should not give in to that thought and feeling; thinking about it adds energy to that very thought of feeling cold. You should turn that thought around and remember the last time when you were feeling really warm. It can be when you were sitting in front of a fire or when you were in a bathtub or tucked really warm in your bed. Then you picture yourself in that warm and comfortable situation and visualize how this warmth spreads through you again. My parents said that it was important to utilize the last memory, because that one was more vivid and closer to you and the energy was still with you. When you're out in the cold and you focus your attention on this memory moment of warmth and heat, it will actually return to you.

This whole process you could describe as constantly shifting your focus while primarily having an attitude of gratefulness inside of you. You focus on a thought or a perception for a while, but never force it. You don't dwell on it either. You shift to another focus and stay with that for a while. At one point, your mind isn't important anymore and you are in a certain state where you experience great awareness with hardly any physical discomfort.

Essential is: no matter what kind of weather you encounter, the cold, the heat, rain, snow or wind, you have to welcome it in. It is all part of Nature and there is a reason and purpose that it is there in that form at that time.

Many people claim they want to connect more to Mother Earth. Yet they continue to see her in a negative way. They want to get closer to nature but at the same time, they want it the way they like it and not as it appears to them. I hear people talk badly about it or I hear them complain. Sentences like: "Oh, I can't handle it anymore. It has been raining for a week! It gets to my mood! I wish it would stop!" or: "This stupid wind is so terrible and awfully cold." Some people even use cusswords and swear. They argue with the weather and express a dislike or a fear of it. How many people are resisting the weather that is outside? How many people say they hate the cold or the rain? Most people react by wanting to put on a lot of clothes because they think they are going to freeze or be uncomfortable outside. They don't like to get wet from the rain and they put sunglasses on as soon as the sun is out. Many people are afraid of the darkness and don't dare to be outside then. It's too scary for them because they were taught that 'bad' things could happen at night. They were taught that if you don't put the right clothes on, you'll get sick, catch a cold or get sunburned.

They do not appreciate it the way it is. But that is essential! We have to see the sacredness and beauty of Nature at all times, instead of perceiving it in a negative way. We should be grateful for it and acknowledge its presence, whatever kind of weather might show up and just be happy for it. If you welcome it in, you'll start off with having a positive relationship with nature.

Embrace the beauty and the sacredness of nature and welcome all aspects of life! If you respond with fear, you actually fear your own being, as you consist of those exact same elements. You are a part of those things; you are not separated from it.

When you start practicing this later in your life, you have to overcome the layers of habit in your way of thinking and your automatic emotional responses, which is a challenge, but you can always start making little changes. Don't expect straight away to sit outside in the snow for hours. Be patient with yourself and watch yourself and your responses closely. Little by little your way of perceiving will change and it will reflect in how the weather affects you and your body. We also have to keep in mind that our physical bodies do have different abilities and limits. We are not all built in the same way.

Think about and imagine yourself speaking positively about the weather and observe how it affects you. Notice how you automatically are defensive about the weather and think and speak negatively. Turn those thoughts and words around consciously: speak about the good the rain does, how the sun's rays warm the earth and how the night brings peace and quiet to everything. Use your imagination and remember all the different aspects of the weather you can think of that are actually beneficial.

I also witness people who say they appreciate nature and are aware of how important it is and how close they feel to it, yet when it comes to their own issues, all of a sudden there is a separation. Partly the old prejudices and belief systems seep through; partly it's negative experiences they have been going through that are in the way.

I am not saying you should go out and let yourself freeze and harm yourself, but you can open yourself up, leave your comfort zone a little, and in doing so, get much more in tune with nature. When you start feeling cold, you can still make a decision to put something warm on when it gets to be too much for you and you really feel you can't handle it anymore. It shouldn't lead to the point where it's hurting you, but you can gradually get used to being outside more without any need for protecting yourself.

Respect for nature is different than having a fear of it. Your chance lies exactly there though - to turn something around where you feel the most resistance. If you go out for a little bit when it is snowing or below zero without putting on extra layers and you just sense the cold and welcome it in, then you are actually connecting with that part of nature and it doesn't rule and have power over you.

Corbin Harney, one of the elders who taught me, has said many times that what made him sad the most was that people nowadays are afraid of everything. They are afraid of being alone; they are afraid of nature; they are afraid of their connection to the earth and to spirit. If you have so much fear inside of you, you can't live life. It stops you from being alive, you just walk through life existing but not fully living. You do your work, wait for the holidays or until you are retired.

The way I see it, we can choose to live our lives with love instead of fear. It is the love for Nature and for Spirit, for Life as a whole that makes it so worthwhile and wonderful. Reality is magical when you carry love and appreciation in your heart. I was told if you walk a spiritual path, in the end you will love everything: the water, the sun, the day and the night, the cold and the heat, the birds, the trees, the visible and the unseen… You truly have love in your heart for all things and every aspect of Nature. There is no good and bad and no judgment. Everything that comes to you, you embrace it with love. It is all there to teach you.

It was helpful that I practiced a lot as a kid and was able to be out in nature a lot too. It came natural to me – so to speak.

When you do not separate yourself from nature but recognize that nature is a part of you, you can actually work together. You shouldn't take the weather as something that goes against you personally, because the weather just is. When you make it into a personal fight, you are basically harming yourself and you are bound to lose anyway. It doesn't mean though, that as a person you can't learn from the weather, because it can teach you a lot, as everything in nature teaches us, if you are open and willing to learn.

Growing up in the desert, I had to deal with great heat in summer, hardly any rain, and cold nights. Wintertime brought extreme cold with a lot of snowstorms. My body has physically adapted to those big differences, even without deliberate practice: it was used to it. The teachings and exercises as described before enhanced the process of adapting on all levels. My way of thinking was shaped; I wasn't overreacting to any kind of weather emotionally; my spiritual connection to nature became deeper and more intense; my body developed an extra- thick layer of skin that protected me both in the heat and in cold. Doctors and nurses have often told me that they have a hard time going through my skin with a needle and actually measured it once, which gave a surprisingly thick result. I still hardly ever wear a jacket or a sweater. Even when the top layer of my skin is getting chilled the inner parts of my body are nice and warm. My body has adjusted to it and can adapt to the temperature as is needed. Only growing older, and my recent suffering from diabetes unfortunately make it where I am more sensitive than before. Most ancestors would be able to handle the weather much better, because they had to deal with it and were able to take it for what it is and not fight it.

All in all, when it comes to the weather and our behavior towards it, it is about changing the energy of resistance into a positive energy. The same principle applies for the wind, the rain, the heat and the darkness, anything from nature.

The fear in our minds makes the cold or the heat more intense. To get in touch with all the elements of nature, you need to know what it is about and how it works on you. You start to communicate with an open mind and heart to understand its principles.

You will find you won't lose as much energy as you would otherwise while being in that constant battle. The battle isn't just physical; it has turned into a mental and emotional one and has power over you. That leftover energy will be set free to help you stay warm and that is how it works. All things are there to help us.

Separation from Nature and Spirit

Very often I have witnessed when people talk about the Mother Earth, they see themselves separate from her. We talk about her as if she is something else over there, while we are here, as if she is something that is outside of us. Yet we consist of the same elements; we come from the Mother Earth -- our bodies with all the different features and parts -- and at the end of our lives we go back to her. Everything that nourishes us comes from her. So we are not separate at all.

Besides being physically a part of nature, we have a spirit in us. That is how we as Native people call it. Others speak about energy; some call it a soul. It doesn't matter what you call it; those are just names. Every person has his or her personal spirit. As we sit together here on this grass, our spirits touch each other and they connect and create a kind of energy field, which has its own spirit. Not only between you and me, but also between the grass we sit on and us, or those trees around us, to the sun, the wind, and so on. In the Native Way, this means that everything is connected through a spiritual energy. You can widen this to the Grandmother Moon, to the stars, to everything in Creation. As this spreads out, everything is affected by each other and everything affects everything, vice versa. In this way, everything is connected like in a giant web. The Shoshone people have Creation stories which tell us about how the world and life on earth got started, and they usually have Spider Woman at the center of all the legends. She creates and recreates the everlasting Web of Life that connects everything. Among the various Native peoples there are many different stories told that each put a little different emphasis on something. I heard many of those stories when I was young and listening in on the elders. I am afraid I am not a good storyteller in that sense, as I don't remember the details very well. But I have always been fascinated by them and kept wondering about their meaning. We refer to all of Creation also as the Great Spirit or speak about Grandfather and Grandmother Creator.

In all the stories there is an energetic, spiritual part that developed into a form. The four components of the sacred Circle of Life -- fire, water, air and earth -- are present and form the Mother Earth and are symbolized in our Medicine Wheel.

If a Native person speaks about "all my relations," this refers to that concept that everything is literally related. There are groups or as we say tribes, formed in all those relations that are more closely related. Human beings all over the Mother Earth are closely related to each other, even if they don't know each other. Deer are more closely related to other deer and we call them the Deer people, but human beings are also related to the Deer people.

Throughout their childhood, indigenous children who were brought up traditionally were made aware of their spiritual connection. They gained knowledge and understanding about it all in a natural way. This inner feeling of knowing could grow stronger over the years with the help of the tribal community. When I say we are connected to Nature and Spirit, this is what it comes down to.

Every child has this natural connection to Nature and Spirit of course, but if you are not brought up this way, a whole different mechanism unfolds itself. In the beginning you were able to hold on to it and nobody was making you doubt your connection. As you grow older, the remarks start to settle in: "Oh, that is just your imagination." Or they say: "It was just a dream." They claim: "What a coincidence!" Or:" That cannot be real!" As a young child you had been able to stick to your own feeling, but from now on this gets harder and harder. At one point you don't believe in it yourself anymore and you block all the experiences and perceptions in that direction. That is how we become separated from Nature and Spirit.

For whatever reason, the white people have gradually separated themselves from the Mother Earth over time. They started to live more from their minds than from their hearts. But the Mother Earth is also a living being with –- as indigenous people see it -- a beating heart. During this whole process, a lot of things have been created and invented, and technology and industrialization thrived, but the connection to nature was lost more and more.

We sit on these chairs and at this table; these things also have spirit. They are made from wood which has a spirit. The walls of a house, made out of brick, have a spirit. It has changed into another form, further away from its natural, original form, but it still has a spirit. But what I was told though, is that the further away from its natural being, the more confused the spirit becomes, and it's harder for it to stay connected to its natural origin. Like this piece of metal here: it is connected to the rock people, but has been melted down and has changed, and maybe something has been added to it, another element, and it's been forced into a specific form for a specific purpose. The connection to the rock people is not as strong as it was before, but it is still there. So its connection to Nature as such and to the Spirit of Mother Earth is less strong. And this goes for all things that we humans have changed and worked with. This also applies to electricity or other forms of energy that we use nowadays.

In ceremonies, Native people like to use the most natural materials, so that it is easier to connect to Nature and Spirit and the ceremony becomes more powerful. Also this rule applies in what we use for our housing, and so on, but it doesn't mean we don't have modern housing with heating systems and refrigerators or we don't drive a car or use a computer.

The good news is that even when people have lost their sense of connection, Nature and Spirit, in truth, never abandon you. They are there all the time for you. The only thing you need to do is open yourself up again. It is up to you to change your way of perceiving the world and what you believe in. Once you start listening again, you will get responses. You can watch Nature itself on a physical level and you'll get answers. It can be in the wind, the rustling in a tree, or the song of a bird. It can be how the water flows, how the colors in the sky form, or that an animal appears at a certain time of the day. It can carry a message if you are aware with all your senses.

Sometimes people ask me: "How do I know if nature is actually talking to me and it isn't just how nature is working at that moment?" Well, first you do have to know about how nature usually works and how the different life forms normally interact with each other. You'll have to spend time in nature, observe and learn all the aspects of it. You will start to connect with the natural flow and become aware you are a part of it. You'll recognize when Nature does something out of the ordinary or you'll realize when it speaks directly to you. It can teach you through its natural ways, and it can also draw your attention to it because of a special kind of behavior or timing. Both are good ways of connecting and both deepen your communication with Nature.

Nature talks to us all the time. It gives us warnings and signals when things are about to happen. We need to be very aware and listen carefully. The traditional indigenous people of the Mother Earth had, and some of them still have, this awareness and capability. I know of an indigenous tribe in Indonesia who watched the signs in nature when the big tsunami in South East Asia hit a few years ago. They noticed the behavior of the animals and birds of the region and followed them up into the hills away from the ocean. These people were so in tune with nature and trusted the signs, so they survived. They had a very strong connection to Nature and Spirit. Most people on the planet have lost this connection and most of all they doubt the connection. They don't know how to watch for the signals; they don't know what the signals mean and they don't trust their hearts enough to follow them. This in itself leads to suffering and destruction. Whenever we have the feeling that Nature is going against us, we really need to look at ourselves and at our connection to Nature. In truth, Mother Earth will guide us and take care of us. We just have to learn to listen to her again, observe and get to know her again. If we do this, then we can find water in the desert again, we will know where a spring is, we can work with the wind, we can find and grow food, and live a good life upon her.

The problem is that we are very stuck in our value systems. We think the world functions in a certain way and that is what we firmly believe in and hold on to. Everything that happens is always explained according to that system of values. Our judgments come out of those values. The truth is that the world doesn't work in just one way; it has many faces and layers and perceptions. Usually we are resisting anything that comes in from an unfamiliar angle. It makes us uncomfortable and we don't like to look at it. Truly learning about something different is unsettling and might shake your foundations even, but it is also where true growth lies.

In order to overcome the separation, we have to dare to go out there and put ourselves in an uncomfortable position in order to learn. A lot of people see challenges as something negative which they would like to refuse or surpass. It can be physical things like sickness or injuries. It can be an emotional issue or a mental process too. The first response from most people is to resist it: " I have to battle this thing! I don't like this!" In the indigenous world we say: "Welcome it in. It came to you for a reason. Actually you brought it to you for a reason!" It is there to help you. If you welcome it in, you may have to go through some struggles and pain, but with effort and willingness to learn, you grow from it and you come out stronger than before. You could look at it as a blessing. If you can only see it as something that is hurting you, that is, in the end, what it's going to do: hurt you. If you are able to change the energy of it and see the hidden blessing that comes along with the struggle, you come out of the experience a little different. You might have gained some awareness or a certain ability that you didn't have before. That is what you call growth.

The main thing is to embrace the lessons from Nature and Spirit, however a lesson shows itself, welcoming it in to be able to connect, flow and learn from it.

Growing up in two Worlds

Whenever I introduce myself I emphasize that I grew up in two worlds that were very opposite from each other. At home I lived in a traditional Native American household, and outside my home white people around me were very judgmental and were racist towards Indians. A lot of cowboys, miners and railroaders lived in the area and they especially had a strong dislike of Native people. They shared the opinion that Indians were just a problem they had to get rid of. In Elko, about 20 miles from where we lived, the only bigger town in the area where we would go to get groceries, you would see signs like: "No dogs or Indians allowed". That showed the attitude of the time in that area. Sayings like: "All Indians are drunks" or "The only good Indian is a dead Indian" explain it all.

There were some white people who thought differently, who were willing to look at the heart of a person and not at the color of a person's skin. We became friends with those people, but they really were exceptions. Out of every 20 to 30 white people, you would come across one good person. I had two white kids whom I played with when I was young. I was taught and warned by my family and elders to leave my traditional customs behind when I was in the "other" world and not show too much of the Native way of thinking 'cause usually that would mean you'd get in trouble. So I have learned to adapt and lay low and although I was proud of being Native, I didn't share our spiritual approach of life with Westerners. I wouldn't tell them that for me it is natural to talk to animals or to the trees and the rocks, for instance, as that would have been considered something extremely odd. I have kept the two worlds separate for a long time.

A lot of negative things happened in my youth but I have lived through those experiences. I was taught by my elders and have come to understand over time that everything happens with a reason and purpose and luckily I have learned a lot through it all. Although when I was young I would experience the two worlds as opposite to each other - one as very positive and the other with an extremely negative, limiting impact - I have come to realize that it is important to bring the best of both worlds together.

Let me give you a funny example which actually turned out okay in the end. Once when I was already older, and I had my driver's licence I drove a white friend home, who had stayed for the night and did sunrise ceremony with us. On the way to his place, which wasn't that far as Elko is only a small town, I was fined with 21 tickets by a cop, who had a strong dislike of Indians. He drove behind us the whole time and stopped us with howling sirens each time when he had thought of something again. "Your tires are too weak. That is dangerous." "You are going one mile over the speed limit. I have to charge you for that." "You didn't stop at the stop sign properly. You'll get a fine for that." Sure enough, he wrote a ticket for each thing and I had to go and pay them at the courthouse. Luckily the judge didn't take this seriously, and he let me off the hook: "This is too obvious. You will not be charged for this." It was pure harassment. This was just an ongoing thing and one of the more innocent ways to show their power, but in fact it was also done to provoke you so you'd get aggressive and act up. Then they would have a real reason to bust you.

I went to a public school. There was also the possibility of going to a reservation school, but those schools were really bad.

The reservation schools developed out of the original boarding schools run by the Catholic Church and Christian missionaries, and their quality was very low. As we know today, around 50% of the children didn't come through this system alive and there was a lot of abuse and violence in those schools. My father was lucky to have been able to avoid a boarding school as he lived with his grandmother and was able to escape this fate. My mother though was forced to go to one of the boarding schools, called Steward Indian School, which was in Carson City, Nevada. It is now a museum. I remember she didn't like talking about that time much. She did mention some things that were done there in general and were also done against her personally. As she referred to them: "they were not nice" –- but mainly she preferred not to talk about this at all, since it was so negative.

My parents wanted to prevent us from going to a boarding or reservation school and so they paid the local school district for us siblings to go to public school. Of the 350 children attending this school, from kindergarten through 12th grade, there were only about six to ten Native Shoshone children. Another peculiar fact was that of those that were actually Native, most of them claimed they were Mexican. In those days, being an Indian was considered very bad and being a Mexican you would be looked down upon a little less.

As for myself, when I became a little older and more aware of the situation, I was very proud of my Native background. I grew my hair long, and I was very outspoken about my Native heritage. Both my parents came from a traditional Native American upbringing and taught me, through their examples, to be proud to walk this path.

My father was a political activist and became a strong speaker for the Shoshone people. He hadn't gone to a boarding school, as I mentioned earlier, but he didn't go to a public school either, as he lived with his grandparents in the hills until he was about 19 or 20, which was too old to go to any school. He was very intelligent though and loved to read. I remember seeing him reading through all kinds of law books all the time, especially on Native American law making. He had a way of remembering all the information that was in there. He simply taught himself. He became extremely outspoken towards the government about the injustice done towards our people and was always advocating on their behalf. Our people, the Western Shoshone, were a very poor tribe. There was no money at all to pay lawyers that could represent us, so my dad offered to help and take certain cases to court. Before we had always believed it when people would claim: "Well, that's the law!" But in fact it wasn't the law at all! It was their way of getting away with something. We just didn't have any way of knowing what the law was for real. My father actually started winning quite a lot of the cases, just out of the simple fact that he knew the law so well.

I remember one time when my dad took me with him to appeal at court for a certain case and the district judge took my father and me aside before the hearing. He told us: "There is something I want you to know before we even start. In a courtroom, in my courtroom or any other courtroom, you have two strikes against you: first, you people don't have much money and money talks and helps win cases in court, and second you are Indians and Indians have fewer rights than other people in the United States. I really want you to understand this if you want to defend your people." We appreciated his honesty, but because my dad had taught himself so much on the law, he was able to win many court battles despite the two strikes against him.

He even won a case for me one time. I had chosen to wear my hair long and in my school there were no other kids who had long hair, not even my brothers. I was the only one. In Nevada, back in the sixties it was unheard of for boys to wear their hair long; it simply was not done and not allowed. In California, with the hippy movement, it might have been possible, but not in Nevada, an extremely conservative state. But my father defended me and even took the case up to the Supreme Court of Nevada with the claim that for religious reasons I was allowed to have long hair, as long as I kept it tied up in a ponytail at school.

Of course, at school the teachers and the principal took advantage of this. Knowing that my long hair was important to me, they used this sensitive spot against me and would sneak up from behind and drag me through the hallways by my ponytail.

One of their favourite things was to lock me up in one of the lockers, where you normally store away books and things, so they could mark me as missing the next class. Even the principal would do that.

After a while, when I was older, in my teens, I must admit I became a sort of a rebel myself, you know. I found ways of getting back at them. School and I became strongly at odds with each other.

I would go up to the principal's office and sit down, light a cigarette in front of his face, put my feet up on his desk and would start talking to him... you know, to provoke him.

One day after they had done something to me, I was really angry and determined to do something back so I went to the boy's toilets and stuffed them all with toilet paper and then kept flushing them until everything was blocked. It flooded out the whole gymnasium. Luckily, they never figured out it was me.

Another time, after they had done something to me again, I even tried to make Molotov cocktails on my own, filling up some jars with gasoline. After school I waited till everybody was gone, and made sure nobody was in the building anymore and then threw in those self-made bombs. But the problem was that brick doesn't burn very well, so I didn't get very far with that.

School Time

Overall, I didn't have many friends in school, maybe four or five in total. My brother wasn't as outward about his nativeness, as I was and had a lot more friends. Didn't claim he was proud of his Native heritage, and so on. Kept his hair short and also went drinking with the other guys. You know, those things that you do to be part of a group, so he fit in much more than I did.

Anyway, they did a lot of things to me, that I do not like to be reminded of and normally do not talk about. One time I remember when I was in 8th grade, we were outside playing American Football at PE (Physical Education) lessons. Since I was so different from most of the other kids, being Native and growing my hair long and everything, I wasn't allowed to take part in the game very often. Most of the time I just stood around at the side or would be left to wander around. This specific time, the principal and the vice-principal were watching the game and I saw them talking to the coach and janitor at the sideline. They called over the guy who catches the ball and throws the ball into the field, and talked to him too. This guy then called me in the game and said: "Mala, I want you to run out in the field and catch the ball." I was really happy that they had finally decided to include me in the game, so I said: "All right, tell me what to do." He said: "All you need to do is keep your eye on the ball so you can catch it. Don't look around, just keep your eye on the ball and keep going." So I did what I was told, and felt so happy about playing I didn't question it. While I took off running with my eyes on the ball, I did sort of know which direction I was going, towards the group of people that were standing around watching. Later on some of the other kids told me what had happened. The janitor had a T-post in his hand, which he used for making fences. It was a thick metal post about six feet long and had a metal sharp point at the end. The kids told me that the janitor aimed the post at me, right where the ball was heading, at about the height of my stomach-chest area. What happened though, was that right at the last moment I jumped up to catch the ball, so the metal end of the post only went through my leg. I was hurt pretty badly. Of course they claimed it was an accident. And I guess I was lucky I wasn't injured worse.

These things went back and forth. As my father was a well-known Medicine Man, a woman came to see my father one time for healing. This woman had a reputation of her own. She came from California and was heavily into drugs. She even had a special nickname, the Acid Queen! When she came to our house, she brought a whole suitcase full of marijuana, all kinds of acid bottles and other illegal stuff. My father told her if she wanted a healing, she needed to dispose of all the drugs, otherwise he wouldn't treat her. I don't remember what kind of sickness she had, but I know she was in pretty serious condition. So she agreed and my father handed the suitcase to my older brother and myself and told us to get rid of all that was in there. We flushed most of it down the toilet and were thinking what to do with the marijuana. Some of the marijuana was of really good quality; there was for instance one kilo of Acapulco Gold in there. We were brooding about getting rid of it and wanted to come up with a good idea. At one point I thought: "You know, we could turn them into cigarettes and hand them out in school! That'll be exciting." It was back in the sixties and a lot of people were really into smoking pot and everything, so we knew everybody in school would probably really enjoy it. At that time I was still smoking ordinary cigarettes and also possessed one of those cigarette rolling machines. You could put some tobacco on a piece of paper and the little hand-roller would help make it into a cigarette. So we bought lots of those tiny papers and rolled all the marijuana into normal cigarettes. In the end we had around 200 cigarettes. We took them to school the next day and divided them amongst our friends, who again passed them on to their friends and so on. Pretty much everybody in high school had one of those marijuana cigarettes. Smoking wasn't allowed on the premises, so we all headed for the bathrooms to secretly smoke over there. Very soon the toilet stalls were packed with people all lighting up and smoking, and sure enough, soon the fire alarm went off. I remember how the smoke was spreading through the hallways and the teachers got alarmed too. They were running around trying to figure out what was going on, yelling: "What's going on? What kind of funny smell is that?!" By this time my brother and I were getting nervous and thought we would definitely get busted for this. We were sure somebody would tell on us, but to our great surprise, nobody said who initiated it. Of course the teachers suspected us and were questioning us, but we just insisted: "We don't know anything about this!" The rest of that day everybody sat in class in total bliss, feeling very high. Yeah, that was a good laugh and we were really proud of ourselves! And for a short time, we were popular in school and considered very cool.

The end of my schooling came when I was in 10th grade. It was in the first few months of the semester, when we had American History. I was sitting in the back of the class -- that's where they always told me to sit -- when we got to the few pages that were written about American Indians. Out of this very thick history book, they covered all of Native American history in just a few pages. What was said in there was basically how horrible the Indians were and what a primitive people the white discoverers had encountered when coming to the Americas. Now, this history teacher even took it further and was saying that it was the manifest destiny of the white man to come to this land and save it from the godless heathen savages who were there. He said the Indians didn't have any language, no real communication and they only grunted. He also claimed that the men abuse their women and make them do all the work. He just kept going on and on, and all I remember is that at one point I stood up and I told him: "As a history teacher you should know better and I want you to tell them the truth." And in front of the whole class, he said: "Sit down and shut up, you stupid savage!" I don't know what happened inside of me: I got real angry and very calm at the same time. I walked towards him, all the way to where he was behind his desk; I walked around his desk, and all I know is that I hit him as hard as I could in his face. So hard that it knocked him down. And you must remember he was a grown man and I was only 16 years old and not very tall. At that moment I thought: "Well, this is it, he is going to kick my butt." You know, in those days -- it was 1968 -- it was absolutely unheard of to hit a teacher! But instead, he just stood up, looked at me and left the classroom. When I turned around, I saw my classmates all with their jaws wide open... they couldn't believe what they had just witnessed. I just walked back to my seat and decided to wait. After 15 minutes or so two police officers came in and asked me my name. They came up to me and yanked me from behind my desk onto the floor onto my stomach and handcuffed my hands behind my back. They didn't allow me to get back up on my feet to walk but dragged me out of the classroom to the principal's office. They threw me into a chair, and I found myself surrounded by the principal, the teacher himself, and the cops. They all kept saying: "Now we've finally got you! You really did it this time. There's no way of getting out of this one. We're gonna put you in Juvenile Reform School.... until you're 18 and then you are going to prison for real. You assaulted a teacher and this is very serious. We've got you!" All the things they said to me didn't really matter to me. I was actually at peace with the fact that I had stood up for my people and said what I believed in. So I didn't care what was going to happen to me. They did have to follow the official rules in a case like this and were obliged to call my parents. I remember they were kind of worried if my father would be around since they knew about his fame and his way of dealing with things. My father had a job at the railroad at that time and worked shifts for three days and would be back home for three days. Of course, they hoped that he would be out of town, but I was lucky that my dad was around and he came to the school immediately. They untied the handcuffs and cleaned me up a little, smoothed my shirt so I wouldn't look roughed up as much before he arrived. They explained their version of what had happened, that they really had tried to work with me but that I had a history of violence and aggression in the school. They had seen it coming for a long time already. I had had no reason at all and just came up to the teacher and had hit him in the face, and so on. My dad turned to me and asked for my side of the story. So I told him. My dad knew I never lied about anything, so he believed me. He came up to me and shook my hand and said to me: "Son, I am really proud of what you have done. Your school days are over now, let's leave and go home." Of course, they all protested and hollered at us that I had committed a crime and was under arrest and that it wasn't possible for me to leave. But my father insisted and repeated: "Ignore them. Just get up and come home with me." So that is what we did and they didn't come after us.

After a few days we got an official letter from the School District stating that I was permanently expelled from school and that I wasn't allowed to enter any education system in the entire Elko School District. Ooh, I can tell you, I was so happy! They actually gave me something good. It was no punishment at all! According to American law, you have to be in school until you are 18 years old unless you have some sort of confirming proof like a GED diploma that you've finished your education. Otherwise you could be arrested. So basically with this letter, I was free from this obligation and that was the end of my schooling.

Youth and Living with Animals

It became known in the area where we lived, not only to Natives, but also to white people, that my father was a healer and could offer help in situations where people didn't know what to do. So very often, animals that were found in nature and were sick or wounded would be taken to our house so my father, with the assistance of the rest of the family, could take care of them and heal them. Over time, we built lots of cages where some of the animals were kept until we could set them free again. We had many kinds of animals, birds and reptiles there. I remember one time a rancher had killed a mother mountain lion on some dirt road, leaving two cubs behind. So he brought those mountain lion cubs to us and we took them in. We had eagles, a fox, badgers, a rattlesnake, and ground squirrels. We even had coyotes. We had just about everything you could imagine living in the desert. Our house was like a little rehabilitation zoo.

My dad was always telling me: "You know, if you're gonna work with the animals, you need to know that the animals will respond to your energy. They can feel your energy very well. So whatever you feel, they are going to know and they will respond to it. They will know if you have a fear of them and that is how they will respond to you. If you respect them, they will know just the same. So whenever you are around them, you have to be aware of that and keep that in mind. If you don't have the right energy, they might easily attack you."

One of my jobs around the house was to feed the animals and help with the rehabilitation. Our goal was to get them healthy and strong again so they could survive on their own out in nature.

My father helped the animals in different ways. Partly he used herbs and plants, partly other things and specific energies too. He would show me these things, though at that time I wasn't always so interested, especially not in how herbs and plants worked and how to talk to them to make them work in that specific medicine way, and how they would try and talk to you too.

But with the mountain lion cubs, we had to find another solution. After we'd gotten them, about four or five days later, they got really, really sick. They manifested their heart pain into a real sickness, with pus coming out of their eyes, sneezing all the time and being very weak, not wanting to eat anything. We were afraid we were going to lose them. My father said: "They have lost their will to live because their mother died and they feel heartbroken. You have a special healing energy within you and I want you to do something for me. Tonight you will take them both into your bed and have them sleep with you." So that's what I did. I took them in my bed, under the covers, up against my belly. I could hear them sneeze and crawl around a little but after a while they did sleep. The next morning after I woke up I noticed that they were playing on top of me, all happy, and they were actually healed. This was all they had really needed; in this case no herbal medicine would have helped. So, after that, whenever we had sick and lonely animals like that, guess who ended up lying with them... but of course I didn't mind that at all!

One time I found a crow myself and raised him. He stayed with me for a long time and was amazingly smart.

We had quite a few hawks and eagles over time. Of course, eagles are much bigger than hawks: from wing tip to wing tip eagles can span six to seven feet, which is pretty big. I would put them on my arm and walk around with them or put them on a tree stump to help them sit by themselves. To protect my skin from their incredibly sharp claws, I wrapped my arm with lots of old rags, but I could still feel their claws on my skin right through all those layers. Their beaks are astonishingly sharp too. And they would always look at me with their piercing eyes, observing me, checking me out, looking right through me as if they knew everything about me. Actually, a pretty amazing, almost scary, exhilarating feeling. I always made sure to be in a very good and harmonious place in myself whenever I would work with them because they would pick up on my emotions and thoughts immediately. But I never got hurt while working with them.

The two mountain lion cubs that I talked about had to be raised somehow now that they had survived the puppy stage. It was the responsibility of my brothers and sisters and myself to take care of them, feed, and exercise them. Every day we took them out into a fenced-in area where they were supposed to be left to themselves. But we wanted to play with them -- we were young kids -- because they were a lot of fun. We made a game of sneaking up behind them and yanking on their tails so they would turn around and try and hit us with their paws. We would then quickly roll ourselves up into a ball and once they had hit us, we would be rolled away by the strength of the blow. The game was seeing who would roll away furthest.

Of course, the cubs became bigger and stronger, but they always kept their claws in and we never got hurt. One time my father saw what we were doing and became very angry with us; obviously it was pretty dangerous, you know. If at some time a mountain lion felt provoked and decided not to keep his claws in, he would surely have ripped us open. Once they smelled blood and sensed a reaction of pain and of fear, things could have gotten out of hand. They could have then even tried to kill us. He scolded: "Wild animals are not something to be fooled with!"

After that, he realized he had to get rid of the mountain lions, but he could not let them loose in the wild because they were too familiar with humans and didn't really know how to survive out there. So he looked for another place where they could stay. Nobody would take them together, but at last we found this couple that lived on a ranch and didn't have any animals there, no sheep or anything. They said they would take one mountain lion. So we drove there and stayed a few days to see if and how he adapted. Luckily, he did very well; he was able to run free but he would come back to be fed and even slept on their porch. They said he was very protective of them. We were very happy to hear how that developed. The other one we gave to an old man who had come to our house a lot of times and who had always seemed to have a special liking for the cougars. He took the other one in and we would see them driving around in his old pick-up truck, the mountain lion sitting next to him, looking out the window, just like a dog. It was great seeing the two of 'em together. When the old man died, the mountain lion went into the desert and wasn't seen any more after that.

Normally we don't take owls in since they are considered close to the spirit world, but this owl came to us when it was sick, so of course we took care of it. You know, we Native people are careful when it comes to owls. Owls are, among other things, considered messengers of death and when you are around that kind of energy you can also attract it. When it was time for the owl to go back to nature after it was well enough, it wouldn't leave. It just kept coming back and even flew into the house! We weren't able to remove it from the house, so for some reason my dad decided it was okay for the owl to stay. "Eventually," he said, "It will leave, whenever it wants to." It wanted to live with us. It would ride on our shoulders while walking through the rooms and it had its own little place in the corner where it would sit. Yeah, that was pretty neat. As kids we would play with him and try to see how far his neck would turn while he was following us with his eyes and we were running circles around him. My mother would scold us: "Quit teasing that poor owl, you're gonna make it dizzy and have him fall off his pole!" We had the task of feeding it, so we would give him little balls of hamburger and toss those in the air. Or once in a while, when we caught some mice with a mousetrap, he'd be fed those. I guess that must be the reason he liked staying in our house so much, being fed and always being taking care of. A lazy owl, eh? (*Mala chuckles*). He tried to sleep during the day, which was his natural rhythm, but us kids didn't make it easy for him. We had cats that tried to go after him, but the owl pecked at them and the cats stopped bothering him. After about two years he flew outside and stayed outdoors. In the end he decided to leave us for good.

Snake Stories

Later on, when I was already older, my father gave me a task to make sure that our piece of land was clear of rattlesnakes, so that they wouldn't harm anybody and the people living there wouldn't harm the rattlesnakes. I would seek them out every week and talk to them, reassuring them I wasn't going to hurt them. Then I'd pick them up and carry them away into the desert. I don't think I have snake medicine, but more a way of being able to communicate in the right way with them and putting myself into a certain space and energy. They allowed me to touch them and didn't harm me. They would curl themselves around my arms and neck, but they never once tried to bite me.

There is a story that has to do with my father that explains some of his special abilities and what it means to carry Snake Medicine. I was about 12 or 13 years old. My dad was already working with medicine powers. He was telling us he kept having dreams about snakes. He wasn't quite sure what was going on. He was working shifts for the Pacific Railroad at that time and was away for three days. Somewhere in the middle of the desert the train stopped and my father was wandering off a little through the brush. Sometimes they had to wait for other trains to come by or they had to do work on the tracks themselves, so that wasn't unusual. I remember him telling me afterwards that while walking there, a vision came to him: a snake was telling him he should have a rattlesnake bite him in order for him to use it as Medicine. As he was approaching the train again, there was a rattlesnake right in the middle of his path. It was sort of looking at him and he started talking to the snake, explaining about the vision he had just had. The rattle was rising up and started rattling. My dad decided to keep walking with the thought: "If it wants to strike me, then that is what should happen, if not, then that's ok too." The rattlesnake did strike him and bit him. My dad grabbed the snake and gently took it off of his leg, because sometimes they stay in you to really put the venom in you. He thanked him for biting him and put him aside. Luckily he only had a few hours to go on the train before he was back at the house. When he arrived, he was beginning to really feel sick and my mom asked him what had happened. He told her everything and she understood. Soon you could see his body changing to a yellowish color, and he was starting to sweat all over. My mom helped him into bed and asked him if we should go and get a doctor. But he refused: "No, I am not allowed; I have to survive this without a doctor to receive the Snake Medicine." My mother and I both stayed with him and we could watch his body color change from red to purple. His leg was getting swollen and smelly pus was starting to come out. We could observe that the color streak was going up to his heart, which was getting worrisome and very dangerous. He was going in and out a feverish state of trance and hallucination. At some point he got out of this state and told us: "The snake has told me what to do. He gave me instructions for healing." He told me where and which herbs to get and my mom how to prepare them. So I went out immediately for the herbs and together we prepared them in the kitchen, quietly but quickly, because it was getting to be a close call. We made them into a poultice and put that right on the wound. By that time you could see the streak with the venom had almost reached his heart and he had a hard time breathing, so we really started praying hard. After 15 to 20 minutes we saw, to our great relief, the streak retreating a little, so we kept on changing the poultice, refreshing it so the poison could be taken out totally. During that time, my father went into a way of communication with the rattlesnake people. They taught him things about the Medicine and revealed to him secrets about their people. After that my dad was able to use Snake Medicine and could call upon them and they would never bite him. They even protected him. In fact, we had a rattlesnake living underneath our porch, about five feet long that had been run over by a car. My father worked on him and it survived. We wanted to put it back into the desert, but it kept coming back to us, over and over again. It just didn't want to leave. So my dad talked to him and offered him a deal: he could live underneath our front porch and would not be bothered by us, but in return he would have to let us know whenever somebody was visiting if that person was coming with good energy or not. He should rattle as a warning if he considered the person not OK. Usually if a person heard the rattle going off they'd be so scared they'd leave straight away anyway! It became our perfect guard snake that warned about anybody entering the house that was coming with the wrong intentions. The snake warned us a few times and my father developed a strong relationship to snakes in general and to this one especially.

During another personal experience I once had with snakes, I got a little help from Spirit. Our family was driving to Oregon and I really felt a need to pee. We were way out in the country and no gas station in sight, so I decided to stop by the side of the road.

I walked off a little bit through high grass that almost came up to my thighs, though I could still lift my feet. At one point I heard a voice hollering in my ear: " Stop!" I froze instantly: when a Spirit comes through loud and clear like that, you better listen! So I stood there with one foot up in the air and I looked down and saw a ball of black snakes with yellow and red stripes on them. I don't know if this kind was heavily poisonous but I 'm sure the snakes would have bitten me if I'd stepped on them and I would have had a lot of pain and discomfort. I thanked Spirit for warning me on time. It saved both those snakes and me a lot of trouble!

Medicine Teaching

Snake Medicine is very powerful and also very effective. It's a way of sniffing to smell sickness. If you've ever watched snakes, you can witness them sticking out their tongue to sniff and smell what's in the air. My dad didn't stick out his tongue but used his nose (*Mala chuckles*). Snakes are very sensitive to sounds; though they don't have ears, they sense any kind of movement through the vibrations that are carried from the earth into their bodies.

But Snake Medicine is also one of the hardest kinds to work with. It's like the snake's forked tongue with its split ends: it has two sides to it. It can be used for really good Medicine but can also be used in a bad way. Working with this Medicine is a constant struggle in keeping yourself in balance with the Medicine and not going in the wrong direction since it is very powerful and therefore very tempting.

The choice which Medicine to use when a person comes with a sickness depends on who asks and what is asked for. There is no Medicine that can heal everything. Usually, when a person needs help, he or she brings some tobacco along that has been held in the person's hands for a while. In this way the energy is taken in by the tobacco, which is a very sensitive plant and is offered to the Medicine person, who will pray over it and see if it is appropriate to help. The attitude of the person who comes for help needs to be in a place where he or she is ready to make certain changes in order to receive healing. Then the Medicine Person will ask Spirit and Nature which Medicine will work best. Sometimes they direct you to another person who might help in a better way, or more than one person will work on the same issue.

Every Medicine has its own qualities and works differently; each has its own nature and its own abilities. I don't want to get into much detail, but you can imagine that, for example, Eagle Medicine has to do with focusing and being able to see clearly.

Each Medicine also works differently on each person and might have different effects. That is the same as for Western medication. You have to make a choice at some point. Our way of choosing the right Medicine is praying over it to clarify and get a yes or no to continue. You always have to remember that true healing only comes when the person is ready for it. Half of the success of any healing comes from the patient himself. The other half comes from the medicine that was used, how it was used and who was the facilitator. It is also important to take into account if the patient trusts the healer and has a supportive attitude.

I believe the reason our Medicine works so well is that more than one level is involved. Obviously the physical aspect usually causes the problem that you are dealing with and that you would like to see healed. Then there are the emotional, mental and spiritual aspects of the sickness or the problem. In our way of thinking you cannot separate those. When our Medicine People use their personal Medicine, which can be Bear, Water, Snake, Eagle or Elk and many more, then all those aspects come into action and need to be taken into account. It gives the Medicine its quality and characteristics that will be effective in its own ways. The reactions will differ depending on how the person responds physically, emotionally, mentally and spiritually. This makes every healing unique.

Wickiup with the Eagle Feathers Story

When I was 14 years old, I had a dream about an elder teaching me how to build a traditional wickiup, the old kind that my people used to live in back in time. A wickiup looks like an upside-down basket and is mostly made out of willow branches. It was totally laid out to me, exactly how to build it, how to gather the material, how to make the structure and everything that's important when you make a wickiup in the traditional way. After waking up, I told my parents about the dream and they said: "Well, this is very clear. You need to follow up on that dream, build your own wickiup and live in it."

The Shoshone people used wickiups in the areas where they stayed more permanently. Back then, they didn't just live in Nevada but in many more states. Once the Shoshone were a very large tribe. There are Western, Eastern, Northern and Southern Shoshones. They came mainly from Oregon but also from Nevada, Wyoming, California, Utah, Arizona, New Mexico, Colorado, Idaho and a couple of other states. When the white people came and asked which tribe they were from, they would often answer with their clan-name: like the Paiutes, the Utes, the Goshutes, even the Comanches, but they were actually all Shoshones. Later on, the clans more or less became their own tribes. It is said that even the Hopi and the Aztecs are originally Shoshones. There is a series of books that document how Shoshone migrated down south. The author did years and years of thorough research before he published all the material he gathered on Native tribes.[3]

The Hopi clan had a specific purpose within the Clan System: of all the Shoshone clans, it was they who had to focus on spiritual matters and take care of the right spiritual balance. The rule was that they were never supposed to fight and there were treaties designed in case this would ever occur. When the Hopis were under attack at one point in history and in great need, other Shoshone clans went south to support them. Some of them decided to stay and some of them even went further south to Mexico and became known as the Aztec over time.

So I was determined to literally make my dream come true and planned my wickiup. Nobody helped me with it, nobody explained or gave

---

3 "Thunder over the Ochoco" by Gale Ontko

instructions. I gathered the willows and started weaving them together really tightly. I was able to make it work somehow, although it wasn't the best. I covered it with rugs and blankets to make it fit for colder temperatures. I could sort of stand in it and still have some other things in it besides a bed. It took me about three days to finish it. I showed my parents and they nodded: "Yeah sure, that is a wickiup. You did a good job." So I moved into my own wickiup, which stood a little away from the house, and from then on for the next 14 years I slept in wickiups of different sizes that I built myself.

A few years after I built my first one, I lived in a newly made wickiup, three square meters in circumference. Since we no longer have buffalo hides for use, I had it covered with blankets and plastic tarps instead, with a door flap also made of tarp.

Wickiup

When I was growing up I had a special relationship with eagles, as is also shown in my name. All through my youth I kept having numerous special experiences and encounters with eagles that lived in the wild. Constantly I would find eagle-feathers; sometimes I would come across whole wings or even a whole eagle. It would happen far more often to me than to other people; it was exceptional. Eagle feathers are extremely important for the indigenous peoples of North America. They are considered sacred and carry a lot of meaning. Eagles can fly the highest of all birds and bring our prayers to the Creator. The feathers are used in many of our healing ceremonies too.

So many of those eagle feathers kept coming to me that I started putting them up on the walls in between the willow branches of the wickiup. More and more feathers came, and more and more I stuck in between the branches. At one point I thought: „Wow, that would be neat if I could cover all the walls of the wickiup with just eagle feathers. That would be great! It would be incredible to sleep in a place totally surrounded by all those eagle feathers. That must give off an incredible energy!"

But I knew deep inside that this wasn't the right thing to do. Because in life you should only gather and use as much as you actually need, and pass on to others who are in need also. I chose to ignore that traditional knowledge and continued with my pursuit. So the day came when all the walls were actually fully covered by the feathers. I had to go somewhere in the area and I was gone for a few hours. When I came back, I noticed that the door of the wickiup stood open a little. When I looked inside, I saw that every eagle feather inside was broken in half. They told me that for some reason the dogs we had had broken loose and gone into the wickiup and had deliberately gone for the eagle feathers. There was not one feather left whole. We had to hold a special ceremony to bury the feathers and return them to the Mother Earth. In our people's way, there was nobody in our community telling me that I had done wrong or who accused me of my mistake. They thought that life had taught me my lesson and that it spoke for itself. I felt very bad and was ashamed. I knew it was my responsibility. Since then eagle feathers still come to me, but only once in a while. The spirit of the eagle thought that I had used my special gift of being able to find eagle feathers easily for selfish reasons and that I had not appreciated it enough to share with others. That's why they took the gift away.

This teaches how important it is to be really grateful for the gifts we are given in life and not to take them for granted.

Turning Point

When I was 14 or 15, something shocking happened to our family. We had gotten word that my oldest brother, who didn't live at our house anymore at that time, had gotten killed in a violent way.

It really saddened my heart on a very deep level. We had already suffered so much loss of so many cousins and relatives through the racist behavior that surrounded us as Native people, and all these deaths had accumulated over time into a pool of anger and despair inside of me. The more I thought about it, the angrier I became and finally I went into my bedroom, took the 22 rifle I used to go rabbit hunting with, loaded it with ammunition and tucked all the extra bullets I could find in my pockets. When I opened the front door to leave, my dad asked me: "Where are you going? What are you up to?" I told him: "I am tired of losing our people, our family to all this violence and racism! Even if we try and make use of the law we aren't helped or listened to. The police and the judges don't care about us. It is all so pointless and unfair: there is no justice! They can do pretty much anything against us and get away with it. I am tired of it and can't live like this any longer..." So my dad says: "What are you planning to do then?" I answered: "I'm going out there and kill the first white person I see and after that try and kill as many others as I can until they kill me. At least I know when I die there will be less white people left to harm my people and cause the misery they do wherever we encounter them." My dad got quiet for a minute and then said to me: "Well, if that is what you feel you need to do, you should go ahead with it. But remember one thing!" "What is that?"

I asked him reluctantly. My father continued: "The first white person you kill will die out of hatred and hurt and you will have become just like those you so despise. You are then no different than the ones who are doing this to us." I stopped and thought about his words. It really shook me up and I realized that the last thing I wanted was to become like people who are doing the exact same hurtful things to my family. So I turned around, went into my bedroom and put everything away. I went into a deep depression for a while, as I didn't know how to handle my grief. It all looked so hopeless and I understood why the suicide rate among my people was so high, as it seemed there was no hope for the future and no positive sign in sight.

A few days later an elder dropped by our house and asked me what was wrong. We started talking and he told me: "You know, we can still win. " I exclaimed: "But how? There is no way. There are far more white people here now. They have all the money and the power. They rule everything!" The elder stayed patient: "If you would teach the truth to the heart of their children about the loss of connection to themselves, each other and to the Mother Earth and show them how the path they are on is leading to self-destruction, there will be those you wake up and who will eventually stand next to you. When the day comes and that happens, things will start to change. We will have allies and become stronger. Not only we will win, so will they and eventually everybody and everything on the Mother Earth will win." I thought about these words for days, turned and twisted my thoughts around that and realized that I wanted to dedicate myself to that way of thinking and behaving. It became a turning point in my life and I have tried to live like that ever since.

Time in the Desert

All through my youth I kept going out into the desert on my own, roaming in different directions every day, taking my rifle with me to hunt for rabbits on the way back home. We were always in need of some extra meat for all the people that stayed at our house. Now that I didn't need to attend school anymore, I'd be gone the whole day and was very happy being alone in desert where I felt at home and at peace.

When I was a little over 16 years old, I decided I'd had enough of being around people all the time, enough of all the problems they caused, enough of dealing with the difficulties of living between the Western and the Native culture. I felt the desert call me and I wanted to be out there for a while. So I went out to an old ghost town in the middle of the desert called Palisades where they used to search for gold and which was now totally abandoned. You could only reach it on a gravel road that wound up along tall cliffs about 200 ft. high and came down to the river that ran through the canyon. The old buildings of the mining company were still standing and there was even a small graveyard nearby. The river, the only natural one that runs through Nevada, was close to where I camped and there was a spring that had been in use before, so I managed to fix it and could get fresh drinking water from the well. There also was a beautiful cottonwood tree courtyard that provided shade. My parents had my brothers check on me once a week though. They usually brought some canned food with them too, since my mom was worried I wouldn't get by.

Besides those supplies, I ate herbs and plants that grew there, the kind I was told were good and healthy. I wanted to put all the things the elders had taught me into practice. I had taken my 22-rifle with me and went to hunt for rabbits or ducks. Now you can hunt by looking for animals, trying to search them out and then shooting them. There's also a specific way, if you have the right power of heart and mind, where you wait for them to come to you and offer themselves so you may kill them. What you do is go look for a trail and a good spot for yourself right next to it. Then you sit and wait while you sing the song of that particular animal. You also make an offering and say a prayer to explain your intention and what you are asking for, to let them understand. You reassure them that you will use their gift in the proper way, you come in a respectful manner and will utilize all the parts of the animal in the best way you can. You ask for a sick or an old one to come, whose time would come soon anyway. So that is what I wanted to do: hunt in that way. I sat by a rabbit trail for about four days and no rabbit ever came. But then on the fifth day, when I wasn't really expecting it anymore, sure enough an old rabbit came hopping along. As soon as it saw me, it stopped and sat quietly in front of me and even looked at me. So I took my rifle and shot it. I thanked Nature for allowing it to happen in this way and gave thanks to the rabbit. I prayed over its spirit and for its people, its own rabbit tribe, to honor the rabbit that gave of itself so that I could continue to live.

When I didn't need to hunt because I had enough from an earlier shoot or when I used the canned food they brought me, I would just sit by the river, surrounded by nature and watch the water go by. It made me feel calm and good inside. There were many birds flying in and out.

I would also just try and chase rabbits for fun, trying to keep up with them and catch 'em while running. I was in pretty good shape back then and was a fast runner, so I also did it for exercise. The rabbits would run between the sagebrush and I'd be jumping alongside over the sagebrush. At some point the rabbit will get winded and stop, then it's easy to grab it.

One day as I was after this one rabbit and I was hopping high up over one of the bushes, I happened to look down and saw a big rattlesnake curled up on top of the sagebrush! He was startled by all that movement and got up ready to strike. Luckily I jumped high enough and he missed me. Otherwise he would have gotten me right between my legs. Man, I was so happy I didn't have to have find somebody suck the poison out of that spot! Yeah, there were many rattlesnakes out there. They like doing that, crawling on top of the sage, especially in the morning to avoid the cool earth, trying to catch the first rays of sun from higher up.

At one of my wander-abouts I entered the so-called foothills, rolling hills with canyons in between. While I was in one of those canyons, there was an area with a lot of loose shale rock. I was aware that this is a good place for snakes, because they like rocks when they heat up in the sun, but I didn't hear any snakes at all. As I walked further into the canyon where it gets narrower and narrower, all of a sudden I heard rattles all around me... There were snakes everywhere and they were all rattling fiercely. I don't know how I even got that far without being bitten, but there I found myself, surrounded by all these rattling snakes ready to strike. You know, rattlesnakes mostly rattle to warn you. They are actually afraid and do not want to be stepped on. They don't deliberately want to hurt you. The thought goes through my mind: "Oh man, this is serious. If I get bitten by only one of them, I'm in deep trouble. I'm about a half-day's walk away from home where they can help me. Nobody out here and I gotta walk myself, but then again, if I walk, I stimulate the poison through my veins, which I should avoid because the poison will reach my heart muscle soon! I wonder if I am going to survive this."

So I started praying to the snake people, realizing I had to be really careful and calm my energy. I talked to them: "I am sorry I disturbed you and walked unknowingly into your home. I don't mean any harm. Many times I have been taking care of your people to avoid you being stepped upon around our house and property. I would like to leave your home now and leave you be."

Snakes are very sensitive to a person's energy. They pick up somebody's feelings easily, so it was important to not show any anxiety or fear. I was respectfully apologizing to them. As I was sending out all these prayers and thoughts in all directions, changing my energy into a quiet but clear mode, the rattles little by little started to become quieter and after a few minutes it was silent again. I could leave without any problem, retreating slowly from their den towards the little path I had taken before. This time

I could see them clearly; they were keeping an eye on me too, making sure I was really leaving.

Rattlesnakes love to nest together. They make these huge balls, lying together to keep warm. It can be groups of a hundred or more snakes. On this sunny day they had all spread out to catch the warmth of the rocks and also do some hunting for mice or other little animals they could find. I just happened to walk right into one of those nesting areas, but I had survived another day.

Something very special I observed while living in the canyon and which I treasure in my heart to this day was a group of eagles, 13 of them in total. One looked really exceptional: it was a big, all black eagle and carried under both of its wings two solid white circles that you could only see while it was flying. I had never seen a large group of eagles flying together before and didn't even know that such existed. Later in Alaska I witnessed that there are actually even larger groups of eagles, up to a hundred, that hunt and roost together, but down in Nevada it is rare. The black eagle was their leader and made them come or go and fly with him into the canyon.

I got really curious where the eagles went every time, somehow disappearing into these cliffs of the canyon. So I decided to get a real close look and try and see where they went. I had noticed the eagles flew there every evening and every morning.

I saw a kind of cave halfway up the cliff, like a break in the wall. I hand-scaled up the cliff and estimated it was about 100 ft. high where the break in the cliff was and gave way to the cave, and I started out climbing. The cliffs of the canyon were of shale stone that broke easily, so I was careful in making my way up. I could look into the cave, but it was shallow and of no further interest and so I climbed further up. Then I reached a point that went deeper into the cliff where the stone suddenly changed to a gray color, with holes in it, almost like lava. And the stone was formed into columns. The whole area gave an ancient impression and I was able to climb onwards towards a little opening at the end which gave way to a beautiful green valley. In the middle of the valley a spring bubbled up and I realized: "That is why the eagles come up here! They can drink pure, fresh spring-water completely undisturbed." The water only bubbled up a little and then seeped away back in the earth, so no one would ever guess there was fresh water up here; no stream came from it. I noticed a big flat stone about 150 ft. away from the spring and I decided: "Ah, that is the perfect spot to go sit and wait for the eagles!" First I took out some tobacco offering and made a prayer to let the area and the eagles know what my intentions were: that I would like to observe them, learn for them. I left the tobacco close to the water.

The next day I went up really early in the morning, way before the time when I knew the eagles would come to drink, and waited. I had a feeling inside, almost like a spirit telling me that I had to sit very, very still, not moving at all when the eagles appeared. If not, they would attack. An eagle has very long and powerful talons and a strong beak with which it can do a lot of harm. So I knew I had to sit absolutely still. The first eagle, the big one with the spots, came in on its own. It made a full circle all around the valley, flew over to the spring and started to drink. Then it spotted the tobacco, looked up and turned its head straight at me. He looked at me for a few minutes, very intensely, then after a while he felt comfortable with me and started to drink more. I knew he had accepted me. When he had finished drinking, he made his call and the other 12 eagles started coming in, taking turns drinking. During that time, the leader stood off to the side and kept watch for them. When they were all done they left, following their leader.

I figured I wanted to keep doing this and I went up there every day early in the morning, always making sure I was there before they arrived. One day I was there a lot earlier and had time enough to wander around the valley, when a special stone caught my eye. It was a very old grinding stone. There were also arrowheads in the area. At one time, my own people, the Shoshone of that area, must have used the spring too. I still have that stone today. It is a special connection to my ancestors. For quite some time, I went up there every day to be with the eagles and they really learned to accept me. It was extremely healing and peaceful for me to be with them.

What happened at some point though, was the following. Like I told you before, once a week a truck came to bring me supplies. One time, my brother, my sister and a girl I had never met came up to visit and check on me. The girl took a real liking to me, I could feel that right away, and she asked if she could spend the night up in the canyon with me. The next day, somebody would pick her up again. I had nothing against that, being a young guy without any kind of company for a long time, let alone female company. I showed her around the ghost town and the canyon and we spent the night together. At one point I mentioned the eagles to her, where they flew in to drink and everything. Since I wanted to impress her, I did a stupid young male thing. She wanted me to show her the spot and so early next morning, we climbed up to the hidden valley together. I knew in the back of my mind this wasn't a good choice. The eagles had given me permission to be with them, but they knew nothing about the girl, so I really shouldn't be doing this. But when you're young, your ego is strong and stubborn, so I ignored that inner voice. So we sat on the rock and I told her, no matter what would happen, to sit very still and not move at all. I told her: "You may not understand, but this is a matter of life and death. Please do not move. The eagles will be angry if you do so and they will attack." She promised and we waited for the eagles to come. Sure enough, the leader comes and does his circle. He looks at us, but she is doing really good, not moving. He makes another circle and then starts to drink. After he finishes, like every day, he calls in the others and they're all drinking from the water. The leader is doing his lookout. Then out of the blue, the girl throws her arms around me and is saying: "Thank you so much for this incredible experience. This means so much to me!" And as soon as she did this, the big eagle gave out a loud scream, never heard an eagle scream like that before, and flew straight up above us in the air. The other eagles followed him. I knew instinctively this meant real danger. I hissed to her: " Do not make one little movement or seriously, one of us could die..." She got real scared and almost froze on the spot. All of a sudden, the lead-eagle flew from high above in the air straight down at us and it looks like he is going to collide with us. Just a little before he veers off; we could feel the tips of his wings touching and the dust kicking up as he went by us. All other 12 eagles did the same thing. There was a lot of movement and dust everywhere around us. Only the two of us were still. It repeated two to three times. We never moved an inch. I knew inside if we had, we would have been attacked and they would have ripped us open with their claws and beaks. At one point, the leader gave his call and they all left. I turned towards to her and then I realized that she was totally white in the face, like a ghost, in deep shock. She couldn't move. I actually had to slap her face a little to have her respond. She snapped out of it and screamed at me and ran off towards the cliff. I was really scared that she would fall down, as upset as she was, but she came to her senses on time and got down in one piece. My brother had just driven in with his truck and she started babbling to him, still not fully recovered and very out of it: "I want to get out of here!" When I reached them, my brother immediately started to attack me, thinking I had done something to her. My sister then intervened and got him to stop and I could explain what had happened. My brother calmed down and took the girl back to town. She never again wanted to see me after that. Neither did the eagles. It was clear that they had decided, because I had disrespected them, that they would not come to the valley while I was there. They only flew in when I wasn't around the water. After the third time of trying without them showing, I stopped doing it and never went back up. It was very saddening, but my own fault.

I stayed for a couple more weeks and at some point, I had a few friends come to visit me for a few days. They wanted to hang out a little and also came to see the old graveyard that was close by. Some of the graves went back to the 1800's; there were probably over a hundred graves all in all. The graveyard was on top of a small hill and we were wandering around it, reading the signs with the names, all of them from white people. Then my eye caught a rusty pipe sticking out of the ground, about three inches thick and sticking out about three ft., going down into one of the graves. One of us kids started yelling something into that pipe, like: "Hello, anybody in there?" We were all laughing and kidding around, each taking our turn. I was a little reluctant, but didn't think about it too much and also called something down through the pipe. All of a sudden, we all freaked out cuz we heard a long deep "Hellooooo..." back! It came from that pipe, from the depths of the earth and we all heard it loud and clear. For a second we looked at each other, terrified, noticing that we'd all heard it at the same time. It wasn't just my own imagination. Then we started to run, getting the heck out of there, tumbling over each other, heading for the car. We left in a hurry, passing Carlin and went all the way to Elko where there was a casino where we stayed all night in the midst of lots of people and noise. Ooh man, we were all so scared!

After that I thought: "My time in the desert in that ghost-town is up!" The experience with the eagles and now this spirit responding to me on the graveyard, whatever it was, I took it as signs to return to town. And that is what I did.

Mushrooms and Mountain Lion Story

All of my life I have had a dislike for mushrooms. It is a funny thing, but they never really appealed to me. There is an explanation to it and a story that goes with it.

In the desert you are grateful for whatever food you can find. Especially plant life is scarce, so when the rains come – and they do come once in a while - you take the opportunity to go out to see what has come to blossom.

In the desert where I grew up there is a special kind of grass called buffalo grass, which is really thick and grows up to your shoulders. Because of its extreme thickness, only buffaloes are able to eat it, hence the name. Although we didn't have the big herds of buffalo like in the Northern States, we did have buffalo in Nevada. Back in time, it was a less dry desert state. We had more rivers and creeks with lots of beavers in them. It was greener and we had trees, especially in the mountains and around the waters. But when the settlers came through, they cut down a lot of the trees and in the desert, trees take much longer to grow back so that influenced the whole ecosystem into a much dryer and more barren place then before.

When the rainstorms would come, a big kind of mushroom would grow in between that buffalo grass. It's called button mushroom and you had to search for it, but if you knew where to look you could find them. The big ones could grow to one and a half feet and after cooking they were really good to eat. My dad used to send a couple of people spread out over the desert area to go find them. He noticed I had a special ability. I would go up to the side of a hill, scanning the area where we were going to search for the mushrooms. I would stand there for a bit and then I knew where to go. What I did was smell the mushrooms and this led me to them. Nobody else did it this way and nobody had that ability either. My sense of smell never failed me, but I hadn't realized it was something special. My father told me: "You know, there is a reason why you don't like mushrooms. You are not supposed to eat them. You have a special relationship to them and you are not meant to feed on them." I was relieved and thought: "Well, that makes sense. It is a good excuse not to have to eat any mushrooms! I can politely refuse to have them on my plate from now on."

One day while I was looking for some mushrooms and was walking through that high buffalo grass, all of a sudden I stepped into an opening in the grass where the buffalo had roamed and flattened it out. They do this deliberately so they have space to eat and rest. It was about 10 feet across and a nice round space. In the center of this circle my eyes caught two little mountain lion cubs meowing on the floor, cuddling up close to each other. At first I was touched by this sight, thinking: "How cute they look!" Quickly it dawned on me that there must be a mother close by too, because when the cubs are that small, the mother doesn't leave them alone for long. As I think this, I hear a hissing sound and I look up to see her standing on a little hill staring down at me, about 30 ft. away. She was really upset I was at such close range to her cubs and she was getting ready to attack and jump. I knew I could never outrun a mountain lion, so that was no option. Once you start running, she will go after you no matter what, because then you become prey in her eyes. I had to think quickly and remembered what my father and others had taught me. The first thing I did was change the focus of my eyes. I still looked at her, but instead of looking straight into her eyes, which would challenge her, I looked downwards on her chest, still keeping in touch with her. If you totally turn your head away, chances are big she will think the game is on. Secondly I had to change my energy field immediately to make her feel I wasn't a threat to her cubs. We carry this energy field around us at all times and it contains who we are at that moment. We are able to project it outwards and we can send messages with it too. I knew I had no time to lose since the mother lion was going to defend her cubs at any moment. I projected my energy towards her in a very strong and yet gentle way, telling her I didn't mean any harm to her cubs. I saw her muscles tightening and I knew it was close. I had to be careful not to be too strong and powerful because that in itself would be threatening, but also not too gentle because then my energy wouldn't come across to her.

My message to her was: "I apologize to you that I have intruded into your home. I mean no harm to you or to your children. I am going to slowly retreat now." I started sending that message out to her, watching for signs how she was responding to it. She was still growling a little, muscles still tense, but then I saw her body relax somewhat. I knew that was my signal to back off from the area. Slowly, very slowly, I stepped backwards, keeping my eyes just below her chest to check on any movement. After about 20 feet I saw her sitting down and getting calm and I was able to walk out of the area, knowing I was safe, turning away slowly.

It was quite an amazing story. And I was quite relieved when I was back home again. She would have definitely killed me, although she didn't consider me prey she'd enjoy feeding on. Mountain lions and bears usually don't consider us as food. In fact, they don't like the smell of humans. Only grizzlies are known to eat humans, but it is not common.

If I had gone into fear, she would have been able to smell that and she would have definitely attacked me. So what I did in that split-second of sensing the danger of the situation was not give in to the fear and then turn the energy around immediately. Since I had heard stories of elders with similar experiences and because I was aware you can always have an encounter like this, I wasn't totally unprepared. It does take practice too, though, to change your energy that quickly and I was lucky I had that ability.

Of course, you can't go out to practice with a mountain lion so that when you have something like this happening, you could say: "Oh, I remember, I've done this before!" (*Mala laughs out loud*)

As a matter of fact, in the desert it is very unusual that you hit on a mountain lion, since the terrain is flat and mostly open so the animal can see you coming and will go into hiding, keeping away from you. They are also more night active and live a rather secretive life. But ever so often it happens.

Most animals will do anything they can to avoid humans. Wolves and coyotes try to avoid people too. In Nevada there were no wolves anymore when I grew up, they were all killed and poached. Only recently have wolves returned to the Western United States.

Blue Dolphin Vision

Not only did I grow up in Nevada, which basically consists of high mountain desert, much of my family's food came from the desert and we literally depended on the land. I grew up hunting rabbits and deer; I gathered food from the desert bushes and roots from under the ground. I spent so much time out in the desert that people used to say: "Mala is never going to leave Nevada. He has sagebrush in his blood!"

Although I grew up in a very dry, water scarce area, I somehow had a strong pull towards the ocean too. For some reason, the ocean fascinated me and I have always felt drawn to it.

One time I had a powerful dream, or vision, as some would call it. I saw myself as a young man, living in a village at the coast. I knew inside it was somewhere along the Northwest of the United States. I saw the lodges with the people working on their fishing nets and some people gathering shells and seaweed. Others were working on their fish catching baskets and making utensils. I knew I was among them and part of the village community. In the dream, I was living my life there on a minute-to-minute scale, as if living it for real.

It was early in the morning and I was asked to come along with some others in one of the canoes. We stayed close to the coast and each of the canoes had four to five people in it. In the center of each boat there was a big basket with a lid on it, where we put in everything that the ocean provided us with and gathered along our ride: little fish, octopus and shells to bring back to the village. We had a good day and were catching a lot. We stayed out all day, and a few hours before sunset another canoe coming from the ocean approached us. There was an elderly man all by himself standing in it. The canoe was guided by his thoughts only; there was nobody at the paddles. I knew he was our Medicine Man. He looked in each of the big baskets, giving his approval and sometimes even tasted a little piece. When he came to our canoe, we were all hoping he would take some out of our basket, because that was considered an honor. He did and even looked me in the eye and smiled at me, which gave me a good feeling inside.

After that we all headed back to the community, emptied our baskets, and others prepared and cooked our ocean harvest. We had a nice little feast that night with singing and dancing. At some point, I wandered off a little and found myself walking towards the beach. It was right around sunset and the colors were exceptionally beautiful that evening. Then I heard my name, which was, funny enough, the same name as I have now: "Mala, come over here!" I looked towards the ocean where the sound was coming from and saw a blue dolphin really close to shore, almost standing up half way out of the water. "Mala, over here!" I saw him speaking to me. He approached as close as possible, showing himself to me. I knew inside he came as my spirit animal, and I felt an incredible love for it. It was warming my body up and filled my own spirit with great appreciation and love.

My dream ended at this point but it explains my love for the ocean. Ever since, this sense of strong connection has remained.

Years later we moved to Oregon and I felt blessed being able to live so close to the ocean, just as it was a blessing for having lived in the desert for so many years. While working in the area around Salem, Oregon, I met a man from the Siletz tribe named Walt Klamath. He was the main spiritual leader of that coastal tribe and was a very involved and active man. He also ran sweat lodges and that is how I got to know him. He came over to visit me at my home one day, together with his helper Rick, who was a wood-carver. Walt presented me a gift because, as he stated, he had seen this in a vision he'd had of me. He gave me a rattle with a wooden top, carved in the shape of a dolphin and it was painted blue. I was thrilled when I saw it. Incredible how the blue dolphin from the vision had actually taken form! It was a beautiful design with a star in the middle of its forehead and also two-quarter moons on each side, all symbols that have meaning to me. I was so stunned and happy with this gift. I still use this rattle and it has accompanied me in many ceremonies.

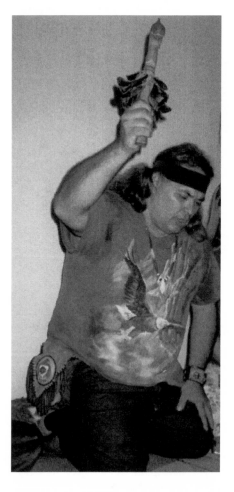

Mala using the Blue Dolphin Rattle

Spirit Helpers and Spirit Names

Spirit animals or spirit helpers can come to you in many ways and can appear throughout your life. It is a connection that you have towards a certain part of nature. If you are aware enough, this relationship reveals itself to you. It can show itself through a vision or a dream. Something can happen where the animal or whatever the connection is actually appears and you have an encounter of some kind. This spirit helper can guide and help you, and you can also make use of its qualities and powers to help others. You are supposed to never hurt this helper or take it for food, because that would violate the trust between you and is considered extremely disrespectful. Although you call this your spirit helper, you actually work with this helper on a physical level. You work with this energy on a more daily basis, with the spiritual and the physical aspects of it at the same time, so to speak. Sometimes this appears in a person's name too. Like the Eagle in my name is also one of my spirit helpers.

If you were given a spiritual name that has something to do with nature, like an animal, a bird, a flower or a tree, then you are obviously connected to that part of nature and are also guided by it. This can also be the name that humans know you by, again, like in my case Spotted Eagle. You can talk about your spirit helpers to others and can also be connected to more than one.

In our way, you usually have another name that goes deeper and is even more spiritual: this is what Nature and Spirit know and recognize you by. If you enter a forest or come up to the ocean, you introduce yourself to Nature through this name. This spirit name is very private and not used openly in front of humans.

This connection exists on a deep and powerful level and is what we refer to as our true spiritual name. You are careful and respectful in using its energy, and call upon this energy only in times of need. You do not share the name or your relationship with it to others. It is just between you and Creation.

In the traditional way, this Spirit name was given to you by a Medicine Person, either already at birth or it would appear during your Rites of Passage ceremony at puberty. We also had a special ceremony called the seeing- or looking-into-ceremony, where the Medicine person looks into your spirit and finds the connection. Only very few people would know this name. Nowadays, this is hardly done anymore and so it has to come to you in other ways. Some people go on a vision quest. In some cases, it happens to you in a time of hardship or sickness.

Sometimes when a connection to a specific spirit helper is very strong, a name can be revealed. Also this name stays between you and Creation.

Power animal is a word not used by Native people. It is used by the white people and refers to the more common spirit animal and not to the deeper spiritual one.

Encountering Spirits in the Desert

Around 1971, I had recently gotten together with a young Native American woman called Georgina. Her brother, named Wild Cat, was a good friend of mine too. He was very dark skinned and walked with a limp because of polio, which he had caught as a child. We were friends with another Native, Cha Chio, who was a big heavy guy, who was also around our age and very strong. I'd known these guys for a few years already. Georgina had traveled to Arizona to the reservation she came from to talk to her people about how she and I had gotten together. My friends and I were supposed to join her a few weeks later. We planned on taking my old car and starting from Carlin, which is in the middle of the desert. Most of the towns are about 50 to 100 miles apart from each other. In between there is nothing but desert and the roads that connect the towns are usually simple two-lane roads, that's all. Not a lot of traffic on them in those days either. Nevada doesn't have a big population, even now, but back then, it was even less.

The three of us finally got the car ready and took off in the direction of Tonopah, a small town with a Shoshone name by the way. After a few hours of driving and still 15 to 20 miles away from town, all of a sudden a lot of smoke came out of the engine and we had to stop. When we looked at it, I soon realized the transmission had blown and there was no way we could fix that ourselves out there. We saw all the transmission oil leaking out. No duct tape and baling wire, the usual repair kit for an old beaten up Indian car, could hold that together so we had to wait for help. We pulled off to the side of the road. It was late in the afternoon and we hoped that at some point another car might drive by. If we were lucky enough, one of us could catch a ride. Like I said, not many cars on those back roads. We waited and waited and not one car came by. It was starting to get dark. We thought, we have some water, but we didn't really wanted to spend the night in the desert and wait again the next day to catch a ride into town. So I suggested that I'd walk to the next town. It would take me 8 hours or so, and I preferred walking through the night, because in the daytime it would be too hot. I was in pretty good shape back then and in Tonopah I would be able to call up some friends of mine who could help us. Luckily the moon was shining and I was able to see something. We didn't have a flashlight either, so I just had to make sure I'd stay on the road and not wander off in the desert, because you don't want to do that and get lost or step on something like scorpions or rattlesnakes.

So that was what we decided and I started right after dusk, just as I saw Grandmother Moon coming up over the hill. She was about three quarters full and there was plenty of light coming from her that reflected on the road. I figured I would need the whole night to reach Tonopah, but I'd done things like that before, just for fun, walking the whole day from town to town. I used to love to walk or run when I was young. So I was pretty confident about doing the same thing now.

After about 15 minutes of walking away from the car, something strange happened. In the distance I noticed some kind of dark shadow alongside the road. At first I thought it was a coyote moving around, so I didn't pay too much attention. Coyotes don't attack you, they don't like being around humans. Then another shadow appeared and I thought, oh well, there is a pack of them. No big deal, they will take off when I get closer. But pretty soon, as I kept walking, there were a number of dark shadowy figures ahead of me of all different shapes. I noticed they didn't get any clearer; though I came closer, they stayed black. So I knew something else was going on. By then I realized they were some kind of spirits. They had faces, some had horns and some had these glowing red eyes. They were beings in all different kinds of shapes that I had never seen before. No spirits of human beings but spiritual energies that could take on any shape they wanted. They looked pretty scary.

As I got closer, I could feel what was going on: these spirits had come to test me. I was taught that spirits by themselves couldn't harm you. It is our fear of them that causes the problem. It makes you do things that eventually hurt you. Maybe you take off running; you stumble or run into something, those kinds of things. Because you're not thinking clearly, it makes you do dangerous things, which are hurtful to yourself or to others. I had heard of stories by people who had lived through something like this, but I had never experienced this myself.

When you are on a journey like I have been on my whole life, you have had a special kind of teaching on how to deal with such things. This test was about if I was worthy of walking the spiritual path and continuing it. Before allowing you to go on to another level in your development, the spirits want to see where your heart is at, if you stay strong in mind and spirit. So I felt this was going on.

But I was also told that spirits are not always very gentle. Sometimes what they put you through can be a matter of life and death. If you give into your fear, you might end up losing your mind and even your life. I knew if I left the path I was walking on they could end up taking my own spirit and then I'd be dead... Then I'd just have to start over again and come back another time in another life.

So I kept on walking -- I was about 30 ft. away from them -- and I started to sing and pray. By now they had fully blocked the road, they were coming from both sides and they had built like a wall in front of me that left no space for me to walk through. They just kept moving but left no space. I knew I just had to stay focused and continue to walk in a positive way. The Native songs I sang carry a lot of power in them, so I trusted in that positive energy coming from the songs, singing from my heart and focusing on where I wanted to go, not giving in to fear. As I was getting closer to them, the spirits started to move away from the center of the road and they left me a little opening. I remember, they were making little noises; heavy breathing was going on and little whistling and mumbling noises as if they were speaking. I could feel, they were really talking about me.

I stayed focused. There is a way of splitting your attention in two directions so you can be in two different realities at the same time. That is what I did: one part of me shifted into being fully aware of what was going on with the spirits and walking on that road with all those beings next to me, and another part was focused on staying in a strong, yet calm and positive energy, singing quietly, being in another spiritual realm of peace inside. The physical one was aware and watching, paying attention and kept on walking forward. The other part was on a more emotional and spiritual level: that one guided me.

So I kept walking and they made space for me, moving to the sides of the road. For a while I kept singing, then I looked back and saw they had dissolved as a group and the last one of them was disappearing into the desert. I must admit I was a little proud of myself that I got through in a good way, using what I had been taught. There was great relief too! I had passed the test! (*Mala gives a big sigh*)

I kept on walking all through the night and the next morning around six o'clock I arrived in town, where I treated myself to a hot chocolate while waiting for my friends to get up for the day before I called them.

They put a tow bar on their pick up truck and the three of us got back to the place where my friends were with my broken down car, so we were able to tow it back to Carlin. I noticed when I came close to the car that my friends were not sitting in the front seat. They were both curled up in the back of the car, covering themselves with blankets. I called their names and when they saw me they jumped up, all startled and making big eyes. They screamed at me: "What? It's you? We thought you were dead!" And I said: "What do you mean?" They said: "We saw the spirits coming and thought they had taken you. It looked like that group of spirits on the road swallowed you!" They had gotten so scared that they went into hiding on the back seat under those blankets. They had thought the spirits might also come after them.

I feel I want to add a little more to the story. Actually a funny part; it has to do with those friends I called upon who helped me. The woman had already been my friend for a long time and she had taught me to play pool, which is still one of my favorite ways to spend leisure time. She had been married before, separated and then gotten together with one of the only black guys in the whole town. Not many Afro-Americans in Nevada in those days. I liked him too and we all got along very well. When they came to pick me up, we first had some breakfast together at the diner. The three of us were sitting at the counter in that small cowboy town of Tonopah that did not like white women being together with men of any other kind of race. So here she was, an attractive white woman with a black guy on one side and an Indian on the other side of the table. They stared at us while we were eating but we sort of ignored them. The three of us were used of being treated that way, as wherever we were, people would always give us funny looks and rude comments. What we didn't know though was that they had called the police on us.

What had happened was that right at that time a famous kidnapping was all over the news in the US: a very rich young woman named Patty Hearst had been kidnapped some time before by the Symbionese Liberation Army. But she, quite sensationally and voluntarily, joined this group and turned against society herself. She was hanging out with all kinds of outlaws, hippies and, let's say, people that weren't very accepted by most white American citizens. They had been robbing banks and doing all these provocative things that were constantly covered by the media. Word had gotten out that Patty Hearst had fled to Nevada. So when the police in that little town saw us three sitting there they thought: "That's her! We're going to catch her!"

When we left the restaurant, about half way to the gravel parking lot where the car was, all of a sudden, police cars were showing up from all directions: sheriff cars, local police, and federal police cars. They had informed everybody in the area about whom they thought they were going to bust. So all these cars came rushing in, surrounding us and circling us in. They were prepared for Patty Hearst and her gang! The police were armed with machine guns and other weapons and all these rifles aimed right at us. Of course we were shocked! Didn't know what was happening! Through one of those big megaphones we heard yelling: "On the ground, on your bellies, arms and legs spread out! Don't move! "Well, that was a moment where I knew: "Oh yeah, real physical danger! They are not kidding." And I was on my stomach right away. I knew singing wouldn't help me now. (*Mala thinks this is very funny and laughs out loud*)

The police really thought that they had made the most spectacular catch in their history! When they searched my friend's car, there were a couple of guns in the back of the truck because he likes to go out hunting. Also my female friend had a couple of warrants for some minor things out for her arrest. They thought she had gone under a false name. The signs looked all pretty negative for us. Oh, those policemen were all so excited about their big luck, patting each other on the back, smiling and being proud, saying: "We're going to be national news!"

It took about three quarters of an hour before they realized something was wrong. It turned out that my friend had a license for all the guns he had in the car. The warrants for the woman had actually already been dismissed at some point but were never taken out of the system. So everything turned around and they had to, very reluctantly, while grinding their teeth, let us go. We left quickly after that, had survived another adventure and had a good laugh afterwards!

Spirits and Spiritual Energies

I would like to share a little on the different aspects of spiritual energies, or what we as Native people call spirits.

Spirits have been part of my reality as long as I can remember. Amongst indigenous people it is common to talk about them or refer to them. You weren't considered to be out of your mind as seeing spirits was a part of every day life. So you would also not make a big deal about it, as they now sometimes do. There are spirits of many different sorts and people in the West might prefer to call them energies.

I know there are a lot of spirits out there. I don't know how many, but there are a lot, maybe a million or more, I have no idea! Not only are there huge amounts of spirits, there are also many kinds of spirits.

There are the spirits of Nature: Father Sun, Grandmother Moon and spirits in trees, rocks, of animals, in plants, or the water. Everything on Mother Earth carries life and therefore has Spirit.

Mostly, spirits are of a neutral nature. There are those that help you, guide you on the path you are on, sometimes showing you a possibility, a direction. It depends if you call upon them, if you are willing to listen and be aware of them. Sometimes they warn you, give you some sort of sign.

I was told to be very careful with using names and asking for certain specific spirits if you call upon the spirit world for help. When you go ask for a specific spirit to come and help you, you think you know what is the best spirit for you in this case and you actually limit this help. It's your personal ego telling you to do so and is considered arrogant. But in fact, you don't know at all what is best for that situation and for that particular moment, and you have no idea what is out there. So I was taught that if I need help and ask for spiritual guidance, I ask from my heart for the best possible help from whatever spirit is willing to help for that situation and for all involved. That's it. When we put our hearts into the right energy, we keep the doorway open for whatever is meant to happen and for whatever guidance may come in whatever form. Otherwise it's showing that you claim to know what is best. If we go out there with the right heart and the right mind, we leave that door open and the right one will come in. Every time we put out there what we want, we limit what is supposed to be. So it's better to leave the option open for whatever is best for us. [4]

Our ancestors, those who came before us and have crossed over already, have transformed into their spirit form and can guide and help us. There are those that are really good and beneficial in nature. Certain people have lived really good lives, living their lives purposefully, being of service and

---

4   Unfortunately I have met many people who practice it this way. They call upon Chief Joseph or upon Sitting Bull, for instance, all kinds of famous Native Leaders of the past, claiming they are their personal guides. We know none of that is true.

doing a lot of good, coming close to that point where they, once they cross over, can choose to stay on the other side and not come back to this realm. But they can also choose to help us whenever they can as a positive spirit being down here on planet Earth.

Sometimes a spirit of a human is caught between this world and the other realm and is really not feeling happy about it. People who have experienced a lot of violence in their lives, either as a victim or also as someone who caused a lot of harm to others, can get stuck in between the realms. Especially when a person hasn't had the chance to make it right yet or when death comes violently and abruptly, the shock hinders preparation for the moment of transition. Some spirits might have been doing so much wrong in their earthly lives that they struggle to release this before being able to make the total step to the other side. They just haven't crossed over fully yet. Sometimes they make themselves known to us and can be hurtful, show their pain and desperation, might try and scare you. They can't harm you directly, but they do try to get you into a frightened state. Sometimes, when they are powerful enough, they are able to move objects, but the reason they do so is because they want to make you afraid, not because they purposely want to harm you. When you then get scared you might start backing off, start running and fall down the stairs or get run over by a car, lose your mind or whatever. In a sense you could call spirits behaving like this "bad spirits."

You also have to be aware of the so-called trickster energies: they try to trick you into saying or doing things that you actually shouldn't, as if they are trying to play a joke on you and test you a little.

When I was young I was taught to sense the difference between all the spiritual energies. We all have these premonitions and feel spiritual energies, but most of the modern people don't know enough to understand them. It is like walking into a room and you all of a sudden get an unpleasant feeling, almost like getting goose bumps on your skin or your stomach tightens up. Your spirit reacts to it and your body is also affected.

Maybe something really bad happened in that room once. It can be the other way around too: you enter a place where you feel a very welcoming, warm, relaxed sense throughout your being. It can be a place where positive ceremonies used to be done or a wonderful place in nature where all flows together harmoniously.

The spirits I encountered in the desert that night I felt were neutral. They just wanted to test me and did what they had to do. They thought: "Well, here is Mala at this point in his life. He needs our spiritual help. But we need to make sure that his heart is in the right place. We want to see if he is ready to continue his spiritual journey, where we will be of assistance to him at a later point."

You can look at it and say: "But they really wanted to hurt you and might even have taken your life! " But I never saw it that way, because it was a test that I could pass or fail, no more. For me, it was okay. If you are brought up this way, it fits in the picture and you don't question it. For everyone who walks a deep spiritual path, these are just challenges that you grow from and accept because that is part of it. The spirits wanted to know if I was worthy enough for any knowledge they might want to share with me in the future and that I could, from there onwards, carry this knowledge forth with the right heart.

I have a question for you: "If you meet an angry bear that attacks you and you lose your life, does that make the bear evil?" No, it's just how he is and you have to take in account the circumstances how and when you met him because this is part of the whole picture. We have to be careful with our judgments here. I see this happening over and over again when it comes to nature. Some animals kill to survive, others give their life in order for the circle to continue. Some people say it is so hard for them to see this killing and they claim this is a bad and harsh thing, feeling sorry for the animal that gets killed, but that is just part of nature. You have predators and you have prey. Also there is no life higher or lower than the other. It is life no matter how big or small, whether animals or plants and there is no comparison about their worthiness.

If you come with a judgment that is based on fear and you keep thinking these spirits are evil, this emotion will grab you by the throat and make the situation worse for you. If you can instead see what the true purpose of their presence at that time and place is, you acknowledge them and yet are not overwhelmed. Then it is not a reaction based on fear but an actual action on your behalf.

Also, to think because they have red eyes and horns they must be evil, you give in to an association you have. But you know, in nature there are many animals that have red eyes in the dark, like cats or martens, and there are all kinds of horned animals too. The fact that the spirits were dark doesn't mean anything either: the night is dark and not in itself evil.

It really depends on your way of thinking and how you are programmed to respond.

When I encounter something like this, when I know the challenge is not on the physical level but actually on a spiritual level, my first reaction is to actually feel the energy of it. I allow it to be there so I can really feel what kind of energy it is. Is it good spirits, is it bad spirits, or is it neutral; what kind of feeling do I get from them? I opened my senses so I could find out if these spirits purposely wanted to hurt me. My fear dissolved and I knew I would come through all right. Those spirits were not human and weren't necessarily evil. But this all happens in a split second, I guess. I knew right away, in the case that I described above, from the way the spirits were coming in and from the way they moved, that they were testing me. They came in the images that would create fear in me.

Once I had a person in one of my workshops, who spoke of his fear of getting onto the subway, as he was very sensitive to all kinds of energies. Whenever he entered a subway compartment, he'd see some people with spirits hovering around them, spirits of dead people in turmoil and in pain. It affected him so much that he felt threatened and became so horrified that for a while he didn't travel by subway anymore. I answered him that whatever the reason was that he saw what he saw, it had something to do with himself and that the importance lay not in the fact that he was actually seeing it. I told him this was happening to him, because it was trying to teach him something and it wasn't about those people or those spirits. "For you to react this way," I told him, "means you need to learn to balance something within yourself. If you have such a strong reaction and even avoid the encounters totally, it means you need to learn to change your response to it. When you are able to stay calm and balanced within yourself, it might be that those spirits won't bother you so much anymore. Maybe they will actually disappear and you will not see them anymore because they no longer need to teach you. If you do keep seeing them, you could look at them, give them recognition or even a smile. It could well be that they change their energy and smile back. You could also ask them what their purpose is and if they are in need of something. Then you have healed something in yourself and helped them as well."

Because spirits have been around me all my life, because I was used to them, because I had heard stories too, this wasn't an unfamiliar situation. That's why I was able to sense it so quickly and as I walked on I was determined and quiet. I have been in training for this. If this had been my first time, I might have freaked out. My body would have had a sense of alarm because the situation was unknown and therefor it would have responded with a warning. If your mind doesn't recognize something, it gets classified as unknown and this message is sent to the body. In my case there was no fear, only a sense of knowing that it was a crucial moment that depended on my actions how I would come through. I actually deliberately sent out:

"Is there danger for me?" The answer came back: "No." Although I knew it was a tight situation, it was really only up to me.

So I chose to sing, because that gives me power and helps me to focus. What I knew I shouldn't be doing was focus on them, watching them all the time, because then they would be able to take my energy in and I would lose my power, and I would actually add to their power.

I had to stay focused on something else so I sang my songs. I know they carry positive energy, they strengthen me while singing them. Even if I had had some fear, the songs and prayers would have helped to bring me out of it. That is what they do. So either way, it is good to sing and pray!

The more you practice and are aware of the energies that are around and within you at all times, the more you will be able to actually see spirits and spiritual energies. It is because we as human beings have separated ourselves from them that we don't see them anymore. Usually people are still able to feel or sense something. You use all your senses for this and seeing is just one part of it. But in today's world we often rely on visual confirmation as proof. If you truly open yourself up to Nature and Spirit, you'll be able to clearly see the spiritual energies flowing and connecting in all kinds of different patterns and forms and shapes. Mostly we aren't capable of doing this all the time, but we can develop this capability as we go along. There are those who are able to smell a spirit or those who have more a strong feeling sensation. There are those who can see an aura around a person and those who have a natural sense for plants and herbs and their energies.

All energy has shape and form and that is why we name it as a spirit. It is like when you look at a cloud: it has a shape but it changes constantly. Looking up at the sky, clouds might be visible and all of a sudden dissolve, become stronger or change color. When a lot of clouds come together, you have a cloudy, overcast day. That has energy and shape too, just not as clearly defined with straight borders. If you looked at it from above, you would recognize a point where there is no overcast or fog anymore. In the end, all energy has a form. It is just that with our limited vision we can't see it. But we learn to be aware and be conscious of it while we practice.

In my perception it feels totally normal to talk about spirits, as they are so much part of life. For a lot of people who are willing and eager to learn, I have noticed it is the blocks in their heads that make them want to control and structure things so they can make sense of them. That is okay. Your perception changes as you learn. You redefine what you perceive and it also gets fine-tuned over time. It is about changing your way of thinking and this affects your belief system and mind concepts.

I have encountered numerous energy workers over the years and everybody has their own systems with its own names. I have heard people talk about the energy grid of the earth or the matrix. In Eastern traditions they talk about the different sorts of Qi that affect us and they make use of it through Qi Gong or acupuncture. We can learn from each other and it can add to our own system of understanding. A lot of these energy workers have a hard time with their clients not believing in those energies, as they don't feel comfortable with the so called "unseen" world. It's what I witnessed in my youth when the white people I grew up around made fun of the way we talked and sang to the spirits. Instead of wanting to learn, they refused to acknowledge a different way of perceiving and got defensive and aggressive about it. Throughout my travels I've been happy to see that so many people are opening themselves up again and returning to what they once knew inside naturally. It is part of why they come to my talks and workshops, because they want to learn and relearn. Many people nowadays start to feel comfortable using the word energy and aren't phrasing it as spirits, but that is basically a detail. What is essential is that awareness grows for the spiritual energies that are everywhere around us all the time.

It is interesting to see how technology is helpful in this way. Sometimes when you take a picture, you can discover a spirit in it. It is like the camera can see what we with our human eyes are refusing to see. You can see spirit balls moving around or forming certain patterns on the pictures, whereas with the naked eye you don't see it when looking in that direction. The camera has a different awareness. Modern technology is capable of making visible or measuring what a lot of cultures have claimed for ages, like the aura around a person or the energy field of the heart. It is beautiful to see how these things come together. It will help us to understand and combine more!

That is why I say that it is essential to bring the different worlds together, whether Native traditions, the Western modern world or other worlds. I can only add what I have experienced of the Native and the Western way. I can share about what I was taught about following your inner guidance. When you have a strong sense inside yourself, you follow that guidance and open your senses even more, trying to see, hear, smell, taste or feel the energy. The first thing is that you have to ask yourself: "Is it coming in a good way?" If it comes from a good source, you follow that lead. If you have doubts and there is confusion, you stop inside and wait a little before reacting. You need to sit with it and sort it out. Question yourself: "Are my doubts getting in the way? Is it my own mind that is playing tricks? Am I being warned? What is it that confuses me?" If there is a negative feeling inside, of course you don't continue because that is a sign of warning. You need to practice and sometimes you will make mistakes. It is like with everything else: you stumble and fall but eventually you'll walk.

Extraterrestrials and Star People

After having met with her parents and family at the reservation, Georgina and I moved to Las Cruces in New Mexico, close to the Mexican border and

Texas, close to El Paso too, where I had been offered a job and worked for a few months. It is basically a military town, centered near the White Sands Military Base named after the area around it, which is desert with really white sand, quite special. It is also known for the sightings of extra-terrestrials and UFOs. Actually, over there they apparently shot a UFO out of the sky, which then crashed and they moved it to Area 51.

Area 51 was a classified military base in Nevada whose existence the government of the United States always denied even though people tried to get close and take pictures to prove its existence. It was a top-secret project where the most advanced technology was developed. They tested aircrafts and other equipment and did research on extra-terrestrial life-signs from other planets. All the information and material from all over the US concerning the topic "extra-terrestrial life" was gathered here. People, who have gotten too close to the area, literally have disappeared. In 2013 the government admitted that this base had been a testing ground for many things. They didn't explain too much about it, but at least its existence was acknowledged. If some sort of communication with beings from outer space or any kind of captures or findings of spacecrafts occurred, this was the place where they were taken. And it still exists today.

Area 51 was well known around the world for the work they did, although not admitted openly and to the public. There was a similar place in Russia, I believe, but I don't remember the name. [5]

When I am asked about my personal belief in this matter, I say: "I believe that it would be really crazy to assume we are the only life form in

---

5   In recent years, more and more scientific evidence is building up claiming with a high
     possibility that there are other life forms in the universe. And there are probably more than
     a billion galaxies with even many more stars out there.
     Already early on, well known astronomists and astrophysicists like Frank Drake (1961, The
     Drake-Equation) and Carl Sagan (1985, in the book 'Contact') made assumptions in that
     direction. The astronomer Seth Shostak from the Seth Institute in California eliminated a
     lot of uncertainties in 2015- 2017 and is concluding that even in our own home galaxy there
     is a probability of another intelligent life form about 2000 light years away from earth.

the entire universe." Yeah, so I believe there are many other life forms out there, in different stages of evolution, some ahead of us, some behind us, if you can actually put it that way, because probably it is just different and it has nothing to do with hierarchy. Also on the Mother Earth, there have been many stages in evolution; long before there was human life, there has been other life.

Many indigenous peoples have a strong belief and connection to what they call the Star people. In fact, one of my tribes, the Cherokee people, claim they originally come from the Pleiades. There is evidence of many old pictograph writings on walls of cliffs in numerous places all through the Americas from long before the white people came that show aircrafts coming down and beings that look different from human beings, some even wearing masks.

Various elders have told me different points of view and beliefs. Partly it depends which tribe they are from; partly it is a personal choice of what they believe in. Personally, I do recognize the existence of star people. I don't know if they are among us, but I believe they exist. There are all kinds of possibilities: it could be true or not, I like to keep it open.

I knew of a couple around my age, who both were Medicine people; they were Yurok and Hupa Natives from California and they had a strong belief in the star beings whom they envisioned to be among us. Together with my family we stayed with them for a few months at a later point in my life. They claimed there are two races of star people, who have been at war with each other for a long time. One race looked more like the classical extra-terrestrials with bigger heads, large eyes and smaller bodies and the other race were like lizards. The lizard ones saw humans as a source of food and the other ones have been trying to protect us. Also they said that the star people have been coming down to our planet to breed with us but that they then take on a human form. The Medicine that the couple carried made it possible for them to recognize those people. They told me that I was one of those that came from the stars, not the lizard ones luckily, but the other ones. They told me that it was why I was on the path I was on, to help and support the people down here. The woman actually drew a picture of me of what I looked like in her eyes. Of course that is quite a statement and I don't know if that is true or not. It really isn't important to me and I didn't relate to it. Each person has his or her own perception on life. In the end, it depends on what we choose to believe and consequently end up seeing.

Important for me is how I am walking my path and live my purpose and that I carry it out in a good way. There is no need for a title, to give it a name, you know. The path itself is all that matters. How am I living, what am I doing in my life now, am I of service to the Mother Earth and to the greater good?

Numerous people have told me similar things about being a celestial being. My choice is not to give too much energy to it, because you can easily get carried away and get caught up in such information. The moment you start putting energy into it you'll have expectations. Expectations only lead to blocking the flow of things, the flow of life. They don't allow things to evolve, to just happen. Expectations block your heart energy. You are not open anymore to the experiences that life offers you. You blow things up, out of proportion; you think that you are special and you need a special treatment or that people need to behave in a certain way around you because you are so special. It becomes a self-fulfilling prophecy that you have created.

But I admit it's a very thin line, because we all have beliefs that we grow up with, things that stay with us all through our lives and become like a frame for our life. In that sense we create our own reality while living our lives, gathering experiences and learning from them or maybe not learning from them.

This is a real important issue in my point of view. It touches the heart of what spirituality means, of what "living a spiritual life" means. On the one hand, we are creating our own path, within the boundaries of our concepts and belief systems. On the other hand though, we also want to allow Creation to flow and let life take its own course and we do not want to be led by our expectations.

Even if you are deliberately trying to live a positive life, which sounds very good and logical to do, you close yourself off for learning experiences. Instead of being guided by Life and by Spirit, you direct it and want to have it a certain way. You are, in fact, limiting your experiences.

Living a spiritual life really means allowing yourself to be open to anything that happens. I try to have as few expectations as possible and be totally open to what comes and what is. To be fully in the moment and be totally present. Of course, I am still learning and it doesn't function all the time. But I try to go with the Flow of Life, to be in a state of accepting whatever comes, to be open to the lessons, open to how my path unfolds, open to how my journey develops.

I try to do good, but not with the thought in my head that I will get something in return. I know that in the end, for my path as a whole, something good will come out of it, but that can still mean that I will have to struggle while living my life, that I will encounter hardship and difficult situations. I try then to embrace that difficulty and hope to grow from it.

I was always told: give from your heart freely, don't expect something to come back to you, don't have any expectations about it at all. Let go and let it flow from there.

Of course there are times when it is necessary to have goals in our lives. We visualize, we put energy into something and hope it will manifest; that is all good. But as Native people we ask for those things only when it is good and meant to be. What you ask for in your prayers and visualizations always comes into the context of the Greater Good. As human beings, we cannot oversee everything, we don't know how our wish is going to affect other living beings so we always want to be humble in what we ask for and we are accepting of how things happen and unfold.

That's where it gets tricky and where we've got to be careful. Allow yourself to be guided and yet also put your best personal energy in it to accomplish something that you believe in. This asks for a constant process of reflection: do I want this for my personal gain, do I do this for the greater good, am I pushing or am I lazy and is that the reason why things do not work out, or is it just not meant to be? To reflect on that moment where you have to let go and allow it to be or where you just haven't given your best yet and you can put more effort in it to make it work is one of the greatest challenges for us humans.

These matters are influenced by our upbringing and cultural definitions of what is important to strive for. Depending on their history and background, humans have different standards and various concepts about what they think is important to accomplish for themselves, others and the community.

Here an aspect comes in that I think is important to consider: on which level do we want certain things to manifest? There are emotional needs and there are physical, material wishes; there are spiritual hopes and dreams and there are mental longings. Very often it is our mind that is trying to convince us how important it is to reach a certain goal. The other parts of ourselves do not get a say; we don't even notice them. Exactly that is often a cultural influence. Are we taught to listen to our hearts? Are we taught to let our spirit guide us? Or are we told by our community and surroundings to reach material goals at the cost of others? What example did we have at home? What kind of schooling did we have?

In my opinion and how I was taught, it is really about checking and listening on all levels, getting a response on each level and letting it be filtered through your heart center. If it is positive and gives you a good, happy feeling, continue with what you are striving for and be guided from there.

CHAPTER 2

THE WEST

Hermine:

Our following meeting was in February 2013 in the USA, where we started the next part of the book journey in Santa Cruz, California. We stayed with a good friend of Mala's, Bob Saenz, an Apache Native he knew from his younger years and who had known Mala's parents very well and had always been committed to the "Red Road". We gathered stories from long time back, many memories of Mala's father Rolling Thunder and Meta Tantay, the traditional Native community in Nevada where Mala and his family had lived for many years. Afterwards we traveled to see his niece, Rhonda Morning Star Pope in the Sacramento area, where we stayed at the Buena Vista Miwok reservation. Rhonda's father was one of Mala's brothers, who had lineage to the Miwok Nation through his mother. Rhonda became the key person restoring the reservation and bringing back the traditional cultural ways of her people. After a long and hard process in which she fought against the local government, she had been able to get part of the original land back and we witnessed her pride and joy in sharing what she had accomplished. At the Miwok Reservation Mala and I wandered around the traditional brush arbor which is now used for dancing and ceremonies. A permanent sweat lodge area with special places designed for the people to change afterwards had also been built. There was a small graveyard for the tribal members, where Rhonda's father's bones were also buried.

On our way to Nanish Shontie in Oregon, the community where Mala lived at the time, we made one important stopover in Mt. Shasta, which became a blessing for our journey so far and a key to proceeding onwards.

During this trip I was guided to give a crystal I had been carrying with me on many travels back to Mother Earth. Crystals have a special capacity to carry information and radiate frequencies. They are born and grown beneath the surface of the earth, so it felt natural to return this crystal to its nourishing source.

I was lead to a spot at the bottom of the peaks of Mount Shasta. The night before, I had had a strong image of how the ancestors of that area are connected to the mountain. I saw an open meadow within the forest with Mount Shasta towering at the back. Lots of Native people were lining up, forming a circle around the meadow, dressed in traditional clothing, coming from different tribes, young and old, men and women, quietly standing there, waiting. In the middle, the Bear People were taking the lead going into the mountain, followed by all kinds of four-legged-ones. The Native people followed after them into a huge cave tunnel system, going into another realm beyond time and space as we know it.

Mala shared with me that many years ago, a Medicine man of the Californian area had told him a story with the same content as my vision. During the time when the white man came, the lives of Native people were threatened to the extent that they were shown a way to go into hiding and stay there until it was time to surface again.

Coming up the mountain by car the next day, I recognized up front where that spot was, and in honor of the ancient ones, placed the crystal I had brought with me under a layer of snow beneath a tree in the earth, it was vibrating with that old energy and was connected to today's world.

When we left the mountain area to head north to Oregon, we heard an eagle cry close by while driving the car. It was loud and clear, but when we were looking for it, we couldn't see an eagle anywhere. It was a Spirit eagle, giving a powerful sign that we had been seen and were being watched and guided. With a blessed feeling we continued on our journey.

In that same year, Mala, accompanied by Sky, his wife and life partner came back to Europe in the fall, doing talks and workshops together. We continued working on the book whenever it was possible.

Tribal Organization of Nature

In our eyes we say that Mother Earth is organized in a tribal way. We talk about the Stone People; we talk about the Water Beings; we talk about the Tree People; we talk about the Insect Nation; we say the Winged Ones or the Four-legged Ones and so on. There are tribes, clans and families wherever you go and it applies to anything in nature. They all have a task and a purpose. There is a dependency within a group and also between the groups. That is the Web of Life where everything is connected.

You can witness the symbiotic relationship of plants, insects and animals very clearly if you take time and are willing to learn.

They take care of each other: some groups nourish the other; some protect and defend each other, but in the end there is always a balance.

Each form of life has their own way of being and their own connection to everything around them. Whenever you enter an area in nature, you will find the necessary ingredients for survival are available: medicine, water, and food.

I was taught to be open upon entering a forest for instance, a beach or mountains, it doesn't matter, to the energy and information that is present there. If you are open, observing and listening, nature can teach you many things and you get knowledge and insights that are very helpful. My father was very gifted in this kind of communication, especially with plants. The plants would talk to him and might share which one would be good to eat at this time. He told me: "Be aware of the life energy that the plant is sharing with you. It can share many things: what is medicine, what is edible, what it could be used for, what is poisonous." Animals communicate in the same way with plants: they will sense the plant energy and know if it is OK to eat. If you pay attention, your understanding of a certain area will grow.

It is often a combination of knowledge that was gathered by your own experience or was passed on to you by others and specific information that you can only get by talking to a specific plant. They are communicating and are being helpful. All this information accumulates into knowledge that you have at your disposal and can make use of if needed. So you become aware of the connection and dependency of these forms of life.

If you are willing to observe closely and listen to the language of the area, you get to a point where you can feel inside that it is talking to you, sharing its information and energy with you. As you listen to the different languages around you, you raise your awareness and connect more deeply to Nature and Spirit.

You can also recognize certain patterns in nature: for instance, in a stand of Redwood trees, you often witness that the trees grow in circles of seven: it is like a family that takes care of each other. For Native people the number seven is sacred: we have the four directions, below (earth), above (sky) and the creator. It always makes me happy to see a family gathered like that.

As humans we are part of nature and should be aware of that connection and not separate ourselves from it. Influenced by the nature that surrounds us, we influence the nature we are living in just as much. If you grow your own food or have a garden, you can put that connection to use in a positive way. When you are watering your vegetables, trees or plants, let the water run over your hand toward the plant. The water will carry the message that is in your heart: you want to tell the plant life that you are grateful for what it gives, that you want it to have a long, happy life for the time that it's here, and that you will take care of it in a good way. Greens offer oxygen, food, shade, coolness, shelter, medicine and things you can make from them, like baskets, or wood for housing and furniture and making a fire.

When you communicate with the plant, it knows it's not alone and will be taken care of. Don't think in human terms in regard to the plants though. Plants have feelings, but are not caught up in issues. Don't worry that the plant is lonely: they are both tribal and yet OK on their own. Maybe get a second plant so that it has more of a family feeling, but when you offer the water with what is in your heart, it will know it's not abandoned and know it's being appreciated. All life wants to know it's fulfilling a purpose. Just give it thanks for what it's doing and don't take it for granted.

When taking cuttings from a plant, you can thank them for the time you had with them, and offer them back to the Mother Earth. Whenever you are working with plants, talk to them and let them know what you are up to. In this way, you will start to understand their needs as well and a relationship develops over time.

Plants are very sensitive to our energy and to noises in their environment. I know about experiments where scientists played different kinds of music to plants: when softer music was played the plants showed increased growth and when hard rock or heavy metal music was played their growth decreased; they were not that happy about those frequencies and sounds.

Obviously their environment affects their health and growth, slow it down or speed it up. They are sensitive to moisture, temperature, soil, the amount of light they get and the insects and animals that visit them. They respond accordingly and have their own ways of communication. They can curl up or withdraw to protect themselves if they feel threatened. Some plants can produce something poisonous or offensive to animals. There is an incredible variety in how plants function and survive, each adapted to its specific space on the Mother Earth. Some endure cold and harsh conditions; some live in abundance. I am not elaborating on this, since my knowledge is limited in this area and it's not the main topic of this book; I only wanted to mention some examples that jumped into my mind to show how to be aware of the connection and of the influence we have, both voluntarily and involuntarily. With more awareness, a more respectful treatment can follow and we can start reconnecting again.

Of course, animals take care of each other too. For most people this is more apparent than it is with plant life, but there are always nice, surprising elements. Once I saw a cow that tried to get an apple but couldn't reach that far. The bull standing next to her held the branch down for her so she could eat it. Even domestic animals, taken away from their more natural state of being, still respond the way they would in nature and take care of each other. It was touching to see and it showed me once more how we are alike and related.

Saying: "all life is tribal" also applies to people, even in urban settings. Maybe you don't think in terms of "tribes" in a city when you visualize the different groups in a city, but the tribal principle remains because it is in our nature. People seek out other people of like mind and like heart. They form groups when they work together or they play sports together or they meet up to have fun. It makes them feel better, gives them security and a sense of belonging in life. It fills a need inside and makes people happier knowing that they are not alone and have other people they can communicate with and that will help them in times of need. This is common for all life forms. So, as I always say: "All life on Mother Earth is tribal!"

Sunrise Ceremony and Sunset

Native People believe that everything has spiritual energy: trees, the grass, the wind, water, birds, animals, stones, you name it. It all carries spiritual energy, just like we as humans do. A group of beings also carry a certain specific energy. We create energy in coming together, because our energies affect each other. If you take an example from nature, you see the similarity and get a deeper understanding of how all these layers work according to the same principle: a forest has a different energy than a tree alone; a mountain carries a different kind of energy than a single pebble or a rock. All beings interact with each other and through the connections a whole web of spiritual energy is built. The Mother Earth, in our way of thinking and expressing, stands for all the different energies combined and as such, she has an energy pattern of her own too with constant interaction.

Day and night each have their qualities too, and there are certain energies more active during the day and some more active during the night. At sunrise both of these qualities are strongly present and a lot of movement occurs as the two energies meet. That is why indigenous people go out at sunrise for prayers and give thanks, because all of life is present and you can connect easily. It is a very powerful time to be out and talk to the Mother Earth: all life can hear what is in your heart and all life can help you when you ask for guidance.

When I look back at my youth and younger adult years, I came to experience a variety of ways of doing a sunrise ceremony. Corbin Harney used to perform a traditional ceremony that took four hours, with seven dances and songs. He'd be up way before sunrise and the whole time he'd be singing and drumming for all Life on Mother Earth. My father came from the Cherokee tribe and he did it in a different way. Both ways though were about honoring, respecting and giving thanks for all life on Mother Earth, each other, and yourself. That was the basic idea of the ceremony. The reason that some of it was different is not just the tribal ways, but also the individual differences. My elders told me to learn from at least seven different teachers before doing a ceremony myself. You can see how each one conducts it and notice what you like about it and what feels good inside. You may combine some of the ways and add your own personal note, without forgetting what the essence and purpose is of the ceremony as a whole. Anything you do should come from the heart. It shouldn't become something that you copy. If it comes from the heart it has a far more powerful energy.

When I am asked to lead the sunrise ceremony, and we have enough people coming together, I like us to gather in a circle around a little fire.

The circle to Native people is essential because we see that most things in nature flow in a circle. Planet earth is round; the sun and the moon are round; water flows in circles down a drain; animals move around in a circle before they lie down; the seasons repeat in a cycle. Circles are the nature of life.

Among the Native People of America, we like to start our gatherings and ceremonies by lighting a little sage. Every plant, every stone, everything on this Mother Earth has purpose and contributes to the whole. Sage told us long ago it has the gift to chase away bad spirits or negative energies and negative thoughts. The energy or bad spirit doesn't like the smell; it wants to move away from it. At the same time sage brings in good and positive energy and puts a protective layer around us. My people have known the special gift of sage for a long time.

A special tobacco mixture is passed around, and we each take a pinch from it to be able to give thanks to the Mother Earth after our prayers are done. The one who leads the ceremony starts with a prayer out loud and then everybody else follows. We offer the tobacco to the fire, so the smoke can carry whatever was said and what wasn't said out loud and is still in our hearts, up to the Creator. The gift of tobacco is that it is sensitive to the information in our hearts.

Then we walk one circle around the fire: it symbolizes the Circle of Life and you are reminded of how you started your life here as an open, spiritual being that was totally connected to Spirit and Nature, while gradually losing that natural spirituality you were born with as you lived your life. While walking you aim to return to that original state as much as possible.

We usually sing songs then. I always sing and drum the "Welcome Song", which goes out to everybody in the circle but reaches out even more to everything on Mother Earth. When somebody else wishes to add a song, that is fine too and we sing more songs depending on the mood of the day and what feels good. It doesn't matter what the language the song is in, as long as it brings in good energy and creates harmony. On my travels I have had children songs being sung or melodies from different traditions, also Christian songs. For me that is all good. To finish the ceremony in a clear way I sing a closing song and then we greet each other, going around to each person with a hug or a handshake.

In fact it is very simple and yet there is a lot to it, as it has to do with how your attitude is and how much you are consciously aware.

If you can't make a fire, then you make do and still be out there together. Sometimes a drum is too loud for the neighbors. Sometimes it really doesn't fit in the day's schedule due to work or young children that need to be fed and brought to school. You adapt and find a solution that works for you and for that situation at that time of your life. Sometimes when I am alone,

I just find a little spot on the Mother Earth to say my morning prayers and maybe sing a song.

Important though is to never forget that you shouldn't be taking yourself too seriously. People do that all the time, and I have witnessed it especially amongst those who are trying to learn and implement a ceremony like this in their lives. Because of their own insecurities they can be very adamant about a certain way, how they believe it should be done, only because they once were taught a certain way. Never lose the essence of what it is about. You do the best you can. It doesn't mean there is only one way and that it has to be perfect.

Nature and Spirit are happy when you try your best and talk to the Mother Earth and to the Spirits in whatever form. If you show that you recognize those energies and are respectful while opening yourself towards them and being guided by them, they are satisfied. That is all that matters and you can start from there.

If you get too serious about anything, you are doing it from the mind and not from your heart!

Life is meant to be enjoyed and also to have fun. Life is not meant to be too serious. Accept that you are not perfect and that you are on a learning journey to experience and grow from.

Many animals and birds also do their sunrise ceremonies. If you pay attention, you can observe this behavior all over. One person in Vienna told me a story about her crow that lives in the middle of the city and visits her on and off on the balcony. This crow always sits still at sunrise and looks quietly in the direction of the sun. After about 10 minutes after the sun is up, he comes and fetches the food put out for him on the balcony.

In the desert of Nevada, where I grew up, you could see the ground squirrels -- we call them "zippies" in our language -- coming up out of their holes at dawn and each one of them would be facing east where the sun rises.

Doing a sunrise ceremony every day is part of the Way of Life and connects you to Nature and Spirit. You give thanks and start the day consciously, raising your awareness and becoming guided with a sense of purpose.

During my talks I am often asked how to connect to Nature when the person in question lives in a big city, has to be inside concrete buildings at work all day, and has through this lack of nature a feeling of separation and loss. Well, Nature and Sprit are always around us. In fact, we are Nature and Spirit! Our bodies consist of the same energies and elements so you can always guide your awareness towards that miracle that you, as a human being, are. Be thankful for your body and give it your full attention. Of course, it helps when you are out in a forest, in a park or meadow to relate to Nature as a whole and therefore to relate to your own natural being more easily. You can look up to the sky or stand firmly on the ground, listen to the birds or the wind and be touched by them. I consider myself very lucky to have had nature around me for most of my life. Sometimes when I would be in a city for a long time and all that concrete and noise was affecting me, I would think of my Native brothers and sisters who are in prison where they hardly ever get to go outside and are closed in. And yet I know stories of how they do their morning prayers every day to give thanks, even under such difficult circumstances. They never gave up making the connection between Nature and Spirit and themselves. I remember what I can be grateful for and to not take it for granted.

Even in cities you can usually find a little patch of green, some grass to stand on. Just stand quietly on the earth, take a moment and say a prayer. You can give some tobacco or a strand of your hair and speak what is in your heart. Ask for help and guidance in getting more connected; let the

Mother Earth know you are willing to learn and grow, be a good caretaker and a better human being.

In the end it doesn't matter what time you do this. The most important thing is that you do it. You offer what you can offer and what fits for you at that moment of your life.

My habit is to do sunrise ceremony every day, no matter where I am. At times we had big groups coming together for the ceremony: then we had the sacred fire going, circled around it, did our drumming, singing, praying, and giving thanks. Then there are times where I can't make a fire and I just stand on the Mother Earth, maybe together with a few others. One time I was in Hannover, Germany, where I had arrived late at night and stayed at a hotel close to the airport. When I left the hotel in the morning for sunrise, I was shocked because right outside the hotel there was an incredibly busy street with lots of traffic, cars honking and people everywhere. No trees, no patch of green in sight. After some searching I found a little piece of dirt peeping through a crack in the concrete pavement, where I was able to leave my offering. Realizing I had forgotten my tobacco pouch, I went in search of a newspaper stand where I bought the most natural cigarettes available with the least chemicals and went back to the spot. I spoke my prayers quietly and put the tobacco from the crumbled cigarettes on the earth. This was the best I could do. Creation and Mother Earth appreciate that effort and are happy that you are trying to make a connection.

Of course, we are never really totally disconnected: there is always the heart connection. It is just that we don't believe in that connection. We doubt it, question it, belittle it, and place ourselves above or next to Nature and Spirit. It is the source of all problems we are now facing on this planet.

So the problem lies in our minds, where we need the physical reassurances of a natural appearance outside our body. It reminds us of our true nature and it is easier to connect again on a heart level. The word: "re-mind" is to be taken very literally here, because the mind needs the "re-membering" and "re-activating" of that channel of mind and heart together.

You can pray at all times and in any situation. You don't need tobacco or a fire to do that. You don't even have to stand on the earth for it. But you can make use of the physical act of standing on your two feet, deliberately on the soil in a natural surrounding, using the physical presence of fire, tobacco, a drum or your singing voice, which makes it more tangible for the senses.

Also, you have to keep in mind that humans have denaturalized a lot of the resources. We have used wood from trees to build houses and make furniture and floors. We have turned stone and sand into concrete houses. Concrete still comes from nature; metal structures also originate from nature. It is just that they are further away from their natural state. If you speak your prayers straight to the tree or the stones, those prayers are much more direct and have more power since it is sent to the original pure being. The spiritual energy of that tree or stone is much stronger, so their response is also much stronger towards you. It makes it easier and more powerful at the same time plus it goes in both directions, back and forth. If you are sensitive enough, with practice you will find you can connect more easily and without much physical help. Nevertheless, we are here on the earth plane to have physical experiences and become a balanced human being with spiritual and physical presence.

In the end we'll find that all the ceremonies and different practices are just tools. They are not the journey itself. If we really walk our path with the right intent and have grown inside, we don't need the ceremonies anymore. We have become sensitive enough to do without. During the journey we need help and support and that is why throughout history we have come up with the tools of a ceremony or certain cultural ways and practices. There is nothing wrong with those tools: the drum, the sage, and the rattle are a physical support to connect with Nature and Spirit and reconnect within myself. If I take the example of the sage, maybe at one point I'll be able to purify myself just through pure energy and without lighting the sage to smudge myself.

Easily said, but for me it is all about the journey and not about the end. So it is of no use to cut out anything from that journey. I want the full experience with all that belongs to it. At least that is my choice. It takes what it takes. Time doesn't matter.

> *(Hermine:*
> *Please feel invited to read the poem called **Sunrise**, put separately as an attachment at the end of the book)*

My tribe also has ceremonies for sunset: the energy is very different at that time. There is incredible beauty in the colors of the setting sun and it has a gentle and soft quality. We line up facing the sunset and also have a tobacco offering and some songs we sing in a mellow way, fitting with the time of the day. The way you sing the song is from the heart: it is the intent you have with it that matters. Through the heart you give it power. When you sing at sunset, it doesn't really have to be a specific song, you visualize the beautiful colors in the sky when the sun is going down, and you listen to the movements in the trees of the wind or the sounds of the birds and other animals preparing for the closure of the day and the starting of the night. These visualizations or the actual awareness of those colors and sounds give the song guidance, direction and strength.

Signs from Spirit

When I grew up, I was taught that the spirit world could communicate pretty clearly to you. It was considered important to listen to the spirits, follow their instructions, take them seriously. It is like somebody standing right next to you and talking to you, giving you information, literally whispering in your ear.

Many times, spirits can see things more clearly, have a better overview, see where things are supposed to be heading because they don't carry the confusion we humans do.

Back in the early seventies my dad was traveling a lot, going on speaking-tours, and he met many people along the way. He always invited those people and said: "Whenever you are in Nevada or in the area, you can always stop by, have some food and spend a few days, always welcome sharing our ways!" People took him up on that, so we had lots and lots of visitors dropping by.

One day there was a knock on the door and I was standing close to the kitchen in the back of the house. Somebody else went to open the front door. As soon as I heard that knock, there was a voice whispering in my ear: "This woman at the door is going to be your life mate. You are going to have children together and you'll spend a long time living with her." My first response was: "Well, I hope she is cute!" I was really thinking that. It never crossed my mind to doubt the message, and I didn't question that it was actually going to happen, but I was worried what she would look like. Yeah, I was a young man back then. (*Mala chuckles, as he thinks back*)

So when this young woman comes in and I looked at her, I was relieved to see that she actually was cute. She said her name was Sky.

At that time, I looked kind of rough. I was going through some hard times, struggling with living in a racist environment with all the cowboys around that were harassing us. To make sure to be left alone more, I tried to look really tough on the outside. I remember I had a cut-off jeans jacket on, with a skull painted on the back. I had some kind of hat on and was wearing dark sunglasses. Sky takes one look at me and was thinking: " Man, I don't want to have anything to do with that guy!" This is what she told me later on.

Sky had met my father on one of his travels and helped him when he was speaking in San Francisco, the area where she lived and then traveled along on one of his speaking tours, together with others that accompanied my father's tours. So she stayed around for a few weeks, but we only exchanged some polite words. I could tell she was not interested in me at all. I was getting a little worried how to approach her, but figured: "I have to trust Spirit here and somehow have to let her know that she is supposed to be my life mate!"

Finally I go up to her and say: "Sky, would you be willing to take a walk with me out in the desert?" She agreed, although I knew she only did this out of politeness. Once we were out a little bit in the open space of the desert, she asked me: "So what is this about? What do you want to tell me?" And I told her what had happened when she knocked on our front door. " I know it sounds crazy to you, but the spirits told me, we are life mates and we are going to have children together!" I was expecting she would slap me in the face, accusing me of a phony way to make a pass at her or she'd start laughing or would run off, but she got quiet for a moment. While the both of us were standing there in the desert, I looked up and pointed out to her what I saw: two eagles, a male and a female bird, were flying right over the top of our heads, circling. We both knew that it was a powerful sign.

But Sky wasn't convinced yet and left a few days later. Professionally she was a certified teacher and had a teaching job over in the San Francisco Bay area, plus she also attended a university over there.

I knew I had to let it go and put my faith into the Creator's hands: "If it is meant to be, this is not the end of it." She did tell my parents that whenever they were in need of something, she would come out any time to help out.

What happened was that a few months later, one of my brothers got killed in a very upsetting way. Naturally my parents were in a lot of grief over this and my mother asked me to go and call Sky. My mother had already grown fond of her during the time she had stayed at our house before, so both my parents chose her out of all the people to have around them during such a difficult time for our family. At that time, we didn't even have a phone at the house, so I went all the way through town to get to a pay phone and called her up. Sky was true to her word and agreed to come as soon as possible. She showed up and a couple of weeks later, Sky and I were together as a couple. She never really went back to California, got her teacher license for Nevada as well and stayed.

Looking back, it is quite amazing how it all worked out and things fell into place. Sky already had been interested in our kind of ways, had some understanding of the concept of the spirit world, but she had not grown up in that traditional indigenous kind of thinking and living. She had of course been listening to my father as he spoke about our way of life and had been drawn to our place to learn more. Through it all and how things unfolded, it became a clear path for her too, to which she is fully committed to this day.

After we were together for a while and actually lived like a couple, we felt a strong connection develop and we both knew it would last for a long time. We didn't get married legally though; we felt we were married on a spiritual level. The law in the State of Nevada was very strict and children from non-married couples were considered bastards. After nine years we still lived in Nevada and already had two children together; we realized that if something would happen to Sky, I would not have any legal rights over my children. If anything happened to the mother, they would take away the children and put them under Social Service and into Christian homes. Of course we wanted to prevent that and decided it was time to get the paperwork done. We didn't tell anybody of our plans and we didn't want any celebration because it didn't mean anything to us. On a heart level, we had been married all these years already. So we ended up signing those papers and at the ceremony we gave each other cigar bands to put on each other's fingers instead of real rings as was considered appropriate at a proper wedding. Afterwards we ripped them off and went home. Only weeks later we told the rest of the community that we had gotten married officially.

Sky and Mala dancing at a traditional powwow

In the old days, Native people didn't have any big marriage ceremonies like is done in modern times with fancy clothes and all kinds of festivities.

But before a couple would move in with each other, they would usually each spend a few days separate from the chosen partner and be with their own kin. The man hung out with the men and the grandfathers in the community, just the same as the woman spent time with the women and grandmothers. They were spoken to and learned about the responsibilities of living as a couple and forming a family. It was a ceremonial time where they'd purify themselves to start the relationship in a good way. According to old Shoshone traditions, a kind of commitment ceremony was done when couples chose to stay together. The tribe was present and would show their recognition, respect and appreciation to the couple, for as long as it was meant to be to stay together. Of course there are tribal differences to all these customs.

Since there wasn't much privacy in the earlier villages -- a drawback of community life -- we had a nice way of signaling the person we had a crush on and wanted to be together with. The man would go up to the woman and would put a blanket around her shoulder. If she was positive about his request and approved his gesture, she lifted the blanket above her head and shoulders and he joined her underneath. The rest of the tribe knew at that moment what was going on and out of respect they would leave and give them space. Nobody would disturb them. It was like a first date and the two of them could talk and get to know each other. From there a relationship could take off. Nowadays we still like to joke and say: "Let's toss a blanket around a girl and go for it". Blankets have great meaning for Native people everywhere in North America. In Nevada before the white man came, we used to make them from rabbit hides. You needed many hides and had to strip them in their total length and then sew them together. Especially for a big blanket that could cover two people, it took an incredible amount of time and resources to make. When the first wool blankets came to our continent, we were all pleased by the quality and relative ease of how they were made. Later on, the Pendleton Company, especially, combined our Native designs with their blanket making, and those pieces are still very much prized and cherished by our people as giveaways at gatherings and powwows.

Relationships

In the Native American culture we have a specific kind of perception when it comes to relationships. We never see a relationship in terms of ownership. Relationships are there for as long as they are good and healthy.

I remember the missionaries who came to our lands and listened to our elders speak. They were very upset when they heard us talk about relationships and family life. They didn't understand our concepts and told us what they thought it was right. White people couldn't grasp that women in our way of life had equal rights to men, also had a voice in daily life and were involved in decisions that concerned the tribe as a whole. They heard that couples do not necessarily have to stay together all their lives. Unfortunately, they forced many of their principles upon us and a lot of the original understanding of relationships within a tribal structure has gotten lost or been mingled with.

When a couple chose to be better off without living together, the rest of the community respected that. You packed your stuff and left. It was not a big deal. Children were never a reason for a couple to stay together because it was the tribe as a whole that was helping to take care of the children and that was responsible for their upbringing. It was never just the responsibility of the parents alone so children wouldn't be harmed by the choice of separation of their parents. Back then, when Native Americans lived according to the tribal ways, it wasn't frowned upon when one of the two people that formed a couple felt a desire for another person, whether the man or the woman, and actually acted upon that desire. As long as it was done respectfully and not in a harmful way, nobody would be jealous or start to make a fuss about it. The community as a whole was accepting of this and didn't interfere by giving judgmental comments.

Basically there was no need for control in relationships. It was about sharing life in a good way, taking part in each other's journey for as long as it felt good. When it didn't feel good anymore, you'd leave. There was no more to it.

Nowadays things are different because we don't have this kind of tribal life anymore. At my parent's home and later at the inter-tribal camp we created in the desert of Nevada, we incorporated the old tribal ways as much as possible. As a couple Sky and I lived according to those traditional principles and she became the mother of three of my children. We have experienced a lot of good times together. After a little over 30 years Sky and I decided to stop being a couple and separated. We honored all the years we'd had together, but knew if we pushed to stay together something bad would come of it. We still cared for each other and remained friends. In fact I still consider her my best and closest friend. A lot of people who have known us for years are sometimes slightly irritated by the fact that Sky and I still hang out so much, have fun, work, and even travel together. They think that if you separate, you should not be such good friends. You separate because you don't like each other anymore is what they seem to think. But if you let go and don't try to control something that you shouldn't hold onto, something beautiful and healing can come out of it. This is something that you have to be willing to learn and at first it isn't so easy. You have to be willing to get beyond the fears and insecurities.

Of course any relationship goes through struggles. Sometimes you need to work on issues between yourselves and you learn to overcome those difficulties together as a couple. In our tradition we just don't believe in pushing to keep it together. The elders say: "You do the best you can and when you realize you are forcing it to make it happen, you turn it over to Creation and you let happen what is meant to happen."

One of the most important things I learned when I was young is that you don't push yourself upon the Mother Earth, upon others, and also not upon yourself. Pushing creates disharmony in the end. When you push to make things happen in the way you believe they should be then you go against the flow of life. Even with good intentions, you still push to make it happen according to your own scheme. If it does somehow happen, due to your forceful controlling behavior, it doesn't come out quite the best way. In the end you push what you want to create further away from yourself.

The way you can tell the difference between pushing and doing your best is actually simple. If you struggle to make something happen and need to work hard for it, but it still feels good to put in all that energy, then that is not pushing. As long as you feel good in your heart, it is okay to work for a positive outcome. The moment it doesn't feel right inside anymore, you are starting to push.

When things get out of balance in a relationship, you may get this feeling inside where it doesn't feel good. It is important to look at the issue on your own first. You look where you could change something to bring back that balance. The next step would be to start a communication with the other person involved to both get back to a point of balance. When you keep having that feeling of disharmony and of pushing to keep it going, then you seriously need to consider stepping out of the relationship.

I have always thought it to be funny that when you start a relationship with someone, you do this because you really like that person for who he or she is. But as soon as you are in a relationship with that same person, you start wanting to change the person in how you want them to be. Somehow I don't get that! This sense of control is a paradox that appears very often in relationships, but in truth control has to do with your own fears and your own insecurities. When you feel the need to control your partner, it is showing that you actually need healing.

I was told that when you get together with somebody, you are supposed to support each other on each other's journeys in life. In a relationship you walk together, but you still each have your own journey also. You help each other along the way. It is the same when you have children: you don't own your children either. You are there as an adult and parent to guide them, to support them on their personal journey through life.

Any good life is a life where you are not controlled and you don't control other people. You want to find a way of life that your heart feels happy about. I don't care what kind of way of life. Any religion, any belief, any lifestyle, it doesn't matter. As long as you don't push your belief upon others and start to control and convince them to live like you, it's all okay.

In my way, it is essential to get spiritual guidance and be in touch with nature. These aspects help and support me on my path. If you start to trust both Nature and Spirit, you will start to also trust in your own self and your own spirit. It gets stronger inside you. Then you are able to let go of your fears and insecurities. Nature and Spirit can never be taken away from you, no matter what happens to you. I have experienced some really hard times in my life, but in the end Nature and Spirit have always helped me to come through it, just by me putting my trust in their guidance and allowing things to happen as they were supposed to happen. I went along with the flow of life and things turned out for the best way possible.

Even when you look at the history of the Native people of America, you see how this principle has been used. The invaders of the Americas came and used the system they had brought with them, a system to control and be in power through fear. They were already caught up in the cycle of having lost the basic sense of trust, and fear grew inside. Some hide their fear by yelling and bullying those around them, becoming aggressive and loud. Others are the ones who become bullied and oppressed. This whole system has spread over many areas of the world. When the white people came to the Americas, they found mostly happy people who didn't live in fear, but to get what they wanted they thought they had to get rid of the Native people through killing and threatening them, just as was done to their own kind back in Europe.

But they never totally succeeded in this, although it has had a devastating effect and a lot has gotten lost. Native people have suffered enormously under the suppression and it has cost us most of our land, a lot of our culture, languages and our traditional way of life. But little by little the Western belief system is crumbling. It cracks open and it shows a lot of malfunction. The system is destroying itself. At the same time there is a revival of the old traditions of our people: we are regaining our pride and our sense of identity. This awakening is spreading out not only to the Native people over here but also to the rest of the world, to all people of the world. I see many good signs leading in that direction.

If you look in nature, you can see that Mother Earth always tries to bring back balance. Whenever there is a fire or a flood, she starts to bring in new life and balances it out. It does take time though. It is believed by our indigenous people that the Creator realized that the world had gotten out of balance and that it was time to restore that balance. The two opposites from Europe and the Americas had to be brought together so that they could learn from each other and in the end everybody would benefit. But in the meantime, there was going to be a lot of suffering, destruction, chaos and great losses on all levels and we need to be aware that this process will also take time.

My personal belief is such that once we learn to be without fear we can no longer be controlled. When we feel the support of Mother Earth and our spiritual guidance, we stop being afraid and get away from the controlling need for power.

Although we humans share the possibility of talking and communicating through words, we very often don't understand each other. We don't listen carefully, we don't pay attention, we think we know what the other persons means, we overrule them, we are caught in our own emotions, we are prejudiced, etc. It seems there are a lot of misunderstandings going on between people. While sharing about relationships, this topic always comes up automatically: how difficult it is to have clear and good communication. I am often asked about the differences in communication between men and women. I agree, there are differences between the two sexes but I see those differences mostly coming from the culture, nationality, the way we were brought up, which social class we live in, etc. This has a huge impact and filters through in how men and women talk to each other. The most important thing in my opinion in any communication is to do it from your heart in a clear and honest way, to be willing to share and be open about your real feelings. If you are able and capable of doing that, you can overcome all those things mentioned earlier: the cultural differences, the male-female issues and the personal problems.

Another aspect that influences how relationships function and work out positively is the backup system of a community. Relationships between couples function so much better when there is a community that supports and holds them. It is the foundation of the relationship and provides stability. The same is true when there are children involved. Children need more than just the parents. It is essential for them to grow up with a sense of community. It can be an extended family or a group that they feel they belong to and where there is a common identity. When the focus is only on each other as a couple or on you as parents of the child, it is bound to be off balance. It becomes a one-way street and very often overwhelms the partners, which in the end can lead to an unnecessary breakup. Elders especially play an important role to help solve those issues. They can give advice, coming from years of experience and the wisdom of old age. They can function as counselors to the young ones. This is basically the old tribal way that is healthy and supportive for everyone.

When I talk about relationships between people, I like to end up emphasizing our relationship with everything around us and within us. This means literally everything on Mother Earth and beyond and it consequently means you are never alone but always connected to everything. You can't separate those things. It reflects an attitude in life. The expression: "to all my relations" that we Native people often use at the end of our prayers is a state of mind and heart.

Birth and Guiding Children

Pregnant mothers are very sensitive and pick up easily on any negative energy around them, which then also affects the unborn baby. So one of the mother's responsibilities is to be in a balanced, cheerful mood, because the baby will pick up when she is angry or when she is sad. The community around her has the same responsibility to create a positive environment around her and the unborn child. We were told not to talk bad language, make sure you didn't watch violent movies or fight and argue when a pregnant woman was around. All these energies influence the two in a negative way, especially the little one being formed in her belly.

It was common to sing a lot around the mother just to make her and the baby feel happy. When the time came and she was ready to deliver the baby, we would literally sing the baby into this world. She would be in a lodge together with the midwives to give birth and the rest of the community gathered close by outside to help and support her, to give her strength, make it easy on her. Special songs were sung that carried meaning, brought calmness or strength and trust, and blessings. She could focus on the singing and the drumming and less on the pain. Also for the baby it was something it could relate to: it had heard singing and drumming while in the belly because in a traditional household that was done on a regular basis. The drumming represents the heartbeat of the Mother Earth and of course also the heartbeat of the mother herself. We believe that everything has power; everything has a way of affecting things, our thoughts, our feelings, our actions. So if you drum and sing in a certain way, with a certain frame of mind, you can direct this inner positive picture and energy through your heart to the mother and her little one to help them come through the birth in a good way. As a group, we join our hearts and make a strong connection to each other, to nature and the spirit world.

So the drumming helps the baby to connect more easily as it doesn't come out of the womb into a totally alien world. The baby feels welcomed: it's a sacred spiritual moment. A positive and beautiful beginning of a new life on earth is created.

I have explained this before: in the traditional way, a spiritual person who knew the normal flow of nature and would notice if something out of the ordinary was happening, would stand outside during the time of birth and look for any signs. The moment of birth is so powerful and creates so much energy and movement that something in nature will feel compelled to act in some way. Every person, we believe, has a connection to something in nature. That spiritual connection will show itself and it will have meaning for the rest of your life. It can be anything: water, an insect, a tree, an animal or bird and will be reflected in the baby's name.

Now that the little ones are in this world, they will continue to have experiences with Nature and Spirit every day. Both are teaching us, if only we are willing to look and listen. Usually nature isn't deliberately teaching us, it is just showing us how to do things by how it works and how it flows. Everything takes care of each other and nourishes each other. How perfectly nature is designed! That is how we learn.

Also Spirit flows in a special kind of way. Spirits are constantly trying to teach and to help us. They know we are born here for a specific purpose and reason, with certain lessons that we need to learn. And they care about us, they are connected to us human beings, so they really want to help. They are trying to guide us to do things in the most healing and positive way. So, when little ones are around, we need to pay even more attention, because they are very open to the spirit world. They do not have any restrictions yet. Little ones or little people, as we call children, are very sensitive, they pick things up easily. Even when we are hiding something from them –- like an emotion we are trying not to show -- they know what is really going on. Sometimes we have a quarrel with our partner and leave the room, and when we come back, we act like nothing has happened, hiding that we are upset. The little one sometimes asks: "Is everything okay?" And unfortunately we often say: "Oh yeah, everything is fine!" And the child will not understand and thinks that its estimation was wrong. Each time we lie to our children, their belief in their own sensitivity gradually lessens and their awareness dampens a little. It doesn't mean that you should answer: "Well, he's doing this and that or she was saying this and that..." But you could say: "Yes, I'm a little upset. We're having a little bit of a hard time right now, but we are working through it." In this case, the little one knows that his or her initial hunch was right but that there is no reason for worrying. It feels reassured in both ways. It keeps the awareness strong instead of knocking it out of them little by little when we deny what is actually the truth.

This sensitivity for spiritual experiences needs to be nourished in children. When children talk about some energy or spirit they saw, we often tell them it was just their imagination, that it is a silly thing to talk about or it was just a dream, that you shouldn't talk like that because otherwise people will think you are crazy, and so on. In fact, this is how children -- and all of us -- are being cut off from our spirit and spiritual experiences. It is very important to take them seriously and speak the truth to them in order for them to be able to trust their own feelings and intuitions, and believe in what they are seeing and sensing. Otherwise, pretty soon they will believe what they have been told and will have less and less experiences with Nature and Spirit. This brings forth a negative spiral that disconnects us from our true being, from who we truly are: spiritual beings in human form, connected to Nature and Spirit. Remember: we are Nature and Spirit!

Don't deny what the spirit world is sharing with the little ones. Even if you haven't sensed or seen it yourself, it doesn't mean that it wasn't there. Maybe you have missed it or weren't aware of it, maybe it was just showing itself to the child.

When they come to you and ask you questions you may not know the answers to, you have to be honest with them and say: "I don't really know... but thank you for sharing it with me." In this way, it reassures them they can trust you and they will come to you again when they feel the need for it. Sometimes they'll ask you about a dream or tell you: "You know, it felt like the wind was talking to me today." You can ask them, how it felt to them: "Was it nice, did it make you feel happy or was it disturbing to you in any way?" You can take the time to listen and pay attention, make sure they are taken seriously and cared for. You can also try and figure things out together that aren't clear.

When the little ones grow up, we want to guide them and help them to live their lives, whatever their path should be. It is very important to not push our own problems upon them, and also to allow them to walk their own path, to let them become what they are supposed to be. This is what a lot of people don't understand. Each person has their own gifts and their own path to walk, different experiences they need to make: it is not up to us really, not as parents or as grown-ups to interfere. This is each person's own responsibility and own choice and we need to respect that.

We can help the young ones to find out what their purpose in life is. Without pushing them in a certain direction, we guide them to find out what is right for them. The latter is a big difference to what we think is right for them.

In the old days we used to give our little ones toy drums they could play with. We explained a little bit what the drum stands for in our culture and talked about the importance to be respectful to the drum. Of course you do that in a playful way where it relates to the child's world and reality, but you can teach them at a young age already to take care of things, whether it's their own toys or the adult ones. If you noticed a child wasn't interested in the drum anymore, you left it at that and don't force their interest. This will only drive them away and can block them from ever trying again. It has to come naturally. You also don't punish them when they maybe break their toy. You explain that it is not immediately replaceable and you just remind them for next time to be more careful. Of course, the drum is only an example here.

Especially when they are little, you have to make sure they are safe, but you also allow them to make their own mistakes and learn their own lessons in life. One of the hardest things for parents is that even if we know better because we have been through something ourselves and have experience, that we still have to sometimes step back and let them go through some failures. If they are willing to listen we can tell them about our own experiences, but then we need to allow and trust them to live their own life. We should not go up to them afterwards and tell them: "Well, I told you so, but you were so stubborn!" Or even worse, you forbid them to do certain things beforehand. Sometimes this is the only way to learn, to really fully understand, experiencing it yourself and coming out on the other side understanding all its aspects. It is hard for parents or grandparents, uncles and aunts to watch this process, but we need to trust in how it is meant to be. And we should also remember that when we were young ourselves, we also needed to make certain experiences and mistakes; we also took risks, even if we already knew inside it was maybe foolish or even a little dangerous, but we wanted to try it out anyway. We can hope and pray that they come through it in a good way, without harm and too much damage. But I admit: this isn't always easy.

Very often we think of our children as some kind of possession, that they are obligated to us to do things in a certain way, maybe follow in our footsteps. But it is never supposed to be like that! Like I said before, and I am emphasizing it again, we have to allow them to follow their own path. This is so important to understand. We have to acknowledge their feelings and wishes. We also want to be acknowledged, and be seen and heard. They might see things and act a little different from grown-ups, but they have the same feelings of love, anger, envy, and so on, the same as we have. We should nourish their path so they become what they truly are supposed to be.

It is very important to communicate if there is a problem and work together in resolving it. One of the ways I was taught when I was growing up, and what I also practiced with my own young ones was that whenever there was an issue, I would have them come and sit with me and I'd ask: "Well you know, there is a problem that has been caused by your actions. Are you aware of it? Do you have suggestions on how you think this could be resolved? What can you contribute to help get this out of the way?" Let them work out a strategy together with you that they feel okay about. In this way, they learn to take responsibility for their actions but do not feel punished as such and become part of the solution. If you give them a chance to speak up and give them a possibility to reflect on what they have done and how to make it up, they will realize much quicker what they have caused and get insight themselves.

In the end they will feel good about it. You really talk to them as you would talk to an adult. And you will be surprised at what they come up with! Sometimes they will suggest: "Oh, I should really be grounded for this!" and you didn't actually have that intention at all. Or they come up with an idea to solve the situation you hadn't thought of yet. Kids can be very inventive and are usually aware of what they have done. Other times, if you feel they are missing the point, you tell 'em: "Well, I don't think that is really helping a lot, let's talk about it some more." In the process you give them ownership of the solution and make them feel they have helped create it themselves. This is very important for a young person. Consequently they are much more willing to follow up on whatever is decided. Otherwise it is more likely they are going to rebel against it, because they were told to do something; they feel punished and left out. They feel you aren't listening to them and don't respect them.

You have to realize that if you are angry with them, this is all they notice and they will focus on that anger. In return they become defensive and angry with you. As a result, they won't understand and think about their actions. Anger is a strong emotion and blocks all other things that are going on. Probably the young person will not listen to what you have been addressing and criticizing. You might recognize this as an adult too: when somebody is angry with you, you start defending yourself and often become angry yourself too. So that is what happens here: the disturbed emotions lead to the young ones losing the point of why this discussion started in the first place, and what the cause of it all was, namely something they had done and that needed attention. With angry feelings, you aren't dealing with the issue and this in itself causes confusion.

By gently including them, you honor their feelings and keep them open and aware, sensitive to things. As parents we have an incredibly powerful influence, though the young ones will deny this and say: "Oh no, I do things my way, I do them very differently!" This isn't true, for we set an example by our actions and by the way we deal with them, their feelings, and with situations. They watch all of that.

To Native people, it is only natural to start at a very young age to help them in their relationship with Nature and Spirit, because then they are still more sensitive and aware. They learn much faster and take it in deeply. But, in fact, we can at any time in our lives begin with opening up and raising our awareness. Part of us has to remember how it was when we were young and part of us has to relearn, but it is never too late. Many of us just never have gotten the chance to live this way. Many have been brought up with the idea that the most important thing in life is to get a good job, have a boyfriend or a girlfriend, get a nice house and a car. In other words be secure. But that is just the surface, you know, true security doesn't come from possessions, not from a relationship we have... or anything like that. Real security comes from within, from your personal connection to Mother Earth and to your own spiritual path. That is what you as an adult are trying to do with the little ones, help them find that connection, their own personal connection to their spirit and their path.

Everything in life can be taken away from you, except your connection to Nature and to Spirit, which is connected to your own personal spirit. Nobody can take that away from you!

You can seemingly give up on that connection; you can deny it and go astray, but of course you cannot really give up on your own spirit, because that is your essence.

Many people nowadays have turned their back on Nature and Spirit, but basically it is always waiting for us, deep inside, if we are willing to go that place. It is our fear that is blocking us from making that connection again. Besides, we are not used to it anymore, we have almost forgotten how. It doesn't mean that Spirit and Nature aren't trying to connect with you, you are just not listening to them anymore. The good news is: you can start doing that at any time in your life. Open yourself and commit yourself to it. Learn to be aware, learn to listen, learn to observe and watch for signs and so on. A conversation will open up, you make contact and a connection can grow from there. It does take work and it does take time. All I can say: it doesn't matter when you start. You can even be 95 years old. When you're really young it is much easier because you're still very open to these things. When you're older, it helps when there are little ones around because they remind us of those ways and aspects, how to do this in a playful instead of a deliberate way. They let us look anew through their eyes. But no matter what point you are in your life, your spirit is always waiting for you to renew your relationship with it.

You know, we are truly never alone! As soon as you start working on that relationship with Nature and Spirit, you'll realize this. When you need that help, when you need calmness, when you need support, it will come in some sort of way. You can reach out to Mother Earth and get it; you can reach out to Spirit and get it.

All that matters is that when you are ready, when the time is right, you can start opening yourself again. It also doesn't matter how long it takes and it doesn't matter which path you choose to find that connection again. There are many good paths to the Creator. Each person has to find their own way of connecting and which direction they want to take, which path they find suits them. We have to always honor that.

We have to relearn these ways. We have to think positive again. Learn to take care of each other, take care of Mother Earth in all its aspects. Help our young ones to connect strongly to Nature and Spirit, help ourselves and be good to our own spirits again.

We have been blocked from doing so because of the governments, politicians and religious institutions that want to control us and tell us to live in a certain way. They threaten us that if we don't live that way, they will take things away from us or we will go to a bad place and bad things will happen to us. We were brought up in fear, we learned how to be in fear of everything. Only if we listen to what they think will we be okay. They tell us: "Buy these products, eat this food, or otherwise ... " "Go to this church, believe in these words, follow this leader..." "Do this and that, otherwise..." It is all based on fear and we need to recognize this in order to get our own source of strength back. A lot of indigenous people have been falling into this trap too, because they have also lost their connection.

When we have a good connection to Mother Earth and to Spirit, there is no need to be afraid, we feel secure in ourselves. That is how things will turn positively in the other direction again.

This is what I think of when I share about the upbringing and guiding of our little people.

Teaching on the Value of Inclusion

Around 2012, I traveled through Europe and did a workshop organized by a friend of mine, Anna, in the southern mountains of Austria. It was at a farmhouse out in the country and lasted for three days with a good group of people coming. Some parents had decided to take their adolescents along because they felt it could also be interesting for them to take part in it.

On the first day, the two young teenage boys, who knew each other well and were good friends, stayed with us for about an hour and then took off running and chasing each other. It didn't disturb the workshop too much. The parents probably talked to their kids that evening about their expectations for them to participate more, because the next day they sat down with us quietly at first and joined in a little, but soon they got bored again and went off to play. A little stream ran through the property and at lunchtime we were sitting close to the water. As it was a beautiful day, the youngsters started fooling around, splashing each other. One of them found a little bucket, and tried throwing water at the other boy. While doing so, some adults got wet as well. The young ones were having a lot of fun and were getting more and more excited. The adults started yelling at them, the parents upset and embarrassed at this behavior, and most of the others annoyed. It was time to return to the circle again and as people were coming back to sit down, I could hear the group sort of complaining about the situation. A lot of people felt irritated that the workshop was being disrupted. They asked my opinion about it, also urging me to take a decision: "Mala, you are an elder! You should handle this. You should sit them down and tell them that they are creating a lot of problems." People were clearly angry with the boys and the parents were frustrated with their sons.

I sat with it for a while and finally said: "OK, I'll talk to them." Somebody got them to sit with us in the circle and I could feel how everybody was getting into the mood for a scolding, thinking: "Now they are going to be told off for their behavior. Mala is going to be stern with them and put them in their place!" The boys themselves were being a little provocative, as if they were totally cool with it, with a look on their faces like: "Who is this guy telling us what to do or not to do!" Then I said to them: "I have a task for you." That is how I caught their interest. They were clearly not expecting me to ask them to do something for me. I continued with a little story: "You know, in the old days, whenever people would come to new places, they would send scouts out ahead. They were to scout the area, look for poisonous plants, any dangerous animals and the specifics of the territory, like maybe dangerous spots to watch out for. And they would also have to look for all the good things in that area: where is the water; which animals are there to hunt; are there good places to camp? Scouts were really important for the Native tribes. I realized that we came to this area and never even took a look at the surroundings! So I want to ask you two to do that for us. I want you to go up in the hills and make a big circle all around where we are, then come back here and tell us what you found out. Maybe you can also bring some little things to show us." They were really pleased by this idea. They had obviously expected something totally different and you could see that they thought it was awesome. They were ready to go immediately. I told them: "Please be careful and don't do any foolish things. This is a serious task and we all look forward to hearing from you afterwards. Do you think you are up to this?" They answered: "Yeah, yeah. This is great!"

And off they went, heading up the big hill almost running, as they were so exhilarated at the prospect of exploring the area.

The people in the circle, though, weren't so sure, asking me: "So how is this helping them to understand that their behavior wasn't appropriate?" I said: "Just wait. There is a reason why I did this. I would like you to all be there when they come back and hear what they have to share. I want you to really listen to them." We left it at that and continued our workshop.

About three hours later they returned to the group. There was a loud whooping and hollering from afar as they came closer, and each of them was carrying a little bag with stuff in it. I told the people to spread out a blanket on the ground and the boys to sit down on it. I said: "Don't speak yet. Be quiet for a minute and calm yourselves first." They actually did that very well. Then I said: "Now you can tell the people what you have witnessed and found out on your search. You can talk one at a time or together, as you prefer. What do you have to report to us? What is it you feel you need to share?" They looked at each other and decided to do it together. Then they started speaking about all the things they had seen along the way. They began with what was dangerous in their eyes: rocks that were really slippery and where you could easily fall, a hole in the ground that had been partially covered where you could fall and twist your ankle. Then they laid the things that they had found on the blanket. They pointed to two kind of ferns and explained to us: "They may look the same at first sight, but if you look carefully at the back of this one, you'll see that it has a certain pattern of lines, which means that it is poisonous. The other one has a different set of lines and isn't poisonous -- you could even eat it!"

It was really amazing what they were able to tell us. They knew where the water ran through, they told us about the plant life in the area; they identified the most important information for us. It turned out that these boys had been in wilderness schools for many years.

I saw the people in the circle starting to look very appreciative towards these two young boys. They knew things they themselves did not know and it was apparent that the kids were very happy to share their knowledge if asked and listened to.

I thanked them in front of everybody for their work: "You did a really good job and I want to give you something from where I come from as a thank-you." I gave them pieces we made at the community I lived in at the time and were selling on our trip. The gifts were two bandanas with the community's logo. They both put them on immediately, one tied his around his neck, the other around his head. I gave them the option: "Now you can either sit with us or you can take a break. Whatever feels good. You are two young adults and you can make your own decisions."

They stayed for about half an hour and went off again to play some more. But this time, nobody said anything or felt upset that they didn't take part.

When it was time for dinner, we were all just hanging out a little. I saw the boys sitting under a tree together, some of the adults going up to them and asking them about the other plants they had brought. They were explaining and sharing happily. It was clear to me that they had finally been recognized for what they could offer and had become equal members of the group. They were taken seriously and honored. For their part, they were now being respectful in their behavior and were no longer disturbing.

The next day we only met for the morning session since people had to travel back home. The young ones took part when they felt like it, and the energy never went back to the prior state. It was very peaceful.

Many of the adults came up to me and thanked me for what I had done and how I had handled the situation. It had showed them a very different approach in teaching young people than they were used to. They recognized that this was an important teaching for everyone involved. It was a way of bringing the group together and forming a community. Before, the adults and the young ones had been separated in their way of thinking and in their behavior. Through this process there was a connection that gave everyone a sense of belonging and of taking part. It was a really positive experience and it reflects how the elders back home had taught us many times as young people.

The Name-giving of Mala's Children

I have five children. Each of them got their name in a different way and it shows their connection to Nature and Spirit and, at the same time, is the name that appears on their birth certificate.

My oldest son is called Michael Thunder Eagle Pope and he was born in April 1973.

His Indian name Thunder Eagle came through my father. He was my parents' first grandchild and my father wanted to honor him by giving him a part of my name and his own name. The explanation is very simple: 'Thunder" comes from my father's name Rolling Thunder and "Eagle" from my name. So, his name wasn't chosen in the traditional way. My father chose the name first and then prayed about if it would suit his grandchild. Although the name wasn't chosen at birth in the traditional sense, I feel it fits because it gives a good connection between the three generations. My feeling also tells me when Michael chooses to seek a deeper spiritual connection, he will find his true spiritual name. That is entirely his own choice. The name Michael comes from his mother's side, in memory of her brother who had crossed over at a young age. His mother isn't Native as you can tell by the name.

My second son is called Red Wolf and was born in August 1976, when we lived at the Camp Meta Tantay in Nevada. When he was born, he stayed red for a few days, a really bright color red. People were a little worried that something was wrong, but he was perfectly fine. My father immediately knew it was a spiritual sign and started praying over it. He told us that his name was supposed to be Red Wolf. The Spirits made clear that through this name an important connection was made to the Shoshone People. We were not familiar with any Shoshone history records, but we felt we wanted to go by what the Spirits were guiding us to do. Only when Red Wolf was in his late twenties did we understand the full meaning of it. We were reading the book "Thunder Over the Ochoco"[6] which covers the history of Oregon right before and right after the white people came. We noticed there was a passage about the Dog Soldiers' Chiefs who were the protectors of the tribe in the old days and were known for their willingness to sacrifice their own life in order to protect the women, children, and elders of the tribe. One of the most famous chiefs around the eighteen hundreds was called Red Wolf. He was known as a brilliant man and also a brave warrior, who fought against the invading white people. My father had already explained that there was a connection to a Shoshone ancestor who had played an important role and now this piece of the puzzle had fallen into place.

It was confirming to see that Red Wolf, after finishing his Law degree, has become an advocate for the Native people, protecting and fighting for their rights, which is part of this legacy.

All my children had a blue spot at the base of their spine, which is a specific mark that Native children very often have. It only stays for a few days before it disappears. It is not entirely clear what it means. Some Native elders say it is a sign that you belong to the Native People because it sits right at the

---

6   Thunder over the Ochoco by Andrew Gale Ontko, five volumes,

bottom of the spine where there is a spiritual center. Usually it has a round form. Others have told me that this is a sign of the beings from another planet: the color is almost turquoise blue and it tells my people we have a connection to the Star People or are actually their descendants.

My next child is my oldest daughter, named Winter Sparrow. She was born in December 1978. We were still living at Meta Tantay, the community in the desert of Nevada, which was about 23 miles away from Elko, the nearest town, which had a hospital. Sky felt she wanted to go there when she went into labor, and we took our old white station wagon. You had to drive on a dirt road for about half a mile before you'd hit the paved road, first a smaller road and then a bigger two-lane one. It was wintertime with temperatures way below zero, normal for winter in Nevada, where the ground stays frozen for about two to three months. Sky was sitting next to me in the front seat and when I looked over to check on her, I noticed a little bird at the window. It was a Winter Sparrow, one of the few birds that can endure the long and cold winters of Nevada, and it stayed with us while we were driving. At first we weren't driving too fast since we were still on the dirt road. Then as we were speeding up on the paved one-lane road, it also kept up. The most amazing thing was that this tiny bird even stayed with us when we were on the highway, flying at the side of Sky's window. We knew this meant something special and when we were entering the hospital I told Sky: "This sparrow is coming in a spiritual way and we should keep that in mind when we give a name to this child." I was hoping it was a girl; otherwise, the name would have been a little awkward for a boy. That is how I recall it and how my daughter got her name.

I have another daughter whose name is Virna White Rose and her name was also given to her by my father. When my father looked upon her as a baby he saw a beautiful white rose. The mountain desert rose is an important symbol for the Western Shoshone. She was born in July 1985 in Nevada but moved with her mother to the East coast when she was still very little. For many years we never had any contact. As an adult, she wondered where she came from and who her father was, and started investigating. Luckily with the help of the internet she found and contacted me. Over the last few years we have gotten to know each other better and are meeting up as often as possible. I am deeply grateful for her to be a part of my life again. As she has gotten to know her other siblings, she truly has become a permanent member of the family.

My youngest son was given the name Hunnan Siton, which is a Shoshone name for badger claw. Sky was already nine months pregnant and while we were shopping at a mall she suddenly looked at me and said in a clear and deliberate voice: "I am ready to give birth." So we hurried to the hospital. While we were in the delivery room, the nurses around her claimed that she wasn't fully dilated, but Sky insisted that she was ready. When the doctor walked in, he put on his gloves and talked a bit to the nurses. He then told her to start pushing. Sky said: "I'm sorry, but if I am going to push, he will come out straight away." The doctor laughed and said: "Oh, I don't think so. It doesn't work that way; it takes a little more than that!" They went back and forth on this for a bit and then he agreed: "Okay, you push and I'll be there to watch over you." Sky gave one push and while the doctor was still putting on his second glove, Hunnan came flying out in his water sack. He just slipped right out and the doctor barely caught him with one arm. The water sack hadn't broken and we could see how the baby was making ripping movements with his hands.

We went to see two Shoshone Medicine Women who lived at an Indian colony just outside of Battle Mountain, Nevada, who both were more than 100 years old, named Eunice and Gladys. We knew they were the ones who could help us with the name-giving. They prayed about it and came up with the name "Badger Claw" since he had been trying to rip the sack open with his fingers.

Adoption or Taking Someone In

I would like to explain a little on how these matters are seen in the Native way. We don't really speak about adoption, but of "taking someone in." When you take a person on as your daughter, son, niece or nephew, then that is all there is to it. They are part of the family and there is no difference to the rest. They don't need to be related through blood. We also don't use wordings like stepdaughter and stepson. When you speak of a stepdaughter or stepson, it gives it another energy. They are different from the rest and that is not how we approach family.

We have a different concept of what family is. It was the responsibility of the community to take care of the young ones. A community was like a big family where you'd call the other villagers "aunt" or "uncle." All children were welcomed at any time and were free to go to anybody's home, would be taken care of, given food or shelter, no matter what. The doors were always open to any child. In the old days, children were often taken in as members of the family after a child had lost a parent or even both parents. This was the natural thing you did in a community. This is where the saying comes from: "It takes a village to bring up a child."

Come to think of it, we have brothers and sisters everywhere, as we are connected on many more levels than just the physical.

It is also apparent in our saying "to all my relations." We are truly connected to everything and to all life around us. We consider all forms of life our relations. In other words: we are related to every part of life. In truth there is no distinction, but of course on a human level, we have our families, our clans, and our tribes.

Blessing Ceremonies

When children come into the world, we have certain ways of welcoming and introducing them to the spirit world, the Mother Earth, and the community. There are many possible ways of doing that. The tribe as a whole can perform a ceremony, depending on the custom of that specific tribe, or you can do it more as a family or within a certain community. Depending on the situation and also on the child itself, you would choose a certain setting. Earlier in time, these baby blessings were done in a tribal setting where a spiritual person was able to perform the ceremony and the whole tribe would be present.

We did a blessing ceremony for each of my children, and for each a different energy was appropriate. It just happened that way and wasn't deliberate. Each child had its own unique path and got the blessing that fit. That is where you trust the guidance of Nature and Spirit. Each element in Nature has its power and specific energy and the words spoken at the ceremonies were of a similar nature. Basically you introduce the baby to that specific part in nature and to the spiritual energies and you ask for protection and guidance.

I don't know if this was very common to do or not, but for my son Red Wolf I felt the need to perform a water blessing ceremony. We lived at Meta Tantay, and the creek, which had been dry for many years before we lived out at that Camp, had filled up with water again and was flowing naturally on our property. We had built a little dam so people could go into the water if they wanted. I decided to perform the ceremony in that pool.

You see, water is considered very sacred to our people. Water is the bringer of life and helps all life to continue; it can carry messages, creates great change; it is purifying and powerful in a spiritual way, and in its physical presence. The water from this creek flowed through the desert over a long distance and picked up the energy of the mountains where it sprang from and the energy of the desert earth along the way. All those messages are present in that pool of water. I wanted to take him with me in the water and get him in touch with that energy. In our way we say, we introduce him to the water and the other way around: the water could also get to know him. You talk to the water, the surrounding nature and to the spirits that are present. I used words like: "This is my son Red Wolf. Please watch over him and help him to have a good fulfilling life. Protect him, guide him and nourish him in the best way possible. Make him a part of the circle of life and help him do his part." There were other people witnessing this ceremony, of course. Sky as his mother was present, and somebody even took a picture, which is quite exceptional, as pictures are usually not taken at ceremonies.

With my oldest son Michael, we did a blessing ceremony where the smoke of sage was taken into my mouth and then blown over him in a specific way with the use of an eagle feather fan and prayers were spoken for him.

My daughter Winter had her blessing at a sunrise ceremony, where at one point in the ceremony she was taken forward and introduced to the spirits. The whole community was present, prayed for and blessed her.

Hunnan was blessed at a sweat lodge that was held at Meta Tantay. We do that quite often: you can add an extra element to most ceremonies, like a healing or a blessing of some kind. That is what we did in both Winter and Hunnan's cases.

Rites of Passage

When children become older and are reaching their transformation time into adolescents, we used to have specific Rites of Passage for young girls and boys turning into women and men. There are big tribal differences, but the foundation is the same: the purpose is to give the young ones a sense of belonging and recognition in the community and to connect them consciously to Nature and Spirit. It isn't really about a certain age but more about the transformation performed by Nature and Spirit, showing clearly in physical changes and signs and also through emotional, mental, and spiritual changes that are becoming apparent. It is a gradual process but there is also a clear moment for both: girls through the beginning of their moon cycle and boys with the lowering of their testicles and their voices. The community celebrates and honors this transition and the young adults are welcomed in. The Rites of Passage ceremonies are a form of recognition by the community.

I have seen where young ones were taken in for sweats that took two to four days. Sometimes they were taken into nature for a vision quest. Sometimes it was basically the welcoming in the community as an adult member.

Girls would be instructed about their moon time and about their life bearing capacity. In the old times, the girls were introduced to the moon lodge and the elder women explained all the ceremonial customs around that.

When you don't have a community that supports the customs of the Rites of Passage it is more difficult to perform the ceremony. When your child's peers aren't going through the same process, this can become a blockage for performing the ceremony. It can be then that your child isn't interested in the ceremony and then you shouldn't force it. If it feels right though, and your child gives you the impression of wanting to go along with a ceremony, then move forward. You could also incorporate it in how you talk to your children. As a father you'd speak to your son and as a mother you'd speak to your daughter. You can share that the physical transition they are going through is just one part of it, that it also means there are emotional and mental changes to be expected, which leads to a new responsibility towards themselves and their community. You explain the benefits of growing up and being able to make your own decisions. Hopefully, this will result in mature and responsible behavior.

Once I heard from an elder who didn't have a supportive community in the background how he performed an improvised Rites of Passage ceremony for his son. He took his son into the woods at night and said: "I am going to blindfold you. Simply be quiet and don't move or take it off. Just sit here on this log for the night and listen to the sounds of nature. Once you feel the sun on your face, you can take off the blindfold." His son was a little scared but went along. He heard all the noises of the animals of the night, the creaking in the underbrush. The sounds are much louder when you can't check what is out there, but he was brave and finally when morning came, he took off the blindfold. Then he saw his father sitting right next to him on the log. He had been there with him all night. He told him: "Just so you know, I will always be there for you. Even when you are not aware of it, and in your darkest times, I am there." His son connected not only to nature and his own strength but also connected very deeply with his father.

In the Western society, the word "initiation" is sometimes used when it comes to the Rites of Passage or as an equivalent to our Coming of Age ceremonies, but to my knowledge Native people never use this term in this context. The initiation happens in a natural way and is not done and decided on by humans. Maybe it is just a name that is used for the same thing.

Matriarchal Societies and Clan Mothers

Although I do not really have detailed knowledge on this topic and others are better equipped to inform you on historical facts, I would like to share a little of what I have learned on the organization of our tribes and the Clan system that was common amongst the indigenous people of North America.

The elders told me that the majority of the Native societies of North America were matriarchal, which actually to us means based on the Ways of the Mother Earth. We call the earth our mother, as she nourishes all life: she gives and takes, and balances through life and death. When we talk about the Mother Earth, we actually refer to everything upon and within her. It encompasses the elements, the stone people, the soil, the plants and trees, the insect nation, the winged ones, those beings that live in the water, the four-legged and the two-legged ones, literally everything. Our Way of Life is based upon the principles of nature, the rhythm of the seasons, the daily appearance of the sun, the cycle of the moon, the stars at night, and the movement and flow that comes with this all.

Men and women are considered equal, although in older times they each had specific tasks and roles in the tribal communities, according to their abilities. Women played an important role in how our tribes were organized and functioned in daily life. Not only because the life-giving capacity that women possess were they considered special and to be honored, but they were also considered closer to Spirit. Because a woman is able to pass on life, she has a deeper understanding of what life means. She carries new life in her for nine months, feels it grow inside of her and then has to give birth, going through pain and suffering to ensure life continues. Women know the pain at birth is an important part of the whole, to be able to experience life with both poles, positive and negative, in order to grow and develop as a being. Afterwards she nourishes this newborn life through her breasts and is the main caretaker in the first years. Through this experience her connection to the Circle of Life is strong; she gets an understanding of how everything interconnects and that life and death cannot be seen without each other. Women have a special understanding of the sacredness of life and they carry this wisdom in their bodies and cells for generations, even if they might not have children of their own in this lifetime.

We say: "Women are water and men are fire." They balance each other. Of course every man also has water in himself, just as every woman also has fire in her. These are aspects that you'll find in each individual, but nature seeks balance within a person and in the greater circle between the people.

The matriarchal concept led to the custom that a man who wanted to get together with a woman from another tribe would go and live with the woman's tribe. My father, being a Cherokee, lived with my mother's tribe and became a spokesman for the Western Shoshone. Traditionally we say we follow the woman's way.

Clans formed the structure of our tribes and as our society was based on those matriarchal principles a Clan Mother system gradually became installed over time. The social structure of the clan developed around the Clan Mother, like the heart in a spider web that connects all the fibers. A Clan Mother shows her compassion to every person of the tribe and gives council to anybody in need at all times. She is a mother to all living beings.

Tribal Councils were in charge of making decisions that mattered to the tribe as a whole and which dealt with the surrounding world. You had female Councils and male Councils plus you had mixed Tribal Councils. Depending on what needed to be discussed, the councils were formed and came together, sometimes daily, sometimes for days in a row, sometimes with breaks over a longer period. That happened naturally, there were no set meeting times or anything.

In the old days the Chief was male in most tribes. He also dealt with the political issues outside the community and other tribes, and his task included watching over the young men and taking care of their training and ceremonies. He was the outgoing one, making contacts where it was needed and bringing back important news, also with the help of others, like scouts and hunters. The Chiefs in our communities were admired for their gifts of bravery, clarity, and for having a strong heart; Clan Mothers were admired for their ability to have a totally open and loving heart. Overall, one could say that the Clan Mother was the nourishing one from within and the Chief was the protector towards the outer world. I was always told that the Clan Mothers were more powerful than the Chiefs: a Clan Mother was the only one who could actually "un-horn" a Medicine Man or a Chief, as we would say in the Native way. In other words, she could strip that person of his power. In the end though, it is always about male and female being in balance, and there was constant communication going on.

The Clan Mothers would guide the social structure of the different clans within the tribe and had the task of overseeing the tribal community. On a practical level and on a daily basis, the interaction between the people was guided through the Clan Mothers. It was essential that things were done in the right manner and with the proper respect. When issues occurred between people, a Clan Mother would intervene and help them deal with it, which meant not only survival for the tribe but moreover meant a life in harmony and peace with each other and all Creation.

Clan Mothers weren't necessarily born into a family lineage, but were chosen more for their personality and character. A Clan Mother had to have the right heart, one that showed an incredible love for all living things, and sensitivity for others. She was chosen for her wisdom and kindness, awareness and knowledge. Usually there was one Clan Mother and she had assistants helping her.

Another thing a Clan Mother would do was to help train young women while they were growing up. They would guide the Rites of Passage, the Coming of Age ceremonies. They would oversee the organization of the moon lodge and the moon custom[7] too. She would always be open to helping people when they needed advice of any kind, and both women as well as men would make use of this offer. You could feel free to talk about anything and know that you and the information you shared would stay safely between you and her. She guided the people to find the most healing and peaceful path.

Her task was also to support young people when they were starting to date each other. She talked to the couple together or separately and filled them in on their responsibility towards each other, on how to treat each other with respect. And maybe also to suggest to them to consider refraining from making any new life yet, if they weren't ready as a couple. She could help out with herbs that could protect from becoming pregnant. With her experience, she was able to help people who were going through the transitions of life. She also oversaw the tribal ceremonial activities.

An important part of a Clan Mother's work was to deal with issues like an argument between a couple or quarrels over the amount of food divided. She aimed to create peace for whatever problem that arose. On the rare occasion that men went out to fight a war, they in fact needed the permission of the Clan Mother. Only when the Clan Mother had come to the conclusion there was no other way to save the situation, could the men go out to war. A woman knows about the sacredness of life and doesn't like to waste it easily. Men, we recognize, are a little quicker to fight. Men carry a different energy in this aspect and do not think twice like a woman does, because she has nourished that life from the beginning. She asks herself: "Is the matter really important enough to send this life off to battle? He may come back wounded or not come back at all? Is this the only way left?"

As you can understand by the diversity of her tasks, she was highly respected. To me, a Clan Mother is someone who is a true mother to all people and to all life.

---

7   More on the moon custom and moon lodge later on in Chapter 3

When the white people came, unfortunately a lot of this Clan system was destroyed and undermined over the years and for generations to come. The Europeans came with their own conceptions and belief systems where women didn't play any role in worldly, political affairs. They wouldn't deal with women and therefore wouldn't talk to our Clan Mothers and we didn't send our Clan Mothers to talk to them either as a result. We sent our Chiefs as spokesmen, but the Clan Mothers were in charge in the background. The male leaders who talked to the white people were chosen by the Clan Mother and the tribe to speak on behalf of them. They always had to go back and forth to the Tribal Council where the Clan Mother was overseeing everything, and together it was decided which answer or message the chosen spokesman would take back to the other party.

Only through consensus, which was our way of politics, was a decision made. The Men's Council would start talking and take its time over a certain decision to reach one voice in their group. They would go many rounds to hear everybody out and then finally bring their decision to the Women's Council, where it was heard and considered. The women usually needed just one round of going through the circle to tell the men: "No, you better go back and think more thoroughly!" This could go back and forth for quite some time too. Native people laugh and joke about this phenomena. We men have to bear with that. When the women didn't agree, the decision wasn't verified. Only when the Women's Council gave its okay could the men verbalize the decision to the outside world.

But the white people didn't know our decision-making policy and thought that it was the Chiefs who were in charge, largely because that is what they were used to from the male dominant societies they came from.

Christianity, with its belief that indigenous peoples were primitive heathens to be converted, with no culture of their own, played an important and devastating role in the destruction of our matriarchal tribal system. From the very beginning, in the early 1500s, priests came along on ships from Europe to the Americas. Although they didn't have any direct executive power, their advice was taken seriously to justify whatever was done to our people. They looked down upon us, condemned us and tried to diminish us once it became clear that "our souls weren't ready to be saved", as it was stated. When conversion failed, another approach was used, and that is when they decided to instead get rid of us all.

They deliberately went after our Clan Mothers. This could have to do with the fact that in Europe this turning against women had already been common practice for several centuries. All over Europe during the Dark Ages, midwives, women who healed with the help of herbs, plants, and natural ways or women who simply had a strong and independent voice were demonized, condemned, and persecuted mercilessly. Powerful women were seen as a threat to the establishment, and thousands were accused of practicing nature's ways and of cooperating with the devil on an unprecedented scale. Many of the conquerors brought this perception with them across the Atlantic. To me it is important information to see that matriarchal societies were destroyed not only in the Americas, but that this had also taken place in Europe at another time in history.

The Europeans who came to the Americas were more or less designated to go after the social structure of the tribes, which was basically the Clan system with the Clan Mothers. They recognized its importance and the threat it was to their own ideas and culture at the same time. The priests and clergymen, whom we called "the black robes", and who attempted to convert the people to Christianity, recognized that the Clan Mothers were holding the fabric of the tribes together and preventing the people from changing their belief system. They passed the information on to the higher ranking soldiers and governors, who knowingly went after the Clan Mothers to kill them and leave a crippled and weakened tribe behind.

Another aspect that needs to be accounted for is that the settlers who came not only fled Europe out of starvation and poverty, but they were also fleeing from persecution of their own deviated forms of religion that weren't accepted there. As you can often see happening, people who have suffered something themselves have a tendency to then implement the same harm that was done to them on others, in this way repeating the same cycle of accusation, abuse, and self-righteousness.

In the course of time in the history of the invasion of the Americas, there were literally no Clan Mothers left anymore, and only Chiefs to fight wars with or to win over and sign treaties with. It is a sad story, and it is a heavy burden for Native Americans to carry this memory and we have to deal with it to this day. Much of this knowledge is still being ignored and hardly ever mentioned in schoolbooks. Only slowly is there some recognition and acknowledgement of the fate of our people, which is an important step towards the healing of that entire historical trauma.

The fascinating thing is though, that for some reason they didn't go after our Medicine People so much, since they were not considered as dangerous and of much influence. Later on though, some of those Spiritual and Medicine People became great leaders of our people, like Sitting Bull, Geronimo, and Crazy Horse.

When we lived in our Camp Meta Tantay in Nevada for 10 years, my own mother was considered a Clan Mother too. She had a natural talent, though she hadn't been looking to take on this role and wasn't officially installed. She just had the right heart and attitude and slowly and naturally grew into that position. When the Alaskan people, who do still have a more or less active Clan Mother system, came down to visit us, they confirmed her as being one.

She was an easy person to be with and also a very wise woman. Some of my friends who really liked talking to her started calling her "mom." You just felt comfortable around her. She never put herself up front. She was the quiet force in the background and at the same time the heart of the family and in a sense also of the community around her: a true Clan Mother.

Over the years she blossomed into that role. A lot of people came to her for counseling. She never turned anybody down. She was kind in her words and yet very observant about others. When people would come to visit us, she would watch how they acted and approached things. It could be something seemingly insignificant, like if somebody would put their shoes out of the way so nobody would stumble over them. Or how they would treat animals or talk to the elders. Those things she would pay attention to. To her those actions were important and said something about the person inside.

Once I was in a relationship with a woman and the two of us often had issues that weren't always solved in the gentlest way. When she was upset about something, she would start to yell and holler. My mother used to tell her that she should be aware that if you say things with emotion, it puts a lot of power in those words. You actually send negative energy with the words and this can turn against the other person in a negative way. My mother said: "Please be careful when you use words in such a strong manner. Energy like that can manifest itself in a very negative and hurtful way, depending on how the person deals with it and how susceptible the person is, because the energy itself is created by a hurtful emotion. It is possible for them to get sick from it or they might get caught in an accident." Her advice was that when you have an issue with somebody, make sure the emotions calm down first before trying to solve the issue with the other person. Of course she wasn't saying that you should agree on everything. It depends on the timing and when you choose to speak up. She emphasized that we are responsible for those words spoken out of anger, just as much as we are responsible for actions that are based on anger, jealousy or being upset, and are even responsible for what and how we think about other persons.

Our thoughts, our words, our feelings and our actions have an effect on the people around us, all the living beings around us, the Mother Earth, everything. Especially when you direct this energy towards somebody or something, it becomes more apparent. The more deliberate the more dangerous, but even when it is done unintentionally it has power because of the emotion that is behind it. We need to be aware of this phenomenon and take responsibility for it. This was my mother's credo in everything she did, felt, said or thought.

To me this makes sense, since everything is connected and the emotional energy can turn into any other form of energy and manifest into a physical form as well.

It is like when you are trying to send somebody healing energy. You focus and direct that energy into the other person with the intent to manifest itself as healing on whatever level it should work. So the energy becomes active by itself and you support it with your focus and sense of direction. As a healer you want a physical reaction within the person you are helping.

When you are angry, you send out energy in a hurtful way as a response to something that was hurtful to you, and you might end up creating something far more hurtful than you ever intended in the first place. Even if it wasn't even done with a deliberate bad intention, the energy does have power because of the strong emotion behind it. In the heat of the moment you sometimes end up saying something like: "Drop dead!" or "Get lost!" That is really dangerous and it can actually manifest itself and come true.

So, we sometimes say very stupid things without really thinking the consequences through. My mother would always point this out to us. She was aware of the responsibility we carry. To her, living a true spiritual life meant always being aware in any situation and under any circumstances.

I think she was very good at it too, although she still stayed human and humble about it.

If you think of her youth, it is astonishing how she overcame the hurts and negative experiences she encountered, and turned them around into love and wisdom instead. She is an example of how pain and trauma in your life can become a source of inner strength, endurance, and power. She was very reluctant to talk about the time at the boarding school because the memories were so hard on her, and she refrained from bringing it up.

I heard a little bit through uncles and aunts how she grew up, but unfortunately it wasn't much. I know that on her birth certificate it said that she was part Shoshone and part Mexican. My mother's mother was a full-blooded Shoshone and was married to a Mexican, but she had an affair with another guy out of which my mother was born. His name was Sammy Long and he was a well-known Shoshone spiritual leader and a very good singer with an incredibly strong voice. Her childhood wasn't an easy one, also because her Mexican father somehow must have always known that my mother wasn't his real daughter.

Children in those days were still taken away to boarding school at the age of five to be educated in the way that they[8] thought was appropriate for Indian kids. The boarding schools were a tool to deal with what the US government called: "The Indian problem" and they'd already started with this policy in the late 1700s. Then it became the big thing around the 1800s, up until half of the 20th century. They literally claimed that Native people weren't capable of taking care of their own children and educating them in the boarding schools would be the better option. They were taken away deliberately so that the children would lose touch with their own culture and language, thus alienating them from their parents, and ultimately to destroy the Native People and their future. Their aim was also to indoctrinate the minds of our people by giving them the feeling they weren't worthy

8   Christian and Catholic missionaries / United States government

enough for parenting. They cut their hair, did not allow them to speak their language, forced them to wear western clothing, and took their Native names away from them. They tried to strip the children, who mostly lived on reservations, of anything that had to do with their culture.

My mother told me that boys were never allowed to come home on the holidays and girls were allowed to only for a few weeks during the whole year. The boys had to work in the fields no matter how young they were. Girls were made to be house servants whenever they were available. There was a lot of abuse going on, not only in the schools but also in those homes where the girls were put to work. Nowadays, there are many reports that bear witness of the situation at the boarding schools, and over the years I have more fully understood what she must have been going through. My mother was forced to be in boarding school for many years. Kids who dared to run away were whipped in front of everyone in the schoolyard. They were severely punished in many ways and constantly humiliated. She said she could hear the screams from the teacher's rooms at night. She told me how afraid she had often been and how she always cried and covered her head with her pillow to not hear them. Children who dared to speak their Native language were forced to put their tongue against ice-cold metal so the tongue got stuck to it and tore as soon as they tried to release it. I did ask her sometimes, but she really hardly spoke about it; she just didn't want to share those painful memories.

It was a massive systematic eradication of normal life for our children, and in many cases once they'd become adults it had a devastating effect. There are studies saying that 50% of the children that went to those boarding schools never made it out alive. It has done so much harm for so many generations.

In 1978, Native parents finally officially received the right to put their children in a school of their own choice.

To me, my mother really represents what the Native spiritual path is about. Despite everything she simply just loved. She loved animals, cats and dogs, the birds we took in to take care of, all of them. She loved people too, always willing to help, to feed and host them. She loved life. That to me is truly what the spiritual path is about and it has formed me more than anything else in my life. She has been and is my true example. She hardly ever raised her voice, she would withdraw a little when she was hurt, but she wouldn't show it. She processed it and forgave the other person. She never allowed it to affect her actions. She was able to see through it and still continue to love. It is a beautiful quality and therefore, she was considered a Clan Mother.

Strong Women

Right across the street from us lived close relations, Elizabeth Dann with her daughter Pearl, whom we were together with a lot during my youth. She was one of three sisters. The other two were called Mary and Carry, known to the public as "the Dann Sisters."[9] They became pretty famous over the issue of the land claim that the government was trying to pull on them and they were refusing to give in to. Mary and Carry are examples of strong and determined women who took on a very different approach in how to solve the difficult and threatening situation at hand. Just as in the case of my mother, they responded to the happenings in their daily life and took on a role they hadn't asked for or anticipated. In their case they decided to take action: they fought for their rights in a way uncommon for women of that day and never gave up.

This example shows that there are no clear roles within our tribal communities for women and men as to what they are supposed to do or not do. Sometimes life leads you in a certain direction that might not be

---

9   *Wikipedia: Dann Sisters / Treaty of Ruby Valley Movies on Dann Sisters*

typical for that gender in the traditional sense, but when this turns out to be your purpose in life, this is what you follow up on.

Elisabeth was a beautiful craft worker and she also made my cradleboard, a traditional board used by women to carry their newborn babies with, which I still have in my room.

At this point, I also would like to say a few more words on Sky. To me she is one of the strongest women I have ever known. Since the day we met, which is more than 40 years ago, there have been many challenging situations in which she consequently showed her strength, patience, and wisdom. Since she is a very humble person, she has always been very quiet about it, never claiming anything for herself.

In the last few years there have been more and more people that have recognized this silent force inside of her. When the Council of the 13 Grandmothers was formed in 2004 [10], she was asked to be the helper of one of the Grandmothers and she got the opportunity to travel to New Zealand with them. Sky literally told me not to mention her in that role to the people I met on my travels through the US and in Europe. She is private about those things. In the meantime, the Council has disbanded again but has done important work all over the world, so in the aftermath I feel I can mention she was involved in it.

I told you how we met and how it was meant to be that we ended up being a couple. Sky knew my parents well and the Way of Life also became her personal path. We were married for 33 years and she gave birth to three of my children. My other children she has always recognized as part of the family. We have been through many storms together, and she has always stood by me, which I am forever grateful for.

---

10 www.grandmotherscouncil.com

When we realized that we couldn't continue as a married couple anymore, we felt it was better to separate so we would be free for a new relationship that might come along. We called together our family and the people of the community in Oregon where we lived at the time to inform them of the situation. We didn't know how the kids would react but their response was positive and we continued living in the same community together after we broke up plus traveled together to Europe and still cooperated with each other as we had done before.

Our relationship has evolved into an incredible, deep friendship, which is very supportive, and based on love, respect and understanding. It has become more a partnership for life: she is just part of my life. We help each other when needed and listen and give our support. We have a lot of fun too but give each other space to live our own lives separately at the same time.

What I would like to honor in her is that she was always there for me when I was at my weakest. Whether physically or emotionally, mentally and spiritually, she was just there. She was (and is) a very good mother and took care of the children in a positive, supportive way. She liked to push me up front when there were people around, but often those people wanted to hear her advice on things. She is very truthful in her ways and doesn't have the need to show off or come out strong. She keeps it to herself. Her most important relationship in life is the relationship she has with the Creator. This comes above everything else.

Becoming older, she has become an elder in the traditional sense and she has grown in her wisdom and in sharing those abilities with others. She has a great hand with animals too: she talks and sings to them. One time all the goats and sheep of the community we lived in had somehow gotten out of their pen. We watched her going out there and while she just talked to them, they all started following her back into the animal pen. They literally lined up behind her and she danced a little in front of them and sang to them and back in they went. She is considered the Clan Mother by all the animals.

Hermine:

I remember one time in Schattendorf in Austria, where we'd had a women's circle and sweat lodge ceremony the day before. After breakfast we were sitting outside, hanging out together, when Sky got up quietly. We watched her walking up to the ridge of the land where it goes uphill a little. The land is open and wide out there and on the rim grazing in the field we saw three deer, outlined against the horizon. Sky slowly and consciously walked up in their direction while sort of chatting to them. She just hung out with this deer family for a while, it is the most natural thing in the world for her, and from a distance we fell silent while observing their grace and harmony.

Sacred Circle of Life and Praying over Food

In traditional Native families we pray over our food. It is a way to say thanks and not take anything for granted. We express our gratitude and honor equally all forms of life: there is no hierarchy, no lesser or higher or better.

I was taught it is wrong to put one life form above another life form. When you look at human history, there are many examples where one group has felt better than the other, whether between races or between groups within a country. Human history is full of it. Let me give me an example that stays close to my experience: when the white people came over to the Americas, they thought they were of more value than the colored people they came across. They claimed to be more intelligent and more powerful, and thus more worthy. This attitude resulted in abuse, slavery, and killings on a large scale and in the end in genocide of many of our tribes as well as wiping out cultural customs and many languages.

We can also witness this hierarchal attitude of putting one life form above the other in the treatment of the Mother Earth. Humans like to categorize and put things in a specific order. Human beings claim to be on the top of the list with the most value. The next ones are the animals; then plant life follows. Stones and soil are at the bottom of that pyramid.

According to our belief, that isn't the way it is. If we keep putting one life above another life and keep on saying that one life is greater and the other is of less value, we end up abusing life and taking it for granted. We end up hurting life and eventually we destroy it to the point of no return.

Native People say: we are all part of the Circle of Life and we are all equal. We are made of the same natural elements that all life is made of. It is just shaped and organized differently. All life will die at one point and forms the dust of the Mother Earth. Even the rocks turn back to dust after many, many years. It is the beginning and the end; it completes the circle, and spirals over and over again. To us, there is no separation. We see all life as one and as equal. We are all spiritual beings and if we'd start recognizing our true spiritual nature, we would be able to connect to all forms of life in a much deeper sense.

When I approach a tree, I approach it as a spiritual being and not so much as a tree. If I see it as a tree, I separate myself from it. We just have different forms and different purposes.

Since we are all connected and really see that there is no separation, this means we honor all forms of life and every aspect of life.

All life is here to nourish other life and is part of their specific purpose. It creates a natural balance and works in harmony.

Consequently, Native people eat meat and we do not feel bad about it like many vegetarians want to make us feel. I hear them say: " As a vegetarian I don't want to kill life for food." I answer: "But you do take the life of vegetables." They reply: "That is not the same. It's far worse to kill an animal. I can hear them scream; I can see the fear in their eyes!" I say: "You are closing your hearing off to what the plants feel when they are taken and ripped out of the ground." If you are really connected to Life and to the

Spirit of every being, you will hear their voices. The water has a voice and the wind has one; the trees and the plants have voices. When you choose to believe this, you will start to open the doorway where you can hear and communicate with other forms of life. When you are brought up that way, and have been around nature since you were young, it makes it easier and you do not block the flow of information. It will come naturally. For most people in the western society, however, this has to be relearned. You need to practice and then your awareness will open up step by step.

If someone wants to be a vegetarian because their body or spirit has told them to do so, I totally respect that. Like I emphasize often, we come from different cultural backgrounds with personal differences and we need to find what fits us as a human being. When it comes from the perception that animals have more value than plants, it bothers me because it is the result of the attitude of putting one life above the other.

Another argument usually brought into this discussion is that animals are raised under such horrible circumstances, in factories with no space, and are being stuffed with antibiotics and hormones. Of course, I agree that it's a bad thing but look at what happens to big agricultural farming where plants suffer under enormous amounts of pesticides and are grown in monocultures. They both endure similar abuse, and it's something that is so far off from the natural balance that it creates hurt and suffering. This hurt and pain eventually enters the food chain as a form of energy which we ourselves feed on. The whole Circle of Life is being distorted.

We need to honor all forms of Life, in the best way we can. With this intent I pray over the food. I honor the fact it gives of itself and I ask that any impurities that might be in it be taken out, so that we can continue and nourish our bodies, mind, and spirit. I give thanks and acknowledge, it is deeply appreciated and not taken for granted. I speak from my heart and really believe it, sending out my gratitude to the sacrifice, which has been made so I can live on. I honor the Sacred Circle of Life in this way, and I am aware of the connection. As I do this, I really picture good energy going into the food. I also pray for the Mother Earth as a whole and for the Circle to continue to be strong.

We like to give a small offering bowl into which we put a bit of each of the foods we are about to eat. This bowl is offered to the Spirits: we refer to it as the spirit bowl. We are given all that food from Creation and Mother Earth and show our appreciation.

There is an extra prayer for the food in the spirit bowl, which is taken outside and given back to the Mother Earth. You pray and give thanks to where the food comes from and you offer something in return. You also pray to the ancestors and the spirits so they can nourish themselves symbolically by the food that you offer. The ancestors and the spirits are asked for guidance on your path. It always goes back and forth.

In our garden it is usually the dog that eats the food from the bowl in the end and sometimes a wild animal.

I would like to share some of my thoughts on food and the way I have encountered food being approached.

Many times I get comments about what I eat. People say: "What you are eating is not healthy." They have their own thoughts about what they think is the best food or what is right and wrong in their eyes. But we have to be careful with what we are saying. Our words have power; our thoughts have power! If we say things like that, we direct that energy into the food

So whenever you go up to somebody saying: "How can you eat that? That is not good for you!" you are sending negative energy into the food. You are actually making that food into something that is not good for that person.

I was taught to never be offensive and say things like that. We have to respect whatever other people are eating. It might be their tradition that goes back a long way. It might be that they do not particularly mind what they are eating. It can be that it comes from an unusual habit in a different country or region. People have all kinds of reasons why they eat certain foods. It can also be because they can't afford any other food. It's just not up to you to be judgmental. You are pushing your beliefs and way of thinking upon the other person, which is never okay. Especially when somebody is just about to start eating a certain food and you comment: "That is bad food," you are actually telling the spirit of that food that it's bad, dishonoring the food. Even if it's processed food and far away from its natural state, it still has a spirit in it.

Of course it is far better to eat homegrown vegetables or raise your own animals that lived a happy life, where you don't use chemicals and fertilizers for the soil and so on. In this way you keep the spirit of those beings alive, strong, and connected. No doubt this is much healthier and better for everyone involved, from the soil, to the vegetables and fruits and to the animals and to us humans who nourish ourselves in that way. If you compare, say an egg from an industrial chain with chicken-batteries, with an egg from chickens that run free all day and get good food, the yolk of the latter ones are rich and yellow and tastes so much better, whereas the yolks of the former eggs are whiter, and more watery. This is all very logical and makes sense and has to do with the spirit that is kept alive and still connected to nature. Happy chickens -- happy eggs!

But remember that when you utter negative comments about whatever food is on the table, you are putting that negative energy into the food that somebody else is about to incorporate. You are being disrespectful towards that life that's in there, however far from its original natural state it may be. In our Native way of thinking, you are practicing Bad Medicine. Food is supposed to be good and healing medicine. I say: "More important than what you eat, is *how* you eat it."

There is one thing I have learned over the years and witnessed so many times in my life: you can make anything into something good or bad, no matter what kind of belief you have. It just depends on how you use your belief system. In other words, it's about how you think and less about what you think.

A lot of research has been done on the ingredients in food and many of them contradict each other. So there is no right or wrong in the food itself. It can be something very simple like milk. Some say it's very healthy and good for you and others say it is harmful. What should we believe? In the end, you have to figure out which food works for you, because we all respond differently to different kind of foods. No two people are alike, so we make our personal choices adapt to our needs.

All food has some kind of nutrition to it and feeds us in different ways. Food doesn't just nourish our body. It also nourishes our spirit. And everybody knows that food like chocolate can be a source of comfort; it helps your emotional state. It's important to understand and keep that in mind. When you try and find food that fits you best, then look at all the levels it feeds you. The essence is: all food has life to it.

What you can do is let somebody know what you have experienced or learned about a certain food. You can say: "If you like and are interested, I can share that with you sometime." It's great if you're invited to share your insights, but don't overload another person with your opinions, even if meant in a helpful way.

Another line of thought here is that even if you would use food that is grown in an organic way with no chemicals involved and from healthy soil, but it's cooked by a person who is very sad or angry while cooking, the food will be affected by that energy. The negative energy goes into that food while handling and stirring it. It can then turn into something that doesn't taste good anymore or can even make you sick.

This also works the other way around. If you eat fast food, which doesn't have a lot of nutrition in it and wasn't handled in the most caring way, you can pray over that food and visualize that any impurity that might be in it is taken out. You really have to see that in your heart and give your prayer power and direction. You see the spirit of the food being happy. You give thanks to it and honor it for giving its life so you may continue to live. In this way, the food becomes better and healthier for you and you have turned the negative effects around.

I often mention the experiment a Japanese scientist[11] did with water some years ago. He was able to show the crystal structure of water molecules through the use of a microscope and took pictures of them. They used water from a single source and poured it into different glasses. Each glass had a piece of paper beneath it with words on it or taped on top of the glass. The words expressed different emotions like anger, love, joy, hate etc. The water crystals of the glasses with the positive words created beautiful, harmonious patterns in the water crystals, full of light. The ones with the negative feelings were torn, broken, and dark. To me, it wasn't so much the words themselves that were responsible for this outcome, but when the person wrote that word down, it was their energy, thinking about what the word means. The water felt the person's energy and it was transferred through the written word.

This is such an incredible message, though it doesn't surprise me at all, since I have been taught this principle since I was very young. It was basically instilled in me. It is so essential how we think! We have to constantly be aware of our way of thinking. Our way of thinking affects everything we do, how we act and how we speak.

Unfortunately many people have not been brought up this way and are on the contrary being judgmental. Many people think they want to be helpful and tell other people what to do, but in fact they have judgments

---

11 Dr. Masaru Emoto

about what they think is right and wrong and are pushing their way upon somebody else. The example of the food is one where it clearly comes to the surface. People are not aware of this process.

If we learn to do it in a different way and restrain ourselves from commenting, but instead say and think positive things about whatever food is on the table, it works both ways. Offering our knowledge or suggestions towards somebody's diet without judgment is much more fruitful. You do not offend anybody and the other person doesn't need to be defensive over his or her eating habits.

In this way, one can stay open and willing to listen to the other person's ideas. If a person is not being cornered in the first place but there is a feeling of mutual respect, you can exchange thoughts and ideas. It is also a matter of timing. It is much better to talk about a personal subject like this when you are not actually eating. Then you can share ways and habits without actually putting the energy into the food while eating.

When we learn to avoid pushing our way upon somebody else and avoid judging the other person's way, we have the chance to come together in a more healing and respectful manner, which is beneficial for everyone involved. Paradoxically, this judgmental behavior usually comes out of a strong need to help. You want to help so badly but instead you are actually pushing and judging without realizing it.

Tribal History and Pollution of the Mind

When Native people walk a spiritual path they are taught to ultimately have an open heart. But as you live and walk your journey, going through different phases, there can be times when you close your heart out of anger or fear.

If you look at tribal history, a lot of information about what happened to the Native peoples wasn't even known on a large scale to all the tribes involved. Most of our history wasn't told and taught in classes at school;

neither was it written down in the history books. Quite the opposite, the facts were distorted and twisted, which resulted in many generations of Native people being misinformed. When finally more and more layers of the atrocities towards our people and the magnitude of the genocide and loss became clear, a lot of the younger Native generations got very angry. They felt deprived of their pride, of their culture, of their languages and couldn't fall back on the old traditions of the community. In many cases they weren't connected to Nature and Spirit and on top of that weren't in healthy family situations. You have to remember that the situation on the reservations was mostly desolate, poor and one of deep despair. Alcohol and drug abuse was common. There was no prospect for a brighter future.

Some traditionalists had been able to continue the Old Ways and walk the Red Road; some Natives tried to adapt and forget about their roots; others just wanted to get back at the white people for what had been done to them; some wanted to get whatever was available as a short-term solution.

Intermezzo: the example of 49-er music

For generations, Native Americans weren't allowed to make their own music, no drumming and singing of any kind, especially not any singing in our own languages. Some of us tried to keep doing those things while hiding where nobody could hear us. We were ashamed of being Indians, and the things we wanted to do were often against the law and strictly forbidden. The situation was desperate and many of us only saw a solution in alcoholism, especially on the reservations. For years we had the highest rate of suicides in the United States. Music is a powerful way of expressing your emotions, and around 1949, groups of Indians, in many cases drunks and addicts, started to use the hood of their old cars as a drum to sing songs again. Since they couldn't remember all the original words, the verses came out as a mixture of English wordings and Native tongues.

The police left us alone, because the songs sounded harmless, and it was drunks that sang them anyway.

These songs developed and spread from reservation to reservation. It became a kind of music of their own, and they are called the 49-ers. You could say it was kind of the beginning of our people finding our way back again.

The last 20 to 30 years we have seen a slow revival of being proud of being Native and returning to our culture. Nowadays, white people even like to be Native and claim they have Native ancestors in the family: what a paradox! When I was young, I was taught to be ashamed of being Native and was of lesser importance and worth than other people.

You can imagine that when you are only slowly rediscovering your Native identity, you may be somewhat defensive about it. It's the reason why white people are often not welcomed at ceremonies. On the other hand unfortunately you can also witness the selling out of ceremonies by Natives for money.

If you really practice a spiritual path you will reach the understanding that you need to let go of any anger you may be feeling or any other accompanying, suppressed feelings like lack of self-worth or depression. You realize in the end that anger turns against you and doesn't help to heal anything. You learn there is good and bad in every person, in Indians like in any other people. You learn to look for the good individuals with the good hearts. So in the end it isn't about the color of skin but about how the heart is. If you choose to stay in hurt or in anger, you end up hurting yourself and those around you.

My personal path has been one of looking for people of like mind and like heart. They might appear different and yet under the surface they are similar to you. I'm looking for people who are trying to create something good for the Mother Earth, for future generations, for their family or community. When I see a person is looking for healing in some way, to create balance and harmony in some sense, I feel drawn to that person and want to get in touch.

I have been involved with AIM[12] for a while, which was a pretty intense radical thing. I was on the protest line and have been arrested several times for activist work. But I realized you can protest all you want against something and you can even be successful at times in blocking something from continuing, and maybe end up winning in court, but it doesn't mean you can stop it from happening again at another place. It just shifts, because there is so much money involved, and they will keep on doing it wherever they have the chance. As a protester you cannot be everywhere all the time. I realized if you really want to change something, it has to start somewhere else: you have to change your way of thinking.

First of all, you need to be a good example, do the things you want to see installed yourself in the best way you can. Then you share these ways with others who are interested in learning about them and may want to implement them in their lives. They in turn will be sharing this with other people in their environment and the snowball can continue to grow. In this manner real change can happen.

It always starts with the way of thinking. I have spoken many years about pollution of the mind. When you look around, you see pollution of the air, the waterways, and the earth through factories, through traffic, through exploitation of fossil energies and minerals, you name it. We can all witness this and it is written down in many reports. But the pollution has its origin in the polluted way of thinking. That kind of thinking doesn't care about the future generations; it only sees profit and short-term interests; it comes out of greed, egoism and arrogance, and it lacks compassion and connection to the greater picture. If we think in a polluted way, we

---

12 American Indian Movement

will have a polluted outcome of what we do. If we think in a greedy way, it will never be enough and the craving is for more and more. If we think in a caring and heartfelt way, this will result in actions that show care for the world around you and the world will also give you something in return. It is the way of thinking that influences what you create, what comes out. That is how it works in the end. I know it isn't always so visible for the human eye. It can take time and even a lifetime, but to me it is totally worth it.

There is still a lot to be healed. Much has been lost and only so much can be recovered and remembered. Prejudice and misconceptions are still common, but at least there are positive things happening. In the United States, we can speak of a revival of the Native culture over the last number of years. It is building up and a lot of tribes are working on cultural programs nowadays, trying to preserve the languages, the craftwork, the oral tradition of storytelling, and much more.

One of the big examples is the Canoe Journey on the Northwest coast, where the old tradition of a traditional tribal gathering has been restarted and has grown huge over the past ten years, with thousands of people coming to join in.

The other example recently is of political importance. In 2016 thousands of Native people from all tribes came to Standing Rock Reservation to protest against the pipeline the Energy Transfer Partners Company, backed by the US government, was threatening to build through their ancestral land that would poison the waters. It became national news with a great outcry for support from all over the US. Under President Obama's administration the process was stopped, but unfortunately President Trump has reversed this and advanced the construction of the pipeline in 2017. Nevertheless these protests are a sign for Indigenous people standing up, feeling connected again to their culture and to the ancestors, being proud of their background, and willing to support each other and be strong. It fills me with great hope for the future generations.

Chapter 3

THE NORTH

Hermine:

Already at Mount Shasta the next step ripened, and we had a strong calling to meet the energies of Northern Europe and the indigenous people still living there.

In June 2014 we arranged to stay with a befriended couple in southern Sweden, Mikki and Cecilia Dreijer in the area of Uppvala at their farmhouse to continue to work on the book. We had hoped to be able to travel further North to meet up with the Sami, the Native people living in the northern part of Europe, now covered by the countries of Sweden, Norway, Finland and parts of Russia. Just as the indigenous peoples everywhere else on this planet, they had undergone much of the same fate, suffering under the occupation of newcomers, who dominated and overruled their culture up to the point of extinction or assimilation. Also here there was a history of humiliation, loss of culture and language, boarding schools and Christianization, very similar to what had happened to the Native people of the US.

Our intent was to build a bridge of communication and exchange between the Native people of North America and Northern Europe. My personal vision was to get in touch with the caretakers and spiritual energies present there. I thought I had to go close to the Polar Circle in order to meet them. There were blockages of all kind that prevented this from happening. Going to where the Sami People are during summer, soon showed to be difficult, since they travel up to the Arctic Circle, roaming around, hard to find in the vast landscapes, retreating to their summer grounds away from the villages. Mala's health didn't allow heavy and long traveling and we only had a limited amount of time and finances. But we also didn't seem to find the necessary contacts within the Sami-community to have a meeting-point any closer either. We decided not to worry, put our intention out to the universe and pray that it all somehow would work out. Jennifer Aulie, a good friend of ours, who had adamantly supported the book-project from the beginning, prophesied: „You are on a road trip! Go and be on it without any expectations and you'll meet the unexpected." How right she turned out to be!

Once in Sweden we did manage to finalize two contacts with Sami people. Joannis Marainin, a friendly Swedish Sami elder and scholar, agreed to meet us on very short notice and was willing to share about his life and his culture. He invited us to come to a camp-area on a hill close to a river, which he also used to take out Sami-youth to learn about their culture and traditions. There was a traditional-style Sami-hut built from logs with earth on top. Unfortunately they had to seal it off with glass windows and a lock on the door to prevent vandalizing, since the area was open to the public. The old Sami-tent that used to be out there permanently was taken away for the same reason, since it had been vandalized recently.

Down at the river we enjoyed reindeer-jerky and a special kind of Sami bread while Joannis told us his life-journey from being a boy living outdoors traveling with the reindeer throughout the seasons, being taken away from his family, and then becoming the first Sami in Sweden who went to university. He remains an advocate for his own people, the culture, and the language. We found he also adapted a lot of the western Christian belief system. The old ways of connecting to Nature and Spirit, as Mala knew it, were not so apparent, but his direct open manner, his heart-warming hospitality, and the way he told his stories with wit and charm and the way he cared, showed his indigenous background. He took pride that for the Sami's in Sweden a lot has been restored in a positive way, where children are now able to learn the Sami language in school, cultural festivals are celebrated and some form of political self-governing exists. The indigenous spirituality has not yet lived through that revival, as it seemed.

Since we weren't going to travel up north, where I had envisioned returning an amethyst crystal into the earth, I was hoping to find another suitable spot. We decided to go on a daytrip in the area where we stayed. Under a perfect blue sky we drove along the coast to a neat little fishing-village with colorful and pretty wooden houses, screaming seagulls in the air, and gentle moving jellyfish in between the harboring boats. Being consciously aware of this drifting and floating though the element water, we became inspired to just roam around the countryside not going anywhere specifically. We were guided to a special retreat in nature, a little off the road, a kind of nature-reserve, where you could take a walk. A meadow, some cow-manure, a little stream, a small oak forest, then an opening towards the sea with an impressive old oak in the middle, clearly being the elder of the trees. We felt invited to perform a little ceremony for the area, giving thanks and saying prayers. While presenting the crystals to Grandfather Oak and placing them against his trunk upon his roots, they got blessings in return and Mala commented: „Hermine, we are being watched. The spirit-caretaker of this land is looking at us from within that bush. I can see his yellow eyes clearly; that is where he lives. His energy is neutral but also a bit critical of our intentions." We honored this being and asked for permission to go to the waterfront. There I put the crystals into a small pool, where the water gently caressed them. After a while we left, feeling satisfied and calm inside, knowing we had been in touch with the spiritual world and the energies of the land. I didn't feel a need to leave any crystal behind, but now they carried the energies of the Northern waters and earth, which was a really good and beautiful thing. The rest of my vision and original intention didn't matter anymore. It was fine the way it was.

The second Sami contact we had made before arriving in Sweden, Ronald Kvernmo lived in Norway, and was a cousin of a well-known Sami shaman healer. Also Ronald practiced the old shaman-way, called "seidr" in their language and we set up a meeting in Oslo.

On the day we headed out for Norway, the weather was lovely. I was dreaming away in the warm car, looking out over the countryside with nice farmhouses dotting the fresh green slopes between patches of darker forests. As time was on our side, I suggested to have a little break out in the sun, so we took the next stop at the motorway, where we discovered a sign pointing out: historical site. The picnic-place was not very inviting, as there was a lot of concrete and hardly any grass, but there were large tables with interesting pictures and text which drew our attention. As my eyes were touching upon those images -- it showed large prehistoric stone-circles and burial mounds --, I immediately got all excited inside. There was a sudden stir, some *sense of calling. We had to check out those places! It turned out that these sites were right by in the vicinity where we had chosen to take our break. Great news, time enough, let's have a little detour before moving on to Oslo!*

We went off the main road up on a little hill, leading into a small woody area with a small parking lot. We walked into the forest, said our prayers, and introduced ourselves to the guardians of the land. As we went up the trail, there was a moment of entering through some invisible veil into another realm, and we felt very welcomed. Soon we arrived at a clearing where there were two large stone-circles. It was a powerful moment to become aware of their presence: ancient, standing still each by themselves and yet all connected through invisible lines. I stepped forward into the circle, was drawn to what seemed to be the male stone and leaned against it. Strength and ageless energy supported my back and a warm gleaming feeling grew inside my chest. The circle made of 13 monoliths was speaking to me. Mala stood at the opposite one, which was the female representative of this stone family. It was a very special empowering moment and I just took it in, leaning against it, inhaling and exhaling, feeling the breath of the ancient ones.

I went on to the second circle, which was built with smaller stones and had a more oval form, and walked around the circle. Circling again and again: all my sisters, all the women I knew in my life, young and old, from long time ago or met recently, they all appeared and circled with me, spiraling back and forth in time. We danced and sung, other women were there too, with familiar faces but unknown in my present life. It felt like a celebration and recognition of each other. What an incredible blessed and joyful feeling!

With gratitude and happiness in my heart I followed the path leading towards where the burial mound was. All that time, I felt that this was the place where I was going to leave my amethyst crystal behind, hidden in the earth. My head showed me a spot, which looked beautiful, but my feet decided to move on until I reached the huge mound, about two meters high and ten meters wide, made solely out of rocks.

Mala, who had gone up the hill earlier, was gazing at a burial mound, sitting at short distance. It felt like a trance and we didn't speak. I walked around to the left, stopping at a spot where the rocks were covered with moss. There was a small hole where my hand went in without directing it myself. „No," I thought, „There is no earth here, the crystal needs soil to touch." Without any conscious searching my hand found another space between the rocks, where the amethyst slid out of my hand on a bed of

humus and dry needles. It had obviously decided it wanted to stay there. As I retrieved my hand, it held a flat piece of glittering stone that had broken off one of the bigger rocks. I had gotten a gift in return! Overwhelmed by this unexpected exchange, tears came into my eyes.

The hill, the tomb, the land, it all welcomed me. I was catapulted back into time, some 8000 years ago, when I had lived here in a community and had helped with the building of the tomb. We had carried the rocks from the seashore, which had been at a much higher level back then, up to the sacred spot where our ancestors were and where our people could overlook the ocean and islands, connected to the water, the earth, and the sun. I saw myself as a woman who helped her people when they were sick or when there were problems within our community. I wore a blue cloak, but also had some animal skin wrapped around me. We were kin to the islands, people of water and wind. We communicated through usage of simple words but mainly we connected through our body language, energy-fields and telepathy.

I encircled the whole mound and returned to where Mala sat. Then he spoke to me of what he had seen, interestingly wording the same things I had been going through before, repeating what I had witnessed in my inner visions. He had also been present at that time long ago, but had belonged to another tribe. What an amazing development! We had made a deep connection to the energies of the North, just as I had hoped all along. I had been talking to the North the whole winter, expressing my intention to find my own northern roots and to honor the North and its people. How magically had we been guided there. Trust to let *it flow and unfold by its own time and rhythm, is in the end all you need.*

Deeply thankful and filled with awe, we finally left the place. We returned to "now-time" and to the parking spot where we had left our car. What a trip, what a journey!

Ronald was only in Oslo for a few days, as he was attending a workshop his uncle performed; he actually was a Sami from the coast up North, where he lived with his family. Not being brought up traditionally himself, he had returned to the old spiritual Sami way at some point in his life. Proud of his heritage, which showed in the colors and symbols on his cap, he looked like any ordinary Norwegian, wearing jeans and a sweater. The whole meeting had something surreal: we met in one of those impersonal pizza bars at the central train station, lots of people coming and going, nothing outdoors, no patch of sky visible, artificial noises. He was a tall guy, long hair tied in a ponytail, a moustache and friendly observing eyes. Then he started talking about his vision, his people, how there is hope for a revival of the old ways. Since a few years he organized a week long festival, called Isogaisa[13] on his Sami homeland during the summer-solstice time, where he envisioned to have indigenous people from all over the world come together to share, pray and celebrate.

Here we were listening to this young man, passionate about his cause, eager to learn and at the same time, very relaxed and not pushing, in the middle of a hustling noisy mall and we were captured by his story. Mala's heart felt uplifted by his positive energy: hope for a younger generation that showed respect for the knowledge of the elders and who was eager to make a connection

---

13 For more information: Isogaisa.org: Urfolksfestival Wikipedia - Isogaisa Festival

to the land, without the assimilation to Christianity that was so apparent in Sweden.

A young Sami woman joined us at a later point. Astrid was a Sami from the river-area in the middle of northern Norway and had a very different physiognomy, short with a strong bone-structure, round face, chubby cheeks and a soft voice. They started to talk in Sami straight away, which was nice to the ear. She came from a female-healer tradition, did bodywork, knew a lot about herbs and also knew how to yolk, the art of guttural singing in Sami language.

Driving back we exchanged our thoughts about the Sami people we had met and talked to in the past days. There is good in all, we realized, we all make our efforts as we think fit, coming from different backgrounds and having had different experiences in life. Some similarities were apparent, between the histories of the Native American People of North America and the indigenous Sami People of Northern Europe, although huge differences in approach, current positions and opinions were also noticeable. In Sweden, a lot of good was done when it comes to education in the Sami language and culture, but it seemed there was a sense of loss of the old spiritual indigenous ways, being overtaken by the Christian belief-system. In Norway, it seemed there was an effort to fill the gap of a lost generation and return to connecting to Nature and Spirit.

Meeting merely a few Sami people, we only had gotten a glimpse, which wasn't representative but worthwhile nevertheless.

The Starting of Meta Tantay

As I have said before, my father was a spokesman for the Native People, especially for the Western Shoshone Nation, the tribe of my mother he married into. Besides defending our tribe in court on many occasions, he spoke about the different ways of healing, on herbs and Medicine and on numerous other issues. Back in the late 60's and early 70's, my dad traveled around to universities and all kinds of organizations because he was asked by a lot of people to come and speak.

He founded one organization himself: "The White Roots of Peace". Its aim was to take a closer look at all the treaties made with the Native people and get the US government to uphold what was in those treaties. An example was his involvement in the protest against the chaining up of pinion trees, which the Native people of Nevada had always used as a food source. The State allowed companies to chain and erode all those trees so that they could use the fertile ground for grazing or exploit it in other ways. Nevada doesn't have many trees, and this was done partly on tribal land. Another example was the prohibition of hunting for Native people, which my father worked on turning around. He saw a lot of harmful things being done where Native people didn't make use of their rights, basically because they weren't aware of what was possible. So his goal was to activate people to claim their rights with the help of lawyers, and to undertake official, legal steps for themselves and the land.

As he was traveling to many places all over the United States, he was a guest in many people's homes. According to our tradition, whenever you are invited someplace, you always offer the people your hospitality in return. Whenever your hosts were in the area where you lived, they were then welcome to stay and share food. Even if you didn't have much food, you would make do and everybody would eat a little less. You share what you have. If you didn't have enough beds people could sleep in, there was usually a couch or a chair or even just the floor with some blankets. There is always a way to make it work! That is how it has always been and it's still an important part of our culture. You always have your home open.

A lot of the people my father had visited over the years actually did follow up on his invitation and would show up at our doorstep to be our guest. There were Native people and non-Natives, and they ended up staying for different lengths of time. Some started even talking about staying for years, actually intending to live there permanently. People felt drawn by the way my parents lived their lives, a spiritual way and in touch with the Mother Earth, practicing their tradition. In those days, this was a new thing. For some people, western society with its value system was crumbling and people were eager to try a different lifestyle. They were searching for their own roots and spiritual connection to nature. For most Native people it had only been possible, if at all, to secretly practice their traditional way of life. Others had mostly forgotten about it or been taught to feel ashamed about it.

In the sixties, the hippie movement spread out from San Francisco, California to other parts of the United States. Hippies felt a strong pull towards Native people, as they lived a spiritual life and were close to the earth with no luxury. We became friends with a lot of hippies during that time; they came to visit us and wanted to live and become like us. Numerous times I traveled to Haight Ashbury, the hippie center in San Francisco. You had a group of hippies, the so-called "Diggers", who were the activists amongst them that provided for the others who just wanted to gaze at the stars and get high. The Diggers wanted to change some things in society on a political level. I met with some of those leaders of the active movement.

There is an interesting aspect I would like to mention here. Amongst Native people a prophecy was known that at some point in history the true white brother would show himself and the possibility of great healing for both Natives and non-Natives would become apparent. For a long time, we thought that the hippies were those people of the right heart and mind, and we chose to welcome them in our traditional culture. They were wearing headbands and beaded necklaces, and behaved like us. The once small hippie movement reached far out into the world as a whole. It created great changes in western-based societies and a peace movement originated from it. When the Vietnam War ended however, the momentum of the original ideas for social and political change could no longer hold and the movement as such died out, but all in all it was a milestone on the path towards healing and transformation.

My family lived in the small town of Carlin, at the edge right next to the open desert, where a small gravel road led up to our house. To accommodate all the people that came to visit, we started building willow wickiups for them to stay in. Depending on the size, you could fit two to four people in them or up to ten people in the large ones. We put carpets and tarps on top to make them waterproof, and put some stoves in them for the wintertime. We also had trailers and vans that you could sleep in; everything that you could think of was put to use.

Of course we also had to feed all those people. We started raising some milk cows and goats, had many rabbits, ducks, geese, and chickens for eggs, milk and meat. Our garden became larger and larger to grow crops, and our property was really expanding. Everything went well for a long time. We did our sunrise ceremonies and sweat lodges and were having a good time together.

The townspeople had already long been suspicious of us anyhow, because we didn't live on the reservation and practiced our own traditions at home. They were watching us even more closely now. We just thought very differently from them and mostly ignored them. As long as they didn't bother us, we didn't mind so much.

We did have a couple of incidents. I remember one time one of our guests, a young Indian guy, got very upset with the local habit of spraying a certain mosquito-repellent, a chemical mixture called malathion. During the mosquito season, they would drive around town in a truck with a huge tank, and spray this stuff in all directions. It came out as a cloud that drifted everywhere and everything had an oily residue after that. They didn't have a clue about the other effects this spraying had on the environment, aside from killing off insects. The serious damage was only known years later. Our family had been talking about our strong dislike of this yearly, unnecessary action. The guy's wife was around five months pregnant and he was very concerned about her. He got so mad that he took his rifle out and shot up the tank of the truck! You can imagine what an upheaval that made with the town council. About three weeks later, she had a miscarriage, but we were never able to prove that the chemical repellent had anything to do with it. It was a very sad situation. There were other similar incidents like this and the townspeople were always looking for ways to get rid of us.

One day there was a closed town council meeting and shortly after that we got a letter that they had decided to draw a new outline of the city. This drawing incorporated all of our land and meant that our five acres of land where we not only lived but also raised our animals was now inside the boundaries of Carlin. There is a rule that raising farm animals is not allowed inside a town. An interesting aspect was that a set of horse corals next door, belonging to our white neighbors, was left out in that drawing of the city-limits unaffected by this sudden new decision. We were given three months notice to get rid of our animals; otherwise they would come and dispose of them. That was a real shock for the moment, but we soon realized that this was actually the opportunity we had been waiting for to make a change. We had reached our limits with the land with all the people already living on it and with still more people wanting to come in. So we said: "This is okay. We need to find new land if we want to take care of all the people in a good way." My father, some others and I decided to go look for land in the desert since we knew the area pretty well. There were some places we thought would be suitable. In our traditional way, if you want to find out if you have chosen the right land, you need to ask the land and wait for a sign. What we do is gather and stand in a circle on the land, make an offering and say a prayer. Then we wait to see what happens, if nature responds. You look for unusual things in nature, for something special that appears or occurs. If there isn't any response, you know that it isn't the place. In our case, it was my father who spoke the prayer, but all present for the land search put their intent into it. First, we looked at an abandoned ranch that had a little creek running through it and had a spring. So we gathered in the middle of the land, prayed and waited, but we didn't receive any sign. Nature and Spirit didn't say yes, so we knew we had to keep looking. This is what we did over the next several weeks. We checked out all the suitable places we could think of. Each time we prayed and there never came a sign. After almost three weeks, we were running out of options. We had to find a place where there was water. In the desert you need a source of water to survive, obviously! Just as we were sitting together talking about how to proceed there was a knock on the door. My father went to open it and there was this old cowboy whom we knew had a strong dislike of Indians, saying: "I hear you are looking for some land. " My dad said: "Yes, we are." The cowboy said: "Well I have this piece of land I've put up for sale, it's 263 acres, just outside of town, out in the desert. I'm not using it anymore. I am willing to sell it to you for a cheap price." We were a little surprised at this offer, but agreed to go and have a look. The next day a whole bunch of us went out to the land. There were no buildings on it, just a broken fence line and an old hand-dug well about 6 ft. wide and 15 ft. deep, and bone dry. There were no springs, and no running creek or anything. We walked around a little more. At the side of the property we found a machine-drilled well in a bush with a pipe sticking out. I tried to see how far it went into the ground, but couldn't see the end of it, so I dropped a rock in it. After a little while it hit bottom with just a dry knocking sound and again, no water. At the edge of the property there was a little streambed that has water for only a few months when the winter snows melt in the springtime, but otherwise is just a dry creek. It was very obvious that the reason the guy wanted to sell the place was that there was no water at all on the property.

We felt we probably should leave since this wasn't suitable at all for what we needed. But my father reminded us and said: "Let's ask the land itself and pray over it. Even if we think it is not suitable, the spirits can still see it differently. That is what we should do and accept." We all agreed and told the old man what we wanted to do and he backed off to the side, thinking we were crazy anyway. We made a circle in the center of the land and my father started the prayer. When we were finished and getting ready to leave, somebody said: "Look up!" And what we saw was simply incredible. A whole flock of eagles were flying in a tight formation and circling right above our heads! We couldn't believe our eyes, looked at each other and said: "This is it! The land has spoken. This sign from nature cannot be any clearer! It doesn't matter that there is no water and there is just desert. If we get guidance like this from Nature and Spirit, we follow it and we have faith in it." So we turned to the owner and agreed to buy the land. We got a very good deal, $75 an acre, even back then -- I think it was in 1975 that we bought the land -- that was a fairly cheap price. The cowboy probably thought: "Ah, those stupid Indians, I got 'em!" But we didn't care; we knew it was the right thing to do.

Now we had to get the animals out to the new land pretty quickly. Otherwise they would come and take them away from us. Winter was coming soon and we had no money to build new barns or nice corrals, so we had to think of something. Together we made sagebrush corrals.

Sagebrush can grow up to five or six ft. high, so we used old bushes. We built barns and sheds for the animals from all the scrap lumber we could find in town. Then we brought out all the animals. With winter coming soon, somebody had to stay out there to feed them all, and to protect them from bobcats, coyotes and cougars out for easy prey. We didn't have the time or the money to build all the housing for all the people. Sky, whom I already was together with by that time and I volunteered to go there together and live with the animals. We were going to stay in a canvas tent; there was no other short-term solution possible anymore. Now, you have to realize that wintertime in northeastern Nevada can be pretty rough. It gets very, very cold, with an average of 20 below zero or even to 35 below zero in its peaks. It's so cold that your skin gets stuck to metal if you touch it. You have strong, howling winds with a lot of snowfall and sometimes blizzards. Winter can last up to five months and there are years where the temperatures don't get above freezing for three months, day or night.

But we volunteered anyway. We had a pickup truck that we drove back and forth every day. It was loaded with a huge open tank which we filled up with water at the house to give to the animals each day. And, of course, we took hay with us, and special food for the rabbits and the chickens. We had it all organized very well. Once the snow hit and blocked the roads, we melted snow to give the livestock water and used the hay that we kept sheltered beneath a big tarp.

We were so poor at that time that we didn't even have any pots or pans to bring with us. Sky used some kind of tinfoil that she formed as a bowl to heat up the food. I gathered cow manure and sagebrush to use for heating and hunted rabbits for food. Somehow we made it work.

Halfway through the winter, we got hit by a heavy blizzard that ripped our tent, and the whole thing went flying through the air. All of a sudden, we were looking up at the night sky and getting covered with snow! We had no place to go, bundled up together and hid as much as possible to stay warm and somehow survive. The next day I walked into town and arranged for an old van that had been fixed up which had an oil stove put in to stay warm. This was to be Sky's and my new home. Now we were in luxury!

We had a lot of goats out there and one of them had a baby, which they normally don't in winter because the babies wouldn't survive the cold. The mother usually refuses to feed a winter baby because it's not going to live anyway. That is how nature is. Sky and I heard the little one cry hungrily and we looked at each other and got weak in our hearts. We took the little goat in the van and took care of it all winter. It was hopping around, always crying for food, and we bottle-fed it There was not a lot of room, but Sky had a lot of fun with it.

In springtime everybody started coming out to the land. We were really happy that we had made it through the winter. The animals were doing fine and we could start building up the Camp out in the desert. The community grew little by little and we based the social structure of the community on the Clan System. Plus we could practice our ceremonies out there much easier without anybody giving us weird looks.

The vision of my father and other elders to have a place of our own, away from Western culture, where we could live and practice our ways according to our traditions had come true. It became one of the so-called Indian Camps. At that time there were three Camps in the United States like that. One in California called Red Wind, led by a Chumish Elder named Grandfather Semu Huaute, and one in Oregon run by a Native elder called Chiloquin. Ours was called Meta Tantay. Although it was a Native initiative and they were called Indian Camps and led by Native people, it was open to anybody who was interested in this kind of life.

My parents still owned our house at the edge of town and they decided they wanted to keep it and live there. They told Sky and myself that they trusted us to take care of the daily coordination of the Camp and basically we were the designated ones to run Meta Tantay. We were in our early twenties, so not yet prepared to take on a task like this, but we thought we could give it a try since the elders had put so much trust in us. We learned along the way. My parents oversaw everything and gave a lot of guidance. Other visiting elders also advised us. At times we had up to 50 people living there. We had daily meetings to organize the different tasks that needed to be done and also solve any problems that came up. It was a learning process and we struggled once in a while but were so happy and content with our lives! We could get up and do our morning prayers together: a daily sunrise ceremony, which is such a blessed way to start the day. We had drumming circles and sweat lodges on a regular basis next to other occasional ceremonies.

Since we were way out in the desert, we had to haul a lot of water in from town where my parents had their house. By this time, there were lots of animals out there and we already had quite a vegetable area which needed to be watered, aside from the water for drinking and cooking and cleaning. Each day we took several rides back and forth with a truck to fetch 45-gallon drums of water that we filled up with a garden hose.

One day my dad came out to the land and said to me: "Come on, let's see if we can find water on the land." He took a special willow branch with him that served as a tool to find water, a dousing rod. Willows love water and need it: wherever a willow grows, there is water close by, you can be sure of that. You walk around with this willow branch, which is forked and then comes together at one end. You have to hold it in a specific way, and watch and sense the energy of the willow intensely: it will move downward and point to where there is water. We had already drilled and dug but never hit any source of water. My father insisted that now it was time and it would work. We were walking around and all of a sudden, the stick bent down strongly and my father said: "Well, this looks like a good spot for water!" I also tried and felt a strong pull towards the earth. We marked the spot and the next day we went back to start digging.

We didn't have any equipment to really dig deep but we made a circular wide surface well by hand, about eight ft. across. We used a simple three-pole tripod system with a straight part in the middle where you could pull up a bucket filled with soil with a rope. By now, the hole was man deep and our heads were already below the surface. It was still sandy soil, which would easily collapse if we went any deeper. We were getting worried as it was getting dangerous to be down there, but we kept praying that the walls would hold up. At some point we hit gravel, a good sign, so we continued going deeper until we noticed water seeping through. It was incredible! You still need to dig deeper though, to have the well function with a steady stream of flowing water. In the end we were 12 ft. deep. When we looked up, we could only see some blue sky, way up high. We organized a special kind of centrifugal surface pump to bring the water up through a hose. We figured we were getting about 25 gallons per minute out of the well, which is pretty good. But we still needed to fix the walls, especially now with the water flowing. An elder knew of a way to put rocks on the inside of the wall to press the soil outwards and prevent the well from collapsing. In the old days it was done like this. You would use the energy of the rocks to press the earth outwards. So we gathered stones from a canyon not too far away, very large rocks and heavy too. Sometimes you needed two people to carry one. Following the instructions of the elder, we started from the bottom and worked upwards in a spiral. He told us to look carefully at the shape of the stone and listen to it where and how it wanted to be placed against the wall to make sure that its energy pressed outwards. He said to explain to the stone the purpose of its being there. Each stone got its specific spot, all the way up to the top and even above, though for the part above ground level we had to use some concrete to stabilize it.

We had built all that and were very content with it, but we still had to haul the water up through our bucket system. The pump was only used for pumping, not for bringing it up. We knew that the Redwind Indian Camp in California, the one run by Semu Huahete, had windmills that could be useful to us. At this camp they had some buffalo in need of hay. Our idea was to go trade bales of hay for a windmill. So Sky and I drove there in a good-sized truck, but halfway there we realized we were using far more gas than we had anticipated now that we were carrying such a heavy load of hay. We didn't have enough money to make the whole trip. We pulled over in a little town in Nevada to fill up, and ordered a Chinese meal from our last money. No way we could make it there and back. So, we prayed over our food, and I also asked the Creator for help to be somehow able to finish this trip and come home with a windmill. Now, I never gamble; having grown up in Nevada, I've seen what devastating effects it can have on people. But for some reason, after we'd already left the restaurant, I turned around and said to Sky: "I really need those 75 cents we got for change from the meal, I have to put them in one of those slots over there!" She looked at me and thought that it was a really strange request but gave it to me anyway. I put our last three quarters into one of the slot machines and sure enough, I hit the big jackpot! It was $ 75, which was a lot back in those days. We could make it back and forth with that and have some food on the way too! The Chinese lady who owned the restaurant wasn't pleased: she tried to make us use our money for more gambling, but we just shook our heads: "No, no, we need to leave!" With it we headed for California and were able to make the trade. Everything worked out fine!

An interesting thing happened at Redwood. Grandfather Semu asked me to be present at a meeting where he wanted me to help with an issue they had. Redwind had about 150 acres of land; it was pretty big, with about 140 to 150 people living there. Like I mentioned, they had buffalo on the property but they also had lots of rabbits which they aimed to use as a source of food. But for some reason the people who did the hunting were not able to bring home any rabbits. He told me: "Those rabbits are running around and these guys are shooting all over the place and they empty all the shells but just can't hit them! Mala, you have to show them how to hunt." Well, I was a little embarrassed, all these young guys looking at me in this meeting, but I had to do it and was given a small caliber shotgun that's actually very easy to use for rabbit hunting. We took a car and went out in the country. Pretty soon we saw some rabbits. We got out of the car and I focused on one of the rabbits, which went down immediately. Then I reloaded, took aim at another one and it also went down. So I turned to the guys and asked them: "Do you see what I am doing? What is different from how you are doing it?" And they told me: "When we hunt rabbits, we sort of go after them and they start running in all directions!" And I told them: "That is a classical mistake, we call it buck fever. You get so excited when you go hunting and see your prey close by that you don't focus and stay calm inside, but instead you chase them. You miss or even end up hurting them without killing them." Then these guys who were with me stood still, took their aim and sure enough, they were able to bring some rabbits down. We said our prayers and honored the animals, and with seven shells we managed to bring seven rabbits home. Semu was very pleased. After that we could travel home the next day with the completely dismantled windmill in the back of our truck.

It was a challenging project to put the windmill together again from the many small pieces but we eventually managed. We set up a big tank and the windmill was pumping up water most of the time since we usually have wind in the desert. We also covered the well opening with a small concrete building so nobody could accidentally fall in, be it curious kids or animals or birds. Since it was surface water, which can get polluted by animal manure or other things, we couldn't use it for drinking, but it was clean enough to water our gardens with, and to use for cleaning or for the animals. It was really great and it worked for the rest of the time we were at the Camp. Quite something if you recall that the farmer who sold us the place had dug and drilled for water for all those years and had never been able to find any reliable source.

About two years later we had raised enough money to pay a company to drill for water at a deeper level. We figured that there would be a source of groundwater on the property after all.

We had noticed something promising: the land was changing. Before, it had been covered with sagebrush and greasewood, a kind of plant that grows only in the driest desert areas, with almost no leaves, just a lot of thorns. If you squeeze the tiny, tiny leaves, a greasy fluid comes out, hence the name. During all the many years we had now lived there, we had done our ceremonies and prayers for the land. We did our sunrise-ceremony every day to give thanks and pray for the land. We did lots of singing and drumming and tried to be caretakers in the best way possible. We honored and respected the land, made offerings while working in the garden and also when we took vegetables for our meals. We prayed and gave thanks when we took the life of an animal. We prayed over our food, always remembering that we are part of that Sacred Circle of Life. The elders, my parents and others who were close and involved with the Camp were giving us spiritual guidance and advice and had told us again and again: "If you take care of the Mother Earth and the Spirits of the land, they will take care of you."

Everybody had noticed the changes that were becoming more and more visible as time went by. We had witnessed little rainclouds moving in our direction more and more. But the astounding thing was that they were actually dropping rain right on our land. In Nevada you hardly get rainclouds. When some clouds do appear and actually let go of their water, it is often the case that the rain comes down halfway, evaporates, and then goes back up. When you watch it, it is pretty amazing. It is very rare that the rain actually hits the ground.

Pretty soon, the earth was sprouting some grass. The creek that in the beginning would only carry water after the winter snows had fallen in the mountains nearby started having water for longer periods, and after seven years it was flowing all year round and increasing each year, widening out to become a real stream. At one point, willows started growing at the side of the river and there were little fish in it. We even saw a beaver a few times. With the grass growing, we witnessed birds coming for the seeds. The land was getting much more fertile overall. It made us feel very happy and we felt so welcomed by the land! Really amazing how the land had responded.

So, we felt that as soon as we had enough money, the time was right to try to drill for a deeper well that could deliver drinking water. It costs about $1500 and you only have one chance to use the drill. If the drill comes out dry, they don't reimburse you. You lose your money, too bad. I mean you really have to be sure about the spot where you want them to drill, because they don't go around and dig at a few different spots. It would cost you more.

Again my dad and I went around the land with the willow rod in search of a good spot. We hired the drilling company and had them dig exactly at the spot the rod had shown us. First they hit the surface layer of water, then they still had to go deeper and deeper to a subterranean layer. They drilled through clay, which keeps the two separate. It took a long time and we were getting a little worried since nothing was happening. But finally, after 65 ft., they reached water. They went down another 10 ft. to really make sure it would flow properly and ran a test to see how much water was coming through. It was 75 gallons per minute, which is a lot of water. After that we had good, clean drinking water -- plenty! It was great! And another surprising thing happened: everywhere on the land, if somebody dug in the ground, after three ft. sure enough, they would find water! All of a sudden, it was all over the place, within reach of everybody, incredible. Only the well the previous owner had dug in his search for water stayed dry. Just for fun we did a little test with that spot and dug a hole, really close to that dry well, almost touching it, and even there we hit water! Mother Earth really didn't want to show water to that other guy's hole: he didn't have a good heart. Mother Earth thanked us for having faith in her and praying for her, giving us fertile land in return. All she needed was time.

It showed us that if you really are willing to work together with Nature and Spirit, if you are listening to the guidance, if you are showing your appreciation and respect, that is when Mother Earth responds and will take care of you. It is such a powerful message! It teaches you about allowing things to happen in the right way and at the right time. We often want to have an outcome the way we think is right. We don't allow ourselves to be guided. If you do, it might take some effort and struggle, but it is so rewarding to be part of the natural flow of things. It is truly a blessing. We felt very thankful and connected to the Mother Earth. Living at Meta Tantay was the best way for me to live and I couldn't imagine leaving voluntarily.

The Way of Life and Praying

In this book, we talk about the Native Way of Life, which leads directly to our way of thinking, which leads to concepts that show in our language and culture. How we feel, respond, and act all come from this and head back again to how we live; it becomes a full circle. If you take the words "Way of Life" literally, it is very simple: it is a way of how you live your life. It also affects everything and goes beyond words.

Since it is so difficult to explain, I have been very reluctant to write a book. The indigenous culture has been passed on verbally for generations through legends, stories and sharing repetitively amongst each other. In many cases we don't speak our Native languages anymore and so much has gotten lost due to historic events. When people read my words, each will have his or her own perception, understanding and concepts, depending on their culture and upbringing. Misconceptions and misunderstandings can arise when you take in account how one single word can already have a different impact on different people. And yet at the same time, I see the book as a chance to reach many people and get them interested in another way of thinking. I envision it as part of the bridge that I am hoping to build between indigenous and non-indigenous people, in order to learn from each other.

Corbin Harney, my father, Grandfather Semu and others recognized that it was important to reach out to people from other cultures. They saw there was a greater need than just among their own Native People; the Mother Earth as a whole is in need of help. They said: "We have to join our efforts to learn and relearn the Ways of the Earth, to connect and share with each other." Even their own people have criticized them time and again for this behavior: "Why don't you stick to helping your own people?" But they recognized there are many good people out there, Native and non-Native, who are willing to help make changes in their way of thinking and in their actions, but they lack guidance and knowledge. Consequently, they decided to continue to meet with people of different backgrounds, and I follow that within my own possibilities and limitations.

What we refer to as a spiritual Way of Life is what we also call "Walking the Red Road." Native Americans don't really speak of having a religion.

This means that this is an attitude you are always aware of and that is part of your daily life. You don't just go to church on Sundays and forget about it the rest of the week. It is not an institutional religion you belong to, it is -- in a true sense -- a "Way of Life". You practice it all the time: how you prepare food, how you start the day, how you treat the people around you, how you drink your water... It is about your approach, awareness and attitude, how you connect and work with it. Most people are not willing to commit themselves fully to such a way of life. It takes a huge responsibility and is not always easy. You often have to make choices to stay true to yourself, to just keep having faith.

The Way of Life makes you aware of how the wind feels on your skin, makes you notice how a leaf falls down from a tree or how a bird flies through the sky. It draws your attention to a little bug that visits you and that might carry a message for you. It is really about paying attention and being aware and then being able to welcome it in, whatever the lesson or message might be. Things that seemingly happen outside of yourself are in fact connected to your life as they appear in it. It is not separate from you.

On the one hand, this is very simple. It is a way of how you live your life. On the other hand, it affects everything and goes beyond words. When you talk about it and make use of a detail or a story to enliven it, you leave out the big picture. The culture and tradition it is rooted in can't be covered by that example.

To have faith is at the heart of the Way of Life and it is the opposite of wanting to control. Having faith is not just doing a ceremony but it means you truly let yourself be guided by Nature and Spirit, which you can only achieve with an open heart and mind. To accomplish this, a lot of endurance, commitment and focus are required. You keep practicing; you will make mistakes, you will learn as you go. But the result will be that you enable yourself to follow the flow of life.

It doesn't mean you never struggle and have your doubts here and there. That is where growth lies and where the possibility of change and transformation can show itself. You may not always understand everything about the path you have chosen. It has to make sense on a deep level inside of you and you should let go of wanting to control the outcome. When you reach that point deep down inside, you simply know what is right for you.

It is very important that you find a way to live your life that is right for you and fits you. I was born in a Native American family and was brought up in those traditional ways of the Red Road. Yet it doesn't mean I have to live according those ways. It just happens that it suits me and makes me happy inside living a spiritual way of life. For other people this can be very different and still be very good and in harmony with their life. Of course you can also live a spiritual life when you go by another tradition or follow a belief system according your culture and upbringing. The elders have always told me: "There are many good paths to the Creator. Find the one that is right for you and sings to your heart! It doesn't matter which one."

What I have come to realize over the years is how difficult it is to explain what the Way of Life means and how it is incorporated in everything I do and am. The sunrise ceremony has a certain structure and we perform certain tasks, like smudging, a prayer with a tobacco offering, singing and drumming, but there is much more to it. As you are welcoming in the sun and the new day, you are connected to everything around you. The earth you stand upon, the cool breeze in the air, the trees close by, maybe some birds that come flying through or other animals that appear. There might be some people walking by, who are even listening in, or some spirits that you might be aware of. It is all part of that moment in ceremony and it all adds to the meaning of it.

This attitude of awareness is constantly present throughout your daily life and forms the backbone of the Way of Life. The Way of Life is a concept that trickles through in everything you do, think and feel. It is a mindset and you feel it in your heart at the same time. It is how you understand and perceive the world as a reality.

The essence of our Way of Life is that you live your life from the heart and walk your path from the heart. You can help other humans, you can be there for other living beings, and you take care of life as a whole. This implies you don't just think of yourself. You do take care of your own needs too, but you realize you are connected to everything on Mother Earth and you are not only there for your own "wants". You think about your actions and how they affect everything around you and how it affects the next seven generations after you.

A good heart will stay humble when it works with spiritual energies and will not be greedy and ask for too much. When you pray, you need to keep that in mind. You can ask for things, yet even if you think they are very important for the survival of the earth, you still need to stay humble, adding: "I pray for these things, only if it is good and meant to be" at the end of your prayers. Since you don't know all the answers and since an individual can't oversee the whole picture, you accept what Creation allows to happen. By speaking this phrase, you allow life to take its course and you don't make yourself more important than you are.

Praying is actually a word that isn't Native to begin with. We call it having a conversation with Creation, talking with Nature and Spirit. You share what is in your heart and you look for answers and insights. You are aware of what is around you and what Mother Earth is showing you at that moment.

As a child, you naturally have a strong connection to Nature and Spirit and are close to the source without being blocked by your mind and ego. As this natural state of being changes as you grow up and as the influences from society and your upbringing settle in, you lose that connection bit by bit. That's why people have made up special times and places for prayers, like churches and temples. In modern societies, children constantly hear that they should stop talking to nature and stop sharing their dreams and visions; these are denounced as phantasy and imagination. Children are forced into a certain kind of adult reality and soon they don't even remember that they once thought and felt differently. They lose their primordial, innocent state.

If you, at one point in your life, decide you want to return to a more natural attitude, at first, you'll start from your mind. You'll think about which direction you are facing in a ceremony; you'll worry about your words or that other people might listen in and point their fingers at you. Gradually that will change as you familiarize yourself with different aspects. You can't do anything wrong as long as it comes from the right heartfelt intent and from doing things in a respectful and humble manner. If you get past the head part, you will become more and more free in the conversations you have with Nature and Spirit. The blocks will drop away and Mother Earth will respond and communicate with you much more easily. You will remember things from when you were young and you will see with different eyes. Sometimes I hear people say: "Oh, it's incredible. I am drawing in all these animals and special energies now." But that is not true, it's just that you are seeing more of what was there before, too. You just weren't aware of it.

A key to any prayer is to express your gratitude. There is so much to be thankful for! First of all, there is the gift of being alive and being able to experience this. You can be grateful for every breath you take, for the birds you hear, the wind you feel on your skin, the beauty you see around you. Be thankful for the food you eat, the water you drink, the house you live in and the family and friends you have. When you are consciously aware of what is there and give thanks, you come into a whole different experience and connection to it all.

When you pray, you need to keep in mind to stay humble. You can ask for things, but even if you think they are very important for the survival of the earth, for people who are struggling or for your own wishes you need to add: "if it is good and meant to be" at the end of your prayers. That way you show your respect for the course of things and accept what Creation allows to happen. Since you, as an individual, don't know all the answers you can't oversee the whole picture.

Prayers are between you and the Creator and this has a personal character. Ceremonies give structures that encompass prayers being made by a spiritual or Medicine people.

I always tell people that once you start to pray, you will notice over time that those prayers change. The wording you use, the phrasing and the content develop because you have gained insight or you might have realized something and changed your mind a bit. My prayers aren't the same as they were some years ago. I have changed as I have become older, and my attitude and the way I see things have changed as well over time. I have been influenced by my surroundings and my awareness of the subtle layers of the energies of Nature and Spirit has become more refined. It is a continuous learning and relearning, adding and letting go, of living according the Medicine Wheel.

I have realized that people are fascinated and attracted to the way I live and talk, but it very often stays on the outside, and they can not incorporate it and make that big change. A friend of mine told me once: "You are like a living dinosaur, coming from an ancient time, which somehow has survived in modern society. We all love to come, watch and listen! But we don't want to become a dinosaur ourselves." All I can say is it is just who I am and all I know.

People like to go for the shortcuts and they tend to stay on the surface. Very often people start performing Native ceremonies without having a thorough background on what the deeper meaning is. Yet I understand that you have to start somewhere to build that knowledge again. It is an ongoing process.

The elders have always emphasized there are many good paths on Mother Earth. Our Way of Life is just one of them and I don't expect people to take on the Way of Life. Each person comes from a very different upbringing, culture and tradition and although most people are interested in what I have to share, they will naturally filter it through their own concepts of belief and practice. It is important to turn the information into something that is your own, not to copy it, and especially not to claim it as the only right way. Important is that it makes sense to you and makes you happy at the same time. You don't have to become an Indian for it and you don't have to pretend that this is the way it is done by Indians. There is no "one way" either!

You have people who are very willing and go to all kinds of workshops and seminars, learning about raising their awareness or doing spiritual practice. But instead of really incorporating all that new knowledge into their daily lives, they keep running to more workshops and doing more ceremonies. They even brag about it and tell everybody where they have been and what they have experienced and were a part of. Even worse is when they go around and claim they are now experts. Instead, it is truly about putting it to use in your daily life where you are a part of a community and are a child of Mother Earth. It is not about making your ego happy but it is about becoming a better person, a better caretaker.

I have also noticed people who have been trying really hard to make changes but who keep putting blocks in front of their own spiritual growth. This is often the result of how they have grown up. They are taught to think in a certain doubting and criticizing way. If you think that negatively, the blocks in your own mind become huge and difficult to overcome. To turn this mechanism around is essential for transformation to take place. Turn your energy towards your heart and have faith in your own spiritual being: this is where your true nature lies and where transformation starts. The heart energy is of immense power and radiates far out. It is much stronger than the mind. Be open in your heart and believe in yourself in a positive way! If you keep saying that you are not on a certain level, you put yourself down and limit yourself. You could also phrase it as: "I am working towards a certain level, am just not there yet." In our minds are our fears and insecurities, but also our hopes and desires. As they mix, they tend to confuse us. They sidetrack us and are not supportive if we stay in that energy too long. If you combine your thinking with the feeling that you experience in your heart, you know you are on the right track. Do you have a warm and happy feeling in your heart, even if it doesn't make sense? Then continue with that thought, plan or action. Then you are connected within. If it is only in the mind, you separate yourself from your inner being.

You have to have patience with yourself there, as you are on a learning journey. It just takes practice. Take a moment and relax. Don't make decisions if they don't feel right. Check your heart where you are guided. Your heart is the connection between Nature and Spirit. Over time, this connection will become clearer and you will be able to accomplish amazing things with it.

Whenever I am sharing about something of my culture, I have to keep in mind to let go of my expectations. 99% of the people who come to listen to me will take out little things that inspire them to make certain changes for the better, but will not make a grand transformation towards the Way of Life. That is totally okay. It is never my intention to convince anybody of my path, to convert people so to speak. If someone truly feels this is what he or she wants to learn more about, it is a good idea to ask if you can live with Native people for a while. You then learn as you live together. It may all be a lot less spectacular than you expect; you just live an ordinary daily routine and do not go from one big ceremony to another.

To follow the Way of Life consequently takes a lot of in depth knowledge and commitment. It requires ongoing attention and constant awareness, which is demanding in today's world with its many distractions. Most people are looking for something on short notice that helps them overcome a certain problem they have encountered in their life, without seeing the bigger scale of things and in the perspective of the whole.

On my end, I am also still learning to do better, to become more fully aware, to really live a spiritual life at all times. This requires a high commitment and responsibility towards that path. There are always moments where you are not in a good space, where you are being tested how you deal with a certain situation. That can be quite challenging sometimes and often you don't understand why certain things happen, but you know that one of the rules is everything happens for a reason. If you believe that and have faith, it gives you strength to carry on doing your best.

Community Life at Meta Tantay

Many interesting people came by at Meta Tantay and we formed a community that was constantly changing and developing. We didn't have any major plans or long-term thinking. It was pretty much learning by doing and just living life.

If a person had a good heart and wanted to stay with us, no matter in what condition or what age, we felt it was important to find ways to make it possible. One time we had an unusual request from a guy who was completely blind and we were really challenged to make this possible. Since we lived out in the desert, and he was dependent on other people for assistance with almost every move, we discussed this matter at length. We came up with the idea of helping him find his way around the Camp by using a hip-high rope going from pole to pole that he could follow with his hands, with knots in it if there was a change of direction: one knot for this direction, two knots for the other direction. Since everybody had to participate in some way with the daily work -- you know, this was an essential principle of the camp: if you share the work, you feel you are part of the community, you are responsible and you take part! He helped with cleaning vegetables from our garden or did other little tasks.

The soil in the desert was very acid and besides not having a lot of humidity throughout summer, this wasn't very beneficial for planting and growing vegetables. We tried to get as much manure and old hay from the ranchers as possible and built really thick beds with it after we had let it compost. Now, we were able to harvest some quite amazing crops: beautiful tomatoes and huge cabbages and onions. Not only the fertile beds helped, but also the way we talked to the plants and prayed to them. The blind man stayed about half a year and then moved on.

We also had a guy in a wheelchair for quite some time. He asked us for copper wires one day, which he heated up a little with some solder and started making beautiful little sculptures. They resembled a playing child or a little car. We could sell them so the community would have some income from them. It's incredible to see how inventive people are if they feel secure and accepted.

It still gives me a good feeling to think back: we were creative in finding solutions and it was very rewarding for everybody involved.

I really wish we could all be more like that in our modern society. Nobody was left out and we all took care of each other. Remember: we all have gifts in us that we can share. Usually when a person has a limitation on the one hand, there is a talent on the other hand, but we very often tend to focus on the limitations.

During the ten years at Meta Tantay we have been through the whole range of life: we experienced babies being born in our community, which is such a miracle to be part of, and were also confronted with somebody crossing over while living with us at the Camp. The death of this person hasn't been officially solved but we have a dark suspicion as to how it occurred. One day we noticed a black, unmarked airplane flying directly over the camp at a very low height, an illegal act in the United States. We saw grey smoke coming out of it while the plane kept circling and crossing over our Camp. The smoke dropped down and turned into long, silver strands that were sticky and we realized they had sprayed some kind of chemical on us. It was too late to hide; we were caught by surprise and a lot of us were covered by it. Many people got sick that night. Normally it was my job to wake people up in the morning for sunrise. I came to a lodge where a young man was sleeping and knocked and knocked on his door but didn't get any response. I finally opened the door and went inside and saw him lying there. He had died during the night. We called in the police and the mortuary to come and take the body to do an autopsy on him as his parents had requested. He was only in his late twenties; his name was Udo, a European name, but he was American. They said they couldn't find any clear cause of death but we knew what it had been: it was the chemical substance that was sprayed on the Camp. It was very hard on the whole community: there was a lot of grief and a lot of anger too. We felt this must have been an action from a governmental organization that wanted to get rid of us.

So we have been through good times and sad times together, as always in life.

Sweat Lodge Ceremony

One of the most healing ceremonies in all of our tribal history has been the sweat lodge. It has always been a tool for Native people to connect with Nature and Spirit, and I understand it as a way of doing Medicine in the sense that it reaches people and can bring about a change in attitude. You work with the energies and you aim for balance and creating something positive for all involved. With that I mean not only for humans but also for other forms of life. Since I was a kid I have experienced their power.

Sweat lodges have been held for ages to cleanse you physically, mentally, emotionally and spiritually, and have been used by most tribes in the United States with a basic similarity and some cultural variations. Usually, you enter the lodge through a door facing east and circle around the fire and the lodge clockwise. Women on their moontime[14] don't join in. Most times, there is an altar in front of the lodge. Different people will run the ceremony slightly differently due to varying tribal ways and also personal approaches of running a sweat. It is important to understand this. In our culture you need to do things from your heart and not from a mindset that wants to copy something in exactly the way it is "supposed" to be. Of course there are certain rules and principles but you always have to flow with nature and how things are at that time, doing the best you can and with the right intent. We encourage people to find their own way.

I was in and around sweat lodges for more than 13 years, before I was told to help with the "pouring of the water", which is another expression for running and leading the sweat lodge. Most importantly, everything is done in a respectful and healing manner. From the way we are behaving ourselves, to how we interact with the other people, to how we approach everything that is part of the ceremony, like the fire, the stones, the water, the tree-people, everything is done from that attitude and in awareness of the healing we want to accomplish. Everything needs to work and flow together. Everybody is part of the ceremony and every person has an influence on the whole. It is not just the person who is running it that makes it happen. It is a joined effort to make it work well. When there is a person, who is thinking very negatively and isn't focused, this affects the ceremony. A good approach is to go in there with an open heart and without any expectations.

Usually, we have four rounds in a sweat lodge. In most cases, the lodge is made from willow branches covered with blankets, tarp or, in the old days,

---

14 Moontime is a Native way of referring to the menstruation period of women See later in this chapter under Moon Custom

buffalo hides. It has a door flap, which can be opened and shut by hand. We sit together on the barren Mother Earth around the pit with the hot stones in total darkness, and water is slowly poured over the stones. We join our energies, praying and singing. In between the rounds, the door is opened and we have a little break with some fresh air coming in.

A sweatlodge being built in Schattendorf, Austria

Each of the rounds is for a different purpose. The way that I do it is to have a welcoming round first. We want to start things in the right way for a healing lodge for everyone and all things, so we welcome in the spirits and nature, and also welcome each other. The second round is for the Mother Earth, as momentarily she is struggling hard and is in need of our prayers. We give her thanks for everything she gives us; we remember and honor her for giving and supporting life as it is; we let her know we do not take this for granted but are aware of this deep in our hearts. We also let her know that we are open to her teachings and we want to learn more to flow with her and not push our ways upon her. We want to become better

Caretakers, as we are her children, and in this role, we feel obliged to help and honor her. The third round is for those who are in need of our prayers and who have asked for them. There are many people who are struggling, those that we don't know personally and those that we do know. We try and connect ourselves with a supporting and kind heart. The fourth round is for ourselves. We ask for help and guidance in our own struggles and lessons that we are going through. We ask for a deeper connection to the Mother Earth and Spirit. One round takes up to 30 or 45 minutes.

This is just a quick overview of what the rounds are about and is the way I do it personally. You can fill in those four rounds, as you feel fit. Between the second and the third round we pass drinking water around and there is a bit of a longer break.

Personally, I offer healing lodges. This means that I don't compel people to last as long as they possibly can, or make the lodge as hot as possible. It is not about bragging and being tough. It is my responsibility to lead the ceremony in an appropriately and make sure everybody is coming through in a healthy way. I let myself be guided by Nature and Spirit through this process, and watch and listen for any signs that I need to be aware of. At the same time, I want to make sure it is strong enough for the people, so they can go through a challenging experience -- you cannot be too comfortable in a sweat lodge either!

The task of running the lodge is to make sure it is going to be a good journey for everyone. It is possible to go out briefly in between the rounds when the door is open; no use in forcing yourself and no need to feel embarrassed. When I run a sweat, you can come back in before the next stones are brought in. If you choose not to re-enter, you're asked to stay close by the sweat lodge area since you were part of the ceremony from the beginning and your energy stays part of it until the end.

It is better not to eat too heavily before a sweat lodge. Some people prefer not to eat at all and use this as a period of fasting.

The best thing is to not have any expectations and go in there with an open heart and the right intent. Our biggest fear is actually the fear of the unknown. The heat inside the sweat lodge is there to help you, so it is important you welcome it. Don't try to resist it or think too much about how you are going to handle it and that you have never been good with heat. Those thoughts will only block you. If you can recognize the heat as something helpful instead of hurtful, you will be surprised how much you can take. Your mind creates a lot that in fact isn't real. In the Western culture, the need to control and to understand things with the mind is stronger than in our indigenous culture, and fear can be overwhelming at times. We are used to this state of not-being-in-control much more and are willing to accept the experience, so the heat doesn't have so much power over us.

The best you can do is really very simple. Don't worry so much and just relax. Let it come to you. Enjoy the journey!

How a person experiences a sweat lodge is personal and is up to Nature and Spirit. It can come through the Grandfather rocks speaking to you; it can come through the Mother Earth you sit on or through the willows; it can come in many different ways and forms. It can be the steam that speaks to you or you see something in the darkness. It can even just be an insect.

The way I was taught and how it was done in earlier days is that you don't wear any clothing, but things have changed over time. You must remember that long ago, it was only the men who did sweat lodges. The women have their moontime, which is a monthly, powerful, natural way of cleansing, and during that period they would be in a so-called moon lodge. The tradition of the moon custom has been forgotten and abandoned even more than the sweat lodge. At one point in history, mixed sweats became common because it was felt that now women also needed an extra possibility for a deep spiritual and emotional cleansing. Since Native Americans too, have become separated from the Mother Earth and the old ways, it was felt necessary that women would join in this ceremony. Cultural changes and habits asked for a different custom with the clothing, partly because we now had mixed sweats and partly due to a changed approach to nudity. I have found while traveling in Europe and doing sweats over there that people are far less stressed over nudity than they are in the United States, where it is an issue and you can be criticized for it. Christianity has made nudity something to be ashamed of, has connected it solely to sexuality, and people have gotten very uptight. Of course when you do a sweat lodge, it is not about sexuality at all.

I was taught to be naked, because all the toxins that leave your body while perspiring need to go into the earth. If you have clothes on, these toxins can go right back into your body again. Like I said though, there are no strict rules on this anymore. Nowadays, most Native people have special sweat clothes on. Some even get upset if somebody wears no clothes in the sweat lodge. Some say that you don't want to distract anyone with your nudity, so you avoid this with some clothing. I don't want to judge the different opinions. It is not about forcing anyone into a situation where they wouldn't feel at ease. We want to create harmony with the sweat lodge, so we don't go against the custom of an area, state or country.

For sure, however, you want to avoid wearing any metal in the lodge because it gets very hot. Little piercings are okay, but no earrings or necklaces. And glasses will do you no good, as you can't see anything in there anyway! Hahaha!

If you regularly hold sweats in the same spot, it is important to know that it is better not to lie down on the earth or to lean against the willow branches, because the toxins from prior sweats may still be there and affect you. Your back is especially sensitive in picking up energies of any kind. In our tradition, we use the lodge for one year, tear it down and build a new one close by. The earth is then able to cleanse itself through the weather-elements. We use the old willows of the dome structure of the lodge for making the fire at the new one, which creates a nice circle in connecting the old to the new.

When I run a sweat, a so-called spirit line is made after the fire is lit, which is a line made with an offering of tobacco from the fire, through the altar and right into the sweat lodge. With the exception of the fire keeper and whoever is running the lodge, this line should not be crossed by anyone. We are asking the energies of the East, the Father Sun, the Eagle and other Spirits to come in through the fire to the altar, which is a little earth mound with some sticks on it. We ask them to come along the spirit line to have those energies present with us in the lodge, right to where the Grandfather Stones are. In return we are sending all our songs and prayers out in that same direction. Everything that is lying on the altar will become blessed with all that energy moving in those two directions. You can put something on the altar that means a lot to you and that you would like to have blessed.

Once we had a person who wanted to put his shoes on the altar. This unusual request surprised me. It turned out that this man was crippled on both feet and really needed those shoes to carry him through life. Then it made sense to me!

We try and stick to walking around the lodge in a clockwise manner because on our side of the world, this is how the energy on Mother Earth flows. We watch our language while preparing the sweat, being in it and around it. Having good and positive energy is important at all times.

Usually, there is a fire keeper who helps build the fire and takes care of the Grandfather Stones. This person also brings in the stones at the beginning of each round, and can still come inside and join in. When we have mixed sweats, I like to have a female helper to balance the male and female energies that work together.

Before we enter the lodge, we make one big circle around the lodge and the fire clockwise. Then we line up to get smudged with sage and enter. In the sweat lodge we stay on our knees close to the ground to show a humble attitude. We go in one by one. The one who runs the ceremony will be first and will be to the right of the door. The co-runner will follow. In the Shoshone way, the single women come next, followed by the couples, and then the single men come in. There is one spot left free for the fire keeper and doorman.

We usually cover the lodge with blankets beforehand, together. It is nice to prepare and spend time in the area before we go in. We get to know each other a little bit. We can talk and laugh and work together. Nothing too serious: a lot of people have this concept that being all serious is how you have a ceremony. Laughing is good medicine: never forget that! If you feel you have an issue with someone, please do not start to argue with each other. Leave the area, take a moment within and do not bring that energy with you coming back in the ceremonial area. This is not the time to start any discussions. We share and offer suggestions for a solution maybe, that's all.

Also inside the lodge we will joke around and tell stories. It all adds up to creating good energy and a good healing experience for all.

The firekeeper is very important when holding a sweat lodge. In the fire we keep the Grandfather Stones, where first they will become very hot before being brought into the lodge. The energy of the fire and how the stones are heated up determines what kind of energy is brought in with the Grandfathers. It needs to be done with the right attitude and mindset. You use kind words around the fire. You speak to the fire and express your gratitude, as it gives us warmth. The Grandfather stones are also treated in the appropriate manner. The firekeeper warns when somebody accidentally crosses the spirit-line in between the fire and the lodge. He or she needs to do this gently and handle it in a kind, positive way. If somebody gets burned a little, they aren't supposed to cuss at the fire, as that brings negative vibrations, which we want to avoid. We keep it positive and learn from it when little things like getting too close to the fire happen. The fire is teaching us something at that moment and we welcome that lesson instead of blaming it. Every thought and every action goes into the fire and thus into the lodge and into the people in there in the end.

We usually get the fire going together and say a communal prayer at that point. The firekeeper covers the stones with the wood and needs to make sure the stones stay covered during the whole ceremony as much as possible. He or she also moves the wood around carefully; the logs aren't thrown on the stones but handled with care and respect. There is a spirit in the wood too. They once belonged to the tree-people and we recognize and honor that while using them for the fire. The fireperson needs to dust the stones before bringing them in the lodge. He or she can either stay outside with the fire or come inside and join the rest. I let them join in. You'll have to go by the rules this person sets up for everyone. The facilitator of the lodge makes the decisions, whether the firekeeper stays outside or is allowed to join inside and then leave in between rounds to get the next set of stones.

If by any chance you don't feel comfortable with those decisions, you choose not to go. In the Native way, you don't criticize the one who is conducting the ceremony for their decisions and start arguing about it. In our culture it is considered extremely rude to openly criticize in front of others. You accept it as their way. If it doesn't fit into your belief system, you go somewhere else where you do feel comfortable.

The one who pours the water is the one who is most sensitive to all the energies present at the ceremony and is guided by Spirit. He or she takes care of everyone and everything involved and watches over what is needed while working together with the firekeeper.

The fireperson needs to be aware of the fire all the time. It is a great responsibility and you need to be focused while you are around the fire, since it has a sensitive spirit. Like I said before, you watch your actions, language and thoughts while working with it. It is a great teacher. You can watch the smoke or the flames and learn from the way it moves, maybe get a hint about how the ceremony will be going. If you are open to it, it will speak to you in many ways. How many times it needs to be lit in order to start burning? How does the smoke flow up? Everybody knows how beautiful and magnetizing it is just to watch flames in a fire. And if you do this often, you learn to understand its language.

In the United States, we use lava rocks for our sweat lodges because of their connection to volcanoes, with the elements earth and fire strongly present side by side. You can heat them up to a very high temperature and you can use them 10 to 20 times before they eventually crack and break.

In Europe we often use rocks from rivers, which are okay too, but these rocks do not store the heat as well and they break easily. The stone's origin from the riverbed has a contradictory relationship to the fire. It's okay though; you just make it work. I have been in sweat lodges where there were not enough blankets to darken the lodge. You improvise and make the best of it. Maybe you wait to start the sweat till it is darker outside. You explain and you make do.

Hermine:

Once in Austria, we had set up a workshop with a sweat lodge but we didn't have a firekeeper. Nobody volunteered and it looked like we couldn't continue. I offered to do the job, but explained that I had never done it before and had a personal issue with fire, but was willing to give it my best. We agreed and Mala and I worked out how we could do the process while I learned how to build the fire, cover the stones, dust them off, and bring them inside the lodge with the pitchfork. At the same time, Mala had to be able to run the lodge and guide the people inside who were mostly first-timers. Somewhat insecure about performing this honorable task, I also felt excitement to finally be able to take on the challenge of my hidden fear of fire and flames that originates from a deep and dark place in my memory. Now I would have the chance to face it out in the open.

It was such a blessed feeling to gather the wood, light the fire, pray for healing and guidance, and then observe how the fire built up. The glow became stronger and stronger. A higher state of awareness came over me. Staying very close to the fire, I walked around it, watching where I had to add more wood or close any open spaces to fully cover the stones lying in the middle underneath large layers of logs. As I was focused on getting the work done with the right energy as much as possible, my physical needs were of no importance anymore. A certain rush and flow inside me let me connect to the one and only purpose of making a good healing fire. My body wasn't a separate entity anymore: it served me. I felt an enormous sense of joy and gratitude: true happiness, really. I remember thinking: "Now, don't take yourself too seriously though!" My shins got burned more than once, but there was no real pain and no need to complain about it. I was able to bring the Grandfathers in one at the time, return to assemble the fire again and join the sweat lodge. The experience at the ceremony was much stronger than other times, as I had made a deeper connection to the glowing stones in the middle of the pit. Also I had gotten the chance to positively transform my fear! How wonderfully life offers you chances you can embrace and then enjoy the ride.

In the old tradition the whole ceremony would take around 24 hours, a cycle of one day. It was a custom, not to have any sexual intercourse for twelve hours before the ceremony as a way of preparing yourself. At the end of the ceremony, certain kinds of food representing the four directions were passed around: a little meat, some corn maybe, various kinds of vegetables. People stayed around in the community the ceremony was held at and spent time together in that ceremonial energy. Afterwards you would refrain another twelve hours from any sexual activity. The time after the ceremony was considered special because your spiritual channels were opened up and you were much more in touch with the spiritual world. You'd be open for dreams and insights and sensitive to steps for transition. To complete the ceremonial time a big celebration would be held with lots of food. Nowadays it is no longer done this way. Few people are left who could still lead such a sweat lodge, and few communities that could support the whole day as such.

I was taught the ceremony was given by Nature and Spirit to the people. As you offer the lodge to the people and the Mother Earth and all Life, you give without expecting something in return. The community would provide everything for the people who came to the ceremony and they didn't worry about not having enough and how much it would cost. I have experienced that these things simply work out if you trust and have faith.

You should never charge for a sweat lodge. I understand that there are costs involved for the firewood, for the Grandfather stones and for food, but you take that upon yourself. In the old days, people were aware of this circle of give-and-take and usually brought food or even firewood along, so you would have enough for everyone. Nowadays we use money as an exchange, but the thing is that you get easily lured into expecting a certain amount of income from it and that is when you lose the integrity needed for a good healing lodge. Remember, the sweat lodge is not just for you as a person, but above all for the Mother Earth and the next generations. Again, you need a certain mindset and understanding for this concept in order for it to function and flow well.

At Meta Tantay this was never a problem. It really always worked out, even though we had few material possessions and were even less liquid with finances. Having faith that things will work out is at the center of the Way of Life. You put your trust in the Creator that you'll be able to find stones and gather wood for the fire and that you'll have enough food for all afterwards.

In Europe we have done many lodges in different countries and over there it wasn't always easy to find firewood and the organizers often had to buy it. The stones also turned out to be a problem and had to be bought somewhere. The concept of a true give-away wasn't familiar and we often agreed that the people who joined in met those costs with a certain amount. In America we come to a sweat and usually bring food or something else to give in return, so it levels out, but it isn't planned ahead with a cost-and-income bill. If you want to give the people who put the sweat together a sum of money it is okay too, but it is never expected and totally fine if you can't and won't. It is perceived differently in Europe and we have tried to accommodate everybody's needs and customs when it comes to finances. We had to be flexible and bend our original rule a little, but I have always emphasized this aspect to everyone involved. The principle is without any expected charge, and a giveaway is appreciated.

Frog in Sweat Lodge

Something amusing happened one time when we had a mixed sweat lodge at Meta Tantay. The lodge was pretty close to the little stream that ran by our property. In between rounds, the door-flap was opened to cool off the air inside and some were chatting a little with each other while others just sat quiet. Then somebody said "Hey look, who's coming there!" A little frog came hopping into our sweat lodge. Besides it being nice to have an unexpected visitor, we recognize that Spirit can come in any form and in any situation to bring across a message. So, we watched the frog as it came closer: "What is this little being planning to do? Where is it going?"

The frog is hopping around the circle and sure enough, jumps straight into the lap of one of the young women. She didn't get scared but was pleased about the visit of this little creature. It sort of sat in her lap for five minutes and then took off again out of the lodge back to the creek. I told the woman: "Do you know what a frog means according to our Native tradition? I don't want you to freak out about this though! There is a saying amongst my people that a frog-appearance means fertility. As this frog jumped into your lap, this could mean you are going to be with child soon." She answered laughing: "Oh, I don't think so. I am taking precaution and we are not ready for it. We are going to wait a while still." Two months later she was pregnant from her boyfriend. Sometimes signs come really bluntly and literally. After that, whenever women saw frogs in the Camp, they would make big curves around them, haha!

Rattlesnake Story

We performed a lot of sweat lodges at Meta Tantay, at least once a week. Running Bear, a Yaki Indian who was an incredible singer with a powerful voice, was running the sweat. During the ceremony I noticed something was touching my back. You know, when you build a sweat lodge out of willow branches, sometimes you have those little twigs that stick out and can be felt when you come close. So I thought: "That must be one of those twigs, maybe a bigger one that we didn't strip off enough while making the lodge." Every time I felt the poking at the lower part of my back, I thought: „Ooh, we must have missed one of those little branches!" This happened a few times and I didn't think much of it and kept focusing on the ceremony. You shouldn't lean against the lodge anyway while praying so I kept more or less away from the sides.

When the sweat was over, we decided to take off the blankets right away and let the lodge air out a little. I discovered two little baby-rattlesnakes cozily curled up at the particular spot where I had sat! They had somehow gotten into the sweat lodge -- it was dark and they like heat. Whenever I'd gotten too close to them, they'd poked me to clear their space. Amazingly they never stung me; they just gently let me know not to come any closer. You have to know that the older rattlesnakes get, the less potent they are. Consequently the younger they are, the more powerful the poison they carry. So, if I would have been stung just once by one of these baby ones, I would have been in serious trouble, possibly it could even have killed me, although my father had some helpful medicine. He used the roots of nettles and smashed them into a poultice, which you put into a cloth onto the bite. Success depends on how long ago you got bit, how strong the poison is and how agitated you got when it bit you. When agitated, your heartbeat goes faster and your blood will carry the poison around much faster. Once the poison hits your heart, you pretty much don't stand a chance.

Why did this happen to me? I had the feeling it had to do with the fact that during that time in my life, I had been involved in a lot of ceremonies, sunrises and sweats, smudging and prayer-circles, it was so much part of my life that the spiritual energy had really been building up inside of me. The baby rattlesnakes checked me out and felt I was in touch with Nature and Spirit so they didn't harm me. At the camp I was the one who gathered the snakes and took them back to the desert. I had always tried to be respectful and talked to them why they couldn't stay close to the people. I took care of them and they took care of me, very simple.

I felt honored by the rattlesnake people to have shown themselves to me. Snakes do not have ears, but are extremely sensitive to vibrations and to energy around them. They had come to the decision that I was a good person. (Mala grins)

The second message for me was not to assume. I'd assumed the poking were twigs of the willow sticking out, which turned out to be very wrong. I didn't check, I didn't feel the energy of what was going on, which I should have done. I should have known that in a ceremonial setting like the sweat lodge, there is a teaching in every detail. Essentially, Spirit taught me to be more aware.

Improvisation and Responsibility

Living in the Camp meant improvising all the time and making use of what we could find for the construction of buildings and surviving with hardly any income from the outside. We aimed to become self-sufficient as much as possible, but it all evolved gradually and we learned while making mistakes along the way.

In the wickiups we used little wood stoves to keep warm inside. These stoves weren't really good and we installed the pipes as best we could under the circumstances. In the wickiup Sky and I and our two kids slept in, I was the one who got up during the night to fill the stove with more wood to keep the fire going. One time when we were all sleeping, I woke up with a strange feeling that something was wrong. I looked up and saw a solid ball of flame at the top of the wickiup! It had gotten too hot around the pipe, hence it started burning. It was fascinating to see this round shape up above in the dome and I remember how mesmerized I stared at it for a while. Then the risk dawned on me and I woke the rest of the family and hurried them all outside. Fortunately we had been smart enough to put a fire extinguisher next to every stove and I was able to put the fire out. We had been lucky! If the fire had reached the door we would have been trapped in there.

Due to this experience we became more careful with the building materials we used and decided we needed to learn more about those stove pipes and their insulation. All that time we had just been improvising and were happy about our constructional work, put together with scraps we had found or were given here and there. We realized we were actually putting people's lives in danger if we didn't do better and get more professional with the material. It taught all of us in the community to be more responsible and not take things too lightly.

The Grateful Dead

I don't remember what year it was, but I was on the road with my father and some others. My dad was doing one of his talks somewhere in the Salsalito Marin County area. He had been invited to come listen to a band called "The Warlocks." They had a good sound, although they weren't well known yet, and vice versa they really liked what my father had to say, so they stayed in touch with each other.

At one point they figured they needed a name change, as the current one wasn't satisfactory. They asked my dad if he knew of a suitable name for their band. I don't know for sure if it was my father in the end who came up with this name but it turned into "The Grateful Dead." The band got more popular and became one of the most successful rock bands of that period. The head guy, Jerry Garcia, turned into a famous rock star. At first, they played a lot for free at festivals but later on they had huge groups of followers traveling with them wherever they went. My father sort of became their spiritual leader, giving guidance and help when it was needed. When someone in the band got sick, they would turn to him and he would help them. Of course, it was rock 'n roll music, and the members of the band and the group around them were pretty heavily into drugs and alcohol. It wasn't so much my thing; for me it was sometimes difficult to be around them. But they did mature over time and started settling down a little bit.

When we were building our Camp at Meta Tantay, they started helping us with monthly payments that helped cover the costs for the down payments for the land. They even bought my father a brand new van and really helped out in many ways.

Whenever the band was playing in the area or somewhere close by in California, they would send their schedule so we could join them. My father had me set up a booth right next to the entrance where we put out information on Meta Tantay. This was a great way of getting in touch with many people potentially interested in our vision. We had lists put out that people could sign and I got to listen to the concerts at the same time. Around 1976, the Grateful Dead asked permission to come out on the land and record an album at Meta Tantay. They thought what we were doing with the land and the community would make good energy, which could flow into their music. They were given permission but the rule was no drinking or using drugs while staying on the land. We had some trailers where they stayed and cleaned one of our bigger barns out to be used as a recording studio. At the beginning of this album, they have my father talking about the Sunrise Ceremony, and the song "Susie Creek" is named after the creek that was running through the property.

When they finished the album, they naturally wanted to celebrate it. When I stopped by, I noticed they were smoking marihuana and I got worried. At that time there was a very strict rule in Nevada if you were caught with just one seed of marihuana, you could go to jail for five years. We all knew that if somebody got caught on our property, we had a good chance of losing the land. They were only waiting for a reason to kick us off.

So, when I walked by and smelled it, I had to go inside the trailer--right or wrong--and tell them: "I'm sorry, but you know the rules here. We can't afford to lose the land. I am asking you to leave." The band members were all very upset and angry with me; they didn't understand why I was making such a fuss about it. As far as I know, I'm the only one who ever kicked out the Grateful Dead! (*Mala chuckles about this little joke*)

Since Sky and I were in charge of the daily routine in the Camp, we were responsible for things that happened. I felt that nobody was above the rules and didn't know how to solve it any other way. The cops were really checking on us time and again. The rumors were that we made money because we were growing our own marihuana out there. They were only waiting for an opportunity to bust us and we never knew when they would show up. I felt the band betrayed our trust, but I did offend them by being so principled about it. My dad wasn't very happy about it either because although he understood why I did it, they had, after all, helped us out a great deal. The relationship between the musicians and me went downhill from that moment onward, I must admit. Many years later a book came out called "The Grateful Dead Family," which also showed some pictures with my parents. We were linked together for many years. The band with their music was part of the free-spirited hippy period and we were really some kind of extended family in some way.

Watch Story

A funny story I remember happened when visitors came to Meta Tantay one time. We had already created living quarters for many people, and we had built a cook shed and other structures. Not only in the nearest town Carlin but also in the rest of the state of Nevada and further away, we had gotten quite the name as a hippy-Indian village, run by the notorious Medicine Man Rolling Thunder. People from all over would come and check us out. You had those who were honestly interested in our ways and sometimes ended up staying and you had the more curious kind that came almost like tourists, who paid us a short visit. We always tried to be respectful and show them around, answer their questions.

As the Camp was out in the flat, sage-brushed desert where you could see cars coming from far away, we knew when visitors were arriving. I saw my father pulling in with two cars full of people. He asked me to show them around on our campgrounds and explain what we were doing and how we were living. I said: "Sure, I'll do it this time." and I immediately recognized them as the touristy kind. They were dressed nicely, going on a stroll and looked slightly out of place in that improvised surrounding. As they followed me around and I explained a little here and there, I could hear them talking to each other: "Indians still hunt buffalo with bow and arrows" and "I thought, Indians only lived in teepees. Where are all the teepees?" We mostly lived in wickiups and only had a few teepees. They were expecting to see Indians making fire just using flint and were hooked on the stereotyping of Indians as the 'noble savages'. It was obvious they didn't have any idea of how the status of Indians as the Native people of America was at that time and they weren't really interested in learning about them either. They just wanted to have their stereotypes confirmed.

At one point I heard someone saying: " Hey, I heard that Indians can tell the time just by looking at the sun. They are able to tell the time exactly!" The other one didn't believe that and said: " No, that can't be true. How is that possible?" So they asked me if I was able to tell the time correctly just by looking up at the sun. I answered: "Of course!" I put my right arm, which had my watch on it up towards the sun and told them: "It is exactly 4 pm and 18 minutes!" Everybody was checking their own watches, so they didn't even notice I was able to take my arm down and fumble the watch of my wrist into the pocket of my trousers and I had totally cheated. They were all stunned by that miracle and nodded their heads: "Wow, he really did it. Unbelievable!"

I chuckled inside and after they had left again, it became a great story that turned into a running gag for a while. "Hey Mala, can you tell me the time?" and I would just look up to the sun with my elbow bent in front of my face watching my wrist: "Let's see, it's 7 minutes to 11 am." Funny each time!

Rolling Thunder Making Wind

We didn't have electricity in the beginning and wanted to at least make sure that the cooking shed would have some light so they could prepare the food more easily. We built an electric windmill out of the materials we found at the camp. We had another watermill that we didn't have any other use for, so we transformed it and put it on a wooden base, built from logs we had gathered over the past months. We found a battery in one car and an alternator in another, added a gauge and were waiting outside for some wind to make the blades turn, hoping the mill would work. Sitting on a little hill where you had a good view over the surrounding desert, we saw my father's van coming in, followed by two black, fancy cars. When the visitors got out of their cars, we noticed they looked like church-going citizens. They were all decked out wearing their Sunday best, looking totally out of place out there in the desert with us wild and scruffy looking Indians and hippies.

My dad starts talking to the people, pointing here and there. Then he sees us sitting up there, comes over and ask us what we are doing. I tell him: " Oh, we're just waiting for some wind to come so the windmill will start to turn." My dad says: "Ah I see, to make electricity for some light bulbs… So that is what you are all waiting for, eh?" Then he starts to make some signs with his hands to call upon the wind and sure enough, a gust of wind comes and the windmill starts to turn. The people -- I think they were from a Southern Baptist Church -- were whispering: "Did you see that? What happened here?" My dad ignored them and asked me: "Mala, do you think that was enough or do you need more?" I answered him: "We could use some more wind here to make it really work!" So my dad did the movement with his hand again and more wind came. Now the visitors were getting upset: "I saw it clearly. He made some sort of movement with his hand, like a sign!" Then we heard a voice shrieking out, it was the head guy of the group and the priest of that congregation: "It is the work of the devil! He is possessed! Go back to the cars and let's get out of here!" The people answered his command and starting scrambling for the cars while the priest turned towards my father, calling him all kinds of names and claiming: "You are linked to Satan and are an evil man!" My father is just standing there looking at him. The wind was getting stronger and dust was flying around by now. All the people were already sitting in the cars; only the priest is still out there, trying to pretend he is calm and in control of things. He passes by a shed and all of a sudden, the roof, about 10 ft. wide and 20 ft. long, is loosened by the wind. It makes an enormous screeching sound while breaking off its nails. Even the poles that had held it all together were lifted up by the wind and were flying through the air. It came flying towards the priest and dropped just in front of his feet. He stared at it and all we heard him say was: "Oh Jesus, Oh Jesus…" Then he ran towards the car, jumped in and they sped off as fast as they could. We never saw them again. As we watched them go, my father turned around and asked: "Is that enough wind?" We rolled around laughing!

John Rolling Thunder Pope

When people don't understand something or have never experienced something before, they either deny it or reject it. When they reject it, they usually turn it into something bad. That is what had happened that day and of course my father had been playing it out shamelessly. Our homemade windmill was making enough electricity to power three light bulbs for the kitchen too!

Rabbit Story

We not only wanted to grow crops to become self-sufficient but we also wanted to bring in animals we could use for meat. We started building corrals for the animals and thought of ways to keep them in such a way that they still lived a life as naturally as possible, close to how they would live in the wild. If you use a life form for food, you also take in the energy level it carries. We believe the spirit is stronger when it is close to its natural way of living than when you take it out of its natural surroundings and habits, and use it only to produce food. As soon as you start to use chemicals like pesticides and herbicides on plants, you also kill a lot of that original strong spirit and energy. Cages and fences limit the spirit of animals, just as food with hormones does. We were putting a lot of thought into how to find a good form that would work for our situation; we did have to feed a lot of people. It wouldn't be possible to just go out hunting and gathering and feed everybody. We thought: "We have all this land now. How can we find a way to make the life cycle in such a way that the living beings that end up served as our food will lead a happy life up to that point? With this in mind, we built the corrals really spacious and open. We also had ducks and chickens and gave them a lot of space to roam around freely.

At one point we decided to raise rabbits. Domesticated rabbits are usually put in cages, where their feet never even touch the Mother Earth. They can't stand up and stretch their legs or hop around. They don't have the opportunity to feel the sun and the wind on their bodies. When we had bought our rabbits, they had come in those cages and we felt awful just watching them. "That is really not a good life at all," we thought and decided to try something different with our rabbits. After a lot of brainstorming we finally came up with the idea to use a patch of land about the size of 2 acres. We dug down a few feet along the sides to make it into a huge pen. It was hard work because of the dry desert soil, but it was necessary to make a deep ditch for the fence to go in, because coyotes and bobcats and even dogs dig to go beneath any fence to get to their food source. We used sheets of tin that we had plenty of from all the buildings we had been tearing down. We also used chicken wire from about one foot down to about six ft. up. On top we ran two strands of barbed wire to make sure no coyotes and bobcats would be able to jump over the fence. In one corner we built a huge barn to hold the hay and other kinds of food that we fed the rabbits with. The rabbits could come indoors to feed in times when there was rain or snow. It took us quite a while to finish the building but finally the whole area was ready. The whole community was excited about it and we all came together to celebrate the liberation of the rabbits from their cages into their new free home. By that time we had about a hundred of them. We put the cages in the middle of the pen and opened them. As with all things in life, it doesn't always go the way you expect it to, even if you have the best of intentions. It really is about learning.

They didn't come out by themselves, so we took them and put them on the ground. But we noticed that almost all the rabbits looked afraid and hardly dared to move. They had been inside those cages their whole life; they had never experienced that much space. Everything was new to them: the ground their feet touched, the smell, the air, the sun. They couldn't handle it and weren't happy at all! In fact, a lot of them were eagerly looking back at their cages ready to go back in straight away. They felt extremely vulnerable. Little by little though, we noticed they were getting more comfortable and starting to hop around. What a relief. We kept observing them and after about half an hour, we noticed there was even some interaction going on between the rabbits. Before they all had been separated, one or two per cage. Then we got alarmed as some of the rabbits were starting to fight with each other. When rabbits fight, they can get pretty nasty: they bite off chunks of each other's fur and it can get really bloody. Sometimes they make growling sounds too. More and more rabbits were getting into fighting with each other, so this was not going the way we had expected at all! We were getting worried. About a third of the animals were fighting and the others weren't even paying attention to them. We had to interfere and used a pole with a net at the end of it that we had invented beforehand to get a rabbit out, once we'd wanted to eat it. You could scoop the animal up from the pen without coming too close to it. So we separated all the fighting rabbits and put them back into the cages. The other ones were doing fine out there and we put out some food for them, which they started munching on. One person noticed something: "You know, I think all the fighting ones are males and the others are the females." Then it dawned on us. Of course, in nature you can see that, whenever you see rabbits living together, it is usually one buck with about ten female rabbits. When babies are born, they all stay with the group but at a certain point, the older male sends off the young male ones, until the old one gets too old and is replaced by a younger dominant one. Those that run off will start new families and groups in territory somewhere else. We hadn't given it a thorough thought that this instinct was still alive, though they had been domesticated for so many generations. But this territorial instinct had been sparked as soon as they were in each other's range of smell and sight, and the males had shown their competitive behavior right away.

We were actually thankful for it because it solved a really important question: which ones do we chose to eat and which ones do we keep alive? Now it was simple. We would take the males for food and skin but keep a few to get the colony going. All the females could be kept for breeding. Only once in a while was there what we call a 'bad mother' who kills the offspring of others and sometimes her own too, so obviously those rabbits also had to be taken out.

We made some new cages from the old ones so they became larger and higher. The cages didn't have any floor as such, so the rabbits had real earth to hop around on. Little by little we butchered most of the males. We had a few different males rotating every week to join the females and the system worked well.

Of course, the jokes kept going around in the community about how peacefully women get along and how men always have the urge to fight and be dominant. For months we men had to put up with those gags about nature's examples.

For a few weeks everything went well. We kept watching them and hoping that the rabbits out in the open field would be starting to dig holes in the ground like they do in the wild. Somehow they didn't start any attempts. We were getting more and more anxious about it, because we knew that pretty soon the temperatures would rise and then it would be way too hot for them out in the open. We had a meeting on: "How do you get a rabbit to dig?" We were hardly able to give them a "good example" and do it for them. We couldn't figure the riddle out ourselves and just prayed that at the right time they would return to their natural behavior. Luckily enough, after a few days we saw some earth mounds spread about the pen and noticed that some rabbits had started to dig. Just as we were observing them, they also watched each other and soon enough, there were more rabbits starting to dig. A few days later there were holes all over the place and we were really content.

Sometimes during spring, strong storms with a lot of rain occur in the desert. These last for about an hour or so and a lot of water comes down in a short time. Right after one of those storms had hit our camp, we checked on the rabbits to see how they were doing. There were still pools of water in the pen as the rains had been extensive. A lot of rabbits were out in the open, totally soaked, not attempting to go back into hiding underground. Wondering why, we went into the pen and noticed that each hole was filled with water and a pair of panicky rabbit eyes was staring back at us. They had only dug the holes straight down, without any curves. We were happy that none of the rabbits drowned, as it had stopped raining on time before the holes filled up all the way.

We had another meeting and talked about it, but realized that we couldn't do anything about this either. We could only hope for the better that they would figure it out by themselves. In nature, rabbits dig holes about two to three feet down, then they curve off to the side, and after a little bit they dig upwards again for about one foot, where they eventually build their den. This is helpful for two reasons: when rain comes, they are protected because the water will go straight down into the earth; when a predator strikes, they can hide away in the deeper layer and the predator can't catch them so easily. We really didn't want to put them back into those cages, so we waited again and prayed.

A few days later, we saw some fresh little hills of dirt beside the original holes. Carefully, without disturbing the rabbits, we looked how they dug this time. We were relieved to see that they had started to actually build a hole with a curve! Pretty soon, the other rabbits copied these few initiators and all the holes were built into proper burrows, as they would have been in the wild.

Everything was really working well now. The population was blossoming; the rabbits seemed to be doing very well, kept having healthy babies, and we got meat and hides from them. It was a good situation for all.

From us they got lettuce, carrots and other vegetables the stores would throw away at the end of each day. We made sure there was no plastic or metal in all those leftovers. They loved their fresh veggies so much they would stand up against your legs when you were inside the fence while feeding.

We took care of them in a good way and the ones that we took for meat and fur, were handled with the proper respect. We talked to them, explaining what was going to happen and worked with their energies so they didn't need to be scared while giving their lives.

After a few months however, one of the responsible persons told us that he thought there were some rabbits missing. Naturally you can't keep exact count of all the animals, but when you are a caretaker, you know your animals and you watch out for them. Only during feeding time were they all out of their dens and in clear sight. We were able to count them then, making use of a system to keep track of their numbers. Otherwise some of them would be in their dens, others would hop around and you couldn't make a reasonable guess. You know, 150 hopping and running animals are a lot. We paid extra attention and came to the strange conclusion there were less rabbits than usual. How could this be?

We took a careful look at the fence around and also at the barbed wire on top, but we couldn't find any holes or any damaged areas. There was no hair on top; there was nothing dug underneath. It must have been a bobcat or maybe a coyote? How did those predators get in there?

We left it for that day and shrugged: "Ah well, no worries. Maybe we just didn't count well." Sure enough though, the next day, we made another count and there were even more rabbits missing. So we checked again and couldn't find any possibility how those rabbits could have gone missing. It was a mystery and the talk of the town at the Camp. Since predators hardly ever come to fetch their game during the day when there are people around, we figured we should keep watch at night. We came up with the idea that we'd put two people taking turns sitting inside a car. Bobcats or coyotes are extremely sensitive to little movements or noise, so in a car the guardians would be more hidden and quiet. Also the smell of humans is less alarming then. The next day we had a meeting with those guys, curious if they had seen anything... They told us: "Well, we know what is going on!" "Tell us, what happened?" "We were in the car watching and around midnight, we heard a sound coming nearer: "Whoosh, whoosh! " It sounded like big birdwings. Then we saw a big bird appearing, it was a horned owl. It sat down on one of the fence poles, looking down in the pen. Then more owls came in. There were eight owls circling around the fence and then landing on the poles around the corral. We noticed though, that the rabbits that were out weren't scared at all. They just stared back at the birds with no sense of what a predator was. Pretty soon, one of the owls flew down and scooped up a rabbit; then the others followed and each took a rabbit in its claws and left. The crazy thing was that although the rabbits that were taken were obviously in pain and terrified, screaming really loud, the other rabbits still didn't go in hiding!"

The mystery of the missing rabbits was solved, but now we had to come up with a solution. We couldn't put dogs out at night to scare the owls away, because they would bark at the rabbits all night and that would be beside the point. We couldn't put a guard out every night from now on, not as a long-term solution. To build a roof construction would have been way too expensive, since the area was too large to cover. We were brooding a little and in the end we thought: "Well, they learned how to make holes and be safe in them, so maybe they will figure this one out too! They will have to remember and relearn their natural instinct to hide from predators."

So we had a few people on watch the coming nights to see how it would develop. The next night, the owls came again and took some rabbits. The same thing happened the next night. We were getting a little worried since it had been going on for a while already. The third night they noticed that as soon as the first rabbit started to scream, a few rabbits would jump down in their holes. That was a good sign. The next night a few more jumped into their holes and this continued. In the end, as soon as they heard the whooshing sound of the owls flying in, they started hiding away immediately. They had recognized what the danger was and had gotten a sense of predators. We were very relieved and no other problems occurred anymore. Quite amazing, that development back to their natural instincts, the learning process with the help of a few smart ones, and then the copying behavior of the group!

After a few years we noticed something interesting. When you hunt wild rabbits, the meat is dark and very muscled. When you raise rabbits in cages for food, the meat is white and soft. Our rabbits, who on the outside still looked very much like cage-rabbits with all kinds of colors and dots and not like wild rabbits at all, developed dark and muscled meat. Their behavior had after having been domesticated for thousands of generations -- a generation passes fairly quickly with rabbits as we all know -- reverted back again to a far more natural way of life in which they were moving, hopping and digging again. Just by giving them this opportunity and creating a semi-natural habitat, they returned to their natural instincts in many ways and it showed in their physical adaptation.

We thought it was so cool and promising! We all have this capability to re-learn and to re-member our natural behavior to survive in nature. Humans, too, can rely on this and return to natural ways. Personally, I took it as a hopeful sign for anyone who wants to make an effort to relearn and come back to the ways of the Mother Earth.

Car Accident Story

We were always looking for ways to support the camp, trying to find jobs to bring in some money. For a few years, a guy lived at the Camp, his name was Paul; he was a professional driller for oilrigs and such. One time, he came to talk to us; he had spoken to some locals in town who had drilling work for us not too far away. It was really well paid and a good possibility to earn some money for the community. He explained that the job was done with a core driller, which can drill for water and minerals, on the land with the hot springs outside of Beowawe in Nevada, which some big company had bought. The plan was to make an electricity generating plant out of it, using the power of the water. As soon as he told me, I knew inside that this was very wrong to do. I had visited the area many times. The special thing about this hot springs area was that it encompassed two geysers continuously shooting up huge amounts of water into the air. Usually, geysers shoot out and then return to a small bubbling, after which they gather enough pressure to start the process again. But these geysers had so much pressure from within the earth that they were constantly shooting water, never pausing. When you stood next to them, you could hear this impressive roaring sound coming from deep within the earth, very loud and powerful, like a locomotive. Hot springs are sacred to my people and to stop this enormous flow of water didn't feel right to me at all. Later I heard that these two geysers were the only ones in the whole United States that had this special, continuous power. The company wanted to cap the geysers and build a power plant for electricity on top of them and the geysers would never be able to blow their water freely into the air again. The spirit of the water would not be happy with that limitation.

Everybody else though was getting really excited about the opportunity to be able to have some work, and I ignored my initial feeling and went along, thinking we could really use the money for the Camp. I didn't speak up or tell them I felt hesitation.

In the end, we were eight guys agreeing to go. Paul trained us and we formed a crew together. A few weeks later we drove over there in two vehicles for our first night shift at the drilling place. One car had six people in it and I was driving with a guy named Steve, who owned a brand new yellow pick-up truck that his parents, who were quite well off, had given him. It had all the fancy stuff included, you know, a roll bar over the back, a power-winch, a crew-cab, everything you can imagine; a deluxe pick-up truck. We reached the place and worked our first night. I had this bad feeling nudging me the whole time: "This is not good, I shouldn't be supporting this," but kept ignoring it. We became familiar with the work and everything went well during that shift. Paul had done a good job of training us and we all finished around the same time. Steve and I were the first to head out. The others were still rounding up together and followed a little later. We were driving down a gravel road that later turned onto the paved road, as the drilling area was way out in the hills. Steve was in a really good mood and driving the truck pretty fast, claiming he wanted to race the others in order to be the first at the shower. I remember I was eating a tuna fish sandwich and still wearing my hard hat and working boots from work. Since I was hungry, I was focusing on my tuna fish sandwich, thinking: "Whatever you feel like doing…"

Then I hear him say: "Oh, oh!" And I looked up and said: "What's the matter?" He answered: "Don't worry, we are going to make it." He had forgotten that the gravel road ended in a T-crossing to get onto the pavement. You had to either go right or left and he was driving way too fast to go either direction. He was somewhere half way through the turn and realizing we weren't going to make it. We smashed straight through the little guardrail, then down a very steep hill. The pick-up didn't roll but instead went head to tail, flipping over and over down the hill. The lights went out as they got smashed but for some reason the dome lights inside the truck all of a sudden came on. I was able to see everything very clearly in a bright yellow light. As the truck was flipping, I got into a state of mind where it seemed I was floating through the air and everything around me was moving. I remember thinking it was actually pretty cool, like you see in the movies, and I wasn't thinking about the fact that we were going to come to a halt somehow. It all felt very peaceful and calm, and I didn't care about the future. It felt good, even if it would have been the end. The next thing I know is my head hits the front windshield and I black out. When I wake up again, I see my friend's face above me, asking: "Mala, Mala, are you okay?" Finally, I come to my senses and say: "Yeah man, I'm doing okay but I lost my tuna fish sandwich!" You know me, food always on my mind. *(Mala laughs really loud from deep within his belly)*

I realize then that we are both still in the pick-up, but the car is upside down and pretty smashed from what I could see. My head had hit the window but it had bounced back. Then I heard a sound of fluid rushing out somewhere. I knew that the truck had two huge fuel tanks and the noise could only come from the gasoline leaking out. If that fuel somehow sparked, we were dead meat. I told him: "We really need to get out of this car immediately! Quick!" We were able to squeeze ourselves out through one of the windows that hadn't totally been crunched and we got out on time. I looked back to what was left of the pick-up, and what was once a long truck had formed into a big, round, yellow ball. Both the front and the rear end had totally been crushed, and the car had become a lot smaller, curling itself around the roll bar while it was flipping over. The roll bar had basically saved our lives.

We started to walk up the hill towards the road to catch the others. Looking back, we could see the car with the lights still on inside and we started making jokes and saying stupid things like: "You know what? We should hide and when they are looking for us once they see the truck has gone through the guardrail, they won't be able to find us! They will think we got thrown out of the car!" "Or we could spread ourselves out on the road, pretending we're badly wounded." Of course we realized we were very lucky we didn't have any broken bones or anything and were actually able to climb up, so we decided to just flag them down and tell them what had happened for real, instead of playing a bad joke on them. They collected us and together we headed for Carlin, which was about 20 miles from there, to report the accident. At the truck stop we drank some coffee and at some point, I told the others I needed to go to the bathroom, as I wasn't feeling so well. I stood in front of the mirror, washing my hands and face. Then I pulled my hand back quickly. It was hurting and I saw there was a piece of glass in it with some blood on it where I had cut myself. I took a closer look at the top of my head and saw all these pieces of glass sticking out of my head! This was, of course, where I had smashed into the windshield, but I had totally blacked out that moment. I carefully started to pull out all these glass chunks and cleaned the wounds, which was pretty easy. They apparently weren't so deep, so there wasn't so much blood either. I went back in, nobody could tell the difference, but I kept feeling a little nauseous and was very tired. I asked some of the guys if it was okay for me not to wait for the police to come. It was another couple of miles to our Camp and I was brought home, told Sky what happened and went straight to bed to get some sleep. I did feel a little chilled and dizzy but didn't realize what was going on. When I woke up the next morning, I got up, took a few steps and passed out. I swear it was like the ground coming up and hitting me in the face, it wasn't me falling down. After a little bit I opened my eyes and got up again, nobody had seen me falling, so I went to the kitchen area to get some breakfast. But as I sat down, again, the table was coming towards me and the plate hit me in the face. I had passed out again. This time though, there were people around me and they got worried. I was taken to the hospital and was examined thoroughly. The doctor told me: " You know, you can consider yourself very lucky. You could be dead. You went into shock and it's extremely dangerous to go to sleep without being monitored. Besides, I want you to have a look at this picture." He showed me an X-ray of my head and explained: "This dark spot is your brain and one third of it, the front part, is all bloody; you have a very heavy brain contusion. We can't do much about it, it just needs time to heal and recover. We can only hope your brain doesn't swell anymore." For the next two years I kept passing out frequently. In the beginning, it was sometimes three to four times a day. Later on, it was less frequent, until after two years it finally returned to normal and the nausea and the headaches also stopped. It was a really interesting experience.

Steve, who felt guilty about it all, kept urging me: "You know, I come from a rich family. I have money. It's my fault and you should sue me and get some money out of this." Now, that didn't feel good at all. I had never sued anyone in my life and had no intention of doing this. I was lucky to be alive. I said: "You didn't do this on purpose, deliberately. Besides, you are my friend! I know there is another reason behind why it has happened, which has nothing to do with you, but with me. The whole drilling job didn't feel right to me from the beginning but I didn't listen to my inner voice. No way am I going to sue you."

Half of our crew stopped going to the rig immediately after what happened. A few went back and worked for a few more days and then also quit. It didn't feel right to them anymore, either. The geysers did get capped and there is a power plant right on top of them that is generating energy to this day. It is really sad. I have often thought of ways to somehow free them again. They used to shoot way up high, 100 to 130 feet, I would say. The water stream was big, too, and there was always water flowing back to the desert, never becoming less during any season. I think they must tap into the big aquifers that scientists have proven to be underneath Nevada in very deep layers within the earth.

I have explained before how the spirits teach you lessons and make you aware. The elders always emphasized listening to those voices but this time I had chosen to ignore them. My car accident taught me in a strong physical way not to mess with that kind of information. It is to be taken seriously, especially when you have vowed to walk a spiritual path, like I had done. I consider myself very lucky to have been able to fully recover from the accident.

Coyote Warning Story

It was already dark and Raymond Sensmeyer, Monica Fast Wolf and I drove my father's van on a two-lane desert road from Tecopa to Las Vegas to a meeting. Raymond and I had known each other for many years and were good friends. We were chatting a bit and out of the blue, I see a coyote coming towards us and I slowed down the car. The coyote stopped and looked straight at us, then turned away. We looked at each other, wondering what it could mean because it seemed the coyote was giving a message of some kind. I knew immediately and turned to Raymond: "The coyote has spoken to me: you and I need to be very careful with each other with what we say to one another. If not, we could end up in a really bad argument." It was a very clear and distinct message, so we were a little baffled, as us two had never had any problems or arguments in the past.

Raymond was reading a book about modern technology versus Native American thinking. By the time we had reached Vegas and finished our dinner, he had started bringing up some of the issues in the book. He asked me questions but I told him that I didn't totally agree with the content of the book. Sure enough, he started arguing with me and I told him: "Raymond, do you remember what the coyote told us?" He said: "Yeah, yeah, don't worry..." but kept on going, wanting to prove his point. I had never seen Raymond like this before. I kept warning him, but he even started following me around while talking to me: "No, no, but I need to explain this to you. It is important. You have to understand." I made my point: "Can we not leave this for what it is? The coyote warned us and I don't want to keep on talking on this subject." But he wouldn't stop. At the end of our discussion he threw the book at my head and stormed out of the house. He was gone for a few hours. Monica came up to me and asked: "How did you know exactly what the coyote was telling you?" I answered: "Sometimes it is so clear. I never questioned it. I heard the message inside of me the moment the coyote looked at us, pausing in the middle of the road. There was no need for interpretation or doubt: it was a warning and that's all."

A lot of times, we try to understand the signs we get too much. We start thinking about what it could mean, worrying about the consequences and how we should act, but it's best if we just relax with it and leave it for what it is.

In most cases and with most people, if they come across a sign from nature or the spirits, they choose to not even perceive the message as such because in the moment of the encounter and receiving it, they are not open from their hearts and senses but having judgments in their mind about what it could mean or what it probably means and so on. That blocks the essence of the message. It conflicts with their own system and their own expectations and then things come out twisted.

The next day Raymond and I figured it out and he apologized for ignoring the warning. He didn't understand what had gotten into him either.

Medicine Teachers

Overall, Native people consider elders as a respected source of knowledge and personally, elders have taught me very much. In my case, I also had the exceptional opportunity of being able to learn from different Medicine people when they came to visit us at Meta Tantay.

During that time, a group of seven Medicine men worked together and met once in a while to share and support each other, each in their own way. Let me see if I can remember who they were... there was Mad Bear Anderson (Iroquois from the Big Lakes area), my father (Cherokee), Semu Huaute (Chumash), David Munongye (Hopi), Johnny Begay (Dineh), Craig Carpenter (Mohawk) and Corbin Harney (Western Shoshone), who was still a little younger.

As part of my upbringing, and because of the path I was on, these elders thought it would be good for me to learn from different people about other ways and specific kinds of Medicine.

Rolling Thunder, Semu Huaute, David Munonghye

Medicine people can work with different tools and with the help of different forces of nature. Some work with the water, some through the fire and the sweat lodge, some mainly use an eagle feather for healing. Some can doctor through sucking out illnesses. There are so many ways. The elders used to say that my father was working with the so-called "old powers," which are the earth powers. For this, you need to have an even deeper level of understanding. I was trained in all those different ways and was aware I had a natural connection to the old powers, too. Inside of me there was a sense of knowing how Nature and Spirit flow. I felt comfortable with this and my upbringing supported it. Many of my friends worked really hard at learning about Medicine. They did vision quests and went to Sun dances and yet they didn't attain the natural access that was given to me without even doing my best. They often found it was unfairly divided.

Let me first say a few things on how we view healings and perform Medicine. If you are asked to do a healing on someone, you have to take a few things into consideration. First of all, the sickness that the person in question is dealing with has come for a reason. The person who comes for help has to be aware that he or she needs to be willing to make certain changes. Also the person has to ask deliberately and voluntarily for the healing to take place, so that the wish comes with the right attitude and it can become successful. This is really essential!

If you as a healer would just decide by yourself to heal a person who hasn't asked for it, you'd take away the lesson that needs to be learned by that person. You'd interfere in something that is not yours to begin with. If the lesson isn't learned, it will have to return in an even stronger way maybe. So, you actually end up hurting the person more than helping them.

In my culture, it is very important that a person who needs healing comes prepared and asks for it to take place. That sets the right premises for the actual healing and brings about the necessary awareness. The healer facilitates in the sense that you offer understanding, which is necessary to take away the sickness. Everything that follows from that point is their own responsibility.

Mad Bear

Mad Bear Anderson and his wife came with their RV to live with us in the desert. He was a very big guy, tall and huge, literally looked like a bear but he always had a friendly smile on his face; a very peaceful and happy man. Thanks to his gentle yet strong energy, I related to him immediately. It was really good being around him. He knew of my path, so he decided to also help me on things he knew about, teaching me things along the way. When he started talking to me I didn't realize at first he was actually teaching me, but that is the way the elders do this. They just talk to you and see how you respond; they observe how you behave, how you think, how you listen and speak, how you act. He then started sharing things with me. He told me how important it is to speak your prayers out loud. He said that Nature and Spirit really want to hear your voice; it is a stronger commitment than if you are just thinking about it. Secondly, when you voice something, you yourself hear what you're saying and you reflect on it. After a while, you start to be more aware of what you are saying, your actual wording of things, and you become more careful how you use words, what they actually mean to you, what you really want to express. So, by speaking out loud, you learn to be more focused on your prayer, on your intent and how everything works together: the mind, the heart, the connection to Nature and Spirit.

Each Medicine person uses something different to doctor with and Mad Bear worked with an incredible full-winged eagle fan. When I met him, he was already in his seventies but, like I said, still very strong. We used to sit around the fire and he would tell me about his life. When he was born, it was seen by the spiritual people present at his birth that he had a special gift of healing and medicine power, which shows in his name. He was taught in these ways from a very young age. I remember he had a special necklace with beautiful bear claws. He explained to me once that his elders had told him he had to go out into the forest and face the bear that lived in the area. He had to pray and sing specific songs, prepare himself in the right way and then go out and look for him, asking the bear to show itself. The bear decides where his heart is at and if he is worthy of carrying Bear Medicine. So that is what he did. He called the bear, started singing and praying. Eventually the bear came and stood right in front of him on its hind legs. Mad Bear kept singing to let the bear know what his intention was. Then the bear came up close and ripped his side open with its claws, but didn't harm him any further. It didn't go deep but scarred the side of his body. In this way, the two bonded forever and the bear transferred the Medicine to him. The bear came close to his face and made a snorting sound, sending him the Medicine through his breath. Then he turned around and left. Mad Bear told me: "Then I fell to the ground and cried out loud because it hurt so much! Man, that was painful!" This is what I remember him telling me.

It showed me that he was not only a person with a strong, determined heart and with lots of courage, but that he also stayed human and could admit that he was in pain after surviving the challenge. Mad Bear was supposed to never kill a bear or eat its meat after that. The claws, he told me, came to him in different ways: he found them or they were given to him.

There has also been a lot of hardship in his life and his people had had to go through a lot. He grew up in the Big Lakes area up North where there was a lot of racism and abuse of Native People, not very different from where I lived. But through it all, he had never given up hope and had not become resentful. He remained positive: "No matter what, it's going to be okay, there is going to be a revival someday, we will make it, I am sure of it."

After he and his wife had once again stayed with us for a month, we sat by the fire right before he left to travel on. Unexpectedly he told me to hold his eagle fan. Objects like this are used to doctor with and are very personal; you never touch them without permission. I was greatly honored to hold his eagle fan. He asked me how it felt. I told him: "It feels very good and strong. A lot of good has come from these eagle feathers. I know it has helped in many situations." He got quiet and then continued: "I want you to keep it," and handed me the fan. I felt very reluctant to take it; it was his personal fan and I didn't feel worthy of it, but he was very clear about it: "It is time to pass it on and you will use it as you see fit." On the one hand, I was happy and proud that he thought I was able to carry that Medicine and work with it, but I was also worried because this could mean he felt his time would be up soon. Eventually I had to let that go and I still have the fan. About 1½ years later, he crossed over.

Peyote Ceremony

John and Gracy Begay came over to my parent's house a lot or visited us at Meta Tantay. Gracy was a full-blooded Shoshone and a close friend of my mother's. She was quite a character. When she started talking, she just kept on--she really loved to talk -- but she had a good heart and still knew some of the old Shoshone ways. Johnny was a full-blooded Navaho or Dineh, as they call themselves. Johnny used to be a roadman, one who runs the traditional Peyote ceremony. Originally this kind of ceremony wasn't practiced amongst the Shoshone people, but the custom had spread to other tribes.

At some point, Johnny Begay thought it was his turn to teach me and for two years, from around my 20th until my 22nd birthday, I was involved in the Peyote ceremonies.

One time, Johnny Begay took my father and me and some other young Indian guys to a Peyote ceremony. We had to drive for about six hours from Carlin, Nevada, to get to the Sierra Mountains in California. These ceremonies go on all night long, you don't stop in between, and they consist of intense prayers and are open to both men and women. You start at dusk, going to dawn, very powerful; I know that for a fact. We were gathering deep in the woods in a teepee. This was reservation land, called McDurman Indian Reservation, and the roadman this time was a Shoshone guy, Stanley Smart, well known for his work and highly respected. So we started drumming and singing, and this goes on for quite a long time. Around half way I had to go out for a pee. I went a bit off to the side and remember when I came walking back to where the teepee stood, all of a sudden I had a feeling that I had gone back in time to way before the white people came. I saw a large teepee with more than 35 people in it and they were all praying, gathered in ceremony. I could see the fire inside the teepee, reflecting the faces of the people. I thought: "This is how it used to be!" I felt so happy and connected; the earth was alive and felt very clean; I could hear the animals in the forest, and some birds singing. The stars were clear; there were no other lights, no houses, nothing. This was when people were of one mind, believing in Spirit with their hearts, and being one with the Mother Earth. Everything was just right and this powerful vision of all people working together and believing in Spirit and Nature has stayed with me all these years. I went back inside and we continued the ceremony all through the night.

When we finished, we all came out to lie on the grass to feel the earth beneath us and rest a little. Stanley came up to me and said: "Mala, can we talk? There is something I need to tell you. It is a story that has to do with your father. I want to share that with you, I don't think you know of this story." Stanley spoke: "When your father first came to Nevada, things were said about him: he was supposed to have special Medicine powers and was carrying strong Medicine within him. But we all had a hard time believing that because he had such light-colored skin. He could almost pass for a white man and we doubted that anybody with such light skin could do Indian Medicine. Especially because it was said that he carried the old powers of the earth and there weren't very many people like that around. Once we were sitting together in a teepee, just like the one we were in tonight, with a group of my people and we decided to test him. We asked him to join us in the circle and pointed out where to sit down. We told him: "The Chiefs want to know something about you. They asked us to show who you really are." So your father took out an eagle feather and he stood up and laid it down in the middle of the teepee. He went back to his place where he sat and he started to sing." Stanley continued: "I can assure you, Mala, that I witnessed it myself what happened next. As your father was singing, the feather stood up straight and rose a little from the floor into the air. Then the eagle feather started dancing and came towards him. Your father kept singing and the feather made a full circle all through the teepee over the heads of everyone and returned to your father, where it danced a little more in front of him. Then it went back to the middle of the teepee. After that, no one ever questioned him again. We knew who he really was." Stanley turned to me once more: "I wanted you to know this story about your father. We have great respect for him. I also know that you carry Medicine within you. Use it wisely."

The other day I was thinking about all those elders already crossed over, or those that are getting close. It is not just that we will miss them, but also that many of those old ways are gone forever. So much knowledge of the traditions of how things were done has been lost. We can try to at least remember and share the stories.

Apache Bob's Story

Bob Saenz is an Apache Native and was also a friend of my father's, although he was a lot younger. He came to our house in Nevada a lot and he was known as Apache Bob in our family.

The following story was told by Apache Bob, whom
Mala and Hermine visited in his home in Santa Cruz,
California while taping and working on the book.

Bob:
"One time we drove across the US from Nevada to New York to accompany Grandpa David Munonghye, a Hopi Elder and Medicine Man who was going to speak at a Conference before the National Assembly at the UN building. He had had a vision as a young person about a house of mica in New York City. This vision showed him a spot where the waters meet and where he was instructed to go and speak about the prophecies he knew of. This turned out to be the United Nations building, which is made of glass.

The instructions and prophecies had been kept all those years by the Fire-clan of the Hopi people.

Mala with Apache Bob

A couple of nights before, we were all sitting together: Grandpa David, Mad Bear Anderson, Rolling Thunder, Lame Deer and other Native healers and spiritual leaders from all over, who had come to share knowledge and speak up to bring balance back to the world. A Shinto priest who was also present gave Grandpa David two things. One was a very ancient medallion that had once belonged to the Iroquois Six Nations, whose people have influenced the development of the political system of the United States through incorporating many of the democratic principles into the Constitution of 1787.

He was also given a bottle of bonded whisky. He didn't quite know what to make of these gifts, so he wanted to pray over it and asked our whole group to fast. We fasted for three days. On the day he was supposed to speak, he told us to go to where the Hudson River meets the ocean. So, we got in the car and drove out there, pulling up at the parking lot at the ocean park. Grandpa took his drum and started singing. He told me to take the bottle with the bonded whisky and smash it on the rocks in order to have the whisky go back to where it had come from. I threw the bottle but for some reason it remained whole and was lying there on the rocks. I asked Grandpa if I should go over there to do it once more, but he said: "No, it is meant to be this way, let it be."

It is time for us to leave for the Conference. We have to cross the city from Manhattan to the UN buildings, which are still quite some blocks away. I can see where the main road is that leads in the direction we need to go, about a quarter of a mile away. We are still in the parking lot, so I start to drive up a little street that heads that way. It has a grass sidewalk and belongs to the park. All of a sudden it ends and there is no more paved road, only grass for about 20 feet, and the main road I was aiming for is out of reach. Either I have to turn around and go back or I just take the chance and drive over that little patch of grass to get where I want to be. I choose the last option and while I still had one wheel on the grass and on the sidewalk and the other already on the pavement, sure enough, a police car turns up, puts its siren on, and stops me right there. I need to tell you that on the way down there, I had gotten a speeding ticket in Kingman, Arizona in the morning, coming from LA, cuz we were in such a rush to get to the East coast, and another one in Tulsa, Oklahoma. I was flying, trying to reach 100 miles/hr. The second time, they took my license, but you see, I figured you don't physically need a license in order to know how to drive, so I had kept on driving and now I was in deep trouble." (*Bob grins as he remembers this daredevil action from his youth*)

"These two cops come over, dressed in their blue uniforms, tough New York policemen, not takin' crap from nobody, that kind of attitude. Then your father, Rolling Thunder, said: "Don't worry, I'll handle this." They had us get out of the car, and we must have given quite the impression of a wild looking bunch, long haired, dressed in many colors, dusty from the long drive, definitely not the kind you'd usually meet in downtown New York. Then RT started explaining: "Aho! You know, we have this whole car loaded with Indians who need to be over at the United Nations. We're a mixed bunch, you know: we got Apache, we got Cherokee, Hopi, Iroquois, and we got Shoshone here and Navaho... We are from the ... f'ckarwe tribe. We're not quite sure where we are right now... kind of lost, it seems." The cops started laughing and said: "Oh, is that so, well, we'll let it go this time! We know you are in a hurry." They actually led us through, showed us the way and we got away with it. I'll tell you, I took off immediately, what a relief! I wasn't even asked to show them a driver's license, which of course I didn't possess anyhow. We couldn't stop laughing all the way to the United Nations: the f'ckarwe-tribe! Hahaha!

Sadly, they didn't let Grandpa speak in front of the General Assembly at all. The US delegates didn't want to listen to him and walked out. They had him speak for a few minutes in a little room off to the side for some people who had nothing to do with the Assembly. It wasn't until the late seventies, after three attempts, that he was finally speaking before the whole Assembly and a broader public heard his message. His vision had finally come true.

They always made fun of me after that: "Remember the time when Apache Bob almost got us busted in NY?" Your father always riddled me. He loved to make those kinds of jokes.

Funny enough, this word-joke was actually used once on one of the Soprano shows on television. There is a scene when they are heading for a casino run by some mafia boss and they are lost. They were asked who they are and answered: 'We are the fckarwes!' So, the story has stuck around since 1975!"

The three of us are sitting outside on his terrace near a Redwood forest, enjoying the story and having a good laugh. Bob, whose health was weak as he suffered from a long sickness, leans back happily, rejoicing in the memory of good times. We enjoyed his company and stayed a few days more. Luckily, he has recovered and is now doing much better. He has put his trust in the Creator for help and healing and is a warrior from old times, Apache Bob.

Grandfather Semu

Grandfather Semu Huaute was the leader of the Wind River Camp in California and came from the Chumash tribe. I have accompanied him on numerous trips, amongst others my first trip to Europe, which was memorable in many ways. Many considered him a distinguished elder, but he could joke around too. We honor and respect our elders, but they don't put themselves upon a pedestal.

It just depends on the situation of course, as there are times when you need to be quiet and just listen when an elder is speaking, but a wise elder shows his humanness in the little things. Here is an example of how elders don't take themselves too seriously.

This time, we were traveling with Grandfather Semu and his wife Eneke-Alish by car on one of the highways to some destination in the US. The journey took a while and Grandfather Semu fell asleep. He was really snoring away but woke up when we arrived at our destination, so I asked him: "Did you have a good sleep?" He said: "What do you mean?" "Well, it sounded that way. You were snoring pretty loudly!" He answered: "Ah, that wasn't snoring. That was an old Indian language!"

Rolling Thunder and Losing Focus Story

When my dad did ceremonies or performed healings, I often had to accompany him and help out. I was still a teenager and we had a request from a Shoshone man who was in need of healing. He offered my father some tobacco, and my dad prayed over it and agreed to help. They lived on a reservation about three hours away from our house and we had to leave really early in the morning, as we had to perform the ceremony at sunrise. We had to walk up a deer trail to reach the spot where the ceremony was to be conducted. I gathered the wood for the fire and prepared everything, just before the first glow of the rising sun. My father started the ceremony and worked on the man. He had taught me how important it is to stay focused during the whole ceremony, because, as you are a part of it, you influence the outcome with your thoughts and energy. I was tending the fire as I had already done so many times before, and did everything sort of on automatic pilot. Then my mind began drifting off. I was beginning to think about what we were going to have for breakfast and was hoping for eggs and bacon, maybe pancakes. I wasn't focused on the ceremony and the person who needed healing anymore. All of a sudden I noticed the fire was behaving oddly and I saw a long flash of smoke going straight up and making a sharp turn towards me. It stopped right over my head, where it dropped some of the silver colored ash on top of my head and body. When the particles of ash touched my skin, they turned into maggots and crawled all over me. I knew what was happening and looked at my dad. He was looking right back at me, signaling, "Aha, I am teaching you a lesson here!" As soon as I realized it, I changed my way of thinking and focused on the healing of the person involved, and the maggots disappeared and the smoke cleared up.

This was my father's way of teaching. He could be quite tough on you, but you wouldn't forget those moments. Of course, you can't be focused every second, so don't be too harsh on yourself, but as you notice yourself slipping a little, you should get back on track again and be present with a positive and focused energy.

Rainmaking Story

My father was, you could say, famous for his medicine-power. Anybody who knew him well had witnessed how he could call upon the wind or the rain and how it would almost immediately respond and be there. He was teaching me some of these ways, how to work with energy and with the earth among other things. As shown in his name Rolling Thunder, he was able to call upon the Thunder beings, to have the clouds come rolling in and even have a thunderstorm hit the ground. He rarely used that power since it is interference in the natural flow, but he has done it in some exceptional cases.

He wanted to teach me how to call the rain and there were a couple of different ways to do that. One method has been written down in the first book on my father,[15] where a stinkbug stands up on its head and it shoots a stinky smell out of its butt as a defense. My father used them to call upon the rain.

There was another way he wanted to teach me: I had to design a circle on the earth with three parts that each had a specific drawing in it. Then I had to use feathers from a certain kind of bird, which had a relationship with water and stick them in the earth in certain places. Also I had specific prayers and had to talk to the clouds and the rain, to help the land and the people.

One day at Meta Tantay, he sent me out to call upon the rain, as we had been in a long dry spell. I went to a special spot all by myself, where I performed the ceremony as he had instructed me. About an hour later

---

15 Rolling Thunder by Doug Boyd, written in 1974

clouds came rolling in and it started to rain. And it rained and it rained…
There was a lot of rain! My dad came over to me, saying: "You did pull the
feathers out once it started raining, right?" "Oh, no, I totally forgot about
that!" Then I remembered how he told me to stay with the drawing and
take the feathers out when the rain started to make it just a gentle rain with
enough water for the earth and the animals. So I hurried to the spot, pulled
them out and pretty soon, the rain eased off.

By then, everything was soaked and almost turned into a flood. I messed
it up badly and it was a strong lesson.

You only perform this Medicine when it is really needed. You ask for
permission, you have to explain why you ask this from Nature, that everything and everybody, the animals, the plants, the people are really struggling.
When Nature and Spirit give an okay, you go ahead and do it. My father
and other spiritual people had already talked to the spirits and he gave me
the assignment to practice and learn. You don't do such a thing lightly.

I never performed this ceremony again. I am really careful when it
comes to these things and prefer to think the Earth knows what's the best
for all things better than I do. Once in a while, when things are really out
of balance at a certain spot on the Mother Earth, we can ask and pray for
guidance here: "Is there something we need to change in order for things
to be in balance again? We notice that not only we two-legged ones but also
the animals, birds, insects, the plant-life are all struggling to survive. Is it
about something else that we cannot see and understand because we don't
see the whole picture?"

You have to be careful that you don't ask just for your own comfort. The
different forms of weather and seasons are necessary for balance in nature
and are teachings for us all. Everything is needed in some way. Nature
cooperates perfectly and magically. Sometimes there are also large cleans-
ings going on, that we as humans find very disturbing but are necessary
too. Over the past decades we have witnessed major weather changes that

have destroyed landscapes, taken a lot of lives, and we could see them as a wake-up call for us humans to take responsibility for our actions. Climate change is affecting all life everywhere on the planet. A lot of people see this as something that is none of their concern. It is happening somewhere else and has nothing to do with them, but to me that is an illusion.

Nowadays you hear about the melting of the ice caps due to climate change, which makes it hard for certain animals to survive because they actually need the cold. I know of Native people in the North who can call upon the snow when it is needed in a certain season to cover up the earth, but climate change is an extra factor that makes it very difficult to influence while practicing their old indigenous ways.

Just like when the white people came to this continent, they brought a lot of diseases which our people were not able to find any cure for. The traditional Medicine people, while performing healings, struggled with these new diseases, as they were unable to communicate with them. This is the same with the changing of the weather and pollution of the environment presently going on. Modern technology causes a rapid transformation of the natural world, where the cure is going to take more than just through the traditional way. Before, we could work with nature, as nature was still nature. Nowadays we have come so far away from the original form and energy that it is far more difficult to still reach the essence of it. The layers of toxins and other chemical deviations of the primary natural state make the energy of the new things darker; it has a darker spirit and is more difficult to work with. For instance, we manipulate uranium from within the earth into plutonium, which is far more dangerous and takes thousands of years to disintegrate.

Fortunately, working with the earth through spiritual ways to help Mother Earth come back into balance is what a lot of people, both indigenous and non-indigenous, nowadays try to do again. That is really important and a good thing. Not give up but wake up, and realize that you have a responsibility as a caretaker. In the fall of 2016 huge protests arose against the Dakota Pipeline at the Standing Rock Reservation. From a small local protest it developed into a huge movement of thousands of people, Native and non-Native stood united against the planned destruction and pollution of the water in that area. The elders have prophesized that the 7th generation would be the one self-consciously standing up for their values and beliefs. They see themselves as advocates for the Mother Earth, speak up and work towards more balance on Mother Earth out in the open. The time of hiding ourselves and accepting certain decision-making policies that aren't serving life is over. Witnessing this gives me hope, although all these things need time and it's a slow on-going process. I feel more and more people from all walks of life are rising to make changes.

Let me emphasize that every person can contribute and it doesn't mean you have to be in the front line. You can always make changes wherever you are and the most important thing is you are not stuck in your ways but that you stay open for whatever comes to you, and learn from it. Changing your way of thinking and listening with your heart are the biggest steps towards a different attitude, and in the end this leads to different behavior. In my worldview, it brings forth healing on many levels.

We each have to find the way that is right for us and fits us. Live your life from the heart; that is what matters. You can help other humans, you can be there for other living beings, you can help take care of life as a whole. This implies you do not just think of yourself. You do take care of your own needs, but you realize you are connected to everything on Mother Earth and are not just there for your own 'wants'. You think about your actions and how they affect everything around you, and how they affect the next seven generations coming after you.

So to come back to the topic of influencing the weather, it is the same. We often would like it to rain or to have a sunny day and we can ask for it in our prayers but you always have to keep in mind for what purpose you ask for that kind of weather. Is it only for our own well-being? Are others involved as well? Are we able to think ahead for the other life that is out there and might be in need? Can we understand the effects the weather change might have on a larger scale?

It depends how you phrase your request. If you ask with humbleness and respect, and explain the situation at hand, you might get support. Of course, as a single human being we can't oversee all the effects but it is necessary to always go by what is needed for the larger picture.

Spotted Fawn and Power in a Feather Story

One day my father came out to Meta Tantay and asked if we could all gather, as he had a teaching for us.

He said: "I want to tell you something about a dream I've had. It really taught me something and I would like to share this with you." So, we all came together as this was something unusual and were pretty curious what it was about. My father hardly ever shared a personal lesson.

"It was at night that I had this dream, but it almost had a vision quality to it. I had to fight a really powerful evil spirit. It was the most terrible creature I had to fight. I was punching it and hitting it where I could. Every time I hit it though, there was this blackness coming out of it, flaring through the air and then it would return to its body and it became more powerful and darker and stronger. It kept reshaping itself and there was no way to defeat him. This went on for a long time and there was no end to the battle. I was really getting tired to the point of exhaustion and despair. Then I woke up. A little later I told Spotted Fawn about the dream and asked her for her comment. She replied quietly, shaking her head a little: "You silly man!" I was taken back by this and felt somewhat offended. She continued: "You know there is far more power in an eagle feather than in your fists! You should have thought about that and called upon that power. Then you would have won the battle!" I sat with that remark for a while and realized how right she was. In the dream, I was just reacting and I wasn't thinking straight at all. I forgot about my own resources.

So here I am, always telling people about the power of spiritual ways and teaching about these things, and then when I need it myself, I totally forget it! It was a very humbling lesson for me and I wanted to share this with you all."

This story has impressed me much. The teaching is so true and showed my mother's insight and audacity. It also showed how much my father honored my mother's wisdom.

Corbin Harney: Teaching and Sharing

Corbin Harney, who at a later point in his life was considered the spiritual leader of the Western Shoshone, has had a lot of influence in my life and I honor him deeply for his achievements and trust in me.

When I was still quite young, he already came over to my parent's place, so I have the feeling I knew him pretty much all my life. He was born in 1920 and a little younger than the other Medicine Men who gathered at our house and met on a regular basis. He was supposed to walk the Medicine Path but in his younger years he wasn't following it yet. He did like to be around all those Medicine Men and especially had a liking for my father.

For a number of years he chose to work with wild horses to "break" them, as you call it, so you could ride them. It is actually a fairly dangerous job; you really need good skills to be able to do that in the right way. He lived in lots of different places, was constantly on the road, never really based at one home so much. Born in Idaho, he was raised in the area of Duck Valley

Indian Reservation, which is part Idaho and part Nevada. Those two states have different time zones, which makes it very interesting if you go and cross to the other half of town, you'd be living an hour later.

He spent quite some years in the Indian Colony of Battle Mountain, which was a small community with about 200 to 300 Indian people of the Shoshone tribe living there. There were two well-known Shoshone Medicine Women living there who took Corbin in and taught him a lot of the Old Ways with the hope and conviction he would carry on the knowledge as he was supposed to. They were already of a high age and both crossed over when they were more than 100 years old. Corbin mentions them in one of his books: Eunice Silva & Florence Vega. [16] '

Finally, Corbin took the task upon himself that he was born into. He just needed time to shake off his youth and do some other things. I can relate to that very well, since it can be a burden to know at such a young age you are supposed to be a Medicine Man.

He regularly visited Meta Tantay when Sky and I were already running the Camp and used to tell me stories about my family. We both loved to hang out with each other, I guess because there were some similarities in our lives and in our character. As we say: we saw similar hearts in each other. He started to share more and more, having developed his own Medicine skills over the previous years. He started to become politically active and devoted himself to the Shoshone people and to Mother Earth. Very outspoken on certain issues, he was stepping up and taking on responsibility. Corbin was a natural leader: he was able to reach people and urged them to become active themselves. Although a popular speaker, he talked in simple language -- also because English wasn't his first language -- and had a way of enticing people, reaching them in their hearts. Through his many efforts and powerful presence, he became recognized as the main spiritual leader of the Western Shoshone.

---

16 Corbin Harney: One Water, One Air, One Earth'

For many years, the US government performed nuclear testing experiments at the Nevada Nuclear Test Site. In fact, this still goes on today. Native people and many others too have been protesting strongly against this from the beginning. The nuclear waste was transported to Yucca Mountain and the ground water became polluted by it. Nature was poisoned on every level; lots of abnormalities have been witnessed in the growth of animals and a lot of sickness was the result. Humans got cancer from it, especially Native people who lived in that rural desert area. Corbin was one of the main activists to demonstrate against this abuse and pollution and he founded a Native organization, called Shundahai, which aimed for a nuclear-free world and worked together with activists from as far away as Russia. Corbin was very adamant about the dangers of uranium and spoke on many occasions of the necessity of making peace and stopping nuclear weapons anywhere in the world. He traveled far to state his point and believed a nuclear-free world could only be reached if people from all over would cooperate with a common goal in mind and heart.

When I became an adult, I also got involved in the protests at the Nevada Test Site because they had such a huge impact on Mother Earth. Due to the outrageous cover-up of facts, my family and I simply felt forced to do something about it. You can't stay silent if you care about life, and we have been at the Nevada Test Site many times with gatherings and protests. Since the early eighties, we organized a big gathering around Mother's Day out there for about a week. A lot of people, activists and environmentalists, Native and non-Native, who were seriously concerned, showed up each year. We talked through speakers to get the word out and to raise awareness, but also wanted to reach the press and through that a wider audience. We camped out for a week and there were all kinds of things you could involve yourself in while being there. On the last day of that protest week, we blocked the road to the actual test site. We showed how serious we took it by chaining ourselves to the fence. There was a white line on the road that we were not allowed to cross. As soon as we did that, we got arrested.

Many times we were put in jail for it or the police locked us in huge pens just out in the open heat of the desert, with no shade, no bathrooms, no water, no facilities at all.

Two kinds of police were present: normal police and privately run police that companies and also the government would hire on specific occasions. The normal police were just doing their job. They would take us to the police station; take our names and keep us in for a few hours. After paying a fee, we were usually released.

The other ones we had to be careful with. This group originally started in Germany and was called Wackenhut. It became a massive mercenary force. They would get in their cars and pick-ups and just drive through the crowd trying to disperse us, no matter if somebody would get hurt. When they arrested us, they would throw us to the ground face down and really stomp on us with their knees in our backs. I have seen them dislocate shoulders and body-search the women, which was illegal. They tried to intimidate us by hurting us on purpose. Luckily these extreme things only happened on the last day of the Gathering.

The rest of the week, we camped out there and had a good time meeting people and sharing. Those first days we also used to train the people in non-violent ways of demonstrating. It was important that everybody was informed and knew how to protect himself or herself, how to behave, what to say. Since the area around the test site was contaminated, we wanted to make sure that everybody knew which areas needed to be avoided. Especially in the gullies, where the dust would gather, you could tell the difference, although you can't actually see the radiation itself of course. You wanted to make sure not to swirl up the dust too much. We all knew there was a certain danger in camping out there, but we believed the cause was worth it.

People were kept pretty busy with cooking and preparing meals for every one and we had other activities going on.

One time Corbin asked me to organize a Native American storyteller to come to the camp. He thought it was a good thing that people could also relax a little and have some fun. You know how elders like to joke and make sure the people shouldn't get too serious about everything. He said: "We should bring some fun in here. It is a very important thing in life! Mala, do you know anyone, who could come to the camp?" I knew a Paiute woman who was a well-known storyteller and asked her if she was willing to come to the Gathering. Her name was Judy Trejo, I believe, and she had moved up to Portland, Oregon, where I had met her. She agreed spontaneously and arrived two days later. Everybody was excited about the prospect of a fun evening and we cleared one of the big tents out for the occasion. Over the years we had managed to get huge army tents, which helped stuff away all the equipment. By the time she started to tell her stories, the tent was filled with both Native and non-Native people and I was sort of proud of myself I had managed to organize this event. Corbin and the other main organizers were having a meeting and were not present. In our Native tradition there are all kind of stories. We have stories for children, we have Creation stories that deal with how the world became the way it is. We have stories about hunting or how nature works. We also have stories that deal with the relationships between men and women and those stories can get quite explicit. In the old days, we didn't have the hang-ups we often have nowadays when it comes to nudity and sexuality. We describe and name the body parts clearly and don't hide the intention of what is spoken about. It was not a big deal and considered natural. Nowadays those particular stories are usually not shared with western people, as they might get the wrong idea. As you can understand where this is going, Judy chose one of those stories, about Coyote and Rabbit, I remember: she is very descriptive when she talks about Coyote who is running around holding his penis and how he is chasing Rabbit and is constantly trying to put it inside of her. This continues for a while and as with all stories, it does have a deeper meaning behind it, which comes at the end of the story. I thought: "Oh man, I totally forgot to tell her that her audience isn't just Indians. I am going to be in trouble!" When I look around the crowd, I see that most of the white people present were sitting shocked with their mouth dropped open. The Native people were laughing, as they are familiar with the figures and the symbolism behind it. They were having a good time and thought it was fun entertainment. She kept on telling these kinds of stories and little by little most of the white people were leaving the tent. They apparently couldn't handle it. I guess what got them most was that this sweet looking old lady was telling all these things in such an open manner with no holding back and no shame. Maybe they also expected some other kind of stories and thought it was inappropriate at this time. Sure enough, the next day I hear that Corbin is asking for me. I had kind of tried to stay away and do work further out but there was no escape and I had to face Corbin. Reluctantly I go over to his place and anticipated a Council, which is a group of elders that is called upon when the community is involved. But Corbin was alone and asked me: "Mala, were you in the main tent yesterday? I heard it was quite the evening." I said: " Yeah, I was there." "Do you realize what went wrong?" I said: "Yes, I know…" Corbin continued: "We have to be careful with these things, you know. We don't want to have people jump to conclusions. Here at the Gathering we like to bring cultures together towards understanding and respecting each other. But you have to take things slow. Yesterday evening was a little too quick for a lot of the people." Corbin proved to be a gentle teacher and I had understood my lesson. Judy only realized later on what had happened. She hadn't been aware that so many of the white audience had actually left. She did apologize the next day to me. She said: "I don't know what got into me but I just was on a roll and I heard a lot of laughing!"

Over the years we had quite some adventures with Corbin and I have always enjoyed being around him. In those days I witnessed many people coming to him for healings and for counselings too. He attracted people through his gentle yet strong presence.

Whenever there was a gathering of any kind, he was leading the sunrise ceremony. He went out for sunrise daily, whether with or without people and did it the old Shoshone style as much as possible. These old ceremonies would originally take from about four o'clock in the morning until around eight o'clock. I remember, it felt like the middle of the night when from outside you'd hear his drum and his singing. He had already gotten up to light the fire and would start the singing and drumming by himself. He would never push anybody to come. Little by little though, people would start joining in and by the end of the week of the Gathering at the Nevada Test Site but also elsewhere, he'd have a big crowd present. He turned the songs he used to sing for sunrise into so- called friendship dances. He liked us to dance those songs. Everybody was holding hands and was dancing clockwise on Mother Earth. He used to say: "Our Mother likes it very much when we dance. She appreciates it when we stamp on her and enjoy Life. Everything on this Earth moves in circles, if you have noticed. The Sun and the Moon, the Earth herself, the Water when it spirals down a hole. When you look at a dog wanting to lie down, he makes a few turns before he curls himself up. Birds build their nests round. There are many examples like this, if you take a closer look."

Corbin Harney

When Corbin sang his sunrise songs, we were always surprised how long he could sing and you would think that he was constantly singing the same thing, but he wasn't actually. He just changed a few words and then continued with his prayer-song. I knew, because I recognized some of the Shoshone words he was singing. He sang for all the different aspects of Nature, for the different elements, like water, air, earth, for different animals, for whatever needed attention and help. One of his favorites was the horny toad. He told me the story once: "One time, there was a horny toad jumping upon my foot and it sat there and talked to me. He told me that his people were suffering and they needed our prayers. So I promised him, I would do that and since then I have incorporated his people in my morning prayers."

Although he followed the tradition of his people, he was also pragmatic and realized that times change, and you need to accept that. All he cared about was that people would pray in some way or another. He told me: "You know, the Old Ways don't work anymore in today's world. These modern ways have made it very difficult to take time to go with the flow of Nature. People go to work and children go to school. They all have things to do every day, so there is no time and space for these ceremonies anymore. That is the way it is. But when people at least go out on the Mother Earth each day and say a little prayer, that is something and it has meaning."

To him, the most important thing was that you go out and pray. How you did it was up to you. He suggested things by his example, not by telling you how you should do it. That to me is a sign of true power and having faith in Creation.

Corbin had an incredible gift of working with people. His Medicine was Bear but he also worked with Water. In the sweat lodge I have been at his side while he was performing healings on sick people through the pouring of water and through the damp. He also knew old sacred Water songs.

We used to go to Rock Creek for yearly gatherings. Rock Creek is in the middle of the Nevada desert, and the ancestors of the Shoshone people had their burial sites hidden in the rocks and did vision quests over there. It is still considered a very sacred place. Although in the dry desert, there was a heart shaped pool, which had been used for healing purposes for ages, but had thickened with soil and mud and had lost its original form. We cleaned it up to have it return to its heart form again. Corbin worked with the water of that pool and performed healings in there. Those weeks out in the desert on that sacred spot connected me to the ancestors of my people while celebrating through ceremonies and prayers. I will always treasure them in my heart. Sometimes we gathered with more than 30 people; we put up our tents and had good times with lots of laughter. We brought in lots of food for all the people who were staying and camping there, cooking for ourselves for those few days. Corbin oversaw the work in the kitchen as well as guiding the ceremonies, talking to people and advising them, and conducting a sweat lodge. He had a way of getting people to come together. It didn't matter to him what color their skin was. He said: "You have to look at the heart. That is what defines a person." So white people, too, came with us to that sacred site. Some of the Shoshone people didn't agree with him on this matter, since they were afraid the white people would take advantage of the situation on their own behalf and abuse our hospitality once again. Corbin's own tribal people criticized him because he strongly believed in inviting people from all colors to gatherings and ceremonies, but he used to answer: "There is no time to be picky. Mother Earth needs our prayers and those prayers can come from anyone. We need to overcome our differences and unite as on people. All I care about is the person's heart."

Like I shared before, I have been around many Medicine Men. They all had their own style and way of doing things. My father was very structured and set in his ways, which wasn't easy sometimes. He was a strict teacher and could speak in a powerful way that almost scared you, but was impressive nevertheless.

Corbin was an incredible gentle person and it showed in his teachings. My spirit responded to the fact he didn't push his way on somebody else. If somebody needed to be corrected, Corbin would find a way to bring it across friendly without being harsh. Very often he used humor to loosen up the situation. He just loved to joke around and laugh! Everybody who knew him thought he looked like a loveable bear. He was short but with a firm posture, well rounded too because he loved to eat. He had a funny habit: he preferred to eat his desert before the main meal. The rest could eat the way they wanted as long as he could eat his ice cream or pie before the other food.

People were always willing to do anything for him, especially when he was getting older. They went out of their way to make him happy. I remember one time during summer we were out in Rock Creek and it was extremely hot, as the sun was shining mercilessly the whole day. You could only reach Rock Creek by a long dirt road with lots of bumps and potholes. It was quite the drive. We were in the middle of preparing dinner and one of the helpers asked Corbin if he was satisfied with watermelon for desert or if he would like something else. Sure enough his eyes started to glitter and he said with a mocking smile: "Man, I have this incredible craving for an ice-cream! Ooh, how I'd love some ice cream right now!" Of course there were no refrigerators out where we camped, and we couldn't bring any ice cream. Because the helper really wanted to please Corbin, he and another guy jumped in the car and took off over that long and dusty desert road all the way to Battle Mountain, which was about three hours back and forth, to grant him his wish. Somehow, they managed to keep the ice cream from melting and Corbin was all happy and enjoyed it, licking his lips.

Yeah, Corbin loved to play little jokes on people, but it was always innocent and never with a mean intention.

A short story to illustrate his sense of humor involves a friend of mine from Arizona. She often visited my family while living in Oregon, but was not used to the practical jokes Native people like to play on each other.

We were taking Corbin off to the airport as he was flying out of Eugene. My friend also joined us. Corbin needed to go to the bathroom before going to his gate and exclaimed: "Mala, I am going to see the Jones's." I said: "Ah yes, you are? Okay." Going to the Jones's is a very old fashioned way of saying you need to use the bathroom, but my friend didn't have any idea what it meant. She was curious though and asked: "Oh, Corbin, can I go with you? I would love to meet the Jones's." Corbin said with a little grin on his face: "Sure, you can come along!" She was all happy she could spend some time with him, so there they went. When Corbin walked into the men's bathroom, she was surprised: "Where are you going?" Corbin pointed out to the sign: "I want you to meet the Jones's!" She realized her misunderstanding and came back to our group, all red in the face, feeling a little embarrassed. We were all laughing of course. It was just a practical joke and Corbin used the situation as it came along.

Let me tell you another story on how Corbin played a joke and how he actually got tricked himself. He would often travel together with people that helped him with ongoing things, like driving the car for him or doing activist support work. I wasn't with him that time, but they told me later on that they were driving through the desert, and on those long desert roads not many towns appear where you can stop and take a break. Corbin wanted to pull a joke on these guys.

After being on the road for a little while, he said: "Oh, I need some food, I am really hungry. But I need something special: I want a beef-donut!" The others said: "What is that? There is no such thing as a beef-donut!" "Oh yeah, sure enough. It's a donut with beef in it." He kept insisting he wanted one of those donuts. So, the rest figured what to do and decided to play along and get back at him too. "We'll get him a beef-donut and then we'll see how he reacts." So, they stop at a donut place and buy the biggest donut they can. They get some cooked beef somewhere else and stuff it in the sliced donut and give it to Corbin: "Here is your beef-donut, just like you wanted." And he says: "Ooh, that is good. Mmmh, that tastes really yummy." They get back on the road, as they still have quite far to go, but after a while Corbin sighs from the front seat: "You know, something is missing. It needs a banana.

That would round it off. If only there was a sliced banana in between that would just be the best taste ever together with the beef and the donut!" So, at the next stop, they pull over, find a grocery store and get him a banana, slice it up and add it to the donut. "Now, it should be good for you, Corbin!" Again, Corbin is very thankful for it, sort of sniffs at it and takes a small bite. Sure enough though, he shakes his head after a while: "I know, what is missing: it needs some strawberries on top. That makes the perfect match!" By this time, the group knows that Corbin is making fun of them and they are determined to keep at it. They somehow managed to get him his strawberries – not easy in empty desert country- and added it to the beef donut with the banana. They were all watching him now, eager to see if he would finally eat it or come up with the next extraordinary wish, but Corbin quit the game and broke out laughing. "Okay you guys, you win. I could go on like this but enough is enough. You got me back this time! I better go and eat this and keep my mouth shut." Very practical jokes he played, never hurting anybody. It was his way of loosening up the atmosphere on a long, otherwise maybe boring drive through the desert.

Some people thought a spiritual leader and Medicine Man should act in a certain, more serious manner. On the other side of the scale people called him a Holy Man, something he strongly disliked. I remember he once said: "The only thing holy about me is my underwear!" His opinion was: "Calling somebody holy sounds like that person is better than others."

The Native Way of Teaching

When Medicine people or healers are learning, we handle it differently than in the western world. There are no courses or diplomas. You spend time with elders who help you understand the healing ways and you spend time working and learning from Nature and Spirit. One of the most important things is to learn to have a humble and open heart. A guarantee you will be successful isn't given, because it isn't about your personal ego and success in the first place.

The elders or the people who teach you, look at you if you live up to what you have been learning about. It means that they share and observe at the same time: how is what is shared being understood, and how does this show in your behavior and in how you handle situations. If you are struggling with it, you aren't necessarily corrected but you're offered help in an indirect and discrete manner, like maybe through a personal story that once happened to them or through some hint or example how to manage a similar situation. You realize: "Oh, this is how I could do it." It's common amongst Native People to not correct openly. We don't punish or blame anyone. This also applies to parenting and being around young people, like I explained earlier on. We prefer to let a person proceed in their own learning as fast as they are able to, to let them develop on their own. We try to avoid pushing; things need to take their own course and time.

It is really about observing if the person is putting the knowledge to use in his or her life in the right way with the right intent and attitude without getting caught up in ego. When a person is ready, the next level of learning is added.

Of course, people have different approaches and different characters, and this shows in how each person comes across as a teacher. Some teachers are more structured and strict. Some are gentle and patient. It also depends on the situation and the person they are teaching.

What is most important is your way of thinking and your way of life. The foundation needs to be strong and based on the principles of Nature and Spirit. You need to have a deeper connection to know how you can ask for guidance and help from Nature and Spirit. When that foundation is laid in a good, solid way, you have a much bigger chance of staying humble on your learning journey. If you just go and learn straight away about a certain ceremony, you may not have that appropriate way of thinking and this can really go in the wrong direction at some point. It lacks depth and the ceremony becomes empty.

Sometimes I see that elements of ceremonies are mixed with other ceremonies, which isn't a good thing, as things get blurred.

An example of how it shouldn't be done is when there is a charge for a ceremony, as that is not according to the traditional way. Very often, money has a negative influence because it corrupts and lures people into becoming greedy and taking more than they actually need.

I have witnessed that there are more and more white people who are interested not only in our ceremonies but in our way of healing, too. Overall, the Western perception of how to heal and help people is changing, because they see something has been left out over the centuries and something is lacking in their own approach. The Western approach is scientifically based, but the spiritual aspect of healing has been overlooked and actually been seen as a weakness or defied as humbug. As time went by, the money factor came in. Doctors and other healers are being paid, but unfortunately, overall this system has gotten out of balance. In the old days there was a fair exchange with food, a blanket, or other things, which has gotten lost due to many changes in how we live our lives nowadays. Communities function in much larger contexts. Influences from outside have affected the systems that have been in place for many centuries. Also amongst my own people we are trying to adapt and see what works. I have been in large meetings where we actually have discussed this issue: "How can we work with people through healings and therapy within the traditional boundaries and yet also continue to make a living? "Are we allowed to charge for certain things or not?" It is not easy to solve this.

In some cases though, it is very clear that the line is overstepped. I have seen an Indian guy who went over to Europe for many years, charging large sums for sweat lodge ceremonies. He was running many ceremonies, one after the other, stuffing in as many people as he could so he would end up earning more money. That is definitively wrong. Unfortunately, the people over there didn't know any better and thought they were experiencing the real thing.

Of course I know we can't go back to where we exchange food or blankets for doctoring. We have to make a living and we need money to pay our taxes, our housing, our insurances etc. Money is needed to cover the bills and has become the means of exchange. It is just that with it, greed and negative energy are also involved, and especially when it comes to healings and ceremonies, this should be avoided.

In our way of teaching, there is no time limit how long learning takes. You are ready when you are ready. Learning is actually sharing: things are shared with you, mostly in an indirect way and you just go along with it. At first you just take part, then you might be asked to help out and at some point you might be asked to take over certain tasks. Some things are understood straight away and other things take longer to grasp. That is all good, just as it develops. You proceed in whatever speed fits you, how fast or slow depending on your actions. That is a big difference in comparison to western trainings where there are schedules and programs to be followed. In the indigenous way, things follow their own time. Time isn't relevant, basically. Indigenous people wouldn't call it "being in training"--that isn't a traditional concept. Training in my understanding is something you do repetitively until you get it right. In the Native American way, you also repeat, but not with the specific goal to be able to do it. It doesn't have anything to do with ambition and personal need.

Just to give you an example from my own life: I was in sweat lodges for thirteen years before I did a ceremony on my own. I wasn't expecting to perform one myself after having been a part of it a certain amount of times and I wasn't keen on it. It just took what it took and it was totally fine. There is no hurry with these things. At one point I was asked to do the fire; at some point I was asked to help pour the water; at some point I was doing the whole ceremony. It is important to really get a deeper insight into all the aspects of the ceremony. You need to know about all those different aspects and you shouldn't want to take a shortcut because it affects the outcome of the ceremony.

I knew Corbin had been getting more and more onto the Medicine path and we'd been hanging out together a lot already. Yet I never asked him about anything so much and I didn't expect him to share with me. At one point though he thought I was ready for it and felt the time was right. He hoped I would use the knowledge in the best way possible. He told me if I had any difficulty with applying the knowledge, he'd be there for me. So I asked for his advice in this sense: "You know, I really did my best but I noticed it works easier for you. It doesn't flow right for me yet. I am missing something." It could be weeks later that he would tell me to come along without telling me what he was planning on doing, and he would show me while I was near him, not commenting or anything on how I should do it. I would thank him for showing me and helping me. He didn't expect me to copy him. He just showed me how he did it and at the same time he supported me to find the way that worked for me.

Many times teachers tell you what to do and what not to do. It doesn't leave any possibility open for your own development. This way you can't find out what really fits you and it isn't as effective. Also when you are being told, you often respond in a defensive way. Either you feel insecure and put down or you feel unseen for what you are worth, and you start to react in an emotional way, not really paying attention to what is being said. It is not a safe and open environment to learn and share.

The indirect way is a main characteristic of our teachings. We don't rub it in. We sort of drop a hint somewhere or we suggest another possibility of doing it. We don't put emphasis on a person's mistakes nor on their success.

Things need their time to sink in and there is a right time for everything. It is common to not comment much, but we do observe all the time. The elders observe the younger ones on their path of learning and growing. The younger ones watch the elders, as they are examples. So there is a mutual exchange.

Nowadays there are Native people who have taken on a more Western way of teaching. Sometimes they conduct certain ceremonies and after a while a person gets some kind of permission to perform that ceremony on their own. Some call it an initiation, but as far as I know, traditional Native people do not use this word in this context. I have mentioned that before already in the case of the Rites of Passage Ceremonies.

There is another word we actually never use and that is "holy." This word came to us through Christianity. We prefer the word "sacred" for certain things, but wouldn't call somebody a "holy person." We talk about Medicine People or we name certain persons as our spiritual leaders. You don't become a Medicine person overnight and you don't give yourself a title, either. Even if you are born with certain gifts and you are supposed to follow a certain path in your life, it still doesn't mean that it is going to happen that way. It shows over time, and you become recognized as such by the people. A name is then given to you and it is not seen as a title. And you don't get initiated and give yourself a name to perform a certain ceremony.

You will never hear a person like Corbin Harney claiming: "I am a Medicine Man. I am the spiritual leader of the Western Shoshone." He was considered it though. When he came to Europe to speak at the United Nations, he probably said: "I was sent over here to speak on behalf of my people, the Western Shoshone."

In the modern, western world, it seems people have a need for acknowledgement and permission to use a label in order to perform a healing or a ceremony. Because schools and universities have diplomas that allow you to advertise with a certain profession, you think you need those labels. It is the result of how western society has organized itself. In the traditional indigenous world there was no need for this. When a person felt he was ready to do a certain ceremony, this was a mixture of Spirit telling him he was ready and the community trusting him to do it. It depends on the attitude of the person: if things are done with the right heart, a positive outcome follows. People wouldn't show up if they felt it wasn't done in the right way. Native people usually don't make a big deal out of it and go out and say: "You shouldn't be doing this or that. You are not ready yet!" They just don't get involved.

This way of dealing with issues has led to infamous misconceptions among western politicians and historians. When the white people came over and wanted the Native tribes to sign certain treaties, they asked the tribal leaders to come. Maybe two or three people would show up and sign the treaty, but most of the leaders just didn't come at all. It was their way of disapproving. But the white people used those signed treaties as if all had agreed on them and they use this against us in court to this day.

Back when our tribal communities were still strong and intact, this 'not–showing-up' would lead to a self-correcting process and the person would stop doing whatever it was, reflect on the reasons and hopefully learn from it. If this person kept on doing things in the same way and even risked hurting or harming people that came to a ceremony, the Elder Council would step in. In that case their ego had gotten in the way and it needed a distinct correction.

Nowadays this whole process is much more complicated, since there are many influences from elsewhere and the indigenous protocol isn't clear anymore for many of our people. Parts of our social protocol though, are still installed in our behavior and when white people have been around Native Americans long enough, they become aware of this different approach. But I guess there are also many people who can't tell the difference and who claim to be something they are not.

Lewis Farmer, a Native elder from the Onondaga tribe once stated:

"Do you want to know who is a real Medicine Man? He is not the one who says: "I'm a Medicine Man." He doesn't ask you to come to him. You've got to out and find him. You will find him amongst his own people." [17]

Moon Custom

Native American tribes had certain customs considering the monthly recurring physical cycle for women, which is closely tied to the rhythm of the moon. Some customs are still followed, but a lot has become diluted over time. The word menstruation is also related to month and moon; we refer to it as moontime or we say: "A woman is on her moon," in a simple and clear manner and consider it a highly sacred time.

Women on their moon are experiencing a natural cleansing on a deep spiritual, emotional, mental and physical level, which has a logical reason: women are the carriers of new life and their bodies prepare to be as clean and pure as possible for pregnancy. In the earlier days there was no need for women to go to sweat lodges: they were very much in sync with the rhythm of nature and life through their periodic, internal cleansing. The moontime was a woman's internal sweat lodge. Only later on did this become a habit, since the moon customs mostly became eradicated and some other kind of purification and connecting with Nature and Spirit then became necessary for women.

---

17 Different cultures produce different concepts and belief systems that are expressed in the use of certain words which have their own coloring, taste and feeling. Even within a culture or language there can be variations where the meaning of a particular word diverges, depending on the setting. Here, we have some words (e.g. initiation, holy, shaman, training, doctoring) that often have conflicting meanings, as they set off different mental and cultural images that can lead to misunderstandings. These we have tried to clarify as much as possible.

We used to have a special ceremonial area for women called a moon lodge, where they could retreat and care for themselves on all the levels mentioned above while on their moon. Over time, women had recognized a need for a separate space and a possibility to go within. It became the moon lodge and was usually built a little away from the rest of the community. The women didn't need to perform their normal tasks and they could focus on the flow of energy inside them. The blood they lost was given to Mother Earth, making a strong connection while being part of the sacred circle of life, thus cleansing and replenishing spiritually and physically. During that time, the children, the cooking, and the household were the responsibility of the husband or the rest of the family. A community well organized to support the system of honoring the moontime made it much easier. The elder women, who were past their moontime already, brought special strengthening kinds of foods. These Grandmothers also taught the younger generation about the ways of women, about the energy of the moon and water, and receiving and giving life. Special songs were taught and sung as well. Of course, I can't give all the details because obviously as a man I was never fully introduced to all the customs. There is a lot more to it than I can share.

The energy of women on their moon is very special and powerful. As women need to replace the energy they are losing with their bleeding, and also with the spiritual and emotional cleansing, it is only natural that the body, mind and spirit search for replacement. It just happens and isn't a deliberate act.

That is the reason why women on their moon were not allowed in a sweat lodge according to our Native tradition, because the power of a woman who is on her moon, attracts all the other energies around her, interfering with the harmony of the ceremony as a whole. When on your moon, you are careful about not touching sacred objects or handling drums for the same reason. You carry much power during that time, which even accumulates when you work with that energy consciously and live according to the tradition and customs. If you practice the moon custom, your awareness for the energy gets stronger and you learn to use it wisely. Logically, women on their moon don't help with the cooking for the rest of the community or work in the garden. Not only do they not need to and are taken care of but they are not supposed to either, since their own energy is too strong and could be harmful if directed in a wrong way. Again, since it is a time of cleansing and replacing and renewing energy, you are drawing in energy from outside your body with your power. When you touch objects or work with plants and food, they can lose energy by your touch.

Since the others in the community had to do all the work normally done by the women, it had another beneficial outcome. Those who had to jump in and take care of the children or do the cooking appreciated in a much deeper way what women accomplished for the rest of the month. Their work wasn't taken for granted, and valued much more. Also in a relationship it can be of great benefit not to be together all the time. A little break every month is good against irritations and boredom that creep in involuntarily in any relationship. You learn not to expect things to happen out of habit. You learn to be grateful, even and especially for the little things. When you are separate for some time, you are happy to be around each other again afterwards and appreciate your time together more intensely. Decision-making was also postponed to a time when a couple would be together again, as a woman on her moontime was recognized to be in a special state of mind and her spiritual energies weren't grounded. This very sacred time for her was deeply respected.

At Meta Tantay we had two moon lodges, and as the women were getting so in tune with the rhythm of nature and each other, there were hardly any women around at full moon as they were all in the lodges together. We men had to do all the work and felt very sorry for ourselves, haha!

I consider it really important that women are able to live through their cycle in this traditional and conscious way. In today's world, menstruation has become something which is a nuisance and not handy for being productive and getting your work done. It is in the way and there are so many negative thoughts connected to the moontime of a woman that they themselves perceive it negatively. Naturally, this way of thinking creates physical problems like stomachaches and backaches or feelings of shame and worthlessness. At Meta Tantay, some of the non-Native women, who had had some problems around their menstruation, experienced a lot of healing in that area and their problems mostly dissolved. The power of the mind can affect you both negatively or positively.

Nowadays it's not always possible to conduct all the ceremonial aspects, since in most cases we don't have a community that supports these ways. Women nowadays have commitments outside the house working on jobs and pursuing a career of some kind, so they need to find ways where they can still have their ceremonial time, away from the duties of their daily lives. You can transform some of the principles into something manageable. I have been in situations when I was married where we'd be traveling or living in a house, just with our kids with no support from a community. We would make it work with sleeping in two separate bedrooms and I'd make sure Sky had time for herself as much as possible. It is not always easy but you can try to make the best of it.

The interesting thing that I found, while having had the chance to meet and talk to a lot of people from indigenous tribal backgrounds from all over the world, was a great similarity in our customs. Most indigenous people I met had or had had at one time some kind of moon custom. Over time, I realized that there is a very simple reason: no matter where you live on this planet, we all had the same teacher and that is Mother Earth. Watching the animals, the birds and the flow of Nature, the water, the wind and the trees teaches you about Life and how to keep things in balance. Depending on where you live, there can be differences, because naturally the habitat and the creatures in that specific spot influence what you observe, but there are overall similarities and basic rules we all live by.

With the moon custom, it is important to recognize that women themselves have asked for this time of separation. I have come across non-Native people who were very upset in how they perceived the custom, claiming: "You put the women away, as if they were filthy and to be kept from the rest of the community!" But it is quite the opposite: women have a need for a time-out. They long for this spiritual and physical cleansing, and for this ceremonial monthly period. It is seen as a gift and opportunity and essential for their well-being. Unfortunately, it has also been subject to misconceptions.

Tradition and Change

All throughout history, humans have developed structures to direct their prayers and work with the energy of Nature and Spirit, and have thus created various ceremonies for different occasions. They are based on principles coming from nature and although many similarities are found within the ceremonies, you can also witness cultural or individual variations. A tricky thing is how to stay open and not be too fixed in your mind on how you, as an individual, insist the ceremony has to be carried out, and on the other hand not to lose the tradition that was built over the years through experience, knowledge and wisdom.

Every generation claims that times have changed and that they want to do things differently, bring in a new way, but if you would do that totally, you would lose a lot of the original. It is good to question why things are done in a certain way and to look at it from time to time, but you have to keep that link to the foundation. Some things never change: how to approach the Mother Earth and how to work with Spirit and be in harmony with all life; this stays the same no matter how you turn it. Native Americans call those "the spiritual laws" and they derive directly from Nature and Spirit.

In the United States, there has been a huge loss of the traditional Native culture. Many tribes have lost their original spiritual ways that were connected to the land they lived on, which led to misconceptions people are not even aware of. Some tribes copied certain customs from other tribes, although they didn't really match their tradition. In the North West, for example, there are tribes that dance counter-clockwise, which is in contradiction to what most other Native American tribes practice. Tribes have influenced each other through traveling, trading, intermarriage, exchange of goods, thoughts and habits.

Nowadays many tribes are striving to get better knowledge of their traditions, but it is difficult because the older generations are gone, and how far do you need to go back in order to get the original ways to come to the surface? I see it as a huge puzzle where slowly pieces are being found and put back into place.

To rebuild the puzzle you can lean on two things: you do research and compare amongst tribes; you exchange and bring knowledge together. The other possibility takes more time but is not less important: to get in touch with the energy of the area again and be guided, like long ago when people learned through Nature and Spirit and developed the ceremonies. This means relearning and reconnecting to the Mother Earth in order to restore and regain the knowledge and wisdom from the old times. People have gotten away from the natural path and have been separating themselves from the original way of living, learning and developing. It became more a process of the mind than of spirit and heart. Some cultures experienced this in a stronger sense than others but nowadays almost everybody on Mother Earth is affected by this separation.

So Native people can use those two possibilities to reassemble knowledge, by listening to and sharing with others and by opening themselves up to Nature and Spirit and relearn that way of communication again. This can be a personal process in which you flow and feel in harmony with the area where you live or this can apply to a tribe or other group of people in recreating ceremonies and traditions. At first you get in touch with the energy, open your senses and listen to what it tells you and needs from you. If that foundation is there, you can take another step and bring in your human ability to create something that fits that specific place. This can only be done through time and with awareness and heartfelt attention.

In our communities we had a figure, the so-called Heyoka, who would purposely live life in an upside-down manner, doing everything in the opposite way: laughing when everybody else was crying and crying when everybody else was laughing. The Heyoka's gift was to help remind the people why things were done in a certain way and if the reasons were still valid.

It is important to stick to certain traditions and understand that when we feel the need to simplify or skip aspects, we often just want to make it more convenient for ourselves. How to discern one from the other is a difficult thing but possible if you are connected enough to Nature and Spirit. You can communicate with Mother Earth and ask her if it is appropriate to make a certain change. If you ask from your heart with the right intention, humbleness and respect, you will get answers. Many times, humans think they know the answers already beforehand and do not bother to ask at all. Or they pretend they got the answers from Nature and Spirit and yet it was something they had their minds already set on.

We can't deny changes are going on with the planet, which we need to respond to and go in accordance with. Everything on Mother Earth is in constant transformation and we should also flow with those changes.

As the true traditions come from the Mother Earth and from Spirit, this is the source you direct your questions to and ask guidance from. If you feel an adaptation is required, it could well be this is more fitting for the time you live in.

The danger in changing traditions and ceremonies is that nowadays people go for the shortcut. They want the ceremony but they don't want the Way of Life that goes with it. If you don't practice and live by what you claim to believe in -- practice what you preach -- then the ceremonies become hollow. What it really is about gets lost and it doesn't carry any strength. People just want the quick experience. Very few people are willing to walk the journey and learn from it to truly change from within on a heart level.

End of Meta Tantay

Meta Tantay flourished for ten years. Many people from all walks of life joined us, some stayed for the whole time, others for a shorter period. It was a great learning place and the Camp developed from a spontaneous initiative born out of the need to accommodate a group of people into a strong community that was linked to the other traditional Native American Camps around at that time.

However, there was one weak point how all those Camps were organized: it depended on one strong leader who kept the community together. In those times it was hardly possible any other way. As Native people, we were only just regaining our spirit and pride. There were a few people with strong leadership abilities who were able to carry the vision of revival of the Native traditions and culture more openly. They were spearheading the communities that followed them. At Meta Tantay, my father had that role. We started the Camp in 1975 and in 1985 my mother, who was considered the Clan Mother of the community crossed over after getting a sickness against which no healing was found. My parents had been together for more than 35 years. My father's spirit was broken; he didn't realize how much he had depended on her heartfelt support and loyal backup. He showed no interest anymore in the Camp and in life in general and never fully recovered from this loss. Through this dramatic turn of events, the people of the community didn't know what to do. It created confusion to see my father, who had been known as such a clear-minded, outspoken activist and powerful Medicine Man, in such emotional despair. They lost their example and the people got divided over it. Some thought it was only a temporary phase and things would turn back to normal. Others had the feeling that this was the end of it and started leaving. Personally I knew my father wouldn't come back to lead the Camp again the way he had before. Sky and I were asked to take over the direction of the Camp and others didn't agree. It was the first time in the history of Meta Tantay that we had an atmosphere of unpleasant discussions and conflicts. We weren't sure how to respond to all this emotional upheaval. Sky told me to go up to our ceremonial circle area and pray and ask the Spirits for guidance how to proceed. I do listen to her sometimes (*Mala says with a grin*) and I went out there to pray. Together with a small group of people, Sky watches me while I stand in the middle of that area. Around us is desert and you can see a long way in the distance. While facing east I focus on my prayers and I ask what to do and what I need to understand to make a decision. I explained I loved this place very much, that Meta Tantay was such a gift of life to me and I had envisioned my bones would be buried somewhere in the desert and my children would take over the Camp. I asked: "If there is a reason why this isn't meant to be, I will accept this with humbleness and respect in my heart, because my path is to follow Nature and Spirit." While I am praying, I notice that a really old car is approaching out of the desert. It drives up as close as it can get to the ceremonial area; an old Indian guy whom I had never seen before, gets out of the car and walks up to me. He says: "You know better than that: you don't fight over the Mother Earth!" He turns around, gets in the car and leaves.

I go back to the rest of the group, not sure if I had been the only one who had seen this man and what to think of it and ask Sky: "Did you see the man with the car coming from the desert?" She answers: "Sure, we all saw him!" That proved to me what I had already felt inside: that Indian guy was a Spirit in physical form who had come to speak to me. When I told her what he had said to me, she replied: "Well, then that is our answer. We don't fight over the Mother Earth. We'll have to give up the land."

We called all the people together and explained our decision that together with our children we would be leaving the Camp. Anybody willing to come with us was welcome, although we had no idea where we'd go next. We were going to trust in life and see where we'd end up. A few came with us; some stayed, but eventually after a few months everybody had left and the Camp was deserted. That was the end of it. Around the same time ironically, also the other two Indian Camps dissolved.

This way of life never left my heart. It had all felt so right. It was a blessing to live in a community with like-minded and like-hearted people, where every day you'd wake up for sunrise and be in ceremony together to start the day. We all worked to create a beautiful way of living together, each making use of their unique gifts. The little people could run around freely and were taken care of by the whole community. The elders had a place where they were honored as examples of wisdom and knowledge, which they were able to pass on. We all learned to remember how to live in balance and cooperation with Mother Earth. It gave me a glimpse of what it meant to truly live in a tribal community. It wasn't always easy because in a small tribal community, you are forced to face your issues and you can't hide from yourself or from others. You have to solve the problems that appear and you usually end up with acknowledging a lesson you needed to learn. You have to learn to deal with things you don't like. There is a lack of privacy most of the time, which is sometimes hard but it also provides you with so many opportunities you would otherwise never experience. To me it was a way of life that made me happy and content inside. It never left me.

CHAPTER 4

THE WEST

My people, the Western Shoshone, connect the West to water in all its forms, like oceans, rivers, springs, ponds and lakes. Water has many qualities and most essentially it brings life. Planet Earth is a water planet and all life is dependent on water.

With its flowing nature, it reminds us of the flow of life: gentle and soothing but also bursting with enormous power.

It rejuvenates, cleanses and is able to carry messages and transport feelings.

Grandmother Moon influences the tides of the waters on Mother Earth with her cycle of becoming full and fading. Certain ceremonies are performed at night, facing the West where on our side of the globe the moon stands and we then use water for purification and cleansing.

Hermine:

In 2015, Mala and I stayed at his eldest son's house in Cruise Bay at the Oregon coast of the Pacific Ocean, while taping and working on the book. That day we started driving along the coastline and enjoyed some spectacular views down the steep, rocky slopes into whirling pools of waves crashing in towards the

beachfront. While I explored the surroundings at a viewpoint,
I took a little walk down a pathway. Everything was humid due
to the mist and sprays of water coming up constantly, making
the path a little slippery. It was exhilarating to be part of the
elements up close: the sound of the roaring waves pounding in my
ears, the moisturizing effect of the water particles on my face, the
coolness of the air with some seagulls flying through the clouds
and diving down for fish. The green of the leaves of the bushes
and trees was shining wet and vibrant. A sense of happiness and
being alive overcame me.

When the sun was strong enough to break through the
overcast of the morning, we decided to have a break at a spot
down by the beach, where a riverbed flowed from the coastal hills
into the ocean and sweet and salt water mixed. As we sat down
on a bench, we observed the mingling of the sediments and the
formation of small patches of water in between the rocks and
pebbles and I asked Mala about what the West could stand for
in reference to the process of the book.

I see the creative process of the book as different streams of water coming together and forming a pool. All the little rivers and creeks of information and stories flow together and form something that is bonded and belongs together, coming from various sources and ending up in the same source. Right now, it is still flushing and flowing, but eventually it will be where it takes on a more permanent form. Water is the carrier of information and of feelings and connects everything.

Where the river meets the ocean in Cruise Bay

This is what I saw in my heart when you asked me this question and what pops up in my mind. The two qualities of the river and the ocean, sweet and salty, meet and merge into one and another and become inseparable.

In the West we gather all the diverse information from different sources until it flows together as one. When a picture like that comes into my mind and heart so clearly, I know it is of spiritual nature and to me it represents what I am thinking. It looked almost like an empty hole that was filled by all these streams of water, rushing in and filling up that hole and becoming a beautiful pond.

What I saw next was an image of calm water, from where we will take all that was put into that water as something that can be carried forth and outwards.

Alaska

After Meta Tantay disbanded after my mother's crossing over, we stayed at Grandfather Semu's Camp Red Wind for a while. Towards the end of 1985, my family and I were invited to stay in the village Yakutat of the Tlingkit tribe in the South East of Alaska.

Alaska is an exception in comparison to the rest of the United States in regards to what is left of the indigenous culture. The aim of most of the governments was to destroy the social structure of the Native tribes. All over the United States, there were laws and policies that were systematically implemented to reach that goal. By sending us to Boarding Schools, by not allowing our language and ceremonies, and very specifically by destroying our Clan System, our culture became diminished from within. They killed the Clan Mothers because they knew that the Mothers guided our communities and held them together. Interestingly enough in Alaska it came about differently. The Russians invaded the northern territories and considered the Medicine People a threat and important to erase. This was due to their knowledge of their own Medicine People, whom they refer to as "shamans" and who played an essential, although already hidden role in their communities at that time. They basically killed all the Medicine People, even the little ones who were born with that gift, and left the Clan Mothers alone. When my father and I came to Alaska for the first time, we found out that their Clan system still stood strong but there were hardly people left who worked with their Medicine gift. My dad and others did an exchange for a while and came up to Alaska to share what they knew and train some people in these matters. In return, they came to Meta Tantay a number of times and explained the Clan ways, while bringing out all their Clan gear, the regalia needed for the ceremonies. Each side benefitted from this exchange of knowledge and customs and it was a very good thing to see happen. Both groups have been rebuilding and remembering the old ways.

Yakutat was very interesting for all of us. We lived under quite different circumstances than we had been used to in the desert. There are some nice stories that go with it too. I remember one time we were invited for a big potlatch. Potlatches are a traditional way of celebrating and coming together, where the different clans of the community invite each other to extensive meals and festivities, which I always love because there is so much good food involved! It's still a common thing in the North West, especially in Alaska and Canada, where many of the tribes were able to hold on to that tradition. Potlatches are used for many occasions: for ceremonial gatherings, for a simple get together, for honorings and namings and sometimes when there is an issue that needs to be resolved. A potlatch creates balance within the community, as usually the different clans of the tribe all join in. Many clans carry names of animals, like the Salmon Clan, the Frog Clan, Beaver, Bear, but also Thunderbird Clan. Most tribes have two main clans, which are the Eagle and the Raven Clan, which are divided in sub-clans. Each of the clans has certain specific duties and tasks to serve the community. Everybody can do the work, but that particular clan has to make sure this part is taken care of. For instance, they were responsible for healing and medicine, for the gathering of herbs, for hunting, for taking care of the young ones. Whenever a potlatch was going on, there was one clan responsible for organizing it and preparing all the food for everyone.

This particular potlatch had a specific reason. One of the members of the Raven Clan had not been careful while driving out with his snowmo-bile and accidentally killed somebody from the Eagle Clan. The way the community deals with such a tragic incident is to throw a potlatch. It is important for the person who crossed over to be able to travel on to the other world, feeling at peace within and not feeling attached to the world he has just left, especially after a tragic death. If this matter was not dealt with in a healing way, it could end up splitting the tribe. The Raven clan people really took special care in how they prepared everything. They cooked lots of food, made presents as offerings for the other clan and with a lot of effort they put the whole potlatch together in two to three weeks. Then they finally called for the actual potlatch to take place and the members of both the Clans were present. It was made sure that the family of the deceased person was seated in the front seats of honor. The rest was circled around them. The dancers and drummers came in and they offered all the traditional dances and songs in their special regalia in front of the rest of the people. The head person of the Raven Clan offered the presents to the family: Pendleton blankets and other costly gifts. Later on, other people came to offer smaller gifts, usually made personally by hand, to the family and also to the rest of the Clan. The guy who had caused the accident was present but didn't do anything in particular. Then words were spoken from the heart: "We as people from the Raven Clan come to speak to you to let you know that we take responsibility for what has happened. We feel great sorrow in our hearts and are willing to do whatever it takes to make it up to you. We offer you these gifts and food to make things right again, so that we can continue in a good way. We pray that the spirit of the person who crossed over travels in peace to the other side, trusting that all the people from our two clans will continue as one people and live in a good, happy and harmonious way. We ask you to forgive us for what has happened and pray that things will be good between us."

Beautiful speeches were given with carefully chosen words and the spokesmen of the other tribe spoke up and answered: "We hear what is been said. We accept your gifts and forgive you for what has happened. Let us continue as brothers and sisters of one tribe."

And that's it. Then it's done. The food is brought out and the celebration will start. They all dance and sing together. They share food together and are not supposed to talk about the issue anymore. It is taken care of and is out of the way. You move on. That is the way they deal with difficulties. I have witnessed this more than once and it is really a beautiful way how a community can stay strong and doesn't end up divided.

It is never about punishment. The idea is that you are all part of an extended family and you do not need to defend or attack anyone. It is considered important that all take responsibility for what has happened and not to blame one person. That is the key to the solution and secondly that you don't dwell on things. What has happened has happened and cannot be turned around. You want to set things right and move on as "One People with One Heart."

It makes so much sense to me and I often wonder how far did we as human beings get off that path when true harmony was present and we tried to bring balance back whenever life challenged us? Over in Alaska I could experience great moments of healing, whereas elsewhere I have so often witnessed punishment and hardship in handling a difficult situation.

One other time, some of the guys of the village asked me to join them for halibut fishing. Of course, I was in for it. I didn't know though, that halibut get really huge: some of them can reach a weight of 300 to 500 pounds. We went out on this flat bottom fishing boot, Walter, Raymond and I. It had a really heavy and big fishing hook at the rear end of the boat and I was thinking: "What are we fishing for? A whale of some kind?" When we were out on the water, I was looking down and the water was pure and so incredibly clear that you could see the bottom of the ocean. Then I saw a halibut swimming underneath our boat. It looked almost bigger than the boat, pale white, beautiful and huge. We caught one that provided enough food for everyone; they never caught more than needed to feed their people for the time being. They only took what was reasonable and necessary; whatever was left they gave to other families to share. That is how it used to be done all over Turtle Island, which is our old way of referring to what later has become the United States.

On another occasion Walter, Raymond and I went out for moose hunting. I had been deer hunting back in Nevada, so I wasn't too worried about it although moose are a lot bigger than deer of course. We go out to a little airport where we took off with a brush pilot and friend of theirs who would bring us into the area for the hunt. Brush pilots are a special kind: they are called this way because they fly so low over the ground that they actually almost touch the brush they are flying over. They go right over the treetops and whenever there is an open space with grass and meadow they go down and stay close to the ground, just to go up again as soon as the trees came close. So, it's quite an adventure and not something for people with soft stomachs. They do pretty crazy things up in the air. The pilot asks Walter: "Is this his first time?" He answers with a blink of the eye: "Yeah, first time ever!" I knew something was going on and as soon as we took off and were flying high, all of a sudden, the plane dropped like a bomb and we started turning and doing wild movements in the air, making loops, spinning around and going up and down deliberately. After the second roll, I couldn't keep it in any longer and I had to throw up. It was the first and last time ever that I did that in an airplane, it felt horrible but what can you do? (*Mala sighs and shakes his head*) When they know it is your first time, they really go for it and test you out. Although it was a bit messy, the guys were laughing and cheered: "Now, you are no longer a greenhorn!"

After that, the pilot leveled out a little and it got better and we started looking out for moose. After a while we spotted one and the guys marked the area in their heads and we flew back to the airport. The area around Yakutat is spread out with only a few roads going into the forest, stopping in the middle of nowhere. The inhabitants don't possess many cars. A couple had been brought in on boats and my friends had an old van they used.

We took off taking our guns and knives and also picked up five dogs that would help us with the hunt.

The moose happened to be standing at the end of one of those roads, as if he was waiting for us. We didn't have to go in the brush and go after him. Raymond and I agreed to each go to a side of the moose and hit him at the same time. A moose is a huge animal and for some reason, when it gets hit, it takes a while before it registers and it falls down. Sometimes it even charges you. So, we made our prayers and went out to go and kill him. We both made good shots at the animal, but the moose still stood for a little bit, looking at us, then turned around and ran off into the brush. After about 300 feet it stopped and fell over dead.

The guys were placing the dogs in a wide circle around the moose. I didn't know why that was necessary, but didn't ask. We started gutting the body up, quartering and portioning it. We made stacks of it to the side and were really working hard because it is a lot of meat.

Then Walter asked me: "Is this your first moose kill?" I knew what was coming and I said: "Yeah, this is the first one." "Well, you know what our tradition is…" "Okay, which is it, the heart or the liver?" It was the liver, which I had to eat raw out of the body. It is a way of honoring the species and also of taking its spirit into your body so you incorporate its specific energy. I thought: "Man, this is really my day. First, I throw up in the plane after being fooled by a brush pilot and straight after that, I have to eat raw liver!" But I did it, took a couple of bites and got that over with. We continued with the skinning and were almost finished, when one of the dogs started barking. Pretty soon, a second dog started to bark and the rest followed, all in the same direction. Then I heard this deep sound, coming towards us, snorting and growling and I knew there is danger coming. The guys said: "It's a grizzly! We've got to be fast now. Just grab whatever meat you can. The rest we will leave behind! The grizzly is coming fast and will go after the meat. There is no time anymore!"

So, I did what I was told and we were running with our arms full of the meat towards the van. They said: "Now we have to get the dogs! Fast!" The dogs were still leashed to their spots in the circle around the moose. I had to get just one dog, which turned out to be the closest to the grizzly. The others would both get two dogs each. You see, the dogs are tied because they would actually go after the grizzly and attack once they knew it was around. These are pretty fearless dogs. Since the other two guys went up to get the dogs, I thought: "Well, they seem to be pretty sure what they are doing, so I can't stay behind. I know that sometimes people get hurt or even killed by a grizzly, but not every time, so I'll have faith and be okay!"

I got up to where the grizzly was: it was standing on its hind legs and letting out this snorting loud grunt coming from its belly. I tell you, it is a massive animal, about six feet tall. I had to look up to him and could see the powerful claws from its massive paws. They easily swipe away a dog or rip a man open. The dog and I were about 30 feet away from where he was standing and there was nothing in between the bear and me, just the food it wanted to get. But I'm doing my best to stay focused and back off with the dog.

I had heard stories about how difficult it is to kill a grizzly. They have such thick skin and such a hard skull, that a few bullets don't impress them and they won't go down. Since we only had guns and bullets for moose, they were pretty useless in this case. I thought to myself: "If this guy charges, that's it. I'm grizzly food. There is nothing I can do. If it's meant to be, it's meant to be."

The three of us were backing up with the dogs without turning our back to the grizzly, slowly making our way to the van with the leftovers of the moose still behind us. The grizzly is following us on its hind legs, making loud noises and growling at us. I thought: "As long as he is on his hind-legs standing, we have a chance. When he goes down on all four, he is going to charge!" It kept walking on its two legs until he reached the food. That's when he went down and got more focused on the moose carcass and we were able to get back to the van. We got away safely!

Every so often though, some person gets killed in a situation like this. There are a lot of grizzlies up there. When a bear smells the blood of a kill, it gets into a state of frenzy. You cannot reach him on a spiritual level and communicate with him as you could otherwise do if you encountered one in the wild unexpectedly. The smell of blood makes him go crazy. They are willing to do anything to get to the food. It explained why we only had a few minutes left. If you are greedy and want to take too much of the food and come back for it, that is when the grizzly will charge and you lose your life.

Walter, at whose house we were staying, told me a story that had happened a month earlier. Alaskan Natives don't really have reservations and live mostly in small tribal communities ruled by a village corporation, where also white people can live or start a business of their own. So, there was actually a bar in Yakutat. The tribe owned a lot of land around Yakutat but the town itself was not on that property. At first, they actually thought it was nice to have a bar in their little town to liven things up, but soon things were getting out of hand and a lot of alcohol was sold. One evening an elder who had also fallen for the seduction of the alcohol came home late and was trying to sneak in through the back door. While he was trying to get the keys in the door, he didn't realize that there was actually a grizzly standing between him and the door and he started poking with his key in that massive body. Someone witnessed this scene: it all happened really fast, the bear didn't hesitate; he just came down with his mouth and bit the man's head off.

Bears so often come into the village to look for food or just because they are curious that the villagers have developed a bear warning system. They have dogs tied up all over the village and once the people hear a dog bark and it spreads in a certain direction, they know that a bear is coming their way. Quickly they urge the children inside and watch out for him.

One of the favorite food sources for Alaskan Native people was seal meat. I really like meat but this is a tricky one. Usually I love game meat, because it's much more natural and stronger. But the meat of seals is too much to handle, even for me: it is an earth colored meat, dark brown, and it has such a strong taste that I tried to avoid it, without being disrespectful, but everybody was aware of the fact that both Sky and I weren't fond of that meat. One day we were invited for a special treat: Alaskan ice cream! We were all happy and looking forward to it. It was quite the surprise! In a glass gallon jar with a lid, they stuffed salmon-eggs, fresh seal-fat and berries almost up to the top of the jar, which they thoroughly mixed. Then they put it out in the sun for weeks to let it ferment out in the warmth: it gets nice and bubbly after a while. When the lid is coming up a little and becomes round on top, it is ready to eat and once you open the lid, it gives a loud pop. All the people join in for the feast and grab in the jar with their bare hands. They love it! Sky and I looked at each other and agreed: "Come on, we have to try this." So, we did and after one or two bites, we almost threw up. It is one of the hardest things I have ever eaten in my life. The rest of the people looked at us with happy content grins on their faces: "What's wrong? Eat! Eat!"

We couldn't stay in the village for the winter, because we knew they didn't have a lot of food and we didn't want to become a burden on them, although they would have shared whatever little they had. So, we tried to make enough money to be able to fly out before that. I worked for a logging company, which was dangerous work but paid very well.

I have experienced many special moments in Alaska. The nature is just overwhelming in its beauty and raw power. The people are extremely friendly and of heart-warming hospitality. The tribal traditions were strong in many ways, which made me happy in my heart. I was lucky too to have witnessed special moments in their daily life and I was also taken out on special trips. One trip I will never forget: they took me to where no white person had ever been or was ever taken. I had the honor of visiting their old village. We took a boat and out on the water amidst many small islands -- some have been inhabited, some never have -- we passed an island, which looked almost like it was covered with snowcapped trees. I asked: "How is that possible to have snow in the warm season?" They said: "Look closely and you will see." Hundreds and hundreds of bald eagles were sitting in the tops of those trees. It was amazing! I wondered why so many of them huddled together on such a tight spot, because that is unusual for eagles. They explained: "In the water there are great amounts of hooligan, a very oily, bigger kind of sardine. They come here in huge amounts to spawn. This attracts all the eagles and the island crowds with grizzlies too, which make it an impossible place to be for humans: way too dangerous. The bears feed on all the fish that die while spawning in front of the coast of that island. It is a perfectly functioning cycle.

We kept on going and when we were more in the open ocean, all of a sudden, an orca whale comes out of the water close to the boat. It was an incredible sight. If the orca had been closer to the boat or even underneath it, we would have been thrown into the air: an impressive and powerful animal that is also honored in one of the Clan names.

When we reached our ancient destination, I was allowed to walk around in the old village. Some buildings were half torn down but you could easily imagine how it must have looked many years ago. Beautiful carved totem poles still stood proudly upright. Up in the trees you could see big canoes being placed in the top in between the branches. This was the old way to bury the dead. When somebody had crossed over, it was believed that the canoe would carry the person to the spirit world together with all the gifts and earthly belongings and finish the journey. I saw some of the ceremonial sites: the power was still tangibly in the air and I felt very privileged I was able to walk amongst the remnants and feel the spirits and ancestors close.

The reason they didn't allow any white people to come was they feared they would not keep it a secret and more people would follow and disturb the peace of the ancestors. Once the word gets out archeologists would possibly come and start digging in the earth, which they wanted to prevent. Even with Native people they were careful whom they would show the place: not everybody was trusted with that knowledge and intimate experience. It was a great honor for me.

Tribal Adoption

Native Americans have a special way of adopting other people into their tribe.[18] Spirit and Nature guide if a person becomes adopted and when things point in that direction, it is usually sealed with a ceremony. When in Alaska, both Sky and I were in the process of being adopted by the Tlingkit tribe. Their people have a special way of understanding an adoption. Elders will look at the actions and spirit of the person involved and search for an ancestor that fits that particular person, who will also get a Tlingkit name referring to that ancestor, which you'll carry for the rest of your life. They say it keeps the lineage going. You become placed in one of the two major clans and a potlatch ceremony is given for the occasion and a certain protocol is followed. The whole tribe comes together to witness and finish the adoption on a number of occasions. In our cases, only Sky was fully adopted, as we had to move out of Alaska before winter started and there was no time left anymore to finish my adoption all the way. That is why I never mention myself as coming from the Tlingkit tribe and Sky does introduce herself as such. Our children are automatically Tlingkit since we are following matriarchal ways. Red Wolf specifically was drawn to the people up North and visited more often when he got older. He learned some of the language

---

18 When it comes to tribes, we do speak of adoption; when it is on a family level, we speak of taking someone in and don't use the word adoption as such.

and also became a traditional dancer in the Tlingkit way. He has performed many times, even with a so-called special button blanket, which is an honor to wear. Those buttons are hand carved from abalone shell and beautiful intricate patterns are created, which show the clans and sub-clans, even down to the specific house or family of the person.

The Shoshone people also have the practice of adopting somebody into the tribe but they don't have the ancestral lineage mentioned above. Both ways though, show you can belong to more than one tribe, just as you can have more than one parent, once adopted into a family. It is not like becoming adopted after you are orphaned. You can end up having more than one father or mother and several families you are a part of. The adopted person adds something to the family or tribe and also has a responsibility towards the clan or the family he or she is adopted in. The ceremonies acknowledge the person who was already connected spiritually to the family or tribe, who is now recognized openly and physically accounted for, witnessed by the spirits, Nature and the community. It brings the possibility of an extended family, which strengthens and connects the community in a wider sense.

Nevada Youth Training Center

After our time in Alaska, our family returned to Nevada, where we stayed on the land where Meta Tantay had been all those years and which now was abandoned. First, I was able to get some work at a small factory, a mining company where they made sodium-cyanide pellets, which is pretty nasty to work with. Even when you just touch them, it feels like a really bad burn, pretty dangerous, but we were in need of money. Emergency kits were all over the place to make you have medication and bandages close by if something would happen. I only did this for six months luckily. After a little while we were able to rent a house in Elko. A friend of mine told me of a possibility to work in Carlin, where the State of Nevada had a Youth Training Center, where youth delinquents go before they end up in a prison, which was the only one in the whole state. I decided to give it a try; they had a few positions open but had no idea what they expected of me. We weren't given a tour through the place and didn't get an explanation of the job description, so I went in blank with nothing to lose. Somehow, I did well in the first test and was asked to come for an interview. At some point I got the question: "What is more important in my point of view for the people living there: security or counseling?" I said: "Well, counseling of course!" Although that was the wrong answer in their eyes, I got the job anyhow and I got good pay with some benefits. It turned out that I was hired because the government had put out regulations there should be a certain number of minorities covered in state-employment. Since I was a Native American and had become a minority in my own country over the centuries, I got hired. It was a really interesting experience. About two hundred youth up to 21 years stayed in the facility and you wouldn't believe the crimes they had committed in their relatively young lives. Any of those crimes committed by an adult would have definitely led up to long imprisonment. 70% of them were part of gangs. Already in those days, gangs were getting popular, spreading from big cities like Los Angeles, Sacramento, Vegas and Reno to every part of Nevada, where they recruited kids for their gangs. There were two major gangs in the area: the Crips, who all wore blue, and the Bloods who all had red clothes on. It dawned on me that with this job, I got the opportunity to witness people coming from very different backgrounds than I was used to. In the more than 10 years living in all the Camps, I had been surrounded by people who were trying to do good, make a change for the better, who were idealistic with a strong sense of community and embedded in a tradi-tional lifestyle close to my own culture. All of a sudden, I saw how a lot of people lived in a very different kind of reality, which I got to witness day by day. Some of them had done such horrible things, crimes against animals, against other humans, even babies, besides robberies and car thefts. They hardly seemed to have any consciousness; for them violence was daily life and a way of survival. It really came as a shock to me and taught me to see opposite sides of existence.

My job was as a supervisor. It was a rule to work together with another person of the staff and hardly ever were you alone around the youngsters. There were seven dormitories with about 20 to 30 kids in them. I had one dorm to watch, which was -- coincidentally and funny enough -- called Indian Dormitory.

The staff didn't put up with a lot and were very strict, I guess out of fear. Some of these youngsters were strongly built and sometimes even bigger than the adults. They had a lot of anger inside them, so logically the staff only had security on their minds. During the almost seven years I worked there, I've seen a number of staff get hurt, some with broken ribs; a female staff-member got raped. Whenever they had the chance, the kids made so-called shinks, self-made-weapons, which they used on each other or against the staff.

The head of each dormitory was called a senior and our group had a very nice guy I could get along with really well. My partner and I had to oversee the kids doing recreational work outside or little jobs like mopping or helping in the kitchen. Unfortunately, like in most of these institutions, there was a constant threat of lack of funding from the government and they were always looking for ways to cut back on their expenses. Usually we had two staff present, making sure everything went smoothly and safely. The government started making cutbacks and at one point we only had one staff during the day, which we knew was not enough and could turn out to be risky for everyone involved. At night at least we still had two people on watch.

The kids, being smart, figured out: "If we are going to run, then it needs to be during the day." After lunch I was supposed to bring my group back to their rooms after they had gone to the bathroom and the door of each of the rooms had to be kept open during that time, so I could check. Each of the boys had their own room.

One time after lunch I passed the door of one boy, who was a huge guy, taller than me, weighing about 250 to 270 pounds. He came jumping right out the door on top of me, because he had decided he wanted to give it a chance and break out. He was trying to knock me out, hitting on me and sitting on top of my chest. I knew the situation wasn't looking good for me. He was so much heavier than me and I had no chance to get him off. I had a hard time breathing and called upon my inner strength. All of a sudden, I felt something built up inside. I reached out with my hand and touched his breast lightly, pushing against it almost effortlessly. The next thing I know this huge and heavy body was flying through the air in an arc movement, all the way to the ceiling and then landing at the other side of his room. The other kids witnessed this, because they were drawn by the noise and curious what was happening. While still recovering from the fall, the kid looked at me with shock in his eyes. Then he got up and shut the door behind him. Fortunately, he was only bruised up but wasn't hurt in any other way. The other youngsters were just staring at me, not believing what they had just seen. I called some other staff members in and told them what had happened. Of course, I left out the specific details. I never encountered any problems on my shift anymore; had gotten quite the name after this incident. I have always known that in times of crisis, I would be able to center myself and focus my energy in order to help myself and I was thankful that I hadn't hurt him more.

Most of the youth that was locked up in the facility came from Las Vegas, being the biggest city in Nevada with the largest population, more than in the rest of the state combined. Usually they stayed in prison for three to nine months, so there was a lot of exchange of kids coming and going all the time. When their time was up and the kids were released, we had to bring them back to their homes. Las Vegas was about eight hours drive, all the way through the empty vast desert. We used a school bus for this with a driver but had one or two staff members patrolling the bus. As you can imagine, the kids were really acting up, after having being locked away for a long period at a young age, looking forward to getting out and returning to their lives outside the confinement of the Youth Center. A lot of built up anger and frustration was easily let out on the bus driver or the staff.

At one point it was my turn to be on the bus and it was going to be just me, 'cause they had been cutting down on our budget once again. I was a little worried about how I would manage, since I had heard all the stories about kids throwing things at your head or beating each other up. When the bus was fuelling up, they often took their chance, buying cigarettes or alcohol or worse, trying to steal them. All kinds of incidents used to happen. They were always inventing new things to create some kind of havoc. On top of that I didn't know all the kids, because they weren't just coming from the dorm I worked in. The thing I was looking forward to though was the drive back in the empty bus on my own through the beauty of the desert.

Somehow, I survived the first two trips, although it had been tough and strenuous and on my third trip an idea dawned on me how I could catch their attention and have them cool down. I'd realized they were very keen on how long the trip still would be. They kept asking: "How far are we? How long does it still take?" So, on the third trip I told them: "Okay, here is the deal. Every time you start to act up and there is any kind of incident, I will ask the driver to slow down five miles/hour. Whenever something happens, I will continue to do this up to the point that the bus stops. I'll make sure you don't get the keys and will just take a nap. I have all the time of the world. So, if you want to go home quickly, you need to stay quiet."

Well, they did try me, but I was serious about it and had the bus driver slow down. Every time I heard one of the kids cuss or spank another kid, sure enough, I had the driver pull over and stop the bus. I put my feet up the dashboard and pretended to take a nap. They were all very upset, yelling at me: "You can't do this! This is not fair!" But I stayed true to my word: "I warned you ahead of our trip. This is it. If you're going to be quiet, we'll continue." After a while it got quiet in the bus. They sat still and waited. From then on, we were able to drive to Vegas without any problems. The word how I handled it got around quickly and all the staff practiced it afterwards. It turned out to be a smart trick. I found out where I could get a grip on something they were emotionally interested in, which was time. They somehow respected what I had come up with and it created a boundary that they didn't cross anymore. Everyone involved benefitted from it in the end. I wasn't forced to punish them anymore. Some staff had quite violent ways of keeping peace at the bus. This way, I didn't have to be loud or do anything to stop their aggressive behavior. There was no need for them to provoke or threaten me. It was a peaceful strategy to solve the situation: getting their attention without being abusive towards them with adult authority.

At the school itself there was a strict grading system, which was influenced by their behavior. The grading system was based on daily rapports that added up in a weekly rapport, which gave them privileges for the coming week. If you had shown good behavior long enough, you could end up in one of two fire-crew dorms. The kids would get paid for their work when there was a fire in the area, which obviously they were keen on having. There was always enough crew to supervise and work as fire fighters themselves, which I did for almost two years and for which you had to go through special training. You had to be able to wear 35-pound backpacks and run up and down hills in the forest and it was very dangerous work. Once two kids and one of the staff members were caught in the middle of a fire and they were forced to use a special kind of equipment, called emergency-fire-shelters. In case of danger, when the fire is coming towards you and there is no escape, you have to lie down, put this over you and activate it -- it is almost illuminating. You would still feel the heat but the fire itself wouldn't hurt you.

They came out all right, not hurt too badly. I've seen another kid though put an ax in his own foot.

One time another staff-member and myself were leading a group of 20 youth out of the fire area where there was a lot of smoke and heavy air and we noticed one of the kids was missing: all the smoke had disoriented him. So, I volunteered to go back and look for him and luckily, I found and carried him out, but because of the strain I had inhaled deeply and taken in a lot of very hot air, which burned the inside of my lungs. I couldn't stop coughing anymore and also spat blood. They evacuated me with the helicopter and the doctors in the hospital told me, I shouldn't be doing this kind of work anymore because of the damage that was done to my lungs. So, no more forest fires for me.

What I did start to do though – this only gradually came to life throughout the years - I started counseling: the very thing I had chosen to prefer working with the day I came looking for the job and which the facility hadn't shown any interest in so far. The staff by now had started to like me. I was always there before the official start of the working day hours. They saw I put effort into the kids, so they were willing to let me have my way a little. When I asked the senior of our block: "If I took a few kids into a separate room and did this on my own time, would you allow me to work and talk with them?" I offered to keep records of what I did and what progress was made and so on. Each kid had progression sheets already anyway which helped each one of them to get some privileges if they behaved well. The boss agreed, although it had never been done like this before, but he hoped it would work and so I began with my plan. The kids saw I did this in my own time so they responded positively and got much better results on the point system on their progression sheets. Eventually the senior had all of the staff of our dorm do the same thing: take some time to talk to them, even during shift and just listen to them. The administration of the facility got word of it and eventually installed this as part of the program for all the dorms. It made me really happy to see that: such a simple tool, you know, just give a person some attention, listen with intent and already a positive change is in the making. It doesn't solve everything but it shifts something in their behavior. Two years before I left, they had a couple of professional intervention counselors. Back in those days a novelty for Nevada.

The Move to Oregon

Since I was born and all through my childhood and upbringing, I felt my parents and some elders had certain expectations of me. Sometimes they spoke directly about it, sometimes it was just in the way they'd approach and observe me, talk to me and would show me things. This expectation basically meant I was supposed to walk a path of healing, the Medicine Path, helping and speaking for the Mother Earth and all its beings upon it, including human beings, traveling and speaking up for my people, leading a life in service of the Mother Earth and the future generations. I pretty much followed that path as I was growing up.

After coming back from Alaska, I'd gone a different direction in my life than I was supposed to go. My purpose was to follow the traditional way and I wasn't going to live a western style of life, working a nine-to-five job, raising a family while living in an ordinary house. But I had come to a point where I decided I was going to do just that: get a job and earn money to get my kids some new clothes or go to the movies with the family, just things everybody seemed to have, a little more comfort and extras. Up until that point I had pretty much always given of myself, not asking anything personally and it changed with having the responsibility of a family. I wanted to be able to give them something. According to the prophecy I was also supposed to be speaking for my people and the future generations, but when I started this job at the youth-center, I basically only did my sunrise ceremonies, went to a sweat lodge occasionally, but nothing more. Most of my time I spent at work and then I went home to be with my family.

In 1992 after seven years at the youth training facility, I got thyroid cancer. Within three weeks I had three big lumps sticking out of my neck about goose-egg size. In Nevada unfortunately, racism didn't stop at the hospital-door or at a doctor's office, so the first doctor I went to see hardly looked at me or those lumps and told me: "Oh, these are just water-cysts, don't worry about it." But I could feel they were getting harder and bigger and went back a few times to have him check. So, when he saw me coming again, he said: "I'll prove to you these are not tumors. I can stick a needle in it and pull water out of it. If it's cancer, that won't be possible." So he tried to stick the needle in and nothing came out. He could hardly push it in. He claimed: "Yes, it's cancer, but I can guarantee you that it's probably benign and not malignant." At least I got him to agree on having it tested. When the tests came back from the lab, sure enough, it was a malignant cancer. They also did an X-ray where you could see that it had grown already pretty far inwards as well, coming close to the air pipe. Once it reached it, it would cut off my breathing and be close to important blood vessels. I had to have an operation where they would take out half of my thyroid; there was no other way. Halfway through the operation, the surgeon came out to Sky, who was waiting outside of the operating rooms and told her that the whole thyroid was infected and she had to give permission to take it out totally. So, I ended up with no thyroid at all, which has resulted in life long medication. The thyroid deals with many body functions that affect all the organs, your hormonal and energy system, your heartbeat and sleeping rhythm, to name a few. They had gotten out all the cancer but I needed to be on a thyroid uptake every week just to make sure. After four weeks something was showing again in the X-rays and it was growing fast, going in the direction of the lungs; not all had been taken out and the cancer had returned. Once it would have reached the lungs, the game would have been over, they couldn't do anything anymore. They suggested sending me to St. Mary's Hospital in Reno, specialized in treating people with cancer at this stage, where they would hopefully know how to proceed further. So that's where I went. On a floor sealed off from the rest of the place - I remember it wasn't very hospitable - they did their treatments with heavy radiation. Everything you as a patient used in the bedroom or bathroom was of disposable material. Only one pot with nice fresh flowers stood out as an exception. I was being told to undress for the treatment and got a hospitable gown to put on. My clothes were taken away. Then two men came in the room, both dressed in full radiation-suits from head to toe. I could only see their faces through a mask. They were bringing in a cart with a machine on top with a lead container that must have weighed 150 pounds and a lid to open it up. In there was a very thick ceramic jar and hidden in a small glass tube a radiated liquid was kept. They told me to drink it. I remember I was thinking: "Wait a minute, here are these guys with their protection suits on and there is all this heavy precaution equipment and I'm just sitting half naked on my bed and I should drink this stuff?!" A doctor came in, also dressed in a radiation suit and he told me flat out: "Either you don't drink it and you're going to die in a few weeks, because the cancer is progressing at a high rate direction lungs or you drink this liquid, which has a very high doses of radiation in it and you might have a chance. It's up to you. You can walk out of here and go home and die there, I don't care. This is your choice." What I found out later: the whole so-called treatment was actually an experiment and I had, without being aware of the consequences signed an agreement to participate. They were testing the largest doses of radiation in liquid form they estimated a human body could take without dying immediately. I decided to take it. The moment it touched my tongue, it was like a liquid fire going in and it burned my taste buds on the tongue away. When I swallowed, I could feel it burn all the way down to my stomach. After 45 seconds, black spots were showing on my skin: those are radiation-burns and I started to throw up immediately. I was feeling very sick. The instructions were that I should try eat and drink as much as possible, because the more you do the quicker the radiation would leave my body. But I felt incredibly sick... that was very hard to do. They tested me each day with a pole about 20 ft. long which they pointed at me, whilst standing in the door, and which had a Geiger-counter at the end to measure how radioactive I was. They had one nurse who had no radiation suit on. She had had thyroid cancer herself and they thought at that time, without a thyroid you'd be okay being around radiation, which of course is not true at all. She brought me my food and would also change the flower each day. It stood on a windowsill across the room, but the flower didn't last very long after I had taken the medication. The flower was a morbid indication to look how the radiation-level was affecting other life. I was in there for weeks and they had to wait until the radiation-level had gone down enough in my body. After a week, my hair started to fall out. My hair had been really, really thick, long too, black of course back then. Sky used to say, she had never seen anybody with such thick hair. She could barely grab it and go around it with both her hands. My hair has never grown back that long and thick anymore. It stayed a lot thinner. After four weeks the radiation-level had gone down enough, so I could leave the hospital and go home. But I was told for the next coming months I shouldn't touch my children, because they were young and it could interfere with their growing bones. I should also refrain from going to public places, like restaurants and so on, because that could affect other people without them knowing. Of course, they did check on me every so often and kept doing tests. Two months later, the cancer came back and was going towards my lungs again. I had reached the point where the doctors told me they couldn't do anything for me and I should write my will and go home to die. That's how they left it.

I knew the only other possibility, which I had been ignoring until that point, was my Native Medicine tradition. So, I called up three Medicine persons: one was Corbin Harney, whom I trusted deeply, the next was Johnny Begay, the Peyote Navaho man and another Medicine man from Canada. I explained the situation and they all agreed to come and they came three weekends in a row, while being aware of the fact I had called each one for help. Sometimes Medicine people work in cooperation to try and help someone, but in my case, they came one after the other.

The first weekend the roadman Johnny Begay came and he worked on me all night, praying and practicing medicine in his way. In the morning he told me: "You know, in our way of thinking, all things happening to you, whether it's sickness, disease, accidents or whatever, come to you for a spiritual reason. You know that anyway. The spirits bring this upon you, because they want to teach you something. There is always a lesson to be learned and a change to be made. The spirits told me: "This is happening to you, because you have stopped speaking for the Mother Earth and for the future generations; you have not been following the path you are supposed to follow. That's why your throat is affected, because you stopped speaking. Now you are forced to look at it." The spirits are guiding you into making a change. Each time though a person isn't following the original plan and that person wants to be healed, there is a price to pay, a sacrifice to make. In your case, you need to leave your childhood country, you need to travel north."

For an Indian to do that, that is harder than for most other people. Not only our ancestors are buried on this land, but also our whole culture is connected to the land. The message was very clear though: I had to leave everything behind and go north.

Then the second Medicine man came in, the man from Canada. He worked on me his way and did a lot of singing and drumming all through the night. When morning came, he spoke to me in almost the same wording as what was said to me the week before: I had left the path I was supposed to follow and I had stopped speaking for the Mother Earth and that's why the sickness came to my throat and I had to go north. He didn't know where, just up north.

The third weekend Corbin Harney came and he ordered me to get a strong fire going outside. He told me to bring in the red-hot coals. In the living room, we had a metal pan with a layer of dirt inside, so the coals could rest on top and not burn through. He had somebody help him who changed the coals and bring in new ones. Sky was also present. As he was working on me, Corbin reached for those coals and took a burning hot coal in his hand and started talking to it. Then he put it in his mouth and kept it there for a little while. After taking it out, he started blowing hot air on the spot where my cancer was. I could feel the hot air coming in my body, really hot, although it didn't look like it was affecting Corbin at all. He kept doing this, singing and praying and blowing this hot air on me, each time changing and picking a new one, as soon as the coal became cooler. He did this over and over, all night, never burning or hurting himself once. When morning came, he started telling me the same things the others had told me! It was pretty clear and a strong message from the spirits and not to doubt. Corbin told me to go north, but he was specific:" It has to be Oregon." And I told him: „But I have never been there!" He said: „Me neither, but this is what the spirits told me." And he also said: "For now, the cancer has stopped. If you don't go though and do the things you're supposed to do, it will return."

So, I called up a Comanche friend of mine, whom I knew lived in Salem, Oregon but had never visited. He said: „Yeah, why don't you come up and I'll show you around, take you to some Native people. There are a few tribes in the area we can visit and maybe you can start working for them. I did go to the hospital once more for a checkup for my cancer. They looked at the pictures and told me: "Well, we don't know what has happened, but the

cancer has stopped growing and it seems to have been going in remission!"
Of course I knew it was because what the Medicine People had done for me.

First, I went up north alone and took a plane; I remember when I came
out of the plane and looked around me, my eyes started to hurt, I had to rub
them. You know why that was? I wasn't used to all the green I saw around
me. I had lived in the desert for 40 years and had never seen so much green
in my life! I couldn't believe it. Naturally my eyes adjusted pretty quickly,
but I'll never forget that moment: it was sensational.

My friend took me to different places, to tribal organizations, a boarding
school, drug and alcohol treatment centers, but nothing seemed to feel right.
Then he took me to one of the last possible places: a Native American Youth
Residential Center in Kaiser, right next to Salem, called Nanitch Sahalie.
Native youth from places as far as Alaska, Washington, Nevada, Arizona
and of course Oregon were brought in for treatment. When I walked in, a
guy came up to me and asked if he could help me. I told him, I was curious
what this place was about and he answered, he could not allow me to go
around on my own, because there was a confidentiality-rule. But he started
asking me questions about the real reason of my interest and I told him, I
was looking for a job in Oregon and wanted to do something for my own
people. So, he asked me what I'd done before and told him a little of my life
and the last job I'd done. He was especially interested in my culture and
upbringing, about the ceremonies and how I go about doing certain things
and then said: "You know, I think there is someone here at the facility who
would like to meet you. Would you be willing to talk to him?" I said: "Yes,
of course!" He had me wait on a couch for a few minutes and then he took
me to a room filled with people, half of them Native, half of them white.
I was a little surprised and thought: "What is this about?" They asked me
all kinds of questions, again about my culture, my background. After this
interview I was asked to wait again on the couch for a few minutes. When
he returned from the room he told me: "We want to ask if we can hire

you!" I was amazed, 'cause I hadn't realized I had been in a job interview. He continued: "Let me explain. We run the 12-step program here. This was developed in England by two men in the late 1800's to treat clients with drug and alcohol problems. They wrote a book in which these 12 steps were described. Originally it was against alcohol addiction, as drug addiction wasn't an issue yet. Almost a hundred years later this system is still being used at our center, as in most of the centers all over America, as the tool for treating addictions; nowadays it's called the Blue Book or the Big Book. We have noticed that although this program still works surprisingly well for most people, it doesn't work for our Native youth. We circle around a 30% success rate. The kids can't identify and relate to the program set up for people brought up in a western culture. What is lacking in this program is a Native approach. We have been looking for a solution and want you to help us. We're hoping to bring back a connection to what the kids can relate to as their mutual bond, namely their culture and the old ways. In fact, we think that this loss is part of the reason why so many Native youngsters have turned to alcohol and drugs in the first place. Unfortunately even amongst our own Native workers here at the center, there is hardly any knowledge of that culture left!"

He carried on: "We asked you all those questions to see where you come from and what you could offer us. We are all impressed with the knowledge you carry and what seems to have been a natural thing in your daily life. This could already act as an example in itself for the kids. We are hoping you could, combined with the 12- step program, bring in the cultural aspects and the kids will eventually benefit from this. Do you feel you are willing to give it a try?" I thought about it and said: "Although I don't know what the 12 step program is about, but I am sure you can explain that to me, I don't see a reason why I shouldn't." They could only offer me 7.50 $ per hour on a part-time basis, because they didn't have a job-description for a position like this, so they had to reorganize their budget and create a position for me to step into. They offered to apply to the tribe that was the sponsor of the program to see if a full time job with much better pay could be financed. I counted it through: in Nevada I had earned about 20 bucks an hour and Sky had also had an income of about 15 bucks per hr., which added up to a lot more money. From that money we had bought some land and had put a nice house on it and also had bought our first new vehicle, a minivan. We'd been doing okay. This would be a lot less and it wasn't really possible for us all to live on. I told him: "I have to go back to my family and talk this through." But I knew inside I had been guided here, so I trusted this was the right thing to do.

Back in Nevada I talked to the family about their feelings and they actually came up with different themes than I had anticipated were important to them. They wanted to go to Oregon and see for themselves what it was like over there, how the people were, the kind of school-opportunities and that kind of thing. Money wasn't the main factor. So, we ended up driving to Oregon together and stayed at my friend's house in Salem. One thing we all noticed: wherever we came, we encountered people who were really friendly towards us. In Nevada white people treated us with an attitude of prejudice that all Indians are drunks or "the only good Indian is a dead Indian." Here that wasn't the case, we didn't encounter the racism and discrimination from back home. You didn't need to walk around with this nasty feeling of having to watch your back wherever you went. Our two oldest were in their teens and said: "Here we have the feeling we are being treated for what we are inside, not for what we look like on the outside!" They felt so happy: it was a relief and something they had never thought of as possible. Besides they loved that everything was so green!

We all knew what the Medicine men had said about my path and the journey I had to undertake, so we put our trust in that. Both Sky and I quit our jobs, we sold the car for a lot less than we had paid for and also gave our house to a young white family, whom we knew well, who had been living in a trailer home and had never been able to make enough money to buy land or a house. We told them: "If you are able to make the down payments for the house each month, we'll sign it over to you." Basically, we gave up everything we had and hired a truck to put all our furniture and stuff in and drove over to Oregon: this time to stay and start all over again. I took the job at Nanitch Sahalie and found a house to rent. Sky is a certified teacher, but there had just been big lay-offs in the teaching area, so she couldn't get any job there. Pretty soon, we realized that we couldn't make ends meet and we had to find a solution. So, I took on two more jobs, one was working for the police at the gang-surveillance department and another at a juvenile correctional- center, similar to what I had been working at in Carlin. I got about three to four hours sleep a night and did this for about seven months. Finally, the Grand Ronde Tribe, which the treatment center was linked to, agreed to give me a full-time position with benefits.

Let me explain a bit more on the history of indigenous tribes and their tribal lands in the modern age in order to let you understand the financial situation of the Grand Ronde Tribe.

In 1953, the US government had passed a law, which affected a lot of Native tribes all over the United States. It was a policy called the "Termination Act," which allowed them to unrecognize and disband certain tribes and even kick them off their tribal lands. In Oregon this was going on during the 40s and 50s and Oregon is actually the state where tribes were terminated most in comparison to the other states in America. All in all, I think there were only two tribes the government didn't interfere with. You can understand that people were traumatized deeply: tribes were disbanded, land was taken; they weren't even recognized as Native people anymore and didn't get any compensation whatsoever and were left with nothing. In the 70s and 80s, a lot of the Native people got organized in much better ways and learned more about their legal possibilities. They realized what had been done to them in the past was actually against their treaty rights. They started to go to the court systems to fight this and get some of their rights and land back. Although they did win, in most cases they only received small portions of their original land. The Grand Ronde tribe used to have a reservation that covered many thousands of acres. After going to Court, they only got about 120 acres returned, but it encompassed their old graveyard where the ancestors were buried. They said to themselves: "This is where we can start again!" But basically, it was a start from nothing; no houses or buildings were left. They did the best they could and over the years were slowly recovering. They applied for financial support from Indian Funding that helped them with financing some of the rebuilding. When I came to live in Oregon, the tribe had just been re-established for seven or eight years, and they had also built the treatment center for Native youth where I ended up working from the money from Indian Funding. Obviously after they had been disbanded for all those years, they didn't know much about their own heritage and their ceremonies. After I had been working there for a few years, they wanted to make an effort to rebuild the cultural and spiritual identity of the tribe.

They called upon a well-known Medicine man from Canada with whom a special sweat lodge ceremony was planned for the tribal members in order to get some spiritual guidance on how to approach this. Because I was an employee for the tribe, I was also invited to come to the ceremony, although I wasn't a tribe member. They built a special lodge for the occasion, which was huge because they wanted everybody to join in. I think we had about five rounds of people sitting in circles behind each other and it totaled around 75 people. They decided to use one stone for each person, which meant there were 75 stones to be heated up. Usually you have 24 stones or maybe up to 30 stones, but I had never been in a lodge with so many stones. We ended up being in the sweat lodge for more than six hours, more than double the usual time. The heat was extreme: it was a grill and a really good sweat. There were a lot of prayers and a lot of singing. Since then the

Grand Ronde tribe has really been growing strong in its ways again. It was a helpful, positive ceremony.

One of the first things I decided on was building a sweat lodge right on our premises, which were surrounded by other building-complexes, as we were in an urban area. We asked for permission from the fire department and everything was okayed. I also came in to do a sunrise ceremony every so often. I'd put a sage bowl by the restaurant. When kids wanted to, they could sage themselves before eating. We also started saying prayers over our food.

I aimed to have elders come in to speak and work with them, but it took some time before I got permission from the board. Another difficulty I faced was because of the strict confidentiality measures towards the privacy of the kids, every person I'd invite was obliged to sign papers to ensure that no data, no names or anything about the persons inside the center would ever leak out. Bill White Eagle, an incredible craftsman who did beautiful beadwork and made baskets, came in twice a week for craft work classes. The materials were paid for from a small budget they gave me. We also had movie-night once a week, where we had Native movies playing, which we started collecting. I knew of another Native elder, Chet Clark, who was a very well-known drummer and singer who went around the different reservations to teach. So, we hired him to come in once a week. After a while, he got company from a couple of Native lead dancers who taught round dances, grass dancing and other different styles of traditional dancing. Each time we cleared out the cafeteria to make room, and anybody who wanted could join, but nobody was forced to do anything they didn't want to participate in. We even had a Native woodcarver whom they finally allowed to teach and work with the kids, since the kids had to use sharp and pointy knives. We had to put a lot of trust in them to be using the knives in a safe way, not hurting themselves or another person. Because they made such cool things with it, like rattles and so on, they took responsibility for each other when maybe one of them started to act up while handling the knife. They corrected each other during the process, so to speak. I had explained that if there were an accident or even an incident, this part of the program would immediately be stopped. They did beautifully and nothing ever happened in all those years.

We had storytellers coming in and along the way I even got permission to bring in Native people who had been in prison, occasionally part of a gang, but had found the Red Road which helped bring them back on track. These people have a lot to share, very personal stories with heavy and impressive content, something young ones can relate to and learn from as an example at the same time.

Sky also applied at the treatment center and worked as a teacher in the school. She was able to get them to read books on Native issues and from Native writers who had made positive contributions to their culture instead of always hearing negative information about failures and such. We were able to get funding to buy books and she started collecting, thus creating a small library. We also collected tapes with Indian music or in some cases taught some of the indigenous tongues. Many of the kids couldn't speak their Native language anymore; usually it had been lost already the generation before. So, all of this together brought some of the culture back to life. After a few years of working there, the white administrator, who'd hired me, retired and a Lakota man, Bob Ryan, followed, who was extremely fond of what we did and gave us more funding to support this.

Sky came up with the idea of creating an outdoor-school where the kids would be taught things directly out in nature. She was allowed to take them away from the property. Eventually we had a kind of vision quest week once a year, where we'd camp out with them and they could experience nature. Remember, a lot of these young ones were really city-kids who had never been out in nature much, so sleeping outside in the hills in the forest was already an adventure. When they came to the end of their treatment, we would take the whole group out for four to five days. I had a friend, an elder, who was a friend of mine, Calvin Hecota. He was a mix from different tribes and a good activist, advocating for indigenous people and for the traditional way of life. Together we worked on a program of what to offer the kids in those couple of days. He had the idea of taking them to a place called Opal Creek, which is in an old growth forest in a National Park where you had to park your car a little way out. After a five-mile hike, you reached a cabin where you could stay overnight. There were two creeks flowing there, closely surrounded by huge trees: a wonderful and strong energy. We were even allowed to put up two sweat lodges, which was doubly effective being built in nature and having more time available before and after the sweat, thus offering a deeper impact of the experience. We also took them on long hikes into the forest and taught them to introduce themselves to an area before entering; they learned what talking and listening to nature means, to the water, the rocks, to pay attention. It was such a blessing for them. We taught them if they wanted to take a stone, a shell or anything basically from the forest back home with them, it was considered appropriate to talk to the stone or shell, explaining you were planning to separate it from its family, and ask if it would like to come along with you. We don't just take things home to collect, as they are living beings and so you communicate with them.

One day, Calvin took us on a deer trail and we reached a massive cedar tree, which eight people could wrap their arms around to fully encircle it. He said it was probably more than 2000 years old. It was the Grandmother Tree of that forest, one of the biggest trees I have ever seen, extremely beautiful.

It wasn't possible to pull through a true vision quest in the sense the indigenous people have always practiced on Turtle Island. These kids had too many issues, so it wasn't possible to have them on no food or water for four days. But it was a start and gave them a strong experience of Nature within our cultural tradition.

One of the nicest experiences I recall that moved me personally was at an early morning sweat lodge we did. We had two separate sweats going at the same time, but used the same fireplace for both of them. It was right above one of the riversides, a really beautiful spot. Almost all of them, all boys -- Calvin and I took the male youth out and Sky and another woman took the girls -- were joining in, starting at four o'clock. We each conducted our own ceremony and began with our ceremonial singing and drumming. It was magically timed as we both opened the flaps of the lodges at the exact same time, coming out of the dark and right at that moment, the sun was rising and shone its first golden rays straight into the lodges. Really incredible and such a blessing for all of us involved, a true and peaceful awakening for a new start in life.

With setting up this cultural program that was embedded in Native traditions, our success-rate became 88% over the years, which is exceptionally high. It was quite impressive and I was proud to have been part of it. At one point we had people coming from other tribal treatment centers in the area and we became an example for incorporating the same principals in their programs.

One day after I had already worked at the center several years, a group from the Siletz-tribe, one of the local coastal tribes in the area close to our treatment center, came to visit and asked for me.

Many of their youth had gone through our cultural program and they had witnessed the positive difference in how they returned home. They wanted to meet me, as I was the one who had initiated it and had put in all the work, and wanted to honor me for what I had done for their youth. They presented gifts to me like a blanket and other things, but the most special gift was a walrus tooth. To their people the walrus is sacred, has special power and represents strength. The walrus had been the main meat supply for the coastal tribes of the North West. They used its hides for clothing and warmth. Many things came from the walrus. You can compare it to what the buffalo meant for the Plains Indians. I felt so honored that they gave this to me. Right there I knew I was going to make a necklace out of it. Whenever a Native person makes some kind of jewelry, like beadwork or a bracelet, earrings or a necklace, this is done with purpose and meaning behind it. You want to express something personal with it and it explains something about you or where it comes from. You don't just make it pretty and nice looking but you want to tell a story. So, when I made the necklace, I thought about what my life had been like up to that point, and chose every bead and every bone with deliberate meaning. I got the gift more than 20 years ago and I have worn it ever since. Some years ago, I restrung it some because I felt I needed to make a change to have it represent where my life had taken me in the meantime. Over the years it has been with me on many special occasions, been around ceremonies all over the world and I feel it carries a lot of that energy. The way we put it, it has a lot of good Medicine.

Why I was so touched by this gift also had to do with the fact that my working with so many native youth with such a positive outcome also reflected my satisfaction about it. It gave me a good feeling to see this transition happen in young people. It made me happy inside and on top of that, I was glad to be appreciated for it.

You have to know that when the kids are released from the center, they go back to their communities and you lose contact with them. They will get support from a social worker or somebody else in the tribe, but there is not supposed to be any contact between the center and the released persons. Very often I did get letters thanking me for what I had done and how they felt I had cared about them. It felt really great to be able to do something for my own people, which had such positive impact. Honestly, I would have even worked there for free! Only I did have to make a living somehow as well, so it was nice I did get paid. It was the other way around actually: I was getting paid and at the same time I was able to help Native youth, do craftwork and ceremonies at work. I was very grateful I got the opportunity to meet all these people from Oregon, get in touch and connect with Native elders, learn from them and share where I came from.

That walrus tooth represented it all, besides being so sacred to the people of the area. Now that I lived in the North West, the tooth made that connection to Nature and Spirit possible. Oregon had become my second home.

My cancer has been in remission ever since. I have seen doctors in Oregon too -- they were a lot friendlier up here -- and had my check-ups. They all couldn't really explain why my cancer had all of a sudden stopped growing after all the treatments had failed to work. They went into some theories about a delayed effect maybe of the radiation therapy. One doctor, when I tried to explain what in my point of view had caused the healing, reacted with: "Oh no, let's not go there, that's a nice story, this so called faith healing, but that is not for real!" So I left it at that but in my understanding this was truly what turned it around. I had followed what the Medicine Men had told me and started walking the Red Road again.

By working at Nanitch Sahallie, I did all the ceremonies, the smudging, the drumming and singing again and I had run into a lot of elders I could work with. Privately my family and I also were engaged in our culture. We joined the Inter-tribal Dance group of Salem, Oregon. I got to meet many Natives from the different areas and tribes around, also from the boarding school close by. I noticed that some of the Native organizations did a lot of good work, but none of them ever worked together. So, I came up with the idea of creating a network where representatives from all those different groups and tribes could meet once a month and discuss how we could support each other. Bob Ryan, the administrator of the treatment center, got very enthused by the idea and very generously offered us the meeting room. I set it up; called all those tribal organizations and explained how I believed it was very important for those young ones to give them a good example of cooperation and for the elders to share, and we'd be able to join resources to help each other and become stronger together. They all agreed and we started meeting. We kept notes all those years, but I did come to realize that although they were willing to join, it was necessary to remind them of the meeting a few days before, otherwise they would have forgotten about it. After I left the treatment center and also stopped organizing the meetings, they soon fell apart. Unfortunately the treatment center is closed now, due to tribal politics within the Grand Ronde Tribe and is dearly missed. No replacement is in sight either, which saddens my heart.

The Basket Story

This true story happened in Oregon, where the university of Portland wanted to organise a course in traditional basket weaving for its students.

They were searching for a Native elder, so they asked around amongst the Native people in the area, for someone suitable to teach these skills. After some time, they found out there was an elderly woman living on a reservation in eastern Oregon, who was known to make the most beautiful Indian baskets, and so they drove all the way to her home. They asked if she would be willing to give this specific course of basket weaving at their university. She told them: "Well, first of all, in my tradition, when you come to someone you don't know and you want something from them, you bring some tobacco. You tell the tobacco what your intention is." And she explained its special gift. "Tobacco to us," she told them, "is a sacred plant, which is very sensitive to the energy of a person. When you hold the tobacco in your hand it cannot only hear your words, it can also tell what is in your heart. So, if you bring me tobacco, I will talk and listen to the tobacco and learn about your intentions."

The men left and did what she said. They bought some tobacco, telling it what they wanted from the woman and went back again to give her the tobacco. She said: "Come back in three days, after that I will know if what you want from me is what I am willing to do for you. I'll be able to see where your hearts are truly at." So, they agreed and came back after three days. The woman gave them the answer: "Yes, I will teach your class, but on one condition. I will only do it, if I can do it my way, the way I was taught long ago." The people from the university were glad, because this was exactly what they had hoped for, to have a course in basket weaving in the traditional Native manner.

Everything was set up for the course, and in a few weeks, they had a room ready with chairs for 20 students and one for the Native elder. The woman traveled all the way up to Portland and started her first day of the basket-weaving course. She introduced herself to the students and told them how they were going to proceed. "This first day," she said, "I am going to teach you a song and for today we are going to sing just that." Of course, the students had no idea why they were going to sing a song and what it had to do with basket weaving, but the whole first day of their class time, they were learning to sing a song, over and over again. The next day, she told them: "Today I am going to teach you another song, a new song." And so that second day they were learning another song and they sang it all class long, over and over again, the same song. When the third day came, from the 20 chairs quite a few were empty now as some students felt she really wasn't teaching them about basket making. She told the students: "Well today, I am going to teach you another song." And sure enough, they sang another song during the whole class, over and over again. On the fourth day, half of the seats were empty and she taught the remaining students one more song, which they sang all day long again. Finally, on the fifth day, she told them: "Now we are ready and we go and gather the material for the weaving of the baskets. Still, the students had no idea why they had had to learn all these songs. They went out on the land where willows grow and she explained: "Before we go and gather the willows, we will give them a tobacco-offering and give thanks through prayer for they will become part of our baskets. We will sing the song we have learned on the first day, during the time we will gather. We will take the willows to our classroom and strip them of the smaller twigs and soak them in water, so they become bendable and smooth and we can work with them. During all that time, we will sing our song to them." So that is what they did. The next day, they went out to a marshy area where they searched for reeds used for basket weaving. And they repeated what had happened the day before, only this time they sang another song, especially for the reeds, to give thanks and to honour the plants. This went on for two more days, with two different plants and the two other songs they had learned the previous days.

Finally, the day had come they were actually going to start making the baskets. They had gathered all the material they needed, but she gave them one more instruction: "I want you, during the whole time you are making the baskets, to sing to the plants we gathered. I don't care which song you choose, as long as you sing to them." So that is what the students did and beautiful baskets were made. "Now," she said," I want you to hold up your baskets and really look at them and tell me what you see..."

The students spoke about how beautiful the baskets were, about the wonderful colours, the shape and what they resembled.

The elderly woman said to them: "This is not what I see. I see all the prayers and the songs you sang while making them have gone into the baskets. It was brought into reality in the shape of a basket. It is prayer and song brought into form. If you only produce a basket, it stays just a basket. If you sing and pray to it, during the whole time you are making it, you put all this good energy, thoughts and heartfelt attention in it. A person who looks at such a basket or touches it will sense this good energy. When they put objects into the baskets, those things take on some of that energy too. That is why these baskets are so special."

First trip to Europe

Growing up I was taught how to treat elders in the traditional way. You approach them with a specific attitude of humbleness and respect and you are in service to them. There are many different little things you need to be aware of. One of the things you should always try to do is go out of your way to help whenever an elder is in need of something. You do not want to disappoint an elder. You do not ask twice, even if you don't like what is being asked of you. You respect what is being asked and you can't really say yes or no. When elders came to visit our house, they started noticing I was aware of those ways and were pleased about it. I always made sure I'd take care of the physical needs of an elder, wouldn't disturb when they were talking to each other and only speak when I was asked.

Grandfather Semu Huaute, who was in his early seventies and whom my family had known for a long time, was asked to come to Europe for a month-long festival in Vienna, the capital of Austria, on an island in the Danube river, which runs through the city. It was called "the Discover Life Festival" and a lot of indigenous people from all over the world were invited to be present. Semu was asked to be one of the main speakers on one of the outdoor stages twice a day for an hour. Performances of all kind, dances and music were planned, next to healers who would show their skills and workshops you could attend.

Although his wife, who was about 20 years younger, would also accompany Grandfather Semu, he wanted to have somebody extra along on this trip who could help take care of him in the appropriate way. He thought: "Mm, maybe Mala can come along since he was taught how to be around an elder in the traditional way. I know his family very well, so this feels good." He suggested the idea to my father, wanting to ask him first and see if he was okay with it. My father agreed, but he anticipated that if Semu would just ask me, I would bluntly say no, since I had an irrational fear of going to Europe. My experience with white people had not been very positive. Living in Nevada, I had witnessed much racism, hatred and bad treatment, both physically and emotionally, such that I hardly trusted any white person. I thought to myself: "The white people who came to America a long time ago are the ones who escaped religious persecutions and poor conditions to find a better life over here and are supposed to be the good ones. How on earth are the ones who stayed over in Europe going to be?! They must be even worse! That is madness: if I go over there and meet them, I will surely not survive!"

A few times before I had been asked to come along to Europe and I had always responded with a "no thanks." But an open invitation isn't a request from an elder. My father knew if I was going to be specifically asked to help an elder, I would not be able to refuse. He explained to Semu that he should phrase it specifically and so Semu asked me: "Hey Mala, I really need your help on this trip to Europe. I want you by my side. Can you come?" My heart sank when I heard that and I swallowed hard, but with great hesitation I agreed to come. I remember I thought: "Well, at least I already know my death song!" I was so terrified and so convinced I would not survive that trip that I felt I probably would end up having to sing that song over there. I had been really building a fear up in my mind, which worsened when I saw some people coming back from trips who had gotten sick shortly thereafter. One even died from a heart attack. I wasn't convinced at all.

I ended up going to Austria, living in a little village called Gablitz in the hills near Vienna. We slept in an old building, which had a little courtyard in the middle with a patch of grass and an old oak tree in the middle. There was another American guy staying with us who was responsible for recording. After sunrise ceremony by the tree we went looking for some breakfast on our first morning in Europe together. I knew Grandfather Semu would want to sleep in and have a good rest after the long travel, so I didn't need to take care of him yet. We walked into the village and realized pretty soon there was nothing similar to a restaurant or anything. The people on the streets could hardly speak any English, but at some point, there was a man who pointed us towards a small back alley, which looked a little suspicious, being all narrow and dark. We reluctantly walked down the dead-end alley, which offered no way of escape and I already pictured some kind of a trap at the end, but we ended up at a sign saying: "Bar" on it. A man just came out of the bar and we asked him if we could also get something to eat over there. Clearly not sober and not speaking any English, we managed through sign language to state our point and he assured us to go inside for food. The lady behind the counter also didn't understand a word of English but she had us sit down in a separate room. We expected to be handed some kind of menu, but everything was handled very different over here. We had to wait and the lady came back with a huge metal plate with all kinds of cold meats on it, like salami, ham and such, and some slices of bread. She puts it down and says in German: "Breakfast!" It was not the American breakfast we had expected, but it fulfilled its purpose and filled our stomachs. I had just survived my first European breakfast and was happy to return to my room without being robbed or trapped in that little obscure alley, although I was still very worried about the festival and everything else.

Someone picked us up and we headed to the Danube Island, a recreational, open area inside the borders of Vienna in between two riverbeds. We were instructed how things would proceed and Semu did his talks on the big stage for a few days. He asked me to assist him with drumming in the background while he spoke, which sounded quite nice. I was beginning to relax a little, because everything seemed to run smoothly and the people were friendly too. But unfortunately, after a few days Grandfather Semu got sick with a heavy flu, so it was impossible for him to continue with the talks. He called me into his room and told me: "You know we came over here to raise money for the camp we are planning to build for our people. We really need this money. I want you to take over." I had always said I didn't want to be doing any talks. I had traveled with my dad and other Native speakers and knew enough about the stress they were under and how demanding it was. It was really not my thing at all. Never had I had any ambition in that direction. But here I was again; I couldn't refuse since I was asked to help out. There just was no choice. I realized that maybe the spirits thought it was time to teach me a lesson and I had to overcome the resistance inside of me. I had never spoken before myself, but I had condemned it with a lot of emotion. I had to be able to look beyond my own fears. I thought: "It is not about what I want or don't want. This is about what is needed and asked of me. I need to continue this for the sake of my people. I don't know what I am going to say, but I have to go for it."

The next day, I explained to the organizers of the festival what the problem was and that with their permission I was going to speak instead of Semu. It was a strange moment for me to get up on the big stage alone, speaking to all those people who were expecting an elder Indian to speak instead of me. The stage was at the bottom of a hill, it was a natural amphitheater and the audience was sitting on earth-and-grass benches on the hill. On top of it, there was a tree, which caught my eye very clearly while I was down there explaining the situation. I didn't feel comfortable up on that stage at all with everybody staring at me. I tried to talk but the words didn't flow. After a while, I said: "You know, this doesn't feel right. I am willing to share about my ways, but I would like to sit by that tree up there. You are welcome to sit with me on the Mother Earth in a circle and we'll continue from there." About 100 to 200 people followed me and that first time a big crowd sat around me. All of a sudden it felt good and easy to talk. I didn't really know what to talk about, but I just thought I could share about my life and how I was brought up. That's what I did for an hour and the people liked it. The next time, there were a lot of the same faces and some new ones. All in all, I had good attendance. Of course, it wasn't so suitable for a big crowd to gather in a setting like the one I chose to be in, but I figured it was more natural and fitting to my personality. So, I was happy that there was still a regular turnout of 30 to 40 people coming and listening to me every day. Unfortunately, Semu didn't get well quickly enough and as the festival continued, I kept on doing the talks.

One day a special thing happened. I was waiting for the talk to start and looked up the hill. There were lots of people coming through. The festival really was a big thing. Most all the performances were done open-air, free of charge. The Danube Island is an area open to everyone, all kinds of people commuting through on bikes and on roller skates. Some were interested, some just passing by. My attention was drawn to a woman standing in the middle of the crowd, a bicycle in her hand, talking to someone. All of a sudden, the crowd faded into darkness and the only thing I saw was a light surrounding this woman and at the same time radiating from her. It was one of those moments you could call magic, a moment with spiritual significance since it was strong and unexpected. All I knew was that it was a special connection and this person would have some kind of impact on my life. In our way, we don't push for things to happen, we wait for it to flow and I decided to see what would happen next. The following day, she came to my talk and sat in the circle. I knew immediately it was the same woman, although from the distance where I had noticed her the first time, I hadn't been able to see her clearly. After she had come for a few days in a row, I approached her and asked her to come for a walk. She came along and we talked while sitting on a little playground. She told me she had only moved to Vienna recently, about half a year ago, together with her husband and son. She originally came from the Netherlands. And that is how Hermine and I met. The vision I had of her on that hill turned out to be the start of a deep, long-lasting, heartfelt connection between us with many teachings for both of us, culminating in our partnership in writing this book. Our families met many times too, and visited back and forth. And I am happy to this day that it turned out we met.

During the time of the festival I met a lot of people, who partly invited me to do some talks for them in other places. I got a lot of positive response for what I did and how I did it. It was the beginning of my becoming a speaker. I felt more and more comfortable up to the point later in my life where I really came to love it, and it became a part of my identity and purpose in life. I was invited back to Europe on my own, as well as accompanying other elders. My initial fear and anguish over the Europeans turned into a great appreciation of their openness and interest in our culture. I realized I had gotten into a judgmental state where I stereotyped Europeans as being cruel and violent, just as much as the white people had stigmatized us Natives in Nevada. I had thought that the behavior of a few people from a certain group was a reflection of the group as a whole, which was a huge misperception. It was an important lesson for me to realize I also had an issue with prejudice; it had never dawned on me that I could have prejudices as well!

I felt lucky to have met many good people and have befriended many of them. For almost 20 years I have been traveling over to Europe, sometimes staying for a few months at a time and each time I feel welcomed and at home.

Being a Speaker

Whenever I do a talk or speak in front of people, I like to let people know that I never prepare anything in advance like a speech or something. I explain that I come and talk from the heart. Speaking from the heart means you only talk about what is true for you, what you believe in, what is natural and important to you. How the talk develops depends on my own state and where my heart is at and of course also depends on the people I talk to, because we influence each other with our energies. I always hope I can reach people in their hearts, that if I share something about my way of living, of my tradition, of my culture that might shine a light upon issues in a slightly new way. In return I hope to take something home from the people sharing with me and to learn from other ways.

Mala at the Danube Island in Vienna doing a talk (1995)

We start a gathering by lighting some sage to begin in a good and positive way. We ask the sage to help us clear the room, the space we are in but also to cleanse our own energies, our thoughts and feelings, so that we can be together in a good way. We pray to the sage to help us with its gift and pray to the Creator as well.

I always ask for permission to burn the sage, so nobody is offended or feeling uncomfortable with it, because when I go somewhere new, I want to make sure I respect the customs from over there. I say: "You see, I am in your home. When you are in my home, I also like to be respected in my ways. This has been the case in America where we have been told to do and believe certain things, different from what we were used to. We were forbidden to do it our way actually, so it is important not to repeat that behavior when I come here as a guest in your home."

We always make sure that a window is open, so that negative energy may leave the room.

When I start my prayer, it could be something like this:

"Oh, Great Spirit, Father Sun, Grandmother Moon, Mother Earth, we pray to you. Sacred sage we pray to you. We are asking you to be with us at this moment, to help us and guide us in your ways. We are asking to use your gift to help take away any negative energy, bad spirits, bad feelings and thoughts within us or within this room. May it leave and not come back to bother us, so we can be here with an open mind, an open heart and spirit, to learn from each other, to share with one another. Help us to have a good time together and put a good layer of protection around us so that harmful things do not come to us. Help us to learn from our mistakes in order to grow and become better human beings for the future generations, become better caretakers for the Mother Earth and for the life that is here now. Help us to work together as brothers and sisters, to be able to share through a kind

and open heart, in a healing way, not in a hurtful way. Help us
to look beyond the differences that separate us and learn how
we can use those differences in ways that strengthen us. We pray
that whatever we may learn today, we will take this to become
better human beings. We give you thanks for those gathered in
this circle and we pray they will also have a safe trip home when
it is time to leave.

I pray for these things only when they are good and meant
to be. To all my relations, aho."

The other thing that we usually do when we gather is to make everyone
feel welcome. We like to sing a song called the "Welcome Song." Each song
has its own energy and this one is to welcome those at the gathering, but
also to welcome in the good energies, to invite good spirits, our ancestors,
to welcome the nature. It's important to picture this in your heart when
you sing. This gives it strength and direction. Your heart has much power
in it and when you picture what the song is about, you give power to the
meaning of the song, besides giving it a sense of direction. Everyone present is asked to join in the singing or you can also just picture this image of
the song in your heart and how it goes out to everything and everybody.

The song has four verses, each verse for one of the four directions. This
number is sacred in Native culture: there are the four directions -- east,
north, west and south -- the four seasons and the four colors of mankind.

There are a lot of differences between the indigenous approaches to life
and how things are seen in the Western culture and this also shows in how
we speak and how we understand things. One of the things I always seem to
encounter is that I seem to take things literally. In my culture it is considered
normal when you say something that you also act upon this. There are no
maybes and second thoughts. You act the way you speak. How you speak

comes from the way you think and what you believe in. You speak the way you think and feel. This is a literal and direct way.

It doesn't mean we don't like to joke. We joke a lot and we fool around. We try to do it in a respectful way though. We do not make use of sarcasm so much or speak in a cynical manner. It also doesn't mean that we constantly share our thoughts or feelings at every moment. I was taught that if asked, I could share my thoughts in the best way possible and this means to be honest but always respectful. It is not appropriate to burden other people with your own feelings and problems. You only share when it is asked for and necessary.

Another thing that is very different in the indigenous culture is that it is considered very rude to stare someone directly in the eye. We see this as pushing our energy upon the other person. If we truly trust someone, like a family member, our children or our partners, then we can look deeply into their eyes. But in the West, I was told that if you don't look somebody in the eye, this could actually hint that you are lying or trying to hide something. This is a good example of how misunderstandings are created between people. When an indigenous person speaks to you, you may notice the person will briefly look at you and then quickly look away. This pattern repeats while we are talking to each other. This is how we are taught to behave respectfully and to not push our energy upon the other person.

I don't consider myself a good speaker. My dad did an incredible job, being able to capture his audience and really turn people around in their way of thinking. The way he spoke had impact, no matter what your opinion on the matter was. He had a special way of saying things and people almost went into trance just listening to him. He would weave such a lively picture that people went along in those images. When we still lived in Nevada, my father went on extended speaking tours. If it wasn't too far away, a group of people accompanied him by van. We'd bring one of our big drums and play softly in the background while he was speaking. Sometimes one of us would be asked to also say something. I usually declined when he asked me. I never wanted to be a speaker like he was, as I had seen over the years how strenuous that life was. He did his speaking tours besides his regular job with which he earned his money and was on the road all the time. In the beginning my mother would join him once in a while, but she preferred to stay at home, doing the things she felt a calling for. She wanted to be available for counseling people who needed help and advice. They both had so much going on in their lives and hardly had any private life. It was basically a life of service.

He spoke at universities, at people's private homes, for some tribes and for certain organizations that invited us, just wherever we were asked. It was mostly about political issues: Native rights, AIM (American Indian Movement), the Leonard Peltier case[19] and such.

My perception on being a speaker was that it was a hard task. My dad used to explain the ins and outs of it to me. Speaking itself is one thing, but afterwards people from the audience usually want to talk to you. Especially when they have put you on a pedestal, they ask for extra attention. All these things I didn't like. I just wanted a simple life, working and living with my family, doing things that were needed but not out there in front. The work with Meta Tantay already fulfilled me and I thought it was a good enough contribution to help my people. I just didn't see myself as a leader being in the center.

You have to remember I grew up with the prophesies on what I was supposed to do. I'd gotten tired of being told how to live my life and what I

---

19 **Leonard Peltier,** born in 1944, North Dakota, U.S.), American Indian (mostly Ojibwa) activist who, after becoming one of the best-known indigenous rights activists in North America, was convicted in 1977 of having murdered two FBI agents. His case became a cause célèbre after the irregularities in his extradition and trial came to light, and his supporters consider him a political prisoner.

was meant to do with my gifts. My father was very set in his ways and could be dominant towards others, especially with his family. It was not easy to step up against him and follow your own choice. I knew inside that I was being resistant to things that came from him and stubbornly said to myself: "Well, the speaking is my father's thing and I'm not going in that direction!" When I came to Europe, this was the trigger for me to change my attitude towards being a speaker. Creation had something else in mind for me.

What I do know and have also been told is: I may not be a fancy talker but when I speak to people, I speak from the heart: people feel this and that is how the connection is made.

Heart and Emotion

I would like to explain something that is very often confused. When I speak of the energy of the heart, this is not to be mixed up with emotions that stir you up.

Emotions like fear or anger are usually amplified by our way of thinking, coming from our insecurities and a lack of control. Let me explain: there might be a situation of misunderstanding and we feel uncertain; we respond in wanting to control the situation with strategies and thoughts; when this fails it leads to anger or accentuates the original fear.

The heart energy is a more pure and real connection to what is and not something we think in our minds. The heart connects us to Creation, Mother Earth and Spirit. It is direct and not about our concept of the world. Human perception of reality and human concepts both change as we travel and evolve through time. Nature works according basic laws that do not change. Water flows, the sun shines, the tides rise and fall, birds fly, fish swim and animals jump, crawl, run or whatever they do. Certain things happen in ways that will always stay the same.

When Native people drum and sing, we use the heart energy to give the song purpose and direction. There is a feeling of warmth and radiance that comes out and we direct it. This is not connected so much to our emotions, as those come and go. This pure heart energy is steady, gives faith and a sense of belonging and connection. The power of the heart energy is immense and yet we neglect it and instead depend on our mind and brain energy. Even the emotion we call love becomes confused and mixed with expectations and isn't always as pure as we'd like it to be. Attraction can be mistaken for love and sometimes an interpretation of love grows out of feelings of insecurity and self-doubt, which leads to dependency. True, infinite love is of another dimension and quality.

When human beings are born, they bring a history along that carries a certain amount of fear and anger coming from unfinished business from previous earth visits if you go along with the concept of reincarnation, destiny or family genetics. This results in different personalities. The way we are taught how to deal with emotions depends on our culture and upbringing. Often patterns develop that are guided by the mind and unfortunately strengthen those emotions in a negative spiral. Sometimes traumas worsen a situation; sometimes experiences diminish the negative emotions and you are able to overcome them. I think the heart energy is the key for that healing to happen.

The way I was taught is that you are born into circumstances, which are optimum for your growth and development. It might be an easy and smooth running life; it might be a difficult and challenging life. At first, those emotions like anger, fear, sorrow, or jealousy may grow, but you have the possibility of choice and might change for the better once you learn to deal with them in a different and positive way. Trying to become a better human being is something you can best do from the heart. It means you are gentle on yourself and not judgmental, because that again would be your mind telling you what to do. If you are gentle and patient while striving to become better at or aiming to overcome, this is the best approach, as it will allow you to make steps towards joy and peace.

When we speak about living from the heart, it doesn't mean you just express all your feelings freely all the time. Like I said before, feelings come and go, and you shouldn't give them too much power and react to them all the time. You don't want to suppress them, but you should be aware your feelings affect all forms of life around you. When the emotions are negative, it is best to learn to channel them away from others and understand where they come from or how they have accumulated over time, especially if your reactions result in destructive behavior. You shouldn't underestimate how your unfiltered emotions can be hurtful to others.

Mind gives emotion its power, although feelings don't necessarily originate in the mind. The emotion triggers a memory and a certain pattern in your mind responds to it. Negative emotions live from the attention you give them, so you can choose to act differently. When you are afraid of something, you are giving it power over you. The feeling of fear overcomes you and takes your personal power away. If you keep focusing on the fear, you will only make it stronger. You need to understand how this system of action and reaction functions. You have to deliberately change your mind-set, which feeds on the fear. Then you start to practice focusing on something else, so the fear diminishes and instead your confidence grows. Find a positive way of thinking and you'll have a different turnout. One possibility is you start singing: when you sing, your way of thinking changes and it will automatically distract you from focusing on the fear of what you think might happen. You can pray and talk to Creation and ask for help and protection, so you are guided in a good way to overcome whatever you are afraid of. If you visualize how the help actually comes, the fear will -- as you focus on something else -- go away; besides you are now focusing on something that brings your own personal power back. Break through the automatic habit of giving in to the fear and giving it extra power and energy, and the result will be quite satisfactory.

If you feed your fear or anger too much, it can actually overpower you and you will no longer be acting consciously anymore. You are then overwhelmed by your emotion. Of course, this takes practice and we are humans on a learning journey. As you grow older, you will come to understand how your responses are and how much you are able to guide them with wisdom and clarity or how much you are directed by those emotions and thoughts.

The following is a simple example of how you can deal with anger. If you get angry, your physical body gets tight and your muscles harden. Usually your head goes down and the anger really builds up inside of you, taking more and more of your energy. The elders told me that is when the anger-spirit is taking over. Native Americans understand that emotional states like fear or anger carry spiritual energy. Changing this can be done with a simple trick: look up and straighten your back and shoulders. It doesn't matter where you look; just make sure the energy isn't stuck inside you but is flowing. The tension will release and the anger no longer gets the chance to grow. You change the flow of the energy physically and after this you can work on it more easily on an emotional or mental level as well.

Although fear is sometimes tied to very old patterns that we are somehow unwilling to let go of, you can use the same principle. As soon as you notice fear starting to build up, try letting it flow, concentrate on something positive and change the energy of that fear-spirit. Of course, fear can also be something useful. An adrenaline-based fear when you encounter a danger of some kind is necessary and can be life-saving. In that case, it is more of a warning and makes us watch out and be careful. You have to discern though when the fear turns into something that sticks with you and pops up when there is no need. Then it can be very limiting and blocking. This fear accumulates over the years, because your memory makes it worse and adds to it. It can end up controlling you and you aren't able to respond openly from your heart.

Heart energy is pure energy. If you strip away all the controlling mechanisms I described above and on top of that you strip away your value system, you'd be left with just the heart energy. Values are connected to judgments and we constantly confuse and mix them. We judge to justify a certain behavior that we have actually performed out of fear, insecurity or anger. We may think we are acting from the heart but instead it is our value system that takes over and makes us react, which is different.

A pure feeling is what it is. It can be true joy or just as well true sadness or deep satisfaction and peace. It culminates in being at one with everything. So, in that sense, a pure emotion is felt as heart energy. Sometimes you have such pure feeling for a brief moment but then you lose it again. As soon as you doubt those feelings, which are the expression of the heart energy, the feeling as such is gone and is being interfered already through thoughts and expectations. Young ones still have the ability of pure feelings and as an adult you can tap into those memories and remember what it felt like. You can practice and get parts of that pure innocent state of heartfelt emotion back.

With your heart you direct energy. The mind gives a hint and an idea of a picture and then you let the heart do the work. It is about having faith in your heart and in your own strength and letting go of expectations. That is why I say it is the heart that directs the energy, although the mind helps where to send it. The picture you paint in your heart, for instance when you pray or sing, is clearly seen and felt with all your awareness. Your heart will open up in the process, you actually are able to listen to your heart and give it space to act from deep within.

Allow the heart to take the main lead. The mind shows the direction and the heart gives it power. You don't have to think about the direction anymore. You focus with your mind and the heart takes over and it happens by itself. We say: trusting your heart. Our heart and our mind each have their own energy; they are connected and can't work fully independently. They need to work together in order to function properly, coordinated and balanced. The more you are able to combine and direct the energy from mind and heart together, the better you are able to manifest and become aware and present.

Another aspect is that the heart connects you to Nature and Spirit with the heart at its center. You can be in nature and see beautiful trees and smell nice flowers, but while looking at it from your heart, you are aware of the spirit of those trees and flowers and the sensation becomes stronger and more imprinting. The heart makes it a stronger and a more valuable experience. Just as much you can have an experience with your eyes closed and see in front of your mind's eye beautiful nature with strong, rooted trees and nice smelling flowers. You engage yourself with spiritual awareness, and it starts to have meaning for you and becomes stronger once you connect the image with your heart, as the spirit is at home in the heart.

Eagle at Sunrise Story

While I was staying in Gablitz on my first trip to Europe, I was staying at the edge of the town. I wanted to do sunrise ceremony just like I always did when at home and searched around in the neighborhood for a nice spot. I discovered a little paved road going up a hill. I didn't see any houses but I did have to climb over a small fence. When I walked further up the meadow, a big tree came into view, from where you had a beautiful view over the town towards the East, where I imagined the sun would rise majestically. This was the perfect place for my sunrise ceremony and I started gathering some rocks to make a little fire pit. I had no idea about the rules in Europe on outdoor fire making and also ignored the fact that I had actually been trespassing by climbing over the fence. I figured: "If they catch me, I'll play the dumb Indian, hahaha!" I started doing the ceremony, singing my songs and playing my drum and all was going well. I walked up that hill every day by myself and was content having found such a great spot close by. On the fourth day after I had just gotten back to my place from the ceremony, there was a knock on my door. When I opened it, I saw a very tall man in a business suit. My first thought was: "Now you're in trouble. You'll get busted for trespassing and making a fire!" An odd thing though, I noticed he was wearing bright orange shoes, quite striking, as his feet were so big and it somehow didn't fit the picture of the suit. He politely asked if he could speak to me. I answered: "Sure," and then he asked me: "Hi, I was wondering if you are the one going up there every morning and making all that noise?" This question only confirmed what I was already afraid of and I wondered how high the fine would be, but I was being honest and said: "Yes, that's me!" He continued: "May I come in and we talk a little more?" I nodded and he ducked to come in through the doorway. After sitting down, I offered him a drink and he said: "I would like to ask you what that is about?" I explained I was a Native American, what my background was and talked about the ceremony and that I was visiting here as a guest for the Discover Life Festival in Vienna. He got quiet and then he really surprised me by asking: "Can I join you?" "Of course, I don't turn anybody down who would like to join. You're welcome as long as you are respectful." He explained his interest: "I am a stockbroker and work at the stock market in Vienna. I have been doing this work for too long and don't feel happy with it anymore. It is time for a new direction in my life. I don't like being in the dark energy of that place anymore." I gave him my point of view: "Well, you have to understand that whenever you're embarking on something like this ceremony, you'll open something within you that might make you look at life differently afterwards. Once the awareness has opened, you can't ignore it anymore." He acknowledged that and agreed to go along with it, as this is what he wanted and needed.

The next day he showed up at the appointed time and surprised me again. He drove up in a car, a fancy looking, brand-new red convertible Mercedes Benz and he opened the door and said: "Come on, we'll drive up there." I objected: "But there is the gate!" He jingled a pair of keys in front of my nose: "That is taken care of. Don't worry!" We drove up the hill to where the tree stood and I remember thinking: "Boy, am I glad that no other Native people can see what I am about to do... driving to a ceremony in a brand-new Mercedes. What a way to arrive at a ceremony!" So, we did the whole ceremony after I had explained it all to him. I was not sure yet if he was coming again the next day, but sure enough, he showed up and for the next week we spent our sunrises together while drumming, singing and praying. We befriended each other, and started talking on all kinds of topics. Soon he began mentioning animals being present around that time of day. He saw a rabbit at the edge of the forest; he noticed some birds up in the air that settled down on the trees nearby. One day, a deer appeared and stood there watching us. He was very pleased with it and I told him: "I want you to understand something. They were there before too, as this is their home, but you only now have started being aware of them."

My time in Europe had come to an end and we were going up the hill for our last ceremony together. As we were getting closer to our fire pit, we saw something unusual: a dark, round-shaped figure stepped around in the fire pit. We stopped the car to give it a better look and realized it was an eagle! We drove on carefully and as we approached the tree with the pit, it flew off and sat down on the tree right where we performed our ceremony. We went ahead while it sat above our heads and closed our ceremony with the "Mountain Eagle Spirit Calling Song." As we were finishing this song, the eagle took off and flew towards the East into the orange colors of the rising sun. It was so powerful that this huge Austrian man fell down on his knees with tears in his eyes, exclaiming: "I will never be the same man again."

I left and a little later I heard he had quit the stock market. He owned a shop that sold semi-precious stones and became a painter. In recent years, he also began practicing as a laugh yoga teacher.

Coffee shop Story in Amsterdam

I have an American friend whom I met on one of my early tours through Europe. Eleanor didn't know much about Native issues but got more and more interested and over the years we became friends. She saw how much work it was to organize my European tours and offered to start a business, which could help to promote my talks and workshops over there. In order to really know what was to be expected of the programming and get to know some of the people, she accompanied me on a tour through the Netherlands and Northern Germany. While in Amsterdam we met up with a bunch of people from all kinds of nationalities. They wanted to take us on one of those boats that they use for transportation on the canals of Amsterdam. They are narrowly built and very low, close to the water, pretty wobbly too. You had to rope yourself down from the quay to get on one, which I thought was probably not such a good idea with my posture and heart condition. We decided not to join and walked around a little when it started to drizzle. We came by a neat looking place and went in to stay dry and have something to drink. Now, I admit I am a little naive when it comes to things like this and I had no idea that in Amsterdam a so-called coffee shop meant something totally different. We are hanging out in there and ordered a hot chocolate, but were also tempted to go for the delicious pastries they had put out. Just as I am about to take a big bite, the owner comes by and starts making conversation. I complement him on the cakes and he asks: "You do know what these cakes are, don't you? They are not just ordinary cakes!" I said: "What is so special about them then?" Then he explained: "They are hashish cakes! You are in a coffee shop!" Only then did we realize what was going on. We both don't do drugs, so we returned the cakes, finished our hot chocolate and left, wondering what we would have looked like returning all stoned without even noticing it. Something like this just doesn't happen to you in America. I am always amazed in what kinds of strange situations you can end up in out of sheer ignorance. In Holland this is commonly known but for us the place just looked friendly. It wasn't shady to me at all and we had a nice encounter. You learn about different ways as you travel!

Misconceptions and Stereotyping

One of my powerful lessons coming to Europe for the first time was that I had a lot of misconceptions about the people here, because I thought that all Europeans were racists and would go after me as an Indian. You build up your own negative thoughts and have a certain expectation about what you think you will encounter. What a blessing to find out it wasn't like that at all! Of course, you meet all kinds of people -- good and bad -- wherever you go but that isn't determined by a country or continent.

You can witness cultural differences all over the planet though. Historical circumstances and social developments form and transform cultural identities. I have witnessed an interesting development myself. In the sixties, the hippy movement spread out from California and took an example in Native people. These youngsters started wearing headbands, beads and necklaces just like Indians. We were revered for our closeness to nature and for our Medicine people. Indians were finally getting some recognition and a positive sense of self. In the late seventies, the Vietnam War gave many Native young men a sense of pride and direction. It was a common goal to -- what they thought was a good thing -- fight for your country. They were seen as patriots and part of America, which nowadays you can still witness at Powwows[20] where the Veterans are honored at the Grand Entry. After the war a lot of Natives –- and also many white Americans as well -- were disillusioned. At the other end of the spectrum there were the "old hippies", who had been very much against the war and were putting their fists in the air to stop all the crimes and atrocities: the Peace movement became an important outlet for feelings and gave focus to many lives. In the eighties, this movement transformed into something bigger; the idea was to create an environmental-friendly way of living through farming, foresting, and use of energy. A new vision of organic living and being examples on land of your own created communities of all kinds. In the search for land, a lot of the people ended up in Oregon, which still had space available. When we came from Nevada, which was still very conservative and racist towards anything other than white and moved to Oregon, nice and open-minded people welcomed us in. Where I live now, there are more than a hundred intentional communes or communities. Eugene is one of the most liberal cities in America. Here, women literally have equal rights, in the sense that because men can walk around bare-breasted, women are also allowed to do so. Once I took some friends from Tennessee to Eugene on a very hot day. Right before our eyes a young girl took off her top, not wearing anything beneath it, as a police car was just driving by. Nothing happened and my friends were amazed she wasn't arrested. In Eugene you see people dress or have hairstyles different to what is mainstream and you aren't harassed. A large hippie festival is held annually close to where I live: an amazing number of people of all colors and gender identity gather for a week of music, theater, joy and happiness. With these communities also a lot of green business and companies were founded, which affects the atmosphere positively.

---

20 A **Powwow** is a social gathering held by many different Native American communities to meet and dance, sing, socialize, and honor their cultures with different types of traditional dances, music and regalia.

What I have learned from traveling to Europe and leaving the comfort zone of familiar America behind was that you just can't expect to be prepared for the differences of culture and habits. You think about certain aspects where you expect the differences will show themselves and then something will totally catch you off guard. Many times, it was the little things that were surprising. Before coming to Europe, I had never even thought about the fact that people could be using a different electricity system, which of course they did. Luckily, I was warned on time not to plug my device into the 220 V used in Europe, since that would have ruined it. Another fascinating thing were their toilets. When I came over to Europe the first time and went to use the bathroom, I couldn't find the lever to flush! It was very awkward and I kept searching for that lever, but nothing even similar to what I thought a lever would look like caught my eye. In America you have a small metal lever on the side of a toilet to flush, but over there it turned out to be a little button on the back in the same color as the tank. Something very silly to not have understood, but it can really set you off, it being very embarrassing having to ask somebody to help you.

It is important to ask questions if you come across something that strikes you as different from what you are used to. Asking is essential, but you have to do this with an open heart and mind without judgment towards the actual difference. It may sound easy, but it actually isn't. Especially with those small practical daily habits we are often limited in our flexibility. We judge and denounce a habit as ridiculous, old-fashioned or inappropriate. We just don't want to change our habits and criticize harshly so we don't need to accommodate ourselves to any changes. If you are able to ask questions, you are also able to learn!

Traveling and moving around taught me that besides getting around your own prejudices and fears, you can learn to see new ways and about how things can be done differently. There is never just one way, but you forget this if you are stuck in a place for a long time. My own people criticized me for leaving Nevada. They said: "How can you leave your home and your land? These are your people! You have sage in your blood!"

I could understand what they were saying, as there is another side to this. Everything is multi-layered and not that simple. As Native people we feel a very strong connection to the land we live on. There are spiritual ties to the land and to the ancestors, which make it far more uprooting to leave than it might be for other people. Since in my case there were spiritual reasons to go live somewhere else, I came to the conclusion that in the end the ties to the land were physical and emotional. I had faith to find a new spiritual connection just as deep somewhere else, since there are no boundaries for Spirit. We can have a connection to our ancestors wherever we are. I was able to create a beautiful and strong connection to the Mother Earth in Oregon as well. I fell in love with the land and being close to the ocean. In my case, my path was guided in this direction. In another case, it can be that you really need to stay at a certain spot your whole life.

It is true that it is easier to connect to the spirits in the place you were born and where your whole family has always lived. There are many stories and shared memories that keep this connection alive, so it is easier to tap into.

Let me speak about an example that might illustrate this further. I was told that if you take a piece of wood from a tree, it carries the spirit of that tree in it. If you make a table from that wood, the spirit is hiding deeper within. The same applies to metal: if you take the metal directly out of the ground, it has a strong vibrant spirit, but if you create something with that particular metal and it ends up becoming a car, the spirit is hard to get in touch with. It has gotten further away from its natural state and it is more difficult to communicate with. It just means you have to go through more trouble and effort to make that bond again and that happened to me in Oregon. I went out on the Mother Earth and prayed for sunrise, talked to the life around me and because I stayed open, it was possible to find a strong and open connection and communication that goes both ways.

In the end it is not about the physical: it is the spiritual and heart guidance to Nature and Spirit. This insight is essential and it is more important than ever today. In modern times, a disconnection exists because we have different ways of commuting with trains, cars and planes. We are in touch with things that are further away from their natural state, like computers and all kinds of machines. We move around, live and work in different places and you feel at a loss because of the pace it all happens in. This is part of our evolution and it is happening for a reason.

What often happens when you enter an unknown situation is that you feel disconnected and immediately close your heart instead of staying open for what is coming. You block what is actually in front of you. But remember: the ancestors are always with you. Mother Earth is always there in all kinds of forms and your own spirit connects to the spirit world all the time.

Even amongst my own people, these limiting thoughts of getting attached to a certain place out of habit or refusal to change reside. You can have a healthy relationship to where you come from and might prefer to stay in that ancestral area, but sometimes life shows you a different option and you have to follow that flow. It becomes unhealthy when you choose to hang on and aren't open for new possibilities. This is what life teaches you and yes, I admit, quite often it is a challenge.

People prefer to stay in a familiar situation, even when it isn't good for them, rather than make changes. Change forces them to leave the comfort zone of their habits and familiarities for the land of uncertainty. That stops them right then and there. It is a paradox, but people prefer to stay in pain and sorrow instead of opening up and facing something new. It takes courage of the heart to leave your comfort zone and take the risk of the unknown.

Faith helps you to continue your journey, supports taking a risk and following the flow of life. Faith to me is the key and faith is installed in you with the help of your community. It is much more difficult to do it all on your own.

One of the most important messages the elders have told me again and again is that everything happens with a purpose and a reason. This is to be taken literally: everything! With our limited human minds, we only see so much of the whole picture. That is where you can make peace with a difficult situation. You can't control everything and you are not asked to do so. Let it flow and use the doors that are opening for you. Embrace the journey!

I have told myself many times when I was in a situation where I felt left out or alone: "Hey Mala, you know your ancestors are around you. Maybe you feel lonely and you long for your family, but Mother Earth is right under your feet." That faith helped me to step out of the loneliness and the illusionary feeling of disconnection. In fact, you are never alone, you are always connected.

> *Hermine:*
>
> *This last part of the conversation took place in Sweden at Mikki and Cecilia's place. At that time, they had a so-called woofer working for them, who came from the United States and surprisingly enough, happened to be a young Native American Indian. It was his first time abroad and it was all very new to him. After this long talk from Mala, he shared that he had been feeling homesick and been on the verge of calling the whole thing off and going home. He had asked for a sign for his plea and when Mala showed up and shared his experiences, he felt it was an answer to keep going. It helped to open his heart again to be brave and hang on. It was beautiful to hear him being thankful for the lesson.*

Stereotyping is always about misconceptions. On my travels I have encountered so many concepts on how Native Americans should look or act and behave. It is amazing how a fixed image of a group of people sets a stage that turns out to be very powerful.

Especially when I came to visit and talk in schools, I heard the questions: "Do you also live in a teepee? Do you still hunt a buffalo from horseback? Why don't you have feathers on your headband?" Those are the pictures children have in their heads when they hear about Indians and this might seem just harmless images, but they go a long way. Those things are still told in the history books and also come from the romanticized picture painted in movies and books, but doesn't cover the reality of modern Native Americans driving around in cars, mostly buying their food in the store and drinking soda pop. Very often people are disappointed when they have to let go of these inner pictures and aren't willing to get past their illusions.

They prefer what they have in their heads, which is either this romanticized picture or a very negative, violent one. Neither is true. We aren't the saviors of the earth who know it all but we also aren't all alcoholics. These are generalizations and it's important to reach people on an individual basis: heart to heart. We need cooperation on that level and to learn from each other. Only together can we make the change happen that is beneficial for all. This is something Corbin Harney has worked very hard for. He kept saying: "We need to overcome the differences and look for what connects us, no matter if you are indigenous or whatever color. What truly matters is the quality of your heart." I strongly believe in that, too.

In Europe, the books of the German author Karl May inspired the biggest part of the misconceptions towards Native Americans. He had never been to America -- although he claimed he had first-hand experiences and was an expert on Indians -- and wrote a whole series of books with the main characters Old Shatterhand and Winnetou. It installed the picture of "the noble savage" in many people's heads. There are numerous festivals in summertime in Europe that still use the same symbolism and draw in large audiences. It is hard to get rid of those stereotypes, as people just prefer to be lulled in and entertained.

One of those romanticized ideas was that of becoming blood brothers. That was never a custom amongst our people. Maybe the idea was born because we do consider people family, even though we don't come from the same blood, so to speak. We introduce someone as our brother, sister, grandfather or grandmother and so on.

I went to a festival held near Vienna that intended to portray the history and modern way of living of Native Americans a little differently. Part of the intention was indeed met, but there were also horrendous mistakes made. What really upset me was the fact that they sold bottled beer with a well-known Lakota chief's head on the label. It was very disrespectful, considering the history of our people, on which alcohol has had -- and still has -- such a devastating, addictive effect. One of the Native musicians who was Lakota and played Native rock music refused to participate anymore, but unfortunately his contract forced him to. Another group of Apache dancers and musicians were told to keep their regalia on for the whole day while hanging out on the premises of the festival, which they otherwise only wore on stage. Half of them were in their teens and had T-shirts and jeans on. They felt like they were exhibit pieces in a zoo, you know. They also didn't get any permission to leave the premises, which was extremely rude and restrictive.

I understand there are misconceptions and misunderstandings. I have been through my own share of those, too. Important is that we open ourselves up to the opportunity to learn new things, facts and experiences. Sometimes it saddens me that even then, people often refuse to take on a new concept or at least widen their horizon. The problem is how to incorporate new knowledge and experiences into that specific reality that works for you, without losing the basics that have been part of your life, culture and upbringing. You still have to stay true to yourself.

An example at the other end of the scale is sad to witness: traditions and certain ceremonies which have been followed for many generations became hollowed out once they were taken over by people who didn't have the knowledge and background to understand the concepts behind the ceremony or the specific custom. I have witnessed it many times where something became just an outer structure to reach quick enlightenment, but without responsibility or a heart for the community. Ego was in charge and aimed for short-term advantage. I have seen both white people who pretended to do things the Native way or were "initiated" by Native Americans and allowed to perform a ceremony or carry a pipe or whatever, but also Indians who went for the money and even sold out sacred Native objects. You should never charge for ceremonies, as Nature and Spirit gave those to all people.

But you know, I have come to understand how difficult it is to discern where you need to stick to a deep principle and where it really only is about a superficial layer that can be adapted. Once I was over in Europe together with Corbin and we were asked to do a sweat lodge ceremony at a certain place. Other Native Americans had taught the people who had invited us, and when we arrived at the area for the sweat everything was already set up. Corbin and I come from the Shoshone tradition and have certain ways in how we perform our sweats. When we made some comments on how we would like to proceed, it became a huge problem and they said: "No, we are taught to do it this way and we're not supposed to do it in any other manner!" We tried to explain that amongst the tribes there are many different customs and that there is not just one way of conducting a sweat lodge. All those ways have the same essence and are all good. They stayed very adamant about how they were taught and didn't let loose. We asked them: "But why did you invite us then, since you knew we came from another tribe? We can teach you something from our way and from our hearts!" In the end we decided to take our stuff and we left. It was actually a shame, as they missed out on a chance to learn from a highly respected and knowledgeable elder from another tradition. They thought they were doing the right thing by sticking to that one way but weren't showing any respect for another way. Their minds couldn't get around it and they had a fixed idea about what was right and wrong. I have seen this happen time after time: if people just start to learn something new, they grab on to that little knowledge so hard that they lose the heart of the matter and their flexibility.

My Vision of a Native American Guided Community

The way we lived at Meta Tantay never left my heart and a vision of creating something similar in my life grew inside of me. After we moved to Oregon, I started writing about what it means to live in a community out in nature based on tribal ways and what it contributes generally to people's lives.

Time went by, both Sky and I had our work where we found fulfillment and the kids were doing good in school. My longing for a community life I shared with Sky, but she was satisfied with how our lives had turned out and didn't feel the need to change that radically again, although she did understand the passion that I felt for it. During those ten years at Meta Tantay, we both hadn't taken a single day off; we'd worked hard and long hours and had been on call 24 hours a day, 7 days a week.

During that time, Corbin and I traveled and worked together, partly in the US and partly to Europe. On many occasions we shared our thoughts and realized we carried a common vision in our hearts: we both wanted to create a community where like-minded people could live and work together and which was based on the Native American traditional Way of Life. Corbin's vision was a Healing Centre for the benefit of Native people, where he could practice his medicine. Mine was the building of something similar to Meta Tantay, the community where I had been so happy and would have loved to live for the rest of my life.

We started sharing our vision with people and found a lot of positive resonance. Little by little my personal dream spread out to other people's hearts and more people became convinced this should be created. We started to look for land and get funds for it.

In the ways I was taught, you put out your ideas and wishes, while having faith in the Creator. You don't push for what you want to create. I didn't have a business plan; I didn't have any money in the bank. I did it through energy. First, I visualized and prayed myself; then the energy gained in power by the positive thoughts of others who also started to believe in it: the energy accumulates and it comes into reality when it is good and meant to be. Wherever I went and whenever I could, I talked to people about it. There were people who didn't believe in it or thought it was impossible, who were skeptical about my ideas and called it all a phantasy. I always answered: "I have faith; we will bring this energy together; when the time is right, it will happen."

As years went by, Sky was also ready for change and supported the vision fully. Although we didn't have the money together yet to buy any land, we felt we had to find the right place first and then find a way to finance it. All together we looked at over a hundred properties both in California and in Oregon.

Californian Camp at Zacka Lake

Around 2002, Sky and I were offered an opportunity to go live on a piece of land in the Los Padres National Forest near Santa Barbara, California. The property, named Zacka Lake, was on private land in a National Forest, really beautiful and with two lakes on it. The owner had a vitamin-company, which made good money. He was really into Native things and that is why he wanted us there. Around the large lake there was a resort with some buildings, like a café and a restaurant, and some cabins. There was a campground too. We had to run the resort for him and in return besides being paid a salary, we were allowed to start our vision of a Native guided community on the area with the smaller lake.

We decided to give it a go and gave up our house in Salem, Oregon. It soon turned out that we had so much work to do there that there was no time left to start with the building of a community for ourselves, but we did have some interesting experiences on that property which are fun to share.

Bear Stories

The forest had many bears and they came to the campground ever so often. Warnings were given to the people not to leave any food in their tents as bears have an extremely good sense of smell and come to take whatever they consider as food, no matter if it is in a tent or not and if there is a person in the tent or not.

One day I get called to the campground: "Mala, you have to hurry. There is a bear in the campground and someone is having a fight with it!" So, I come running to see what's going on. I see a man and a bear in a tug-of-war over a cooler with meat and other food in it. We couldn't believe it! They were both tugging on each side of that cooler and the guy didn't want to let go. The man wanted his cooler back! As more people showed up, the bear eventually got scared and ran off without the cooler. That guy had been very lucky and he didn't even realize it. A tug-of-war with a bear!

Another funny story happened on a hot summer day. One part of the lake was reserved for swimmers and was marked so that the boats stayed out of that area. On warm days there were quite a lot of people coming from all over for a swim. It was really beautiful to relax and cool off. A co-worker and I were driving around in our truck on the hill that overlooked the lake.

My partner notices: "Hey look, there is a bear!" We figured to keep a close eye on it while it was wandering around. All of a sudden, it starts running down the hill towards the lake and with one big splash it jumps right into the water! It was almost like in the comics-books. The bear was having lots of fun and started to swim around: it was as if you could see it grinning. As soon as the people in the water noticed this big brown animal, they freaked out and ran out of the water, screaming and going in all directions. This made the bear panic and it came running out of the water as well, just like the people. We couldn't stop laughing: it was all very hilarious! The bear thought: "These beings are in the water, I'm in the water. They get scared, I get scared!"

Another bear story happened at the garbage dump area. On a daily basis we loaded all the garbage from the resort and campground up on the back of a dump truck to drive it to the main dump. From there it was picked up every month. My son Hunnan must have been five or six years old and was sitting together with another young Native boy on the back of the truck, which was very old and noisy. They loved to help us and were catching the plastic bags we threw upwards and stacked them in places on the truck. So, we are coming to the dump area and are backing up towards it. We hear the two kids hollering in the back but we think they are just having fun and are being loud. All of sudden though Hunnan really screams from the top of his lungs and I figure: "Okay, I better stop. This sounds serious." I get out of the truck and ask him: "What's wrong?" He says: "Dad! Look!" A bear was standing a few feet away in front of the dump, on the verge of being shoved into it by the truck. That experience scared the kids pretty much and they weren't so keen on coming along on the dump truck after that. But I have to admit we had a good laugh about it.

I have one more bear story to share. Up along a path with pine trees growing on each side, you'd reach the top of the hill where we had built a nice sweat lodge. We had used it a few times already and Sky was running a women's sweat. They started pretty late in the evening, sort of around eight o'clock.

I was waiting in the kitchen with another guy and we had food ready for them whenever they came down from the sweat. It got later and later and nobody came down, so I was getting a little worried and decided to go and check on them, because it seemed to me that it was exceptionally long for a regular sweat. I walked up the trail in the dark with a little flashlight and when I was almost to the top of the hill, I could hear singing, so I thought: "Oh, everything is okay. They are still in there." I turned around and when I'd almost reached the front door of the restaurant, I heard an unfamiliar sound. I discovered a little bear cub sitting right next to me: he was still tiny and really cute. Then I heard another little cooing sound on my other side and there the second one was sitting, also very adorable. It dawned on me: "Wait a minute! I'm standing in the middle of two bear cubs... Where is the mother?!" I know if you get too close to a bear cub or even worse come between the cub and the mother, she will take this as immediate danger and flat-out attack you. I'm standing real still to wait and see where the mother is coming from, so that I can move away in the other direction. All of a sudden, I hear a loud crashing from garbage cans and there she was, about 25 feet away from me. She looks up and sees me. I realize that she was blocking my way to the restaurant, and all the other buildings are further away. There is no way I can outrun her. What am I supposed to do? She is already standing on her hind legs and comes threateningly towards me, making loud grunting noises. I know as soon as she drops down on all fours, she will come and charge me. Although black bears are not that huge, they are pretty impressive and have powerful claws and teeth. Standing up she was about six feet tall, a little bit bigger than a human being. Then, out of the blue comes my rescue: an eye-blinding flash is coming from one of the windows of the restaurant and the bear gets startled and looks up to where the flash came from. That was my moment! I ran off behind her to the back door of the restaurant, where the kitchen was. Next thing I know, she comes running after me; I can hear her coming closer, but I made it inside safely and as I slam the door behind me, she hits it with her paws wildly. My heart is pounding and I notice she is climbing up the roof of the shack and looking around for me. But I'm safe and enter the restaurant where I meet my friend, who is waiting for me, all excited: "Mala, Mala! Did you just see that bear? I just took a great picture as it was standing on its hind legs!" "Well, yeah!" I sighed with great relief: "I was out there and you just saved my life!" Mama bear soon left with her cubs. So, I had a nice story to tell the women after they were finished with their sweat lodge!

Drowning Experience

After we had been living there for a few months already, something really profound happened to me at Zacka Lake.

In the middle of all that dry land it was quite exceptional to have two lakes so close to each other. The big lake went very deep. One time the son of Jacques Cousteau, the famous ocean and water researcher, had tried to go down in a special little submarine to find out how deep the bottom was, but he never made it all the way down. They assumed that the structure of the lake was formed ages ago by a volcanic rupture in the earth: a so-called volcanic vent that eventually leads to the ocean. The swimming area was marked with some buoys along a rope, with a little floating dock some distance from the shore.

We were hanging out there with a bunch of people one day and one of the women kept challenging me to do a little contest. She said: "I bet I can outswim you. I am a better swimmer! Let's go and try it out!" I don't like challenges like that so much, but I gave in to the peer pressure, because everybody was cheering and saying: "Yeah Mala, go for it. Come on, show us what you can do!" So, we all went to the shore. I wasn't wearing any swimming pants, just a t-shirt and jeans, that aren't very suitable because they get heavy when wet. She was wearing some short pants and a tank top. But I thought: "Ah well, let's get this over with." We all headed towards the shore and I took my shoes off and emptied my pockets. The plan was to swim out to the dock first and back along the rope to the shore. We started off and touched the dock, which is about 50 ft. away, more or less at the same time. I noticed I was already pretty tired, as the swimming with my clothes on was making it hard to move my limps. I told her: "Let's call it a tie. I think this was enough." But she felt this was no proof and wanted to continue the challenge. I agreed, ignoring my tiredness and inner voice telling me to stop. The track along the rope and the buoys was a little longer, about 70 ft. and we jumped in again. Pretty soon I noticed my wet pants are really wearing me down; my legs feel heavy and I don't have enough strength to continue. The option to take off my pants to make it easier on myself, for some reason doesn't come to my mind. I try and continue but it is getting harder and harder. Because I notice I am not going to make it otherwise, I grab hold of the rope. The woman is hollering at me: "That's not fair! You're cheating! You have already lost!" I answer: "That doesn't matter. I just can't make it otherwise!" We are still leveling with each other and are swimming at the same speed, just that I pull myself forward with the rope. All of a sudden, one of my hands misses the rope and I feel myself going down but I manage to get above the surface again with the help of the second hand still holding on. When I am able to breathe again, I tell her: " I'm in trouble. Can you help me?" But she answers: "I'm not falling for that. Forget it!" and she swims off. I keep urging that it's serious and I'm not trying to fool her, but she refuses to help me. I keep pulling myself forward with both of my hands on the rope and again one of my hands misses the rope and I go down a second time. I struggle hard and keep working my legs and somehow I reach the water surface and am able to breathe again. I yell at her one more time: "You've got to help me. I'm in trouble!" She looks at me and realizes it is serious. I notice the fear in her eyes, if she's going to help me, there might be a chance that in my panic I am going to take her down too. She can't handle it and swims away. I don't have much breath left to yell to the others for help. I repeat to her: "I'm in trouble. Please, can you tell the other ones what is going on?" She stares at me intensely, not sure what to do and swims off. Then both my hands slip of the rope and I try really hard to get back up and reach the rope, but I'm so exhausted it doesn't work. I can't make it and all of a sudden I feel I am floating down and I remember thinking: "This is it. There is nothing I can do." I flip over, my face is looking downwards to the darkness of the water below me and I am drifting down towards that black space, thinking: "So this is where the Creator has decided my body will end up." Tumbling around again, I see the light of the surface above me getting further and further away. A deep peace comes over me and I see the bubbles coming out of my mouth, the last bubbles of air inside of me. I turn over one more time and float down in a very sleepy state, quiet and at peace. As I notice this sensation another feeling appears inside of me. Around the stomach area there is a warm, tingly feeling, like many little hands are touching me. All of a sudden there is a strong shove that shudders me and gives me an enormous jolt upwards. Some powerful energy shoves me through the water and I break the surface! Later on, the people watching the spectacle from the shore, tell me that I came flying out at least waist high. This force shoves me all the way to the shore, without my own doing and I land still half in the water but on safe ground. People jumped in and grabbed and pulled me out. Sitting up, I cough all the water out of me. When I finally come to my senses, I see the woman that raced me, pacing up and down, very upset: "O my God, o my God!" She realizes she hadn't tried to help me, ignoring my plea and how close I had been to drowning. Just as I have composed myself a little, she walked up to me, saying: "I can't take it anymore. I have to go!"

I have to admit: in that moment I lost it: "I almost drowned. You just left me out there and you're the one who can't take it anymore?!" I got really angry inside and wasn't able to control myself. As she walked away, I put my hand up in a certain way and as I did that, a huge branch hanging from a tree above her, snapped and came down with a loud thump. It landed right in front of her feet. She turned around, looked at me terrified and realized where that came from. Then she screamed and ran off.

Her frightened eyes shook me up inside and I was able to quiet my energy down and balance myself again. I wasn't proud of what I had done, though. It had been an emotional reaction to the woman I was angry at, but it hadn't been her fault that I almost drowned. She just disappointed me with her behavior, but I had gotten myself into the situation in the first place.

My own strong reaction had caught me by surprise and taught me an important lesson: to control my emotions so that the power of my energy wouldn't harm anybody as a result. Before you know it, you have done something regrettable out of anger.

Teaching about the Use of Medicine

If you carry a powerful Medicine but you lose control, you can be quite destructive. You have to take in account that emotions themselves already carry a lot of energy and have an effect on your surroundings. If this is combined with a Medicine you carry and you have been taught to direct that energy in a certain way, the Medicine becomes a well-focused laser. This can go both ways of course: if you add love or compassion to the energy, you can create wonderful healings, but if the directed energy becomes afflicted with anger, jealousy or other negative emotions, the outcome is explosive.

It takes a huge responsibility and is not something to be taken lightly. I have seen many examples where Medicine works beautifully and facilitates a healing process, but unfortunately, I have also seen the opposite, up to the point where the energy of Medicine is deliberately abused.

In the old tradition a person with a gift was taught and made aware of that responsibility, so the person could slowly develop a required ability and attitude for performing good Medicine. The difficulty is that when the power of healing grows, it often gets to the person's ego, which is a dangerous combination. You need to stay humble with that gift of healing, know when to hold back and never to show off. You use your Medicine when it is appropriate. You carry that gift and it is your choice when to use it with purpose and intent. If in an ordinary situation your emotions take over, that Medicine-power you carry comes out together with the flow of emotions and might not have a positive result.

Consequently, as a Medicine person, you need to be very aware of your thoughts, your feelings, your words and your actions all the time. Just let that sink in: all the time!

Knowing this and seeing the consequences made me very reluctant to step on the path of becoming a Medicine person. Already as a small child I was conscious about not wanting to hurt anyone. I don't know why; it's just been that way as long as I can remember that I only wanted to make people feel better. I realized in that aspect I was different from my siblings and from other kids. I didn't want to cause any disharmony and wanted to be a really good person. I remember this with great distinction and clarity. I never really had the urge to become a Medicine person myself so much and wasn't interested in the power that comes with it. A lot of the things I observed as a child were common amongst my people at that time: we talked to the spirit world all the time and spirits were part of our daily life.

On the other hand, I have also witnessed Medicine people going astray. There is a rule amongst Native healers you shouldn't work on your own family and those that you are very close to, because your love and personal needs get in the way of being neutral, which is needed for performing the healing. My father broke that rule in the case of my mother. He insisted on working on her and didn't permit anybody else working on her. I knew instinctively that I wasn't supposed to work on her. When she crossed over, it broke my father's heart and he had a lot of guilt in himself. It was because his love for her that he was blinded. My mother didn't deny him his efforts out of her love for him either. It is one of the reasons why I haven't become the Medicine Man I was prophesized to be. I was disappointed and thought that if people with such powerful gifts didn't know any better and were more humble within themselves –– and it wasn't just my father, I have seen other Medicine people go that way too –– then I would rather not walk that path at all.

Performing healings when you aren't clear in your mind and the longing in your heart blurs your perception just isn't supposed to happen. That is a rule. It is always a tightrope you walk when you help somebody, because the true healing will only occur when it is good and meant to be and when the time is right. This is up to the Creator. As a healer you can be of assistance and open doorways for understanding and translating the information needed for somebody to learn their lesson and be healed.

I have always felt the presence of a strong healing power inside of me, but I realized I wasn't always in control of my own emotions and still got angry at times. If I chose to develop this power more deliberately, this could turn against people in the wrong way and I wanted to avoid ending up seriously hurting anybody. All my life I never got the feeling: "I am there, I am able to control my emotions." After what happened at the lake, I once again realized how extremely careful I needed to be.

Poo Ha Bah

Since we didn't make any progress with our own community at Zacka Lake, we were thinking of not going through with our plan to create the new camp here. Things didn't flow in the right direction. Something triggered the situation that made us decide to leave it for what it was. Sky and I had been invited to come to Europe for a speaking tour for a few weeks in a row. Winter and Red Wolf took care of Hunnan, who was still much younger. While in Europe, we got a phone call from our daughter saying we didn't have our own place to stay in anymore. She had been told by the owner to move the belongings from our room to make way for somebody else. The owner of the property had made contact with a guru whom he offered our place at the resort. He placed a red velvet carpet on all the floors and what looked like a throne for him to sit on and claimed: "Everybody is welcome to stay as long as they worship the guru." So, when we came back from Europe, we just packed up and returned to Oregon. We had ended up staying there only half a year. Luckily, I got my job back at the Native American Youth Treatment Center and worked there for a few more years. We moved away from the city to the countryside of Oregon around Monmouth. We were renting a farmhouse, which put us more in nature and offered enough space to have people stay with us who were in need. The vision of a community became clearer and nearer: we just didn't have the finances yet and we hadn't found the right land for it.

In the meantime, Corbin was spiritually led to an old spa close to a town called Tecopa in California just outside of Death Valley.

This spa was in the desert but had, oddly enough, hot healing waters and Corbin turned it into a Healing Center. Native Shoshone of the area had always gone to the hot springs in order to find healing. Some years before, white people had bought the land and made a spa out of it, with mud baths and swimming pools, etc. Eventually this failed and it was out of use for a very long time. As one of Corbin's Medicines was water, they named the place Poo Ha Bah, a Shoshone wording for "Doctor Water".

When I came to have a look at Poo Ha Bah, I knew straight away that we couldn't build our community here. In the summer, it gets so extremely hot that you can only stay indoors during the day and come out to work in the evening. You can't grow vegetables either, because the soil is very alkaline out there. There is no rainfall and no fresh water at all for people or to raise animals. Although at Meta Tantay we had also endured hot summers and very cold winters, here the situation was even more extreme and we opted out. Naturally, we fully supported Corbin in his choice for the Healing Centre and after raising enough money he made the first down payments. We helped him to find funding and reestablish the place, because quite some work needed to be done before it could function as a Healing Center. Buildings from the former spa were still in place, so they could be used after fixing them up. Next to all the constructional work on the property, it remained important to raise more awareness and money to support the cause. We were constantly trying to get people involved to help out, donate their time and energy. Sky and I were both part of the Board of Directors of Poo Ha Ba, which was guiding and overseeing the development and functioning of the Healing Centre.

Corbin wanted to make it into a Non-Profit-Organization, but due to legal reasons that turned out to be quite difficult and would take a few years. A large Native support organization took over as an umbrella and Corbin also brought in money through grants. Unfortunately, a few years later the umbrella organization started to interfere with how Corbin was to manage the place. Their policy didn't allow any white people who might benefit from healings, but Corbin didn't agree with this attitude of exclusion. Sadly, he became blocked in his financial affairs and couldn't lay hands on the money from the grants he had gathered. Partly it is understandable that the organization had such restrictive rules, because historically there weren't many pure Native organizations and they were really aiming to be of assistance to Native People specifically, as white people had often taken advantage of them. What they ignored was that Corbin had installed an all Native Board of Directors and they simply refused to listen to his view. Corbin's way of thinking was always aiming at bringing people together, not to exclude anybody.

When word had gotten out about this unfortunate situation, a lot of Native people were really upset since Corbin was a highly respected elder and leader. The organization got many angry letters and negative publicity and the chairperson apologized personally to Corbin, who -- being forgiving and not holding grudges -- was willing to let it all go. The positive side effect was that the organization changed its policy: the rule "only for Native People" got handled less strictly.

When our community in Oregon became a reality, we were able to install a Non-Profit Organization with the help of less strict laws in Oregon, which could also function as an umbrella for Poo Ha Bah. The money collected through the grants got released and Poo Ha Bah finally became his own Non-Profit.

Corbin had many talents and unusual ones too. We had already founded our community near Eugene, Oregon. It was about an 18-hour drive from Poo Ha Bah with a lot of two-lane highways in between. Sometimes we visited each other, also to share and work together, but each time we had to make that long journey. Corbin was able to call us up and say: "I'm leaving pretty soon now, so I'll see you then!" Then about 12 to 13 hours later, he would show up. We kept thinking: "How is this possible? This trip takes up to 18 hours! How does he do it?" But we couldn't figure it out. We asked the people at Poo Ha Bah about the exact time he had left, to check if it was really true. So, I asked him: "Corbin, how do you get here so fast each time?" He said: "Ah, I just drive, I just drive. I just sit there and pray and drive." One day we drove up to Poo Ha Bah together in a white Dodge van, which used to be mine but I had given him. It's not the fastest car, you know. Corbin was behind the steering wheel and was speeding a little. You were allowed to drive about 55 miles an hour and he was driving up to 65, sometimes 70 miles. I wasn't thinking much of it, since we took back roads and fell asleep. When I happened to wake up, I noticed the car was at a totally different speed. It felt like the surroundings were flying past and I was thinking: "How fast are we going?!" I looked over at the dashboard and see that the arrow is totally gone from where the numbers are. I was rubbing my eyes: "He must be driving about 100 to 120 miles an hour! I can't believe it!" Corbin was just singing and driving, totally at ease. I asked him: "What are you doing? How fast are you driving?" He answered with a mild smile: "I don't know, but it can't go any faster. I've got my foot down all the way to the floor!" I asked him: "How long have you been going like this?" He said: "I don't know. You have been sleeping!" So, I just sat next to him and watched him drive. He seemed to be relaxed and calm while taking the curves smoothly with no bumping or rocking. It was amazing. Since it had been my car before, I was stunned how he did it, since the highest I ever drove with that car was about 90 miles an hour. I was worried a little about cops that might catch us, but he said: "Don't worry, Mala. They're not going to be here." And he was right: never a cop in sight! From the side of the road, we must have looked like a streak flying by. Unbelievable, at an age of almost 80, without any fear, he did something to the car and something to the road ahead, which he never explained but 13 hours later we magically arrived at our destination. I have seen him do this at other times too: he would show up, way before people would expect him to be there. This Medicine Man sure knew how to fly!

A lot of good work was done at Poo Ha Bah. The buildings were renovated. Groups started to come in for healing work, but then unfortunately, Corbin got terminally ill and wasn't able to oversee everything anymore. Since he was the main one who did the healings, the center emptied out pretty much and it all stopped. Somebody else took over, but the Healing Center sadly enough has never been active the way it was envisioned by Corbin himself.

Hermine:

I still vividly remember seeing Corbin after arriving at a beach at the Atlantic Ocean. We had been traveling in the car for a while, going to a conference in Virginia Beach, to be held the next day. We were all giddy and having fun, happy to be in the open space of the beach and the ocean after being confined to the car for a long time. But I'll never forget Corbin, going straight to the waterfront, drum in one hand, drumstick in the other, singing and drumming to the Water. He didn't ask us to join him; he was just focused on what he was doing. He talked and listened to the Water. He communicated in such an intense way that after a while we all stood there with him, without him ever urging us to join him. I have never witnessed so much focus and deliberate purpose in a person in such a healing and gentle, yet strong way. He told us: "The Water is sick. She needs our prayers. She needs our help and attention."

To me it was a great lesson in how differently you can perceive things. Coming to the beach, the first thing Corbin did was pray to the water and give thanks. He wasn't thinking about his own pleasure or fun. The water was his priority. Afterwards you can still have fun, be happy and playful.

I remember Corbin as an extremely happy and kind man, who liked to make jokes and enjoyed life. My children were drawn to him, especially my daughter when she was very little. She would just cuddle up and sit on his lap, because his energy was so soothing and peaceful. No need for words. While staying at our house in Vienna in summer, he'd be up early for sunrise and was already humming in the kitchen starting his coffee for the day. He felt at ease wherever he was and never claimed any special treatment.

Corbin was an admirable, truthful person, steady in his ways and always authentic. I am deeply grateful for the opportunity to have been around his energy. Thinking of Corbin brings a smile to my heart and to my face and I still hear him singing his prayers inside of me sometimes.

Reconnection and Pushing of the Heart

Corbin and I both found that one of the main problems in today's world has to do with the fact people are no longer connected to the life source of all. Reconnecting to Mother Earth became one of the main topics whenever I talked in front of groups: it literally means to reconnect, to get the connection back in a stronger and more conscious way. The teachings of Mother Earth aren't lost. They are there, right in front of us. Mother Earth is always showing us through her example and has never abandoned us. The elders told me that the ways of the indigenous people are similar all over the world. We all had the same teacher! Most indigenous tribes make use of a drum, sing songs and see the circle as sacred. They use a certain herb to cleanse and purify themselves. They use other herbs for healing and strengthening, depending on the local variety of the plant life. In many cases you can witness a kind of sweat lodge or purification lodge. Indigenous people everywhere have similar views on the sacredness of women as life-bringers and also have some kind of moon custom. Most tribes have rites of passage with similar ideas behind them, because all humans have young girls becoming women and young boys becoming men. Our customs and traditions spring from the same source: the Mother Earth. Obviously, there are cultural varieties, because on our planet there is a lot of diversity in geography, climate, plant, and animal life. It is only natural that these aspects are reflected in how a culture develops. Amongst the many Native tribes of North America, there are many differences and yet there are lots of similarities. It depends on how you look at it.

Once you realize that Mother Earth has been the teacher for all and she is the foundation for all the teachings, you only have to go back to her and reconnect to what she offers. She has never turned her back on us, because she is our mother. We are the ones who choose not to listen. Luckily, I see proof of many people who are willing to look at those roots again, who are open to reconnecting.

Through the tribal ways of living we can understand more easily how Mother Earth is flowing and guiding us. The connection to Nature and Spirit can fill up the holes people feel inside, as if something were missing.

The question that I am often asked is how to reconnect again. It has to start with an honest wish in the heart. If you truly feel committed, you will see doorways opening. Important is that you allow things to flow and you don't try to control life. It is much more of an attitude of willingness, of being open to guidance and of listening and being aware than of doing much yourself. You need to observe first, be willing to sit outside and be still. Look at the Grandmother Moon; observe how she moves across the sky and wanes and waxes. Listen to the wind and look at the leaves in the trees. Watch how the colors of the sky change at night or in the morning. It is very simple. You are open and already making a connection when the beauty of nature touches you. The next steps will follow naturally. Maybe at some point you will feel called to talk to a tree or ask Grandmother Moon a question.

If you observe Nature, you'll notice it has a certain way of flowing harmoniously. Everything works together and has a certain purpose and reason for being there. Nature constantly adapts and changes according to its own rhythm and rules.

In principle, all life is tribal. Most animals live in groups or have some sort of support mechanism for each other. A lot of people try to give an opposing example: "Eagles only live in pairs and never in groups." Yet I witnessed the tribal aspect in Nevada while living in the canyon for half a year on my own and saw it in Alaska, where hundreds of eagles were flying around together. If you look at trees, it is the same. They form a forest or are standing together in small groups, expressing: "We are a family and take care of each other." That is how it is supposed to be.

Nowadays we hear the opposite: "You can only depend on yourself. If you want to be something in this world, you have to do it on your own. Think for yourself!" But Native people don't believe in that. We are supposed to cooperate and support each other. Each individual adds something to the whole and has a unique personal attribute that makes a difference. The community or tribe consists of little ones, of men and women, of youth and of elders, which makes it a circle and a whole. I understand that times have changed and am not saying we should go back to the old days as such, but the tribal principle is necessary for our survival through connection to each other. The larger picture goes beyond just your own life; the tribe looks to the survival of the future generations. Maybe at one point, people will return to living in tribal communities again, but then in a modernized way, even within a city or in a different setup. Some initiatives are already being tried out with day care centers working together with old people's homes, for example; both benefit from these contacts. It is possible when we are flexible and creative and yet have the foundation of the tribal origin.

Whatever I share you are welcome to utilize. And I figure that one day you'll add your own things and you will learn other things too that make sense to you. As you are relearning these ways, be patient rather than frustrated because it will take time. Just do the best you can, as long as it comes from the right intent from the heart. Besides, you never stop learning. That is the beauty of life: to learn each and every day.

Everything can teach you: the fire and the ashes; the smoke that spirals up in the air; the cry of an owl in the night; the first flock of birds in the morning. Nature is alive and vibrant and is constantly getting in touch with you. We often look for the dramatic signs, but it can come subtly too. And yes, sometimes it does come in a strong way like an earthquake or a big storm. It can come in the form of death and sickness or as drought and forest fires.

Essentially though, Nature and Spirit teach you to be in a passive role of observing: you just watch and listen for what comes and open up all your senses.

Over time a connection will develop. Most everybody knows the fascination with fire, how its spirit shows in the colors of the flames, the energetic movements and the physical sensation of its warmth. Watching a fire, you learn about how it responds to the wind, how the smoke rises and the wood cracks and whispers. Water also has a fascinating spirit. We love to watch the flow of water, gently smoothing out the rocks or thundering down a waterfall. Water shows itself in so many forms: the dewdrops in the morning, the mist over a valley, tiny raindrops from the sky and the huge amount of ocean water, rivers, creeks and springs.

There is an aspect you need to be aware of when you are re-learning these ways: be careful about pushing yourself. I have encountered many people who were willing to reconnect and learn about nature, but who are frustrated due to their own impatience and wanting too much. There is a difference between doing the best you can and pushing yourself too hard. Sometimes you really struggle when you are giving your very best: where do you cross the line and where does it become pushing?

The elders told me that as long as you feel good about it, even if you are working hard and even struggling with it, it is okay. The moment you no longer feel good about it, the energy changes -- you have started to push. The energy is no longer flowing and it feels like you are going against it. In our way, we then turn it over to the Creator and say: "I have done the best I can, now I leave it up to you, because I have faith in the way it is meant to be and best for everyone and everything involved." You let it go and accept whatever is unfolding.

I have noticed people who have been really trying hard to make changes, but kept putting blocks in front of their own spiritual growth. This is often the result from how we have grown up. We are taught to think in a certain way, which is always about doubting and criticizing. If you think negatively, the blocks in your own mind become huge and difficult to overcome. To turn this mechanism around is essential for transformation to take place. Turn your energy towards your heart and have faith in your own spiritual being: this is where your true nature lies and where transformation starts. The heart energy is of immense power and radiates far. It is much stronger than the mind. Be open in your heart and believe in yourself in a positive way! If you keep saying that you are not at a certain level, you put yourself down and limit yourself. Instead you could phrase it like: "I am working towards a certain level, just not there yet." In our minds are our fears and insecurities, but also our hopes and desires: as they mix, they tend to confuse and sidetrack us. Do you have a warm and happy feeling in your heart, even if it doesn't make sense? Then continue with that thought, plan or action. Then you are connected within. If it is only in the mind, that separates you from your inner being.

You need to have patience with yourself there, as you are on a learning journey. It takes practice. Don't make decisions when they don't feel right. Take a moment and check your heart where you are being guided. Your heart is the connection between Nature and Spirit. Over time, this connection will become clearer and you will be able to accomplish amazing things with it.

It doesn't mean you never struggle and have your doubts here and there. That is where growth lies and where the possibility of change and transformation can show itself.

Allow things to happen the way they are meant to be and let it happen at the right moment in time. That is when things turn out in a much better way. If you push for things, the natural flow isn't harmonious and balanced and won't have a positive outcome.

We have a saying: "We don't push ourselves upon the Mother Earth, each other or on ourselves." There is a lot to that saying. We often do things that go against our own feelings and natural guidance. We make certain things happen because of our desires and wants and our fear of losing control: "I need this right now. It has got to happen this way." It is a cover up of what we truly need in ourselves: the longing for connection, feeling loved, feeling worthy. If you allow the flow to happen, it is easier to relax and enjoy life.

You need to constantly listen to your own feelings and be honest with yourself: "Am I still okay with it or fooling myself here? Am I going against the flow in myself or in others?" It is easy to trick yourself by claiming: "Oh, I still feel great about it all. I want this to happen and will keep on fighting for it." You see, we have been trained to work hard and obey what is asked of us. To let go and flow with life has a different quality. The Western culture has put a lot of emphasis on setting and reaching a goal, achieving and being ambitious.

Many people who come to my talks and workshops complain it is difficult to quiet down the noise in their heads. The mind is constantly doubting and questioning; it is buzzing and nervously offering distractions or commenting and judging harshly. The solution that I always offer is to just relax! When you are tense, things only get worse: the muscles harden and become tight; the nervous system responds with high activity and it's unhealthy for the whole system. Again, relax, flow with it, and the rest will follow.

Another aspect that might help you see whether you are pushing or doing your best is to ask yourself: "Am I still learning something from this situation? Is it serving me in some way?" If you work hard and learn at the same time, something positive comes out of it. You can stick with it and be persistent. You can always adapt the way you are doing it, change your approach or adjust your expectation. Sometimes you just have to admit: "I was on the wrong track. It doesn't fit me, so I am dropping it." Then the change is the true teaching: you had to change something in your value system and way of thinking. Those are good struggles and are part of spiritual growth. And I am not saying you should stop when the going gets tough! On the contrary, you need to encounter those struggles, learn through them, and become a better human being.

In order to deal with the struggles in an easier manner, a good practice is to welcome them into your life and embrace them. Tell yourself: "You know what? It may not be easy but I am thankful for the opportunity to learn. Welcome!" When you do that, the energy of the struggle changes and it actually helps you instead of being in the way. You don't build up those blocks of resistance and it becomes much easier to learn from them. They can melt away and the flow of the energy resume naturally.

Living your Life with Purpose

These days it seems a lot of people have lost their sense of purpose and don't really know why they are here or what they are here for. They merely exist and do not fully live their lives. When you just work and work from nine to five, going from one weekend to the next, it is really a sad and empty way of living.

Each and every one of us is born with a purpose, with something that is special about us, something we are good at. This special something adds something to the Circle of Life, to Mother Earth, to Creation in its turn.

One of the ways to know your life has purpose is that you wake up each day happily looking forward to what the day might bring. Living your life with purpose is not about the big things; it can be little things that make the difference. It's not so much about a goal you have to reach; it is about how you live your life. In the traditional Native way, spirituality is the main factor in everything we do, say and think at any time, day or night. We recognize that every act, every thought, every word we say carries energy and it influences everything around us. Consequently, you are responsible for your actions, words and thoughts. The smallest things can sometimes make a huge impact. What sometimes looks small to you in the end may cause a big wave. Everything is related. This is how Spirit works.

You try and create harmony wherever you go. Like for instance here in this room, when I look at all the things that are placed on the carpet, where the bowls are put, where my rattle lies down, where I put my tobacco and the sage... each affects the other. Or in the way we cook our food, the way we talk to each other, it really matters how we do things. How do we treat our little ones, how do we relate to our animals? Purpose really is about awareness of how I live my life: giving purpose to everything I do, think and feel. We call this "walking a spiritual path."

The other aspect of living your life with purpose is what I am supposed to be doing and where I am of the most benefit for Mother Earth. In the indigenous culture, we believe that the spirit world and also nature itself are trying to guide us to live our life the way it is supposed to be. If we are trying to control the outcome of our actions, the spirits cannot come through to us. Human beings only have a limited way of thinking and our mind and ego want to constantly control. At the same time, we have ways to go for the short cuts, choose the comfort-zone, stick to the easiest way, avoid difficulties. But sometimes we need to go into an uncomfortable place in order to be able to learn something. You learn through the struggles. If we don't make the necessary changes, we stay more or less in the same spot and stop ourselves from developing.

I was told that in the beginning Nature and Spirit teaches in a gentle way. In most cases, we tend to ignore those smaller hints and continue living our lives. When the person doesn't really want to make a change, a stronger lesson is needed: the tapping and prodding will get stronger. Usually we still refuse to listen and read the signs, stick our heads in the sand and think we know better, until we are forced to look at things and make that change. It would be much easier if we had done it right from the beginning when the lessons were still gentle, but ah well, this is human I guess.

I was taught that when things are getting out of balance within us, it first starts at the spiritual level. From there it spreads to the other levels and finally reaches the physical one, where it is the hardest. Maybe we get sick or we bring an injury upon ourselves. An injury is not a coincidence in my understanding. It is trying to tell you something and forces you by literally stopping you physically. By now we may be really shaken up and maybe we understand a certain pattern and might be willing to make an adjustment or change. We call this the path of spiritual growth. It provides us with a new way of understanding, of looking at things, a new way of thinking.

If you have learned your lesson, these things will leave again, because then they have lost their purpose.

The problem is that we are very stuck in our value systems. We think the world functions in a certain way that we firmly believe and hold on to. Everything that happens is always explained according to that system of values. Our judgments come out of those values. The truth is that the world doesn't work in just one way; it has many faces and layers. Usually we resist anything that comes in from an unfamiliar angle. Truly learning about something different is unsettling and might even shake your foundations, but again, it is where true growth lies.

A lot of people see challenges as something negative they would like to refuse or surpass. Yet you need to welcome them in. The principle behind is it once you embrace it, it loses its power over you. In the indigenous world we say: "It came to you for a reason!" It is there to help you. If you welcome it in, you may have to go through some struggles and pain, but with effort and a willingness to learn, you come out stronger than before. You can look at it as a blessing. If you see it only as something that is hurting you, thát is in the end what it's going to do: hurt you. If you are able to change the energy of it and see the hidden, blessed nature that comes along with the struggle, you can grow from it.

When you put your faith and trust in the guidance of Nature and Spirit, even in hard times things will unfold the right way. If you truly follow Nature, the spirit world and listen to your own spirit, this is for your own good as well as for all Creation.

As you learn to trust in the natural flow of things, your fears and insecurities will crumble. You have to start believing and allow your mind to see change might be possible. Each of us walk our own paths, we are responsible for the choices we make and how our life develops. In my talks, I keep emphasizing that Native people have never claimed that their way is the only way. We say: "There are many good paths to the Creator." This is very true and I would never play missionary. Each of us needs to find our own path.

If you really want to walk a spiritual path, you have to remember whatever you do, it has to serve the purpose for the greater good, for all life and for the future generations. When you are faced with choices or are in the process of decision-making, keep these things in your mind and heart and they will help you to guide you to make the right choice.

When life forces you to make a choice that might involve resistance or even fighting, we have a saying to always choose the most healing and balancing option to try and solve things. If that doesn't work, you take one step back and think about what you can do next. A long time ago when the white people first came to our continent, we welcomed them as our guests. We showed the newcomers our ways, where to find food, how to get around, basically how to survive over here. This worked well in the beginning, but as more and more white people came, they started to overtake us and claimed we were in the way and they no longer had any need for us. The indigenous tribes tried for a long time to keep balance with the white invaders, tried to compromise, but in the end, it didn't work. Eventually we had to take a stand and even make use of arms, which ended up with us risking and losing our own lives.

Sometimes it is wise to fight; sometimes it is wise not to. Remember, there are many ways to do battle. Another important thing is that if you do decide to fight, you should not become part of that negative energy and become like the other party but remember why you started the battle in the first place.

Spiritual Guidance

What I feel a lot of people lack nowadays is that they don't trust their own spiritual guidance. They might get a clear sign from the spirit world and yet they are afraid to follow this guidance. The mind tells them it is a crazy idea and it wants to analyze and categorize it. People feel fear and insecurity inside. Their gut might contract or they start to sweat and get nervous. Then the other three levels, mental, emotional and physical are blocking the spiritual information. You can overcome this by trusting and having faith through the help of your heart energy. When somebody is brought up in a traditional tribal culture, it is easier to follow that guidance. You don't question and simply trust. My example is always how I left my home state of Nevada and went to live in Oregon. It was through the spiritual guidance that came to me after my sickness that I left everything I felt familiar with and went into the unknown. Although I didn't understand everything, I had a strong sense of knowing I had to do this. In the western culture, I witness the battle between the mind and the heart. The missing link is trust as opposed to control.

Another aspect is that immediately after the knowing, acceptance sets in. Acceptance is very important in our tradition. You don't understand it all, but you know there is a reason for everything and you trust and accept whatever is needed. It seems embedded in my culture: "If you have faith, it will all work out!"

I have had many difficult situations in my life, but I listened to this inner voice and with this attitude I always made it. Sometimes the spirits test you if you truly are having faith and they look how far you have grown and developed your skills. In my life particularly, it has often been a balancing act, almost like a roller coaster, I guess. That is because I am who I am.

If I follow those spiritual messages, the journey has a guided direction, but can still be bumpy. This is what is meant to be and I am determined to follow that guidance. There is no doubt, no resentment, no anger when I struggle or encounter difficulties. It's just part of the lesson. You see, time has no meaning in the spiritual world. Things take as long as they take, when we learn what we need to learn. The path put out there for you by Creation is yours to follow. How we walk our path, if we choose to take side roads or to let ourselves be guided, if we walk gently or hard and resentful is up to us. It doesn't matter how long it takes and it isn't about reaching a certain goal, either. As we change our energy, doorways will continue to open and the journey can become smoother again.

We do not always receive clear messages, and it is only natural that we have doubts and questions. We are human and have emotions and second thoughts. Yet even if you have doubts, it is helpful to have faith and trust in a good outcome, understanding that you are guided anyhow, consciously or unconsciously. I have had many situations where I was wondering what I was missing and tried to understand. Sometimes it was helpful to go into ceremony, to try to change something in my thinking, to look at my life and behavior, and open my heart and spirit for guidance and support. Sometimes it is important to seek help from a Medicine person or an elder. Help can come in many ways. It can be a book you read or somebody you meet on the street. Sometimes nature itself helps once you go out and just be with Mother Earth for a few days.

Sometimes the lesson is easy and sometimes the lesson takes its time and has its ups and downs. Sometimes you may have understood it spiritually, but your emotions are reluctant and your body takes more time to respond. Sometimes your body looks healed but you haven't understood what it was about on the other levels, so the illness might come back. It reflects the journey of life.

Living from the Heart

Living from the heart means basically that you are trying to live a good life and it shows in how you interact with others, whether humans, other creatures or any form of life, and yourself. If you tie the energy of the heart to spiritual energy, a lot of good can come out of it. If you tie judgmental and harsh energy, which comes from the mind and imbalanced emotions like anger and fear, to spiritual energy, something negative will come out of it. It is essential that spiritual energy is based in a strong heart connection. A good heart will stay humble and not be greedy and ask for too much.

Listening to people from all over, something I have come across is people who have willing hearts, but who aren't very good with their boundaries and keep offering their help. They feel compassion for a certain person or situation and keep putting energy in to make a change, but somehow nobody is using that assistance in a useful way. The energy gets wasted and the helper gets drained and depressed. You have to be careful not to expect the change you would like to see happen overnight. Things take time and sometimes a person doesn't want help or a situation on the whole hasn't gotten to a point where the transformation can actually take place. You then have to take a step back. Offer help only when you are asked and know when you have to accept the way it is for that time and place. If you don't recognize that, you will end up hurting yourself. Here, too, balance is needed. My first urge is to help wherever I can, but I came to realize that if you keep helping others all the time, you are actually not helping them to get on their own feet. There is a thin line between enabling and "unabling" someone.

Living from the heart is a matter of being truthful and sticking to what you believe in. You don't change and adapt just to accommodate others. This can be quite challenging. People will keep trying to distract you, even when they don't mean to. As an example: I never drink any alcohol and at times I have been invited by friends to join in. You know how that goes: "Come on, have a beer! What difference does it make? Why can't you have a beer with us? We are your brothers." It makes you feel bad, because you do want to belong and join in, but the alcohol goes against your belief. You are being tested and peer pressure is heavy. In the end you define who you are by what you do and not do. At the same time, you don't want to offend anybody and be very principled about your beliefs.

To be truly connected from the heart and living from the heart gives you joy and purpose in life. Isn't that something people are really in need of? To live according this attitude on a daily basis means you are a good caretaker for the Mother Earth and future generations. And isn't that something the world is really in need of?

CHAPTER 5

THE SOUTH

Hermine:

In the summer of the fourth year of our book project, I spent four days alone out in nature. Native Americans used to practice a vision quest under far stricter and harsher circumstances, with no food, no water, no clothing, no protection during the night and no leaving the designated area. Mine was a modernized European style quest and a way to retreat from ordinary reality with all its time frames, distractions, structures and technical solutions. Just spending a night alone in the darkness without a source of light becomes a challenge as we are overwhelmed by our fears and phantasies. We have gotten far away from our original source, are so used being comfortable and afraid of a change in habit. And yet, we can cope with a lot!

I managed to be out in the forest on my own without food, which was already an accomplishment for a spoiled city girl like me. To leave my comfort zone in order to receive spiritual insights and reconnect with Mother Earth had been my impulse. I was allowed to drink water and also permitted to roam around the forest wherever I felt drawn to.

There I was, and I found myself thrilled being able to connect with the earth, the air, the tree people, the plant people, the insect nation, the animals and the birds, all up close. No human contact, just myself and my thoughts, feelings and own being: confronting and challenging at times, but soothing and magical in many moments.

Close to the spot where I slept, I walked around and let my eyes wander about. I was just thinking about Mala and our book project, which had been on hold for almost a year due to turmoil and major changes in both our lives. I wondered and asked Spirit how to proceed, if and how it was meant to be to continue writing and if the book would ever become a reality.

My attention was drawn to some logs lying on the forest floor, each covered with a thick layer of dark green moss. A big old tree had fallen over and the rest of its trunk with large roots going in the earth was totally covered with a mossy fur. It had the shape of a turtle standing on its feet: big, round and very wise. Turtle, moving slowly, carrying a lot of weight, old being from times long ago, living in water and on land. Native Americans call upon you when they refer to North America as Turtle Island. One of the creation stories describes how long time ago a woman fell down from the sky, coming from another world with a few seeds in her hand, and how she reached our water planet where she would have drowned if Turtle had not given her a place to rest her feet. On some soil brought up from deep down under the water she dropped the seeds from her hands and Earth started to blossom: Turtle Island was born. [21] *I saw an image with this green tree turtle with a mother of pearl shield on its back, shimmering with pink, white, violet, blue, yellow and green hues of light as a supporting symbol for our book project.*

---

21 Story from "Keepers of the Earth: Native American Stories" by Joseph Bruchac and Michael.J.Caduto

A fresh, new birch tree sapling was growing out of the old dying tree, very promising and uplifting for my heart. The year before, after I had left Oregon in March of 2015, I had struggled to continue with the book and only managed to do a little transcribing of the tapes we made. In late summer, things changed dramatically. There were transitions in Mala's life and his health condition became more serious. On my end, I had a lot going on in my personal life with an ailing, aged mother in the Netherlands, a big move and a change in both living and working circumstances. This new life coming forth out of the old tree trunk gave me hope.

When I looked at the logs leading up to the trunk, it became clear that it actually was one long log that had broken into three pieces. You could see they once belonged together and came from the same trunk. Those pieces represented the first three years of our book project. Then an obvious break came, followed by a smaller, rounder piece of wood, again all covered with a layer of moss. It looked like Europe and I felt relieved that this meant Mala was indeed going to come to Europe again that fall. He had been struggling with his health the past year and was advised not to do heavy duty traveling, definitely not crossing the ocean in a plane. The break in between stood for a pause with the book as well as a turning point in Mala's life, him leaving the community where he was living at the time, and giving his life yet another direction. My relief and gratitude at the answers of Nature and Spirit were immense!

I realized while standing there in the forest looking down at those symbols materialized into form, only seen in my head through my eyes and with my energy, body and history, that even if you don't understand and it doesn't make sense, you still do

what you sincerely feel is right in your heart. And that it is not
about you at all! You just do your part in the whole. You are
invited to fully welcome it while doing it.

To express my gratitude, I gave thanks to the landscape by
crumbling a long line of tobacco over the logs towards the turtle.

Vision and Realization of Nanish Shontie

We continued looking at all kinds of pieces of land that we hoped would be suitable to carry out our vision. Although we didn't have the money together yet to buy any land, we felt we had to find the right place first and a way to finance it afterwards. Meanwhile, I traveled to Europe quite often and already had support from many people who were enthused by the vision and carried it in their hearts: the word was spreading. Groups in the States and Europe were promising financial or logistic support.

One day, Sky drove by a property up for sale in the coastal hills of Oregon close to Eugene. At the end of a dirt road, hidden in the forest, it had a creek running through it and some buildings on it, which would suit our needs. The price was much too high though, and the guy wasn't willing to negotiate. One year later we drove by again and the land was still up for sale. The price had gone down a lot already. Just as we were visiting the property, a young Indian woman who turned out to be the one neighbor showed up. She was a real estate broker and became very interested in our plans and intentions with the land. She said: "You are the neighbors I want to see here!" and offered to do the negotiations to enable us to become the new owners and start our community. She worked hard to make it happen.

Just as we had done at Meta Tantay, I wanted to see what the land would say to me. When we came to the land with a group of people who were closely involved in the whole process, I walked to the center and asked everybody to be really quiet and make no noise. The first thing that came to me was this sense of overwhelming nature all around me; there was no sound of a car and it was very quiet and silent. The land felt happy and welcoming and inside I felt a yes to the place. We brought Corbin Harney to the land to see what his advice was and after his prayers he confirmed the power of the nature at that place. The creek flowed beautifully with crystal clear water all year round and there were two natural springs on the property. The water carried no contamination and you could use it for drinking. Corbin said he could see a Healing Center built here. So, we went ahead with it and named it Nanish Shontie, which in the Shoshone language means: "To ask the Creator for a Blessing".

On many occasions we had tried to raise money for our plans but had never been successful. When we put the word out this time, we were in need of a down payment of $25,000 and it somehow came together within days. Most of it was donated and not even a loan, it was really incredible! The land in total was $200,000 and we were still in need of collateral to give the bank as a security. A friend offered us 50 acres of farmland just like that. We felt the support of Spirit very strongly when everything came together within a short time. It still needed a lot of faith to continue since both Sky and I had no regular income and had to make monthly down payments of about $1500 plus another $1000 for the extra cost of taxes, gas and such. I got some income through my talks and a workshop here and there, and Sky earned some through the teaching she did, but how were we going to raise 2500 bucks every month?

We had a four-bedroom house to live in but couldn't afford to start renovating anything on the land yet, although a lot of work was to be done there. It wasn't smart to invest in new buildings since we weren't sure if we would be able to keep the land. We focused on the land payments. There were months where we were short maybe $1000 and didn't know how to make it. Somehow a door always opened and a check arrived in the mail with exactly the right amount. At times we hardly had a dollar to spare for food and definitely no money for insurances. It was a close call sometimes, but we just continued on. We did our morning prayers every day at sunrise and kept having faith.

After five years of surviving month by month, a person walked up to me at one of my talks in Europe and wanted to talk to me. After an intense conversation about Nanish Shontie and our plans for the future, I was offered a check that covered the rest of the money open on the down payment. I called Sky back in the US and told her: "Guess what just happened? You won't believe this!" She started laughing: "Yeah sure, that is a good joke, Mala!" She refused to believe it until she saw the money in the bank. It was over the top but it was true!

It is amazing when I think back. A lot of people never believed we would get the land and if we did, we wouldn't be able to keep it. Others told us we would be paying for the rest of our lives and would not be able to put any money in the buildings and the creation of new structures for a growing community. Now we had it made! If you have faith and don't give up, miracles can actually happen, which is at the core of Native American spirituality. Every time before you do something or have an idea, you first think it through: "What is it we want, what do we envision, how are the effects on the Mother Earth, how is it going to influence the next seven generations, with what purpose and intent do we start the project, how will it benefit the people?" First you put spiritual energy into the vision with humbleness and respect. If your way of thinking is pure and connected to the heart and the ways of Nature and Spirit, it results in good things.

My personal vision had grown into something bigger, carried by more and more people and we now had an actual community. We envisioned a place where people could witness an example of what had been passed on to us by the elders and by our tribal traditions and what we believed was a good way to live on Mother Earth. More so, people from all walks of life were able to experience it. Like Meta Tantay, we wanted it to be intertribal and interracial. Since it wasn't reservation land, we weren't confined to the rules and regulations of just one tribe. Alcohol and drugs were prohibited. The vision was to create a community, guided by Native spiritual and traditional values, open to all races and colors as long as people respected our ways and were willing to contribute to the daily work.

We made Nanish Shontie into a legal, non-profit organization with a Board of Directors so it wouldn't be owned by anybody personally and we could accept donations. On a more practical level, we had a Council that oversaw community-life and the daily work and planning of the development of Nanish Shontie. This was based on the way tribal communities used to function, where the members of the Council talked through issues and matters concerning the practicalities of life.

We had some elders living with us for a while, but we also had younger Native people staying at Nanish Shontie. The first years our youngest son Hunnan still lived with us while going to school in the next village. At one point, a man named Ross joined us permanently and for many years he was a strong member of our community who put in a lot of work and effort. Later on he left for Europe to live in Belgium with his girlfriend. Around 2008, my daughter Winter, her partner Abram and our granddaughter Miranda became part of the community. Abram was responsible for the construction of the buildings; he is a great carpenter and also does beautiful murals. They both felt very strong about the environment so they initiated the building of solar panels, a grey water system and composting toilets. Sky took care of the animals and Winter started doing the office work. I provided income through my talks and workshops both in the US and in Europe. Sky, Winter and Miranda are great cooks so we combined all our talents to make things work.

For about three to four years in a row, we had 10 to 20 people visiting from spring through summer. Quite a lot of people from Holland, Belgium, Germany and Austria stayed for longer periods. It was a great feeling to hear all the different languages being spoken on our premises. There is an old belief amongst indigenous people that it doesn't matter if the facilities aren't perfect or you don't have enough room for everyone: you just make it work. The food, even when it isn't much, you simply share. You always find a place for someone to sleep. This is part of the Way of Life. To share and take it as it is. To me this is a beautiful concept and a tribal principle in its core. I really love this way of life and it makes me happy inside.

One project I felt really strong about was the recording studio. The idea was to make a platform for elders to share their knowledge, so we could all benefit from their wisdom and the information could be preserved for coming generations. Eventually we built two little rooms, one as a sound room and one for equipment. Over the years, it became much easier to record with simpler devices and the whole setup with the recording studio became outdated. You basically just need a computer with some software and that's it. Whenever elders came through, we did some recording, but it wasn't enough to make it a continuous project. Unfortunately, it just never really got off the ground.

Intermezzo: elders and old people

There is a big difference between elders and what I sometimes refer to as "olders," in other words, people who become old. In Western society you see evidence of this last group: "olders" are no longer incorporated in society, are put away in old people's homes or senior citizens centers and feel they have become a burden to society and their families. They basically wait for when their time has come to cross over.

Elders in the Native perspective are people who notice they have reached a different stage in their lives, where their bodies are aging and they feel they can no longer do heavy physical work, but who still have a lot to offer. They can support society with all the knowledge and experience they have gathered in life and pass this on to the younger generations for the benefit of Mother Earth and the people. They are considered very valuable and we owe them our greatest respect. It is our duty to take care of the elders, provide for them and assist whenever we can in order for them to take on that special elder role in society. They give their expertise and wisdom freely and are living examples for the young ones. In our tradition, becoming an elder is something you strive for when you get older and it's is an honor to be treated as such. The younger ones help to take care of you, give you food, help in the household and with other tasks and your needs are met. Elders help with their knowledge and wisdom; young ones help elders in return. It goes both ways. It gives you a sense of belonging and purpose in life, connecting to the younger generations and remaining part of the circle.

All in all, Nanish Shontie encompassed eight hectares or about 20 acres. The trees weren't old growth anymore but there were still beautiful redwood trees on the land and it was very green all year round.

We started growing crops in summer and harvested from the apple, pear and cherry trees in our beautiful fruit orchard. Blueberry bushes kept us busy making yummy jam! There was always a lot to do with taking care of our chickens, sheep and the ponds, which were full of trout. Besides our many cats and one or two dogs that roamed around on the land, deer and elk came to visit us from the surrounding hills. They do tend to nibble on the fruit trees or empty our garden, but that is what happens when you live on the edge of the forest. Raccoons or possums also feasted on our chickens and occasionally a bear visited in springtime when it came out of hibernation. Yeah, wildlife was close! We observed a very special thing in our creek: some newts, which are extremely rare nowadays. We took good care of the land and saw it as a positive, welcoming sign.

As far as we knew, there was no other place in the US like Nanish Shontie where people could come and live year-round -- not just a summer camp

-- learning and experiencing the Native American traditions. The original intention was two-fold. We intended a community and also a healing center on our property, where different kinds of healing could be practiced and healers could work together without needing to charge for their help. They would be taken care of by the community, just as it was done in the old days when they didn't have to worry about food and living expenses but were able to focus on their gift and purpose in life, which was healing. If you are a healer in modern culture, you have to support yourself and your family and go out work at a job. Or you are forced to charge for the healing work you do, which in our tradition you are not supposed to do. Corbin Harney put a lot of emphasis on this aspect. He pointed out a flat area for building a traditional healing lodge between the trees where the two creeks came together naturally: "It is the energy of the water flowing from the mountain between the spruce trees that holds power." Unfortunately, before this became a reality, he crossed over. His dream had been to have the forest area of Nanish Shontie in summer and the desert at Poo Ha Bah for the winter.

We eventually decided to let go of Corbin's vision and focused on strengthening the community instead of creating something new on top of all the work that was already in planning. At that time, we had about eight people permanently living at Nanish Shontie.

In the meantime, we got a regular financial support from the person who'd helped us with the down payment, so we were able to start with the renovating of the old buildings and constructing new structures. I still brought in money through my talks and workshops. We applied for grants to bring in funding and we kept receiving donations.

Our aim was to become self-sufficient and we started all kinds of initiatives to make money over the years: printing logos on cloth like T-shirts and bags, or holding drumming workshops. In the beginning we just had the main house with one bathroom and a kitchen. We were able to house guests and visitors in a few old, donated trailers. They weren't very pretty, a little battered and rusty, but functioned quite well, and many mice found a home in there as well. People donated all kinds of things, even a large yurt was given to us. In summer we were frequented much more, since the weather in Oregon is pleasant and our visitors could stay out in their tents or in the teepee that was put up. Winters in Oregon are pretty wet as we get a lot of rain, so it wasn't possible for people to keep camping outdoors.

With Meta Tantay, we wanted to get away from the Western culture and go by tribal Native traditions. With Nanish Shontie, we had a different approach: we wanted to reach out to the local people and contacted a neighboring organic farm where we exchanged drumming and painting for an organic box of vegetables every week, which was pretty cool. We started doing drumming sessions at a center close by. We worked for and with the Native people of the area, getting them to come to our land and enabled them to hold ceremonies on our premises. Sometimes we took in Native youth who were in a crisis of some kind. We also initiated a spiritual sharing group and a traditional drum circle where we invited local people to join us. We shared and learned from each other. So we expanded our vision into what we felt was dearly needed in today's times. The foundation remained a community based on the spiritual and tribal ways of Native Americans.

We wanted to create a place where we didn't just talk about it, but became an example where you could learn about these ways, where we could learn from each other.

I have always seen Nanish Shontie as a bridge between the spiritual tribal way of living in a community and the modern achievements that are available through technology and other developments.

Community Life

For who I am –- and this is not because I am Native, but also because I have lived a tribal life for most of my life –- I can't think of any better way to live than in a community based on tribal values and insights. You share work and daily life; you enjoy each other's company and benefit from the presence of people of different age groups. It gives you support while dividing up the daily work and it enables you to exchange with each other. Moreover, it provides a sense of belonging. Especially for children and for elders it is such a beautiful way of being together.

My goal became to pass on the experience and knowledge I have gathered over the years by living in a community and also through what I have learned from my elders about how it used to be.

First, we finished a new communal bathhouse and the composting toilets, and then we started building little houses for the permanent residents. As the years passed, we were able to build a large community center where we could hold the workshops and the drumming circles and could invite bigger groups. We had ceremonial areas for sunrise and a moon lodge where women could go when they were on their moon. The main house was adapted with a dining room, and kitchen plus an outdoor kitchen. We were able to get some green technology going and combined insights from permaculture with ancestral knowledge that was passed on to us over generations.

The idea was that everybody was welcome as long as you came with a good heart. We didn't charge our visitors but appreciated help with the ongoing work on the property, because there was always a lot to do. Financial help for food expenses was welcomed. Like I mentioned before, in our culture it really is about giving and sharing from the heart so we can learn from each other and can keep the circle going.

Since Corbin and I had become so close in working together and sharing our visions with each other, we both believed in lifting the original Camp vision of the seventies to a much more globally orientated idea, reaching people from all over the planet and finding like minds and hearts to make positive changes towards a better world that included all forms of life on Mother Earth. We recognized that what was needed most for the benefit of future generations was to bring people together to cooperate with each other.

One of the ideas was to make it possible for other non-profit organizations to come to Nanish Shontie and offer them a place to hold their gatherings for free. We contacted groups and activists in the area who had positive environmental and non-violent political goals. So, we had organizations like the Peace and Justice Centre, Radio for Peace International, and Maturla Global School, which gives education to the lower casts in India. They all used our facilities as a place to meet and work for a few days. It didn't matter what their belief system was or if they pursued goals a bit different than ours; the common trait involved people with good hearts who were trying to accomplish something for the greater good. It made me very happy to provide a space for them at Nanish Shontie. It was about a supportive network that created cooperation and communication between different groups.

Through reaching out to others, we got in contact with people who were very knowledgeable in their specific fields. Once we had a local group coming in doing a workshop on growing medicinal mushrooms for your own use. We had an acupuncture school from Lyon, France, offering free treatments for a week. This school had a policy of traveling all over the planet to give free acupuncture treatments a few weeks a year to people who could normally not afford this. They had heard about us and ended up giving treatments to 40 to 50 people from the neighboring area. In return, they got to experience drumming and sunrise ceremonies, talking circles and a sweat lodge, which they embraced as a great gift.

Nanish Shontie really became that place I had always envisioned: a place of learning and sharing for all walks of life, for people who were like-minded and like-hearted, who came to live and work in a community.

Luckily, throughout all those years we had a regular source of funding which provided us with larger amounts. What started out with finishing the down payments of the land developed into sustainable sums needed for renovation and construction. Nanish Shontie wouldn't have materialized the way it has without this enormous generosity in funding. This person not only supported us but also gave lots of insights and emotional support in times of struggle. It is with great gratitude and acknowledgement that I say this.

My Roundhouse

February 2015:
"Right now, as we talk, I'm sitting in my little home at Nanish Shontie. When Nanish Shontie was developing and we were starting to build new structures for our permanent members, I was asked what kind of home I would like to have. I would have really liked to live in a wickiup, just I'd lived in Nevada, but in the damp area of the coastal hills between Eugene and the ocean this wasn't a good option. So, we designed something of similar shape out of wood with an open ceiling and with a dome on the top through which you can see the sky. It turned out to be such a good comprise and totally made sense. I love my little round house!

It has a little porch on the front where I can sit outside, day and night, even when it rains and pretty much stay dry. Especially in the night I love to sit out in my rocking chair and feel the nature around me, how the wind gently touches my skin, how everything is quiet and yet present. Also our cat Furball has adopted this roundhouse as his home and he hangs around most of the time"

Hermine:

The rain pounds heavily outside and it is nice and cozy inside his round home. There is a big bed in the middle of it, some small sideboards with all kinds of objects and a closet for clothes and private belongings. The heater spreads warmth nicely and Furball is happily curled up on the bed.

"Inside, as you can see, I have many objects, presents and purchased, from different cultures and countries. I try to put them in spots where they feel good and can serve a purpose. I look at the energy flow of things individually and how they are in connection with each other. When something doesn't fit or doesn't fit anymore, I know it is time to let it go and pass it on. Sometimes it can be very spontaneous that I feel I need to give a particular thing to a certain person. If this adds specialness to that person's life, it serves a good purpose and that is how it should be. Each of the objects in here has a story to tell and a certain energy connected to it. I am basically honoring the spirit of the things that are at my place for whatever time they are meant to be with me

And I learned a long time ago that when you start gathering too many things, it's important not to get caught up in those things. [22] Proving how much you can collect on a physical level is an ego game and closes down the spiritual part. I don't want to be a person who collects and collects. I feel that these things have to serve a purpose, even if it's just that they make me feel happy to look at or they remind me of someone. They are living items filled with energy. When I touch an object, it may give me energy and I also work with some of them. But it shouldn't just hang or sit there

---

[22] Chapter 1: Eagle feathers in the wickiup story

and collect dust. I would rather give it to somebody else to wear or use in some way than hold on to it.

I am really grateful for how Spirit takes care of me, so I watch and make sure that I also pay attention to those unspoken laws of giving and receiving."

Mala now points to all the different objects in his little cabin:
"For instance, I have this wonderful necklace that is made from bear claws. It has great power and can help you in times of need. I've got necklaces made from seeds from Hawaii, given to me by indigenous Hawaiian people. This necklace is from Taiwan and there is a special story behind it. Sky and I took in a young woman from Taiwan, her name was Ni'wa, and she felt we were sort of like her extended parents while she was here in the US. My son Red Wolf went over to visit her in Taiwan and met her family, who were indigenous to the area outside the big city. The elders of her people asked him questions about his family and how his cultural traditions were. At one stage of his trip, they offered to teach him to hunt wild boar in the old traditional way where you only use knives and spears, no guns. Wild boars are sacred to the indigenous people of Taiwan and there is mutual respect between them. Hunting this way, the boar has equal chances to survive as you do: the boar might charge you; try to get its big tusks in you. My son must have done a good job and out of respect, they gave this necklace made out of wild boar teeth to me through Red Wolf.

This felt bag over here has a Raven on it. A person in Germany who belonged to a wilderness group made it. They wanted to honor me for what I'd done. They can always call me and ask for advice or help in any matters. This was their way of thanking me.

I also have many crystals. This Tibetan one was given to me and is carved in the shape of a scepter. I have worked with it, but I feel that at one point I will give it to someone who comes more from that tradition. Sometimes I am just a link to where it really needs to go, I usually feel that when it's the case, even if the person who gives it to me thinks I should have it. I am a kind of caretaker for a while. I can talk to the crystal and it will tell me when the time has come. Maybe it lets me know it wants to travel with me and then I meet the person who is supposed to have it. That is how everything flows.

Many years ago, a guy who worked for the Bureau of Indian Affairs gave me these chokers and other traditional pieces of jewelry. They told him they had been made from a breastplate that had belonged to the famous Native Chief Red Cloud. A breastplate is made from buffalo bones and beads and was worn as a protective shield against sharp knives. Long ago, the plate was stolen from Red Cloud and these necklaces were made from it. The BIA guy didn't feel right about having it and entrusted me to utilize it in the right way. I knew right there and then that someday I would be able to return it to the Red Cloud family, and that it wasn't for me personally. I had it for 12 years, had put it in a nice, secure place. Oddly enough, of all the places I had been in the US, I had never met anyone I could pass it on to. And then I met a member of the Red Cloud family in Austria, all the way over in Europe! That was actually quite funny. He'd received a prize for the work he had been doing for his people at the Pine Ridge reservation where he came from. He had left the reservation for many years and learned about solar energy. He had managed to simplify the principle in a cheap way so that anybody on the reservation could afford it. Most people there are very poor and living conditions are hard. Then people had a way of having electricity and heat out in the middle of the prairie. So, I knew this was a really good man and I promised to send him the remains of the breastplate as soon as I was back in the US. That way, it got back to the place it needed to go."

Giveaway Story

Once I was traveling in Europe, accompanied by an American friend of mine. She really liked my talks, had never been around Native people much but was very willing to learn. In Holland, we were doing a sweat lodge on the property of a friend of ours. I used a drum that had come along on many ceremonies, talks and travels for many years. The skin was getting really thin and I knew it was getting close to the point that it would break. Just shortly before we started the sweat lodge, it got a hole in it and I couldn't play it. I thought: "Well, that's how things go, I'll flow with it and do the ceremony without a drum and just sing." We went on to Germany and did our talks there, but at the end of our tour, we returned to the same place where the drum had broken. Before we started with our sweat lodge this time, a young man, who had been present the first time, approached me and handed me a brand-new drum he had made in the meantime. He said: "It was such a special experience being in that sweat lodge with you and it has given me so much. This is what I would like to give to you!" He had put a lot of effort and energy into it, I could see that, and it looked beautiful and strong too. It was made from buffalo-hide, which is difficult to get in Europe, and was a very generous gesture. Because of the thickness of the hide these drums endure sweat lodges with all the changes in temperature and humidity a lot easier than drums made from deerskin or other material. I was so humbled by what he said and how he gave me freely from his heart that I decided to give him something in return right there on the spot. It had to be something that meant something special to me, so I looked through the things I carried. There was a purse made by my mother, who had crossed over a few years before, which was covered with beadwork. All over the soft deerskin, she had made a beautiful pattern with a wild rose in the middle. The Wild Rose is one of the clans of the Shoshone people. So, I decided to give him this purse, one of the few things I still had from my mother, but I didn't tell him about my personal attachment to the purse. I just gave it to him to honor what he had done. It felt like that was what I was supposed to do.

I want to explain a little why I felt humbled and not only honored. If he had just gone to the store and bought me a drum, I would have felt honored. But him going through all that effort, really wanting to do something because his heart told him so, not because some part of his mind told him, no ego was involved, really putting his energy into what he made, that made me feel humbled. Something given truly from the heart. You don't often see that anymore. When someone has such a giving heart, it always impresses me.

My friend had watched all of this and when we were back at the room, she told me she needed to talk to me. She was very upset and couldn't understand what I had just done: giving away something that meant so much to me. She said: "That pouch was from your mother, of whom you have almost nothing left anymore. Not only that, she actually made it herself!" I was trying to make her understand that it was necessary to give him a gift that was important to my heart, which gave it more value. When you give something that you can easily replace, it is not the same. The extra value comes from what it means to you and that you are able to give it away without second thoughts. It took her a few years but then one day she told me: "You know, I think I finally understand what you meant at the time."

This little story shows the way of thinking I was brought up with: in our culture, it is called the principle of give-away.

Sometimes, though, it is important to just be able to receive. You don't always have to give in return. It can be that the gift is balanced out on a different level and you only need to accept it. But to be able to let go of things that mean something to you is a good practice to feel the flow of the circle of all things on Mother Earth. We give and receive and we pass on. I have been given a lot of really special things in my life. Sometimes they stay with me for a long time; sometimes I know when it is time to pass a gift on to another person. It never belongs to you, it can linger for a while, but when the time is right, it will move on.

Talking Circle

In our tribal system, we feel it is important to reach consensus whenever there are problems to be solved or decisions to be made. Consensus means you strive for balance. This can take a long time, that is true, but it is essential we all carry the same vision and all feel good about it. We go sit in a so-called talking circle and use a talking stick or talking stone for this purpose.

We conduct the circle clockwise. If you observe nature, you'll notice that almost everything moves clockwise. It is in the movement of the earth and moon; it shows in the animals that curl themselves up before lying down; the movement of water going down the drain flows in a clockwise rotation. We strive to learn from nature and be in harmony with that flow of energy, then nature can support us more easily in return.

We have all had the experience that when you talk in a group, other people often cut you off. We don't listen to one another very well. People have a tendency to interrupt or get loud and comment straightaway on what has been said. Some people are big talkers and others are very shy in expressing themselves in front of others, so it seems it is always the same people speaking. Sometimes people get really way off the chosen topic. The talking circle is a tool to solve those communication problems.

You have one person who acts as a facilitator and makes sure that the rules are applied in a gentle yet clear way: everybody stays on topic, there are no accusations or finger-pointing, and nobody raises their voice. In a talking circle, it is important to be careful with the use of your language and how you word your thoughts. You don't want to offend anybody and you choose your words wisely. The talking circle in its essence is about respect. The moderator does not interrupt and is an equal part of the circle.

The person who holds the talking stone or stick is the one who is allowed to talk. All the others listen and pay attention to what is being said. You speak from your heart and listen with your heart. When you are finished, you pass it on to the next person in the circle and thus it circles around. Nobody is allowed to interrupt in between if it is somebody else's turn to talk. When it's your turn, you are free to say something or remain silent. In a normal discussion, people are often afraid to speak up. Though they have made an effort, once interrupted or overruled, they shut down and stay quiet. A talking circle makes sure that everybody gets the opportunity to speak and is encouraged to do so, but nobody is forced. When you choose not to say anything when it's your turn, your presence is acknowledged and your energy is felt. You are part of the process and the circle, which is important for the outcome.

I find this indigenous way of communicating is different from the western culture in its approach, where people often get into debates and constantly interrupt and interfere. We feel it is important to hear everybody in the circle out. Every person has a voice and is equal in what they feel they want to share and this is essential for problem-solving.

If there is an issue, we continue until consensus is reached. We ask at a certain point if there is still a need to continue or if everything has been said and shared. It is important that everybody has been heard and is satisfied. We will pass the stone around as many times as necessary until all questions are asked and answered and a good decision has been made.

Traditionally, I know of talking circles that have gone on for days. If something was considered really important within the community or tribe, we took that very seriously. In indigenous communities, time is not important. It takes as long as it takes. It continues as long as it is needed.

You can also use a talking circle where it is more about sharing and less about handling a specific problem. You can choose a topic or just exchange freely about what is in your heart. I know that nowadays, this traditional tool is actually used in staff- and board meetings in modern offices, which is a great example of how the old can fit in with the new.

A friend from Austria whom I go back with a long time, once gave a special turquoise stone to me. He had a lot of knowledge of semi-precious stones and brought specialties from his travels. Turquoise is considered sacred to my people. It is able to carry energy and has healing qualities too. It can really pick up what we feel inside. Usually, turquoise appears only in sheets, in small, thin layers of stone. Every once in a while, pockets form, and the turquoise I got was one of those larger shapes. It fitted perfectly in the palm of my hand and I knew immediately what it wanted to be used for: as my talking stone. It has been passed around in many talking circles, held by hands from all kinds of people and spoken to in many languages. It has been held by Native youth that I worked with while they were getting away from drugs and alcohol. The once rough surface has become smooth from all the caressing and stroking while being held by persons talking and sharing from the heart. All the emotions and thoughts of those circles are ingrained in the stone. It is the energy of the heart that is understood by the turquoise.

Meeting with the Spirits and Belonging to Mother Earth

When I came over to Europe for the first time in 1995, I met a Dutch guy named Eric van der Geest at the Discover Life Festival in Vienna. He introduced me to his vision of "Meeting with the Spirits", which saw the organization of a gathering of indigenous leaders from all over the world to help the Mother Earth and the future generations. He had set up a support group in Holland, and after a few years, he had some concrete plans on how to continue. Sky and I got involved and were asked to be on the Board and we worked together figuring out how to have the right approach. For a while, everything looked very promising. The organization got support from Princes Irene from the Dutch royal house and there was financial input from some large companies too, which made it possible to reach out to indigenous peoples in their homelands.

At one point, Eric asked us to accompany him to Hawaii, where he wanted to connect with some of the indigenous peoples over there. We got to meet an indigenous Hawaiian guy, Ikaika, who showed us around on Kauai Island and turned out to be incredibly knowledgeable. He could tell all kinds of stories about the area and point out the different kinds of plants. He knew what they were good for and when to best pick them. He reminded me of my dad, who was an expert on plants, roots and herbs and used them for Medicine. Unfortunately, I didn't inherit his talent and don't have green thumbs at all. Ikaika also was an activist who did a lot for his people. He had gathered a group of supporters around him who had been working on getting a piece of land returned to the indigenous people of the area. This piece of land was so huge that he offered us to split it in half so we could build our community on it. He was planning a Hawaiian village with a center where the children and all the people could learn the old traditions and language. We were very tempted to accept but declined, as it would not have served our purpose of creating a community where Native Americans and others could easily find their way too. Our vision had to be created on the mainland itself.

In the end, the gathering didn't come through. A lot of contacts developed through these efforts of bringing people together with indigenous backgrounds though.

A while later, while in Oregon in 1998, I got a phone call from a man who only lived two hours away in Portland but who'd heard my name while he was over in Europe in Holland, funny enough. His name was Richard Schneider and he was looking for someone who could help him with a similar plan of creating a gathering for indigenous people in the US. Most of the conference, which he had named "Belonging to Mother Earth," was already organized and set up, but as he was reaching the final phase he was encountering serious problems with the local tribes of Virginia Beach on the East coast of the Unites States, where the gathering would take place. Once the local tribes were refusing to cooperate or to welcome the guests at the Conference, a lot of the other Native tribes wouldn't show up either, and a negative snowball effect was starting to roll. The whole Conference was falling apart. His friends had told him about me: "We know of someone, who comes from a traditional background but is okay dealing with Westerners. He could be the bridging figure."

Later on, he told me he'd often thought how hilarious and peculiar it was that he found the right person almost in his backyard, so to speak, while he had been frantically looking all over the place. We agreed to meet and talked while drinking hot chocolate and eating some pie in a small café in Salem. At first, I was a little withdrawn, as he was dressed in a more formal way, definitely not someone to hang around and relax with. Native people often have an immediate suspicion towards the white-collar business suit type of people who come along with a certain arrogant attitude. We had mostly had negative responses with people from the Bureau of Indian Affairs, the government people or lawyers working for companies and big corporations. It very often meant we ended up losing our land or having to deal with rules and regulations that weren't beneficial for us, to say the least. The vast majority of time, these people came to take, so I have quite some mistrust when I meet someone dressed like that. But Richard turned out to be someone who really had a vision and intended to do a positive thing and this is how we started to work together and became friends.

His vision was to get indigenous people from all over Mother Earth to come together and share their knowledge, from which a shared message would be sent to the rest of the world to help create a better place for all. He naturally wanted to include the Native tribes of the area, but he hadn't approached them with the appropriate protocol and the local tribes were getting more and more upset with him and had called out for a boycott from all the other Native American tribes. Time was getting short and he didn't know what he was doing wrong, although he was somewhat familiar with Native people as he had lived up in Alaska and had been one of the top employees at the Bureau of Indian Affairs. He felt committed to helping them, but had apparently never spent time with traditional elders.

I told him: "It is very important to approach Native people in the proper traditional manner. You can't just go and say: "I have a great idea and I want you all in." Our people appreciate it when we get to know each other first. You also need to follow a certain protocol that shows humbleness and respect." Richard asked me if I would be willing to come to Virginia Beach and meet with the local tribes to set things right. I agreed; the vision was strong and came with good intention, so I flew east, all expenses paid. There were only a few weeks left before everything started, so I went directly to the different tribal elders, brought tobacco and other kinds of foods, was patient and respectful and waited for them to invite me to speak. The tobacco is especially essential, as this shows you understand and respect their ways. We agreed to bring all the elders together and hold a meeting that could hopefully solve the issue. The elders, clearly very angry, explained why they had chosen to boycott the gathering. They were very offended by the typical "white man" attitude, of knowing it all and making decisions before it was discussed by the elders. They felt the whole conference would go in a false direction rather than the voice of the indigenous peoples being the heart of the gathering and being respected. I sat quietly and prayed over it and then came up with an idea: "You are correct in what you are saying. Richard hasn't shown respectful behavior towards you. But the one thing I keep thinking about, and I am also an indigenous person like you, is that this conference offers an opportunity for us directly, but more importantly for future generations! Isn't it a wonderful opportunity to host many indigenous people from all over the globe and bring them together to hear them speak? This could be something really powerful that extends far, where we as indigenous people can also connect amongst each other."

They answered: "That is all nice what you're saying and might be true, but we don't want to work with him anymore." They were adamant and still refused to do a welcoming ceremony, which was important to start the Conference with, as Native people consider this the positive sign to come as a guest to another area. If this failed, most indigenous people wouldn't come. Hearing that, I suggested: "I could act as an intermediary between you and Richard, so that any direct contact would be avoided. Would you then be willing to do a Welcome Ceremony for all the tribes coming in, as it is your land? This would start the Conference as it is supposed to be and we would all benefit from it greatly, our own people included." They nodded and it was finally agreed upon. The word went out to all the tribal people and this was a sign to go ahead.

The Conference was very successful: a lot of people came in with indigenous backgrounds but also from other cultures, not necessarily indigenous. We had a program set up with speakers from all walks of life and the possibility for smaller workshops on all kinds of topics. As I constantly had to go between the Native elders and the organizers, I was kept very busy that week. At one point, the elders honored me and thanked me personally for what I had done to make it possible.

Lots of connections were made between different groups, which brought about fruitful cooperation and networks. There was music, prayers, sharing of elders and young ones. A firekeeper tended the sacred fire that was kept alight throughout the days of the Belonging to Mother Earth Conference. It was a very special time for everyone.

Ravenwind and Radio for Peace

Richard Schneider knew about my vision for a community and that I was in search of funding. He called me up and said he had an idea. He already had a non-profit organization named Radio for Peace International, and he suggested having a business meeting together with his friend Eleanor Kedney-Schafer, whom I'd met at the Conference, to look for a possibility to combine our efforts. She had a strong financial business background involving larger companies, which could be helpful.

When I saw her again, I thought: "How am I going to take this woman along to Native people and talk to them on delicate issues when she looks so typically Western-style in her business suit and make-up and all? They are all going to close down immediately when they see me coming with her!" Eleanor later told me that when she saw me, she thought: "How am I going to get funding in business meetings for our projects with this scruffy-looking guy wearing an Indian T-shirt and a headband?" We sure both had our prejudices going on but decided to flow with it. We got to know each other better over time and as the years went by, we became good friends.

Radio for Peace International had been set up on the campus grounds of the University for Peace in Costa Rica to broadcast on positive and educational messages on short-wave, in contrast to all the so-called hate radio that was broadcast in the area. Richard's intention was to bring our individual intents for our non-profits together in a mutual interest, as this would be more effective to create funding, serving under the same umbrella. His idea was to create a business for selling services to larger telephone companies who would provide their customers with the model of donating a little of their profit to our organizations and the good causes we represented. We would all get some form of residual, regular income from this and were very much enthused. When I asked him why he wanted me on board, he said: "We have the technical potential but the heart is lacking. If you want to reach out with those idealistic goals, that would be essential."

The name of our new business became Ravenwind and we started selling some subscriptions. Unfortunately after a few years, just as it was picking up a little, cell phones became the big thing and we were basically out of business. During this whole time, Richard and I got along pretty well. I became a member of the Board of Radio for Peace International and the great advantage was that I got to go Costa Rica for several years in a row! I had never been to the tropics. It was wonderful and lush over there and I met kind people there and returned gladly each time.

Costa Rica: Snapping Turtle and Jungle Story

At the Belonging to Mother Earth conference I met Oannes Pritcher, who was from the Seminole tribe and a little bit older than me. He joined us in Costa Rica. He considered me his elder, although I was actually younger, and a couple of years later he asked me if I could help him to receive his Native name, since he was not given such a name at birth and would appreciate having one now that he was getting in touch with his Native roots. I agreed to do it for him and get back to him. I explained that a name has a connection to you as a person and to Nature and Spirit and there is always a reason and purpose for the name. Oannes had a really good heart but I had noticed that he could snap at people when he was grouchy or irritated about something, and his remarks were often directed at women. During the naming ceremony, the name Snapping Turtle came to me and when I told him, he was really happy about it: "Oh, I can see the significance. Turtles are connected to our legends in which North America is referred to as Turtle Island; they have a long life and may be slow but are wise beings." About two years or so later, he chose to talk to me again about his name-giving: "Why did you give me that specific name Snapping Turtle?" I was glad he finally asked me and I was honest with him: "You know, snapping turtles lash out at anything that gets in their way, for no particular reason. They are pretty aggressive. I have seen you do the same with people. When you are irritated or disagree with something, you snap." He got really quiet and I could see he was upset and not so proud of his name anymore.

One or two days later, he came back to me and told me: "I can see why you gave me that name. You are right. Can I do something to change that?" I said: "Sure, don't be a Snapping Turtle anymore!" He really worked on himself and people actually commented on his changed behavior. He had turned it around and was much more mellow in the way he dealt with people, and had become respectful towards women. So that name was taken away from him, because it had only been a temporary one, as a way of intentional teaching. He then received his true spiritual name, but as it is considered private between him and the Spirit world, I will not mention it here.

He has told me often he had been right about addressing me as an elder right from the beginning of our friendship, because only an elder would choose a teaching like this. Unfortunately, a few years later he crossed over.

In Costa Rica

Another story that happened in Costa Rica involved myself in a humbling way. When we came over to conduct the meetings, we'd work really hard and concentrate for a week and then spend some time visiting different places. I considered myself very lucky to be able to see such wonderful spots in that country. One time, we were staying in the middle of the jungle in a large hotel, which struck me as a paradox: a big hotel and only green, humid jungle all around. I could hardly believe I was actually experiencing this! As I always do wherever I am, I got up for sunrise and looked for a place to do my ceremony in the morning. There is the hotel to the right, there is the jungle to the left but I notice a big grassy clearing up ahead that I could reach following a small trail. When I got to the clearing, it dropped off a cliff and gave way to a magnificent view over the river below with more cliffs and jungle on both sides. The sun was coming up over the hills and I was very pleased to have found this awesome spot. I started doing my prayers and all of a sudden I heard a loud crack: "Ah well, that must have been a branch falling down or something. That doesn't bother me," and I continued with the ceremony. Half way through one of the songs, I heard a sound that curdled my blood: a huge roar! All I knew was that I thought it sounded like a dinosaur! It was so loud, so deep and roaring. I had never heard anything like it before! It was terrifying! You know, I have been out in the desert faced with a mountain lion, but this was in a different category, not a lion or jaguar kind of animal, something much bigger! It was just like in the movies.

I stood still, kept really quiet: "Maybe it will just go away..." but my heart was pounding nervously. Then another loud sound, this time even closer: "ROAR!!" Another branch cracks and I am definitely freaked now, pack up my drum and rattle, throwing things together in my bag. I decided to get out of there quick, thinking: "This is a little off from where everybody is at the hotel, I better hurry up! Man, otherwise this is the last view I am ever going to see in my life!" Now there was even more than just one roar and it was coming closer each time… No time to think, just: "RUN for your life!" All I can do is hope that I'll reach the hotel on time before this dinosaur-creature gets to me. I am running my butt off and sweating and panting heavily, looking back once in a while to see if I am being followed, but I can see no dinosaur coming after me. I finally reach the hotel where there are now some people up, starting to work in the kitchen and I come running in there, closing the door behind me. Someone on whom I must have made a disturbed and weird impression asked me: "What is the matter with you?" "Well, there is this massive beast coming at us out of the jungle! Listen, you can hear him roar!" When they heard the next roar, the locals just rolled on the floor, laughing: "Those are howling monkeys! That is how they defend themselves!" The look on my face must have been so silly and ashamed; I became the joke of the day. Monkeys! I had made my own little movie out there, quite embarrassing and humbling.

All in all, I went to this beautiful country about four or five times and I even got to meet the residing President of Costa Rica at the University. He was very interested in the work we did for Radio for Peace and was extremely friendly as well as knowledgeable and an intelligent thinker. He had done a lot of good for the development of his country. At the next election, he was not reelected, and unfortunately Radio for Peace lost the university as their transmitting station.

I was also involved in the volunteer work that Richard Schneider's wife Ruth did. She had set up a school for the lower cast girls in India, called Maturla Global School. I never made it to India but was on the Board of Governors of that non-profit as well. I am always amazed that there are so many good people trying to help wherever they can and I am thankful I got to know them.

Wilderness Groups and John Young

When I still lived in Monmouth, I was contacted by someone who had created an organization called Wild Lore, which had the purpose of building a platform for Native Americans to share their knowledge with the rest of the world. He was looking for speakers, stumbled upon me and asked me to be a part of it. I got involved in the organization for a while and met many good people. John Young was one of them, one of the main leaders of the Wilderness scene in the US, in which the participants were searching for deeper understanding and knowledge of how nature works. Cooperation between the wilderness people and indigenous traditionalists turned out to be fruitful and worked well. After a few years, I choose to leave the organization since I didn't agree with how it handled its finances, but I kept working with John Young and together we did talks and workshops both in the US and in Europe. In those years, I was already traveling across the Atlantic twice a year, doing one tour in Holland, Belgium and Northern Germany, and another one in the South of Germany and Austria. So I could combine the trips pretty easily and thus got involved with the wilderness schools over there. We also put together large gatherings for wilderness groups, where people had a chance to meet out in nature and learn from each other and from speakers and teachers who were invited. The gatherings were named "The Art of Mentoring" and were held in both the US and in Europe.

The motto of the wilderness schools is: "seeing through indigenous eyes." Willing to learn from indigenous people, they recognize there is much knowledge and wisdom to share. They try to incorporate what the essence of an indigenous approach to life is.

The people of the wilderness schools aim to get back in touch with nature and build a respectful relationship with the earth. They are very committed to the earth-ways; they know about survival techniques or how to build a fire; they have already been learning about how to sit quietly in nature and to get in touch with one's own natural spirituality. It was great to witness and made me happy inside that we could start a program of mentoring and guiding people, young and old, of similar interests to ours.

Many of the attendees are very knowledgeable on environmental issues. Some are good storytellers, others do craftwork or perform spiritual healing work with the earth. Some know incredible details about certain birds in the area or about herbs you can use for medicine.

A lot of research was done on the local history of certain areas. They also tried to reach back and remember the knowledge of their own European ancestors and elders that is still available. I saw groups building networks for women or for elders who did counseling work, basically creating small communities, which is at the heart of tribal thinking. It fills me with hope for the future to see so many young people and families with children being committed to this cause. I have been invited to act as a counselor or mentor for some of these groups.

Out of the enthusiasm of some people in these groups, a few festivals popped up and started to blossom, where literally hundreds of people would gather for a week and camp out on a piece of land somewhere in the countryside. Food was cooked for all in large communal tents and there were all kinds of workshops you could attend. Every morning, people came together for sunrise and there were other ceremonies as well on the campgrounds. The basic idea was to celebrate life and take on responsibility for Mother Earth as a caretaker. Nobody got paid a fee; the speakers, those who ran the workshops and the leaders of the festivals, did it all voluntarily. I took part in many gatherings throughout the years, partly as a teacher and speaker. Great experience each time! I thought that was pretty amazing and I wanted to come back more often, but unfortunately my health prevented me at one point.

I would like to emphasize that in the last years I have seen a movement of awakening to what is really important in life: to take care of each other, the Mother Earth and the future generations. More and more people are opening up and are willing to put energy into that. Sometimes you may have such a big thing as a festival. Sometimes it is in done on a smaller scale and is more tied to your own area. Essential is that people join their forces, as it is much easier than managing everything on your own. A well-functioning community is a living example of how things can be done in a positive way and with a different mindset. People speak of having a "Wilderness family" which is beautiful and gives a sense of belonging.

Humbling Story and Stick Game

There is a nice teaching story that happened when I got invited to visit John Young's place that he leased in Northern California for his teachings and courses. It was beautifully situated in the hills, surrounded by Redwood forest and covered quite an area. He had an advanced group arriving for some extra training. They were starting to get into their ego a bit about how good they were, and getting pretty competitive amongst each other. I had known this group for years, as I had been helping out with the training program for quite a while. Their task was to come from different directions, spreading over the land and then meet at the top of the highest hill where we would be waiting for them. They had to observe their surrounding thoroughly, and along the way we had hung little objects in the trees and bushes, like a cd or a piece of flag. John Young asked me if I could think of a teaching way to humble them since they thought so highly of themselves and had started bragging about it, saying things like: "I have learned all these great skills in this advanced workshop" or "I know everything about bird language and I can tell them apart just by listening." They were missing the whole point, just going from one workshop to another. It is not about gathering knowledge, but how you apply it for the earth and the greater good. I said: "Mmm, let me think about it… Ah yes, I know what I can do!"

I had somebody drive me all the way to the top, which had an open arbor with some simple benches to sit on. On my way up I saw one of the guys who had gotten a little behind. I said to him: "Come on and hop in the car! I'll give you a ride." He was not supposed to accept any help, of course, and was hesitant, but I urged him: "No, no. Come with me. It's okay. I have something special for you to do." When we arrived at the top, I told him to go and hide underneath one of the benches. I covered the bench with a blanket and sat down on it. I told him what I expected of him: not to speak or let the others know he was there until I gave him a sign. Slowly, the others appeared on the hilltop one by one and we all sat together underneath the harbor on the benches. I asked if anybody had had any experiences while climbing up the hill. Some had noticed things were hanging in the trees and some hadn't. We shared some more and then I started counting the group: "Wait a minute. How many are there in your group again? I think somebody is missing!" They looked around and started counting as well. They hadn't noticed anybody was missing while sharing. I asked: "So, who is missing? And where could he be?" They all started talking: "He was with us before!" "I don't understand where he is or what has kept him!" So, I suggested something: "Here I have an exercise for you. You are very connected to this guy as you've known him for years and been working together on numerous occasions. You are trained in awareness and to be more sensitive to nature and to the energies around you. So, this should be easy for you guys. I want you to all close your eyes and really picture him in your heart and connect with him. Once you feel his energy, point the direction where he is at!" Everybody agreed and all closed their eyes to try and meet the task at hand. They thought it was a fun thing to do. After a few minutes I asked them to point in the direction where they thought he would be found and to open their eyes again. They pointed in all kinds of directions, everywhere around them but no one pointed to where I was sitting. I told them: "Keep pointing, but I want you to know, I know where he is at and none of you are right." Finally, I called the guy to come out from under the bench. Of course, they all exclaimed that wasn't fair but I told them: "As much as you think you know and as good as you think you are, always be prepared for the unexpected. There is always more that you can learn!" They all looked down: "Ooh man, I totally didn't get it." Even when I was sitting on top of the guy and of course had deliberately confused them through my action, they still could have been able to sense his energy. It was difficult but not impossible. It was maybe a tough lesson but also one with humor. We could all laugh about it!

As Native people, we used to train the capability of seeing and sensing with a game called "the stick game." You have two rows of people on opposite sides. You play with a set of bones or sticks all painted white, except for one with many colors. If you have an audience, you first have a betting round on who will be the winners. One person takes the colored stick and hides it in his hands. The others take the white ones and hide them too. Everybody puts their hands behind their backs. The opposite party has to find out in which hand the colored stick is. So-called power songs accompanied the game, which supports you to look through a person and enable you to find out who was holding the colored stick or bone. Colors have energy and you can sense and see the differences in those energies. Playing around like this teaches children sensitivity at a very young age. Healers can learn clear discernment in diagnosing illnesses. There are other names for those songs too, like stick game songs or gambling songs. Nowadays when I travel to the wilderness groups, I notice that one of those songs, an old Shoshone one, is even used as a fire song to help light a fire in a strong manner.

An Example of a Dysfunctional Community

While at Nanish Shontie, I got an invitation from a community in Holland that sounded like a positive project, where they used alternative energies and lived a simple life away from society. I am always open to these experiences and exchanges and went ahead with it. The community had gotten hold of an abandoned army base used by the Nazis during World War II. As a cover up, so the Allies would be unsure whether or not to bomb these structures, they had made it look like a big farm-complex. Sky and I were invited for a couple of days to do some workshops and talks or run a sweat lodge.

As we entered through the gate of the premises after driving down a narrow dirt road, I immediately felt something like a warning of some kind that this place might not be as we had expected. There were a lot of old brick buildings, most of them with earthen roofs covered with sod. Some houses had shattered windows, some didn't have any at all. Garbage was lying around and a lot of broken bicycles were just dumped here and there. It didn't look very inviting and taken care of.

The guy we had been in contact with showed us around in the house where we could stay. Everything was very filthy inside. The floors were all covered with a few inches of dirt; no way you take off your shoes in there. There was one bigger room with a little kitchen and a room with a single bunk bed that we both knew couldn't handle the two of us together.

As we walked across the field towards the meeting room where the rest were waiting for us, we saw a dog running around with just three legs. Sky is very fond of animals and wanted to know more. He told us: "Oh, he got into a fight with one of the other dogs and his leg got badly infected, so we had to take it off."

We noticed how dark it was in the meeting hall and he explained: "We prefer not to use any electricity." As our eyes adjusted to the interior, where some candles were burning, we discovered a lot of couches. The funniest thing was that on each couch some dogs had spread themselves out, while the people were sitting in front on the floor. He explained: "We feel that dogs have as many rights as humans, so if they get to the couch first, it's theirs. Just go ahead and find yourself a spot!" I looked at Sky and said: "Follow me!" and walked over to a couch, gently moved the two dogs off and sat down, who naturally curled up at our feet on the floor. That caught most people by surprise. We were served some tea and listened to their meeting. One thing surprised me: the entire group consisted of around 40 persons talking freely, as they felt. They were cutting each other off sometimes; there was no real listening to what was being said, and little groups also talked. We were introduced and explained where we came from and why we were visiting. Beforehand, the community had expressed their wish for our advice on some issues, as we came from a traditional and tribal background, and this topic was scheduled for the following evening.

We went back to the guy's place and had some dinner, which tasted nice but while I was stirring, I kept hitting on some harder pieces that stuck to the inside of the bowl and I realized the bowls were dirty. Sky peered at me and we both nodded with apprehension: "Definitely not clean!" But we were polite and handled it. We were given two thin mats to lie on and some blankets. He threw them on the concrete floor, not thinking twice about having two older people on a concrete floor for the night. Sky asked about the bathroom: you had to climb up a rickety little ladder, which I was afraid would crash if I climbed it. Then you had to turn around with your back facing the ladder, take off your pants and do your thing. There was no flush. It was basically an outhouse, except that it was indoors! An open space with no privacy of any kind was used for showering through a pipe with a lever coming out of the wall. Some black-colored water spouted out, which they were very proud of since it was part of their recycling system. I knew I wasn't going to use that water for showering!

We finally went to bed and I got under the covers. It was pretty hard on that thin mat but at least we had enough space. All of a sudden, two huge dogs thumped in and just put themselves right on top of us. "Oh yes," the guy says, "I forgot to tell you, but usually those dogs sleep on those mats!" Then we hear voices and a lot of young people show up, carrying sleeping bags and luggage with them. "Oh yeah, one more thing: these are all people coming to your workshop tomorrow." By now we are surrounded by a bunch of young hippy punks who are stripping off their clothes and cuddling up really close, while there are two dogs on top of our legs. It was going to be a pretty rough night with some interesting noises of young people making love and others snoring, but we survived it.

For breakfast, our host made us oatmeal and said: "Outside there is a big box with all kinds of plates and cutlery. Go ahead and pick whatever fits you." They were all dirty! When we asked where the clean ones were, we got the answer: "Oh, we don't bother. We just re-use them." By that time, we were getting disgusted but were hiding it politely and managed to eat the food. We offered to clean our own dishes. You had to heat up water for cleanup, so we made a large fire and got started with cleaning ours plus all the dirty plates from the box. Then the guy pulled away a blanket hanging down from somewhere next to a wall. I couldn't believe my eyes. Underneath were stacks of plates, cups, bowls and silverware. Some were covered with green mold; some were black from dirt and fungus. It was horrible and filthy. I sighed but thought: "Ah well, we better start doing this! It is just too grimy to leave it there." The guy apologized, he had to leave for an appointment and I knew he wasn't coming back any time soon. It was obvious that the method had been not to wash anything until they were totally out of any bowls, plates or cups and to just toss everything that was used in a big pile. Later that morning we walked to the place where they had already built a sweat lodge. It could only hold four to five people. The area around the lodge and the altar was covered with rounded, broken pieces of glass. They had actually made an attempt to make it pretty with the glass, but it wasn't how we would treat the earth and the ceremonial area. When I looked in the fire pit, I could see garbage in it. I explained that for a ceremonial fire, you don't burn garbage, but he replied: "Never mind, the spirits understand we need to get rid of the garbage and we don't have enough wood." Finally, I had to come forward and said: "I am really sorry, but we aren't going to make it like this. We can't do our ceremony in this way. I don't see how we can fix this in the short time we are here." So, we never did a sweat lodge and I am still grateful I put my foot down.

In the evening, we joined them for the meeting where they asked us for advice in resolving problems. They had a rule which was actually the opposite of a rule. Anybody could do anything to anybody and nobody was allowed to complain about it and had to be okay no matter what happened. It was supposed to be total freedom of speech and action with no restrictions. Over the years, they had realized some really bad things had happened and nothing was done about it. We had already found out there were two other three-legged dogs hopping around. They refused to interfere when dogs were getting into a fight. We had witnessed one of those fights and a little toddler was standing right in the middle of it. Sky grabbed the child away from the dogs, but the people watching the scene said: "If this child wants to stand there, it has every right to do that. We allow whatever is meant to happen."

My first suggestion was the talking circle principle. I explained: "You need better communication amongst each other. You need to learn to listen to each other instead of constantly cutting each other off and having conversations on the side. You need to be respectful." I laid out all the different aspects of a talking circle and they really seemed to like that idea. Next, we started talking about the boundaries for the dogs and the children. I explained with some simple boundaries you provide safety and care taking. They weren't very enthused by this at all, so we left it at that.

We did see some people who were trying to keep their little piece of land clean and tidy, who tried to take care, took out the rubbish and did some repairing. I remember there was one man who used to be a professional chef-de-cuisine. He made fresh bread in a handmade oven out of clay, which tasted delicious. He did it all by himself without anybody else assisting him. Unfortunately, the overwhelming impression at the community was garbage, chaos, broken things and no care for anything.

The meeting for the next evening got cancelled. We guessed it was because we really didn't say the things they wanted to hear. We had had enough ourselves and wanted to leave earlier. They weren't interested in anything we had to offer from our experience and knowledge and we could see no effort in their attempts to make the place better for everyone involved.

Luckily, we were able to call up a friend who lived a couple of hours away and who agreed to pick us up. We didn't tell anybody, just packed our stuff and left.

In this story, there was great teaching for me personally: you don't have to put up with everything, haha! Traveling around on low budget, I was used to odd sleeping accommodations and different eating habits. I don't mind simple housing at all, but this really wasn't acceptable. The wisest thing is to not be judgmental about the situation or the people involved. As human beings, we have a tendency to become very negative about situations so that it is easier for us to reason why we are stepping out. We become defensive or even aggressive, as if trying to excuse our own failed judgment that got us into that situation in the first place. At the same time, we appear better ourselves. But everything has its reason for being there. It just means you choose to leave the situation if it doesn't serve you and if your presence doesn't serve the situation.

The other lesson was that not everybody wants to be helped or is ready for help. Even though they had asked for our support and help, they were so stuck in their own way of thinking that they don't even want to consider another approach. Very often, the advice somebody is asking for is actually a request to affirm what is already present. The person wants acknowledgment or maybe even a compliment for their accomplishments and efforts. Sometimes the person's heart asks for help but the ego and the mind are in the way of an open discussion and exchange.

Of course, Sky and I talked about the whole situation at length and agreed that although the idea of the community was good at the start, there was a misconception about what a community needs. You could see that the whole project was a response to an overregulated society with a lot of limits for artists and creative people. The attempt was to enable people to live in a community that would support each other and guarantee total freedom for everyone. As Native people coming with experience of living in a community with awareness for the environment and for personal development, we were asked for help when problems arose within the community. According to my tradition and understanding, elders provide a community with guidance through their wisdom and knowledge in how to create and keep a community healthy and harmonious. This is based on respect for all life forms and the act of care-taking of all those life forms. Yes, a traditional community enables everyone to live and follow their own path, but it is not just about the individual.

When you leave your trash and don't clean up after yourself, you create disharmony. You show disrespect to the Mother Earth and to all Life. In the end, nobody cleans up anymore; people, animals and plant life get hurt; nobody seems to care. That is not a positive flow of energy.

How you interact with other people is essential for how communication will function. If I don't listen, just go and do my own thing and don't care how it affects others, it doesn't create harmony. If you feel nobody is listening to you anyway, you stop doing so yourself. You either go silent or start shouting to be heard. This amplifies after a while and each person is soon on their own secluded island. The elders teach you that human beings are only a very small part of Creation. You need to be aware of that at all times and strive for harmony with all Life. As we are a part of the great circle, it is only natural that what we put out is exactly what comes back to us.

Respect creates harmony. What we encountered at that community was out of balance and a form of anarchy, though the intentions of the people had been good and idealistic. I am aware it was an experiment and manifested as an act of resistance to the uptight rules and regulations of the period before. As a result, it was overdone in the opposite direction.

The problem is that when you are living in a certain environmental energy for a longer period of time, it has an effect on you. You start to behave and become like it. You don't bother anymore, you stop caring and trying because it is too much to handle on your own. This can be a very treacherous process. You even start to justify things as they are or you belittle problems or even deny them just to keep the status quo going. When you come from the outside as a visitor like we did, you see things more clearly. All in all, it was a very interesting learning situation for us.

Meeting of Good-hearted People

On my many travels, I met a lot of good people and was repeatedly amazed at how similar our wishes and dreams sometimes were.

To give some examples: I have often been invited to stay over for free or have a meal at people's homes. Many talks and workshops have been organized for me and people gave their time freely to help find funding for Nanish Shontie, Pooh Ha Bah and other causes. I witnessed people trying to create some kind of community or set up an organization. Others got involved in large gatherings like the Peace Conference at The Hague in the

Netherlands. In Belgium the NGO "For Mother Earth" produced special T-shirts for our shared cause. One of the members made a homemade chocolate spread that I could sell as income for Nanish Shontie. I have had offers for interviews on radio and even filmmakers in both the Netherlands and Austria who offered to make videos and a small movie on Corbin and me. There have been people who offered me their meeting and seminar rooms free of charge when I did a workshop or a talk. When I was in a difficult financial situation without any medical insurance, the surgeon and nurses offered to do the operation for free and I only had to cover the expenses of the hospital costs. I could go on and on. Sometimes I am so amazed about the positive resonance and how people have offered help! It fills my heart with great joy and gratitude.

With Raymond (Tlingkit tribe) at the Peace
Conference in The Hague (NL)

What I kept hearing from a lot of those who came to see and hear me was that although the message was very inspiring, a continuous follow-up to incorporate what was said was lacking. Information given once a year was too little to keep a practice going. You start out with a high motivation but it lessens over time as the daily habits creep back in and you feel left alone with all those new ideas. To continue to practice something new, you need a regular possibility to ask questions and become reassured that you are on the right track. This was understandable, but I didn't see a possibility to solve it. I offered everybody to stay in touch, they could always contact me with their doubts, questions or problems through phone or email, but I couldn't be there in person all the time. When I started to go to the wilderness groups over in Europe, this was a different setting, because these groups already existed and met with each other year-round. Over the years, I have watched this community grow and it gave me inspiration and hope. People who have already chosen to walk this path are easier to reach and work with, of course. It is not just talking to the choir but the choir is actually participating!

Rewarding friendships developed throughout the years and I made a special connection with Corvus, one of the wilderness groups in Germany. At a large gathering with about 200 people attending for ten days, the members of this group were especially active in accommodating and help-ing out on the spot. They gathered the wood for the fires, helped cook the food, organized little games out in the fields for the attendees, made sure the sweat lodge area was set up in the proper way and that the ceremonial area was prepared for sunrise. I was impressed with their attitude and commitment. I got invited to their home base in the area around Bodensee in the south of Germany, and I incorporated a visit nearly every time I'd come to Europe from then on. A few of their members came over to Nanish Shontie, which was a beautiful opportunity to strengthen our bond. One day, they approached me and asked if I would consider becoming their

Grandfather, in German their "Opa." I knew that would mean a commitment beyond just the name. Native people give the honorary title Grandfather or Grandmother to a person, usually of older age, whom they consider wise, knowledgeable and highly respected. We welcome a stone coming into a sweat lodge as a Grandfather, because rocks are the oldest people on Mother Earth connected to ancient wisdom. When we go into the forest, we usually look for the Grandmother or Grandfather of the tree people and pay our respects. So, I returned the question: "Do you understand the significance what that means? In my way, becoming a Grandfather results in a relationship for life. We will take care of each other: if you ever call upon me and need me, I will try and be there and you need to do the same for me." They realized it was more serious than they had anticipated and wanted to reflect on it before proceeding. In the end, we went along in a ceremonial setting where we committed ourselves to each other. From that moment on, I was called Opa Mala and became their Grandfather. They still call me up from time to time, even now where I can't travel around anymore. It has stayed a special relationship and I feel honored to this day. Becoming a Grandfather is a deeper layer where you become part of the family: it is of a more intimate nature and closer to the heart.

Ostrich Story and Shifts in Awareness

One time I was traveling through Europe on a speaking tour. Sky accompanied me and we were in Belgium, where we have a good friend, Lutgard, who had accommodated us many times and helped organize talks and workshops. Together we visited a friend of hers who had traveled through Australia for a few years, where he'd had the chance to live amongst Aboriginals, the indigenous people there. Upon returning to Belgium, he had decided to start an ostrich farm and intended to implement the knowledge the Aboriginals had shared with him. He must have had 30 to 40 ostriches of different sizes at that farm. It had horse stables and barns, only now there were ostriches sticking their heads out over the stable doors. He gave us a tour of the land and said: "There is something special about ostriches that you should know. I'd like to do a little experiment with you and see how it works out." He took us to the main outdoor pen, where a group of ostriches was walking around freely and had our group gather in the center. As soon as the ostriches saw us, they all took off in different directions, not wanting to be close. Then he started explaining: "When I was in Australia, the Aboriginals used the ostriches as a tool to train their young ones for a specific ability. I would like to see how you cope with that situation. It's going to be fun and there is nothing dangerous about it, don't worry!" He continued: "As you probably know, ostriches are the largest birds in the world. Although they have very large bodies, their heads are pretty small in comparison and their brains are even smaller. Creation balanced this lack of brain mass with a gift in another area, as everything in nature is balanced in the end and makes perfectly sense. Next to being able to run really fast with that huge body with the help of strong muscular legs, the ostrich was given a special ability. It is able to be totally present in the now; it doesn't worry about the future or the past, is literally in the moment all the time. It is so sensitive that it can feel what a person is thinking when someone approaches. If you plan on catching it or harming it, it knows straight away. The ostrich knows what you are feeling because you are thinking about it.

The Aboriginals thought this was an excellent possibility to train their young ones in the ability of being with two mind-sets. They gave their children the task of walking up to an ostrich and pulling out a feather while it was standing still and wasn't trying to run off. This meant they had to develop the ability to come close without letting the ostrich know what their intention was. To learn to act without thinking, to empty your mind yet still be able to act. Would you like to see if you can perform this task?"

We all thought this was a great opportunity to practice and see how we'd cope. One person in our group agreed to go first and walked up but within a few feet the ostrich already turned away and ran from him. The next person did better but still didn't get near the bird. Some couldn't get it to work at all, as the ostrich took off the minute the person turned towards it. Others did better and got pretty close, but nobody was able to touch them. I was the last one to have a try. I remember how my dad used to teach me how the physical part of you can be present but not really all the way. He taught me to focus on the spiritual presence so others are only aware of that part and the physical part is not visible. It is a way of visualization. So, what I did was the following: while standing a few feet away from the ostrich, I visualized my intention and the path I was going to walk. Then I changed my focus and left that thought behind with a part of my physical body. Next, I started to focus on a flower that was right next to the ostrich and walked towards it. All I thought about was that flower. While walking, I came close to the ostrich and was able to pet it a little. I stroked it a few times and saw there was a feather already hanging out halfway. I jerked on it twice and had the feather in my hand. The ostrich didn't even move and I walked quietly back to the group.

Even at the moment when I took the feather, I wasn't thinking of it. I just did it but there was no excitement or planning. My mind was sort of blank, yet at the same time busy with the flower. It is a way of separating yourself from your physical presence. A part of me was there and actually petting the bird and a part of me wasn't there at all. The forefront of myself was thinking of the flower and this was also what the ostrich was sensing so it wasn't worried. It is a shift in focus, really. So, I ended up with a nice, big ostrich feather!

The rest of the group was impressed, but basically this is something you can practice. I learned this at a young age and have simply gotten better over the years. According to our tradition, if you were serious about living a spiritual Way of Life, this ability was something you wanted to learn, as it gave you a chance to approach nature without disturbing it and be fully surrounded by it. Some people may be more gifted in this area and learn quicker than others, but you still need to practice. Sometimes a gift can even block you because you don't bother to practice and take it for granted.

Hunters use this skill because it makes them blend in with nature and they can get close to their prey. There are actually two approaches in traditional hunting and I have practiced both ways. Either you communicate clearly through the energy you send out what you intend to do and you wait if there is an animal or bird that is willing to give its life, or you make a shift in your consciousness and hide your intent so the prey doesn't sense any danger and you can get close.

When you train this ability, you get to the point where you can shift pretty quickly from one state to another. It can come in pretty handy. I remember when I was at the Peace Conference in the Netherlands, we had been through many long meetings and were pretty tired of listening. I was sitting in a room in one of the back rows and had gone into a certain state where my body was asleep but where I could actually hear what was going on. The woman leading the discussion at one point said: "I would really like to hear Mala Spotted Eagle elaborate some more on this subject." I had no problem answering her request straight away. I knew what she had been talking about and could also give an adequate opinion. Everybody in my vicinity was amazed how I did that because they all noticed that I had been sound asleep and snoring. Yeah, it was actually very funny! My body was resting and relaxing but my mind was fully aware and ready to respond to whatever was needed. I knew how my body is positioned or even that I was snoring, but I was not totally present in my body, either. Even when I'm standing, it sometimes seems as if I'm asleep almost. Many people have mentioned that to me. I wouldn't really know a name for it. But if I think about it, I could go call it a shift in awareness of the physical and the spiritual self. You are aware of both sides, but there is one part that is stronger in its conscious presence than the other part.

Drumming

Mala is speaking to a group of approximately 20 students gathered in a circle around the big drum in the middle.

"The use of drums has long been at the core of Native American spirituality. Whenever there is a ceremony going on, you usually hear the sound of a drum. To us, it represents the heartbeat of the Mother Earth and the heartbeat a child hears when it is still in the mother's womb. You have small hand drums but also larger ones for specific purposes or ceremonial use. Sometimes we use a big drum like this one. Depending on the size of the drum, six to ten people sit around, each with a drumstick in their hand, and we drum together.

We start off with putting tobacco in the center of the drum to speak a prayer. There is a reason and tradition behind using tobacco. Tobacco to us is a very sacred and sensitive plant. It has the gift of sensing energy and feels what is going on in a person, not just their attitude, but deeper layers inside. It can sense if a person is in need of help, is struggling physically or emotionally from a sickness or hurt that is carried inside. When we begin to drum, the tobacco on top will start to dance. And while it dances, it will move in a certain direction towards the person who needs the prayers most. At the end of the drumming session, this person takes the tobacco and returns the tobacco back to the Mother Earth, giving thanks for being chosen. You see, we all need help sometimes: there is no one who never needs help. We shouldn't feel that we are above that, nor that we are not worth it. When the tobacco chooses you, this is something to be thankful for.

Here are some basics on how to approach the drum. You don't put anything on top of it. Sometimes you can lay the drumming sticks on it, but we don't use it as a coffee table or put our feet on it." *Mala makes this comment in a joking manner and laughs but is also very serious about this.*

"This drum was made from buffalo hide on the one side and elk hide on the other. Those hides are still connected to the buffalo and elk people. The wood used was from a cedar tree. So, we want to honor the spirits of those peoples whenever we are around them or use the drum. We know if we respect and honor them, whether buffalo, elk or cedar, they will take good care of us and be there if we need them. If we are disrespectful in any way, this can have consequences, as this information goes back to their people.

I usually sing the so-called Camp songs, which are about certain animals or asking the Creator for something. They are much older than powwow songs, for instance. Powwows are actually only a recent invention. When you are gathered around a big drum like this one, you have one person who is the lead drummer. This person decides on beat and pace and is also the lead singer. He makes use of certain signs that show when to stop or to continue one more round, when to be quieter or stronger in the sound.

I have been around the drum pretty much all of my life and I know a lot of songs, but I have met guys who literally know hundreds of songs and different beats by heart. When you are a practiced drummer, you can also hear when somebody else in the group is offbeat. I had a teacher who would tap the offbeat person on the head during the song and continue playing without a blink of the eye. He would let that drumstick leap out and you knew you had it coming! Drumming needs a lot of focus!" *Mala remembers and laughs his bellowing loud laugh again.*

"When you drum, it is very important to have an image in your heart and mind about what you are singing and drumming for. You give the drumming direction that way and you add energy to the outcome.

If I am singing a song, I think about what the song is about and picture this as a clear image. I then think about whom the song is for and what I am trying to create with the song and give it direction through picturing where it needs to go. It is simple but takes a lot of focus, and at the same time great awareness. You send the song out and it gains strength.

If I sing the Welcome song at sunrise, I deliberately picture all those creatures like birds, animals and people as much as I picture the water, the trees, the spirits, and all of Mother Earth. The song goes out to those beings. If I pray for someone who needs healing, obviously I focus on the person and picture the person. This is how it works.

When you drink a specific tea, when you have a cold or a stomach-ache, you can just drink the tea, but it becomes much more effective if you remember the plant the tea is made from and you talk to that plant and picture it how its gift will help you.

You see the flow of energy going into a person or into the Mother Earth or a certain tree or the water. Although you direct the flow of the energy, you don't interfere with the energy itself and how it should work. The energy will do that part on its own and you just have faith and visualize something positive. You leave the doorway open to how Creation will answer.

As I said, this applies to everything and therefore also to when you are sitting together around the drum. When it is done in this way, the energy of the drum can spread far and do a lot of good."

Training of Spirituality

Spirituality is something that everyone has and it is something that can be trained. If you are brought up in a way that supports the concept of spirituality as an important part of a human life on this planet, then naturally this develops within you. If it is denied by your surroundings or not mentioned at all, of course it remains hidden or shows itself only on certain moments. You might not even recognize it as such.

Nowadays when we talk about awakening, this is in fact what is meant: you wake up the dormant aspects of your spirit and work with it -- as it has been there all along! Together with the physical, the emotional and the mental, spirituality forms the fourth aspect of the circle.

Like you train a muscle to make it stronger, you can train your spirit. The ceremonies are part of our traditional, indigenous culture and help open those spiritual channels and connections. A strong connection to Nature and Spirit can overcome you and you recognize the oneness of all things with a great sense of power. It is what they call the Medicine energy: a flow of energy comes together inside and you know it will have a strong impact on whatever you think, feel, speak or do.

But you can also train your spirituality while being on your own, just by practicing in your daily life, without any aid. What matters is that you choose to walk that path truthfully; then you will always receive support from the spirit world.

It is up to you to train it and work with it. The ceremonies, the sun dance, the vision quest and such are all tools to reach a higher level and become stronger in your spirituality. In the end, spirituality is in everything you do; it becomes so much part of you that it is always present and tangible. It is like those muscles you train: you just have them, wherever you go and not just when you are at the fitness center. The good thing about having a stronger spiritual awareness is that it will affect your words and actions positively, aside from you feeling more connected to Nature and Spirit, which will give you a greater sense of belonging and happiness. The way Native people see it: your ability to work with Spirit will be something that carries you through life.

What you have to be careful about is not to want too much too fast. When you walk this path, you need to be aware that you walk a circle and you have to walk it completely. If you take shortcuts all the time and you think you are already there, you have missed the essence, since you will always continue to learn. It often happens: you fool yourself and jump ahead. This is part of the teaching and okay because you only have to get back on track. As many great teachers have always emphasized, the true teaching is the journey itself. A circle has neither a beginning nor an end, and is very different from a straight line, which sets a goal.

Yet there are times when you seem to go through certain steps more quickly. The steps are different for everyone but each step is important in itself. You shouldn't skip any; they are there for a reason. If you do, at some other point the lesson will return to you. Other steps seem to go on for ages and feel like heavy loads that constantly repeat themselves.

One of the hardest things is to look at yourself in an honest and truthful manner. That is where your own character flaws come in: if you don't believe in your own abilities and doubt yourself a lot, you will tend to overlook your own growth. If you have a tendency to brag about yourself and be quickly satisfied, you will think you are further along than you actually are.

Growing older brings the advantage that you have had many experiences and hopefully have become more balanced within yourself. Not all older people have this: some can get very stuck in their ways and haven't become wiser in the wider sense. If you are a true elder, you carry the wisdom of the heart and mind. Over time, you have learned what you are capable of and where your strengths and weaknesses lie. Time is an important factor as you have walked the journey longer and have gathered experiences that may be similar but still be a little different each time: you have a whole scale of experiences and that gets fine-tuned and more distilled. Your understanding gains depth and you have a feeling for both details and essence at the same time. You become much more conscious of your actions, words and thoughts.

When you are young, it is tempting just to react to a certain situation or person. Over time, you learn that it is necessary to wait and let things sink in before reacting without thinking about the consequences. Yet, the stormy, impulsive energy of youth can also be refreshing of course! An impulse can be very intuitive and correct if it is aligned with your whole being. It shouldn't just be an emotional reaction out of feeling offended or because you feel an urge to lash out because of spite and anger. That is where it is off. If an impulse comes, like when you feel the need to help someone who is in trouble -- say, someone is in the water screaming for help -- it is good not to think twice about it. It is more a reflex that leads to an action and becomes a deliberate act, where you are even guided on a spiritual level without necessarily realizing it. Especially in situations where there is danger involved, it can be life-saving to act upon those impulses and insights about what to do.

Often, however, acting without thinking and reflecting hurts people and doesn't help a situation at hand. Time teaches you patience and consciousness and raises awareness for the whole.

Overall, I would say that just reacting is not what we favor. Instead, acting consciously after having given it a thought, not just from the mind but also with your heart and spirit, is what will help you live a spiritual life.

"Walking a spiritual path" or "being a spiritual person" is what it comes down to in the Native American traditional Way of Life.

Mala is speaking to a young woman, Anna, who comes to his place for counseling once in a while. While she is talking about the significance of walking a spiritual path, she is distracted by a little moth flapping in front of her face, tickling her a little bit and making her eyes restless. She starts to laugh and Mala brings up a related story from his own past.

"When I was a kid, I was playing outside once in our yard in the desert and I got bitten by an ant. Sadly, I have to admit I was mad about the pain and squeezed all the ants to death. My dad just happened to pass by and asked: "Why did you do that?" "Well, there was one that bit me and now I want to get rid of all of them so it doesn't happen again!" He says: "You know, usually they only bite when you're interfering in whatever they are doing and you threaten them. Apart from that, do you remember how we have always told you that everything is part of Creation and everything is connected? In the Old Ways, we were able to listen to all the messages from everything around us. We would hear and understand what the wind was telling us. We were able to sense the animals nearby or what the birds were up to. The connection was total and we were all one. We took care of each other and knew that anything could be a messenger from the Creator, even the tiniest being could warn us or make us aware. You never know what form the messenger will take on. It can be a mosquito or a buffalo... Think about this: did you just kill your messenger?" and he walked away and left me with my thoughts. I asked other elders: "But what if I go out and hunt for prey? I also take a life then." The answer was simple: "If you go out to hunt or gather food from the plants, you talk to the spirit of that life-form and you would know if it is a messenger or not. You work with them and there is a harmony there between the life you take in order for you to live on, as part of the great Circle." That is when I understood. The elders also said: "A lot of times it doesn't even have to be a messenger but it is just Creation's way of seeing how much patience you have. Do you go through the trouble of moving the creature to a safe place? How do you respond to it?"

The woman chuckles softly and we continue to share our thoughts on the subject. Teachings and little "nuggets of wisdom" can come from anywhere. The question is: do I allow it to become a teaching and sit right in the middle of the ant nest, so to speak, or is the teaching to get myself to a safe place where I also don't end up hurting the ants?

Mala comes with another real-life practical story that happened when he was in Europe leading a sweat lodge with a group of people who weren't yet very familiar with the ceremony.

"Sky and I traveled to Holland, where we stayed at a farm outside of Breda that the owner had changed into a spiritual center. The ceremonial area had been used before and the willow framework was already standing. We covered it with the blankets, got the fire going and went in to start the ceremony. When we were doing the first round, I noticed that as it was getting warmer in there, people were moving around and started hollering: "I am getting bit over here!" "Me too! Ouch!"

So, we opened the door to understand what was happening. Apparently during the time in which the sweat lodge hadn't been used, an ant-colony had moved into the earth right beneath us and now the heat was drawing them out. Hundreds of tiny red ants were crawling all over everybody's bodies. People were trying to brush them off and one of the people was killing them. I told him: "You are sitting in a ceremony, praying for the Mother Earth and asking how you can become a better caretaker. Think about that."

I turned to everybody: "This is what we'll do. We need to change our energy towards the ants. I want you all to sit quietly and go within. See those ants as spiritual beings and not as animals that are biting you. Tell them you understand why they are upset, as we have intruded on their home. Tell them, you don't mean harm. Apologize for having upset them. Ask their permission to carry on the ceremony whilst they return to their home deep within the earth where they will be safe."

Everybody got quiet and started focusing on these words and worked on changing their energy. While the door was still open, we noticed all the ants crawling back into the soil until they totally disappeared. I poured some water on the earth in front of everybody, so they could put some of the mud on their skin to help with the stinging. After that we could carry on with all four rounds of the ceremony. It was a powerful lesson!

In the Western world, I often have encountered the need for proof that you can actually talk to the spirit of creatures and to Creation overall. They don't usually believe it. We have a saying amongst our people: "Believing is seeing!" Indigenous people have a tendency to see what they believe. The Western culture applies this principle the other way around. "Seeing is believing" In other words, they first need proof. People of Western culture often don't believe in magic. They claim it doesn't exist and persist in going by the objective facts and scientific proof. If you choose to believe in magic, magic comes into your life. When you carry a strong belief in your heart, the power that goes out is enormous, unlimited.

Even if you want to get past a Western mindset and know that the wind you feel on your skin exists and that the full moon makes you feel a certain way, it is still often hard because you have to unlearn a habit that was instilled long ago. You remain skeptical, as you were taught to observe everything with a critical mind. Indigenous people believe in their hearts that you can communicate with nature and spirits and that their response comes naturally, and you can witness that. In indigenous cultures, it is said that the heart should lead you. The mind is helpful and important too, but it is considered essential that the heart leads and guides you in pretty much every situation you are in.

When you walk a spiritual path in the Native way, you aim to be in a state of presence that fills you with gratitude, joy, humbleness and respect for all Life. You enjoy becoming fully connected and fully present.

Always remember that you are part of the circle and that it is give and take. You can compare it to when you are harvesting fruit at the end of the summer season. You ask for permission to take the fruit; you only take so much and pray that the bush or tree will recover again and you leave some for the birds and insects; you give thanks and acknowledge their presence as part of the sacred Circle of Life and, last but not least, you give something in return, like tobacco or a strand of your hair. In this way, there is balance.

A lot of our ceremonies show our appreciation that we don't take the gifts of life for granted. We choose to go through the suffering of a sweat lodge or a sun dance, in order to show Spirit we are serious and willing to endure something so balance is kept. An offering is also a way of showing the spirit world you are aware of the connection between give and take. Talking to the life you are taking is an important part of the communication going on. Since he was a herbalist, my dad told me to see plant life and trees as tribes and that you naturally would speak to the eldest of that tribe: to explain what you are going to do and what you need the plant for, to never just take from the Grandmother or Grandfather, and to remember to give thanks. If it is done appropriately and if you are fully aware of the Circle of Life and Death, harvesting can be very much a tool to understand the balance upon the Mother Earth.

The three of us talk about the power and the gift of the elderberry, which grows in so many places on the planet and which is seen as a sacred tree both in Europe and in the United States. In Europe, people plant the elderberry on their property for protection of the house and the people in it. In fairytales, the colors white, red and black of the flowers and the berries, depending on their ripeness, refer to the phases of a woman's life. Elderberry is connected to the Great Mother of All, which brings new life and takes life to continue the circle. Mala shares that a long time ago, the Shoshone people would stick an elderberry branch from a mountain area in the ground of a sweat lodge, as in the desert itself there weren't any bushes or trees. The name elderberry is also interesting as it directly refers to the elders and ancestors and their knowledge and wisdom.

To walk a spiritual path and become a true spiritual person, you need to practice constantly and every day. Becoming a spiritual person is a path you embark on and you want to do it in a way that creates harmony and makes you feel good. It doesn't happen overnight. You practice and you stumble but you don't push, just try to be in that space again.

Spirituality is not convenient. It forces you to slow down and take your time to reflect, sit still, observe and be patient. It is about walking gently upon the Mother Earth and becoming more aware of your actions, thoughts and emotions. You can learn awareness by activating your senses both outward and inward. You also need to incorporate it into your daily life, at work, interacting with your partner or your family or when you face challenges and difficulties. At one point, you will see where all those pieces lead to; it becomes a puzzle that takes shape and makes sense. That is a great feeling! You start to enjoy the journey of life more and more. You also know that you will keep on developing and that you are no better and no less than any other person or creature. This keeps you humble and connected in a deep way. If you walk your path in a natural way, you'll find doorways open and your purpose in life becoming clearer, too. It is about having faith and being guided all the time.

No Owner of Spirituality

One of the things I would like people to understand is that we can't own spirituality. You see, Creation gave ceremonies to us and they are meant as a gift for everyone. They are there to help and guide us. No one is supposed to control or own them, but unfortunately people often do just that when it comes to ceremonies and healings.

I met a person who ran a sweat lodge the way he wanted it. Although it was a public sweat lodge, he decided which people were allowed to come and didn't even consider the possibility of allowing an unexpected visitor. A sweat lodge is meant to be open to anyone who is respectful of the tradition and not disruptive. Anything else goes against the whole essence of what the ceremony is about. There are so-called family lodges with a specific purpose for that family, where obviously only the family members take part. As soon as it is a public sweat lodge, it is open to anyone who wants to come and we are supposed to be grateful for any unexpected visitor.

I had a powerful lesson once that may help explain this deeper. I grew up in a time where I witnessed what a destructive effect alcohol had on many of the Native people. I had a very strong dislike of it and vowed to never take any alcohol myself at any time. We had a Navaho Elder living at Nanish Shontie for a while who was a Medicine Man but also had alcohol problems. He was doing pretty well, not falling back and slowly recovering and becoming more stable. Then something happened that triggered his old behavior and he disappeared for a few days, apparently on a drinking binge. We had planned a sweat lodge for the weekend and just as we were about to begin, a taxi drove up the driveway and he showed up again, very drunk. He retreated to his camper to sleep. We went ahead with the ceremony and I remember I had included him in my prayers while in the sweat. After the second round he showed up, ready to come in. I had to make an instant decision since I was the facilitator of the sweat lodge that day. I remembered what an elder had told me long ago while still living at Meta Tantay. Everybody knew I had a strong dislike of alcohol and was pretty adamant about anybody who was drunk not coming near any ceremony and certainly not participating in a sweat lodge. The elder had told me: "It is good that you are explaining to people that according to our tradition they are not allowed to use any drugs or alcohol while in or around a Native ceremony. People should respect that. But what if a person who is addicted to some kind of drug and who has reached rock-bottom shows up, asking you for permission to come into the sweat and you decide to reject that person? What if that person, who chose to come to the only place that he felt could be helpful to him in his desperate situation, is so disappointed by your turning him down that he turns away, continues his path and never again tries or might even choose to commit suicide because nobody cares about him? By keeping that lodge open to anyone who is genuinely searching for help, you still give them a chance for healing. If you reject them, they might never have a second chance." I remembered those words when this specific elder came to our lodge that day and decided to let him join in. He was still a little drunk but was pleading with me: "I really need this right now."

I allowed him in although I knew it could be offensive to some of the other Native people in there. It was a mixed sweat with Native and non-Native. I couldn't explain or defend my decision right then and as I expected, the Native people present were really upset. One said: "Drinking at a ceremony is simply not allowed. That's it!" and never came back for another sweat lodge at Nanish Shontie. I could understand where he was coming from because I had been there, too. The second person stayed away for a while and finally came back again after I had explained the reason why. You have rules and instructions, but there are exceptions if a person is struggling and really in need of help.

I have seen the benefits of being able to go into ceremony for people struggling with addictions. It is not just that they need physical help with the side effects of the drug or medication. They especially need help on a mental, emotional and spiritual level in order to heal and get away from the addiction. I mentioned earlier that I worked at a juvenile correction center for Native American youth with drug-and alcohol abuse. I was working there with kids that came fresh off the street. The sweat lodge was part of the treatment program that was installed to help them remember where they came from and where they could find help by talking to Nature and Spirit. These kids were partly still on substitution drugs. Had I not changed my attitude towards the strict and principled way I was thinking before, I wouldn't have allowed them in either. But time and again, I had seen the progress they all made with the help of the sweat lodge. It is a powerful tool and was given to us by Creation to be used as such.

No one is perfect and it is easy to be judgmental towards people with weaknesses, which is what an addiction basically is. A person might also have been involved in violence or might have had some other imbalanced areas in their life. Some of these imbalances are clearly visible on the outside and others may be hidden in some corner of a person's personality and life. The sweat lodge is a tool to help us find more balance within ourselves and in our lives with others and all Life on the Mother Earth. If a person who comes to the ceremony is sincere in his or her effort to make a change and is eager to go through with it and do better after that, we want to welcome that attitude. Another matter is only wanting to go through the ceremony for the benefit of your own ego. Or if you are searching for some kind of absolution for your sins but still continue with the same kind of regrettable and off-balance behavior. That is like going to church on Sundays to pray there in front of the whole community but still being a hard and dishonest person all through the week. To me it is essential that a person is sincere from the heart and it is not coming from the mind. The mind leads us astray because it tells us that it is important to show up at the ceremony, the church or whatever only to prove to others that we are doing what we are told. That is no true commitment from within.

On the one hand, we need certain rules and regulations to go by. It gives a structure, an outline to the ceremony. But we shouldn't get caught up in those rules. We should remember the heart of the matter, what it is about: to create healing for all involved. It's a thin line sometimes and it depends on the situation, the person and your own spiritual journey through life what you as a facilitator decide to allow or to say no to.

Remember, Spirit and Nature are not structured and tight, they are adaptable and open to change. There is a certain backbone that is kept and stays there as a foundation, but it has enormous flexibility.

We need to flow with the situation, be flexible rather than just stick to one way, adapting to whatever the circumstances are at a particular moment.

I learned a lot while traveling in Europe and observing Elders dealing with certain situations. Corbin Harney, Mad Bear Anderson, and David Munongye especially impressed me. They always kept a smile on their face, regardless what happened around them, but continued with their prayers and ceremonies. They were happy about whoever wanted to join in to pray and didn't judge people if they didn't follow the protocol exactly. What counted was that they prayed. They would say: "Let's find a way that works for the people. Let's find a way to their hearts and see what works." I have been trying to incorporate that in my own approach, too. The healing is more important that the structure.

Life as a Learning Journey

I was taught and have always believed that when we are born into our bodies, we come in as perfect beings. Actually, I do not really like to use the word "perfect" very much, as I will explain later on. What I mean is that when we are born, we start off beautifully and have a very open, natural, spiritual connection to Creation. In our bodies, we can have experiences and learn from them. During our lives though, we become influenced by our surroundings, by our family, where we are born, our peers, by society as a whole. Everything affects us and the cycle begins or, as we believe, restarts again. To my understanding, it is also possible that we carry lessons from our past lives we haven't yet fully understood, that we still need to learn.

So, while growing up, we are no longer perfect: we come here to learn, to become aware, to understand, to heal. It is about inner growth and change. In our way we call this coming back into balance.

When somebody would come up to my tribal people and say "I am perfect the way I am," we would consider that person arrogant and feel sad for them because it would mean that they had missed out on what life is all about, namely that we, as human beings, are here to grow, that we need to make mistakes in order to make changes, so that we experience things in different ways to look at life from other angles. We are here to learn, to become better human beings, to become whole and be healed on all levels. This is an ongoing process and never finishes. It is about expanding your awareness of things. You can learn a lot about one thing in your life but still not know every aspect. You can always learn more. And that only applies to that one thing, what about all the other things that you haven't learned about yet? So, our spirits are never finished with learning, growing and experiencing.

We also believe there might come a time that we have reached a point where we have accomplished a true growth on all levels, whether spiritually, emotionally, mentally or physically, where, if we cross over, we can stay on the other side. When we have reached that point where we have come so much into unison with Life, Nature and Spirit, then there is no need to come back again. Western people would call this enlightenment, I guess.

This state of total awareness is felt in every pore of your being and is present wherever you are, whatever happens around you. It is a state of total bliss. We call this walking in balance on the Mother Earth, in balance with all things at all times. In my language we say: "*Shundahai*" - walk in peace and harmony with Nature and Spirit. When you live your life in this state of high awareness, it means that every action, every word, even every thought becomes a prayer. Basically, life is a learning journey for us and we need to come back many more times until we have become what we are being guided to be. Each lifetime we get a little closer.

> *Hermine:*
>
> *I often hear you use the phrase "becoming a better human being" in your talks and prayers. I have wondered if that could also be understood in a way that makes you feel you are not good enough, that you could and actually should do much better. I guess this is common in the western way of thinking: the concept of guilt and judgment. A spiral of feeling bad, guilty and unworthy goes downwards, getting worse as you keep making mistakes. I know this is not your way of looking at life. But for many people, there is this little twist that needs to be gotten around in their way of thinking. I know I tend to fall into that trap myself of not feeling worthy enough, which has a pretty negative effect.*

To us, there is no such thing as a bad person. We would consider that person as hurting deep inside and in need of healing. So, we don't divide into good or bad with a judgment. Some people are struggling within themselves and need help. Everybody gets an opportunity in life to come more into balance and learn certain lessons, but it is up to us if we take the chance and make choices accordingly to change and work on that healing process.

While trying to become a better human being, you will have to face the fact that you will make mistakes along the way. It is important to be aware of that. Some mistakes are only small and don't have much impact, but others are of graver nature and might cause trouble for others.

In the old tribal ways, if a person behaved in a way that could be harmful to others too, we would gather and try to find ways to help that person on their journey. We all feel responsible and offer possibilities for healing and restoring the balance within that person and also within the community. But we would never talk to the person in a negative way. You see, we think you then actually confirm that behavior and make it worse. In Native languages there are no words for such things as "hate," nor do we use bad language or scolding words. We just don't have those concepts. It was not in our way of thinking. In the old tribal communities, we didn't have jails or prisons either, we didn't punish. We'd offer different ways of healing: a talk with the elders, a sweat lodge or a vision quest. If that was not enough and the person continued being hurtful, there was the possibility of sending him away from the community for a certain amount of time. This could be six months or a year where they would have to get in touch with Nature and Spirit on their own to find healing before they could return.

Striving to become a better human being isn't about being strict on yourself and blaming yourself for mistakes. You need to forgive yourself for your stumbles and falls, as they are part of your growth. At the same time, you shouldn't just lean back with an: "Ah well, so what! I made a mistake, that is just who I am. I can't help it." If you are willing to reflect, practice and stay with it, you will become better. You do the best you can. The consequence is that you will need to practice. When you first learn to hunt, you won't catch anything and only by repeating, you'll manage to become better at it. Mistakes are part of the learning process.

When you go through life, it is important to ask yourself the question: What is the purpose of what I am doing right now? Does it make sense? Am I doing it for my ego or because I am told to live in this way? Is it really expressing who I am? If you keep doing that in your daily life, you will also reach the deeper purpose of why you are here and what you are here to do.

The elders told us that everything you do in your life creates an energy that not only affects your own life at that moment in time, but it also goes ahead of you. At some point in your life, you will come upon to that energy again. What goes around comes around, as they say. It is never about punishment, but in truth about raising your awareness. The journey is life-long learning.

Sometimes life can be hard, but if you are patient and embrace the lessons that life presents you with, understanding can come. If you fight the experience and let confusion take over, it gets worse. Welcome whatever it is, even when it is tough, and see it is as an opportunity to grow. We are all humans and aren't always able to do that, but that is okay. We can make our mistakes and go astray for a while, giving in to weakness and fear. This happens but luckily Creation gives you more opportunities than just one. If you let life teach and guide you, you can continue in a good way.

My own journey has been full of incredible and beautiful experiences. There have also been quite some difficult and harsh circumstances and that gives it balance. It is almost never more than you can handle. It depends on how you choose to act when you're in a problematic situation. You always have the choice. Exactly therein lies your chance and it gives you the possibility to turn things around. Any lesson can go in more than one direction. You can grow from it or you can allow it to weaken or even destroy you.

Another aspect in this whole matter is that you should never look down upon someone who is struggling. Neither should you put anybody on a pedestal and admire them too much. We were always told that nobody is better or higher than another person. Each and every one has their role in the whole and is part of the Circle. We are traveling together here on Mother Earth. A Clan Mother can be highly respected but is still not "better" than any other member of the community. The Clan Mothers or the Chiefs or the Medicine People also make mistakes, but when you look up to them and they stumble, they fall harder in your eyes since you hadn't expected them to be human and make a mistake. You judge them and are disillusioned: "How could they have done that?" You can admire and respect somebody for what they accomplish, but not to the point where you think they are perfect. Position doesn't make the other person better than you. We each have our own journeys and we each have a specific purpose. You cannot swap or compare. Life is just how it is. Sometimes you wonder why a person acts in a certain way and it is okay to try and understand, but be careful not to be judgmental. Also try to avoid copying the other person. You need to follow your own heart and what is right for you.

In our tribal system, we didn't follow anybody. In its essence, our system isn't hierarchal. We never really had any bosses telling us what to do. We each understood our part in the whole and we would listen to the Clan Mother or to a wise elder. Guidance is something different than forced rules and being told to do something and follow the leader. If something doesn't feel good in your heart, you can choose to go your own way.

That's why we didn't have any missionaries, either. We just didn't have that concept and couldn't grasp what was going on when they came to our homeland. We felt sad that people weren't allowed to live their own path. We were taught to flow with Creation. The most important relationship is really the one your spirit has with the Great Spirit.

Once I had an experience where I fell off a pedestal somebody had put me on. I attended a weekend workshop in Holland making hand drums. At that time, I still drank soda pop and during a break, I drank my coca cola as it was pretty warm outside. One woman just kept staring at me. I could feel the intense energy coming from her stare and it was getting really uncomfortable. Then she pointed her finger at me and said: "You're a bad

Indian! A real Medicine man wouldn't drink coca cola!" I was flabbergasted and tried to explain that I just liked it. I told her I was aware it might not be the healthiest thing to drink, but that it was my choice and didn't make me less Indian. She kept going on about what I should be doing in her opinion. Obviously, she couldn't deal with my weakness and was so disappointed that it turned into accusing words and rude behavior.

You often want to convince others if you have found something that works for you, but if you get caught up in that too much and think it is the solution for others or even for the whole world, that's where it gets off balance.

You could simply ask and say: "I noticed you drink coca cola. May I ask you why?" Then you could exchange your thoughts and learn from each other. If you don't agree, leave it at that, no need to try and convince another by pushing your way upon them. When you push, the other person no longer listens anyway, but becomes defensive and you defeat your point. You can be an example but still respect another's path. We all have a right to our own learnings.

I have heard so many people point their finger at me because they thought eating meat was a bad thing since you kill animals for it. They didn't understand our concept where we don't feel one form of life is better or higher than another. We eat vegetables and meat and we don't categorize into low and high. We don't have a pyramid with humans on top, then animals, then plants and then minerals. Native people see this differently: we are all part of the circle of life and we honor all forms equally.

One of the things I was always told and really believe in – and of course here I can only speak for myself -- is to never to speak in a negative way about anything or anyone, including myself. This implies not looking upon the weather, a certain animal or something in nature in a negative way. A lot of times, people do that. When they see an animal kill another animal for survival, they judge it and feel bad about it. But to us, this is part of nature.

Every life form has to take another life form to survive. We all do this, whether it is plants, fruits, nuts, or an animal. For us, there is no hierarchy and it is a natural process.

As human beings, we have a choice and the question is how we take life. Do we honor it, do we appreciate it, do we give thanks? Or do we just take it for selfish reasons? Do we take it for granted? Do we just do it without thinking, maybe just because we feel powerful over the other being, because we put ourselves higher than the other?

When you honor life, it knows how you feel, whether plant life, animals, birds, anything. We used to be able to feel their feelings too, but we have blocked that ability and mostly lost it. But they still feel our feelings. They appreciate it when we honor them. The vast majority of nature knows that they have a certain life span, as long as it is meant to be, that at one point, they will give their bodies to another life form for them to continue. That is just how it is. Our human bodies go back to the Mother Earth too, and it nourishes the life within and upon the earth.

Canoe Journey in the Northwest

In recent years, a very positive revival of Native American traditional culture has occurred in the Northwest of the US and has been growing each year. It's based on an old tradition where people from the coast would visit and gather each year in the summertime to meet, exchange and do ceremony together. It is called the Canoe Journey.

The Canoe Journey used to be a social gathering where tribes all the way from California, Oregon, Washington, and on up to Alaska would come together at a chosen village, a different one each year. Inland-tribes would participate too, those that were able to reach the ocean through rivers. Each canoe, beautifully carved and painted, would fit 10 to 20 people and there were literally hundreds of canoes coming together. People on foot would leave a lot earlier to be on time and could also take part. For a few weeks, people came to trade, share stories, legends and food, exchange and get in touch, dance, sing and drum together and do ceremonies. It built a bond between the people, reaffirming old contacts and establishing new ones.

In opposition to what many people might be taught in school or elsewhere, most tribes in North America got along pretty well. It didn't mean that there were never problems and issues amongst the tribes, but we dealt with them peacefully for the most part.

When the white people came, they outlawed most of our ways and culture. Speaking our languages was forbidden, our dances and singing weren't allowed and ceremonies were banned. We couldn't practice our Way of Life anymore. Thus the Canoe Journey also came to an end. In 1987, a group of elders from Washington State sparked an initiative to revive this tradition.

You need to understand that on most reservations there is a lot of hardship, violence, drug and alcohol abuse, gangs, no jobs, loss of culture and identity, no perspective for the future: simply a lot of despair. Although ceremonies like sweat lodge and sun dance were performed again, which was helpful, it didn't have a lasting effect and people stayed in the same troubled situations. On top of those problems, living on the reservation, you find yourself in the middle of a tense political situation. There is the control of the US government, there is the Bureau of Indian Affairs that mixes in, there are Native people who want to adapt and blend in with the modern way of consumerism they see all around them, make money and profit quickly and exploit the land, and then there are the traditionalists who want to go back to the old ways. When I grew up, you hardly found any traditionalists on the reservation. It was extremely unsafe to show you were one. You'd be harassed, molested or even killed for it, so naturally these people went into hiding. A lot of such people also got into so-called "accidents" or were put in jail to be silenced. Only recently does there seem to be a turning point where more and more people dare to show what they believe in and are more outspoken about it.

This group of elders thought that the revival of the Canoe Journey would be a way of helping the people structurally. They envisioned that the people paddling the canoes had to commit themselves for a longer period before going on the journey itself. They had to meet every few weeks and practice. They had to learn the ways of the ocean, the water and the earth, the spiritual ways of approach, they had to learn the songs in the Native languages, they had to understand the protocol and learn what was behind it. The building of the canoes also takes a lot of time and effort if you do it in the proper traditional way. It was a matter of relearning the culture and at the same time preparing on all levels, spiritually, emotionally, mentally and physically, in order to take part. It would mean a commitment of a full year. Naturally this included no drugs and alcohol and no violence whatsoever during that whole time.

The first time, only two canoes took part with four to five people in each. In the Seattle area, they paddled from one reservation to another. The response was positive though, and more and more people got involved over the years. This has continued to grow to the point that there are now over 80 canoes participating and more than 10,000 people coming to the gathering.

Most non-Natives are not aware of this cultural event, but it gives us as Native People from America great hope for the future.

With Nanish Shontie, we were present at the celebration for several years in a row, but did not take part in the canoe journey itself. Once though, one of my sons paddled together with a canoe family from Alaska. It has been amazing to watch and observe how it has spread so much. Most of the people in the canoes are teenagers. They feel they have something to hold onto all year round, they have a sense of belonging and of regaining their ancestral pride. They have purpose in their life where they put in energy and effort that enables them to know about their heritage and who they are.

Anybody is welcome to join and be part of the gathering at the Canoe Journey grounds. I would say there are about 10% non-Native visitors. They witness how Native people celebrate the canoe families coming to shore after having spent long journeys lasting days or even weeks out on the ocean. The gathering is done in the old tradition of giving. In a lot of indigenous cultures, this principle is at the base of everything. Indigenous people believe that giving is far more important than taking. Not only to give to each other, but also to give back to the Mother Earth, because she gives constantly and in so many ways. It is a way of being more appreciative of what we have and not looking so much at what we don't have. Each year a different reservation takes on the task of hosting the gathering. This means not only a lot of logistics, organization and work, but they have to use all their resources in order to be a host in the traditional way. Twice a day a big meal is provided for all the families involved and for those camping out there, without charge. Considering the number of people coming, you can imagine how much food is needed. The campsites with their facilities are for free. Some of the participating reservations save for years for that occasion.

The principle of giving is also apparent in other ways. The canoe families themselves often present giveaways according to protocol to the visitors who are in the main tent where the celebration takes place. Some elders might be given blankets or clothing, but everyone present gets little gifts. Essential is that they are given freely from the heart without expecting anything in return, and that no money is involved.

The positive side effects are enormous. Recently, some of the young ones made the effort of building new longhouses. These used to be the traditional buildings in the Northwest for ceremonies. They would go in there for two to three months and learn about the culture, the language and the old spiritual ways. The elders would teach them all they knew until they became a walking history of their own people.

Canoe Journey on Lummi Reservation, Pacific Coast, 2007

What is interesting is that although these gatherings have become so huge over the years, they are hardly ever mentioned in the mass media. Maybe some local news station might cover it briefly, but that's about it. We are used to this news blackout: any big action Natives took over the past decades never made the news. Only if there were deaths involved or some negative claim about Indians would they show it. There were so many protests in the sixties and seventies where we blocked off areas, stood up for our rights, tried to save a certain piece of land from exploitation and mining or when we protested against the transportation of nuclear waste on reservation land. We literally blocked trucks with our own bodies and hooked ourselves onto gates to stop them from opening them for the workers at a nuclear power plant. There were helicopters flying over us, even tanks rolling in, lots and lots of police that arrested many of our people! I took part in these protests so many times but they were usually barred from the news to prevent the information from spreading.

In the week of the Canoe Gathering you can enjoy good food from food stalls, storytelling, dancing, drumming and singing all day and night and buy craftwork from vendors. It is really a blessing that the Canoe Journey has returned to the people and I am very thankful and at the same time more hopeful for the future.

The survival of our culture is strongly related to the many languages of the different tribes and how we use words, what words we use and do not use. Unfortunately, most of the languages have been lost, along with the many tribes that no longer exist. This process continues to this very day, as there are only a few people left in some tribes still speaking their Native tongue.

Many efforts are being made to save as much as possible and keep the damage to a minimum. Every tribe has their own approach, emphasizing different aspects of native culture.

All in all, having witnessed the Canoe Journey through the incredible nation-wide engagement of Native peoples, as well as at Standing Rock Reservation where we also stood as one to protest against the pipeline that threatens to destroy precious water and wetlands, it leaves me with hope that Native people are finally moving upwards again.

Continuing and Leaving Nanish Shontie

For many years, I was the one going out to speak on behalf of Nanish Shontie. I went to universities in the US to give talks, would tour Europe for two to three months at a time, sometimes even twice a year. Next to the generous funding we received, it was still necessary to bring in money for the feeding of the animals, the survival of the people and to create a garden we could use year-round. We wanted to become self-sufficient with the help of environmental-friendly technology. Solar panels, a grey water system, green houses, barns and corrals for the chickens and sheep, and a healthy pond system for the fish we were breeding were all on our list.

Through my talks and workshops, I could also reach those who weren't able to afford coming over to Oregon and I could still pass on what my elders and tribal upbringing had taught me.

After some years, I got comments like: "Mala, you're the one holding the vision and keeping it all together. It depends too much on you. For every final decision, the members of the community look to see what you think of it. But when you're not around, who is capable of doing it?" This thought started bugging me and I couldn't get loose from it anymore. There was truth to it and I realized I had to act upon it. Around 2012, it was my decision to step out of my function on the Board of Directors and I no longer regularly attended the meetings of the Council.

Because I was gone many months a year, I couldn't oversee the daily things at Nanish Shontie anyhow, nor be present at all the meetings. This added to my resolution to step back from the decision-making process of Nanish Shontie. Personally, I had been struggling with some major health issues that made me realize I didn't know how much longer my journey on earth would be. It was important to have others take on the guidance of the community. My experience with how Meta Tantay ended was another factor: that Camp had depended on my father and dissolved after he left and I aimed to avoid just that.

Somebody once told me: "If you have a vision and you share it with people, you have to be aware they will take it over and the vision will become different. Every person has his or her own concept of a vision and it will lose your personal touch. That is only natural." I felt there was a lot of truth in those words. I had to trust that. If it's a real vision, all the people should guide it: it shouldn't be one man's vision.

At times it was hard to watch when certain decisions didn't appeal to what I thought was needed. I had to learn not to interfere. It became a process of finding a new balance from the old status quo, where I was in charge of everything to where things were seen and done from the perspective of others.

Little by little, I started noticing that Nanish Shontie was definitely going in a different direction. Some things were understandable, but overall in my view, our community was moving further and further away from the original concept of being an open community where everybody with a positive heart and good intentions was welcomed. Visitors had to fill out elaborate forms for security reasons and visitor break-periods were installed.

When we had the Land Blessing Ceremony at the beginning of Nanish Shontie, we counted 75 people whom we somehow accommodated, although we hardly had any space and very little infrastructure. We somehow managed to cook food for all. Everyone helped out and it was a great thing to experience. It works if you are willing to make it work. For me it is about trust and having faith. Very often I encounter the opposite. In a non-Native approach I hear: "We have a certain amount of space, so we can only take a certain number of people." This way of thinking already limits the outcome. You put up blocks where there don't need to be any. Because you think that way, it then turns out that way. That is how the law of energy works. It wasn't what I had envisioned and felt to be an essential part of indigenous tribal life. If you are open to miracles, they can happen and this lies at the heart of the Way of Life of my ancestors.

I am not saying that there wasn't a lot of effort put into the projects we had planned. Great work was done with all the buildings. A lot of things were put into place to be able to accommodate more people (bathhouse, outdoor kitchen, outdoor showers). The main house was totally redone with extra office space. The kitchen was remodeled and enlarged with extra storage room. Green technology was used as a tool on our path to becoming self-sufficient. We had our garden and fruit orchard thriving. We had ponds with fish and chickens for eggs. There was a beautiful yurt with a heater in it that could be used for gatherings and for sleeping. We got rid of all the old trailers and our parking lot grew bigger. Little solar lights illuminated the pathways in the dark. A lot of cool and nice ideas became visible through a lot of hard work. But for me, the heart of Nanish Shontie became lost in that whole process of material accomplishments.

The development at Nanish Shontie saddened me. The sunrise ceremony that we used to start the day with together was no longer carried out. It became more a working community where everybody did their own thing, coming and going. At one point, it was suggested having drumming sessions and talking circles somewhere else because Nanish Shontie wasn't set up for that yet. I realized then it wasn't going to be any time soon that it would be ready for ceremonies and more visitors again and I had to make a decision.

I spent a lot of time thinking about it. I want to emphasize, I definitely had my weak moments and made my mistakes during this process. We all have our insecurities, fears and anger, which are sometimes hard to face. We try to deny them or start to blame others and the situation around us. We think it is unfair and lash out. I wasn't an exception and have done my share of wrongdoings. My traditional teachings came as a great help though: "There is a reason and purpose for everything!" I had to take a look at that. Why was this happening in my life? What was the reason behind it? Could I understand it or, if not, could I accept it and simply embrace and continue in a good and positive way?" Maybe it wasn't meant to be that I would remain at Nanish Shontie, which I had thought would be the place I would stay until the end of my days. Even though I had been involved so strongly in finding the land and funding the place to keep it going, even though it was my vision to begin with that materialized, it didn't mean I owned it! Slowly I realized deep down: "I need to let go. Something is guiding me to something different. If I am trying to control and hold on, nothing good can come of it. I have to be willing to flow with it."

The last 2.5 years at Nanish Shontie, my health had worsened and I had stopped touring. Everything had really narrowed down and I had to deal with medical issues, one after the other. A lot of questions troubled my mind in those days, but it dawned on me that if I wanted answers I would have to change my living circumstances and follow the guidance from Creation. I told myself: "Keep having faith and be open for what is good and meant to be."

Two good friends in Austria initiated a fundraising for a flight to Europe. Like so often before, I was getting help unexpectedly just as things were getting narrow and difficult. Although my doctors told me they would rather see me stay at home since they considered it risky to travel, I knew inside that this trip would help me and I would benefit from it. So, I insisted on going and the long, intercontinental journey went well. Moreover, I was doing better since I could contribute something and felt worthy and listened to by the people over there, which uplifted my heart and mood.

If I would have put my foot down and said that I wanted to have things my way, it would have forced things. There was a thought that kept going through my head that had happened long ago at Meta Tantay. When Meta Tantay was disbanded, people disagreed on how to move forward and I very clearly got the message: "You don't fight over the land." With all the problems and differences at Nanish Shontie, there was a similar situation. I would have ended up fighting over material things and this memory cleared my mind to make the choice.

Finding out when to still put energy in to make a dream come true and stick to something you really believe in, or when the right moment has come to stop is a tricky thing and you are on thin ice. Especially since you are in the middle of the whole experience and therefore biased. You very easily justify your behavior to persist in doing something, or the opposite, by refusing to quit doing something. You also have to take into account that all those involved go through a similar process. I asked myself: "How can I find peace? Where can I compromise? How far can I reach out without losing my integrity? These are complex patterns and though it looks like there are only those opposite sides of the issue, there are actually many more layers involved.

But it became important to continue my own path without holding grudges. It is not up to me to judge, as everyone involved in the situation has a different lesson to learn.

Finally I left Nanish Shontie in February of 2016 and moved to Eugene, Oregon, to live in a residential retirement community in the so-called independent living section. The last years had taken their toll and my medical condition forced me to stay near medical help and hospital care if needed. Certainly not my first choice and something I had never expected to be witnessing from the inside. My judgment about these kinds of institutions wasn't a positive one. Putting your elders away from the rest of society so they won't bother anyone is such a sad thing to do. In the tribal tradition, elders are honored and therefore taken care of. So, I had pretty strong feelings against living there, but I remembered the words my mother once said to me: "Whenever you feel adamant about a topic and speak against it in a strong emotional manner, you have a lesson there. Creation will put you in a situation to learn about the good and weakness in all things. You're forced to take a closer look, as it's not so simple." So, I learned about the other side of my opinionated judgment and have met good people in this institution. It was a good in-between option and it was important to be able to retreat from my usual busy life and turn my focus inward.

Through that whole process, I grew and learned a lot about myself. For a very long time, I had hoped to have a tribal community around me. I was very happy and content at Nanish Shontie. I loved my little round house, I loved the land, I loved seeing how it was growing and changing, I loved having my daughter and her family and my granddaughter around.

Ultimately, the lesson to let go of the vision made it possible for other doorways to open for me. I got to know new people and build new friendships that enriched my life. I have been able to help people in other ways than would have been possible at Nanish Shontie, which also makes me feel good inside. My life has definitely moved in a different direction than I had anticipated.

Recently, I moved to another Residential Living Center that is closer to the woods. I have a little porch again where I can sit outside and be more in touch with nature again. Furball, my cat is happy there too. There is more space, with even a spare bedroom and I have a sense of freedom and of having my own little place again.

Mala and his cat Furball

It took me a long time to get to where I am now. I have learned a lot and am in fact still learning. My awareness of not taking things for granted and being thankful has actually reached a new level in my life. The blessing of living another day on Mother Earth is already such a gift that I am humbled and happy quietly from within.

Reflection on a State of Flow While Playing Pool

The other day back in Eugene, where I go out and play pool a lot, I watched somebody playing at a table for a while. He was incredibly talented and had a very fluid, beautiful style. I just couldn't stop watching him. For every shot he took he used just the right amount of energy to make it the perfect shot. Nothing was wasted, nothing was done with too little effort. He took his time, every move thoughtful and with a soft smile on his face, his game almost sensual. I realized he had reached a remarkably high level of harmony whilst playing, relaxed and having fun while doing it. Understanding how much energy to put in to make something work smoothly is like art at a high level. You can apply this to anything you want to accomplish. Too much energy and it becomes like an overload and a waste at the same time. Too little energy and it lacks power. To reach that level, you need to practice of course, but once you have made it to that state of flow and balance, it is true harmony.

Again, it is about how you go about doing something. It is not about controlling it or being efficient. Efficiency might look nice: you don't waste energy, which seems something to strive for, but you are losing something very important in the process. In this case, it wasn't about him winning or having the greatest shots to impress anyone. He played with ease and enjoyed himself while creating those beautiful shots. Like a master of martial arts who has reached a level of harmony between the physical and the spiritual aspects of his art, it all becomes one.

The difference between true harmony and pure efficiency is that the first is done from and with the heart and the latter is done from the mind. The first shows a harmonious flow of energy. The other lacks flexibility and becomes static at some point.

Accusations and Negative Campaign on the Internet

More than once in my life, I have been confronted with negative information and accusations against me that I was forced to deal with. Much of it was just simple gossip. Some of it had great impact though, as it became part of an internet campaign with grave accusations. Your first reaction is one of disappointment and hurt, and you would like to lash back straight away. The elders always spoke about being very careful about reacting, especially when you are emotional about a situation, but also because you add energy to the negative information that is out there.

The difficult thing is that words spoken like that meander onwards and are believed by others, so it can create great negativity around you. Being defensive is so tempting as you feel it is unjustified and you would like to put things straight. I chose to not react to any of it, as I was taught.

When I was young, my father had said to me: "Whenever you stick your neck out to help out or do something, be aware that there are others ready to chop it off." I couldn't figure it out at first, but then I watched him being unreasonably attacked on numerous occasions. Others were also blamed for wrongdoings when they were actually trying to do the opposite, and I slowly understood. When you are not doing things the way they have always been done, you get attacked because it challenges people to think in a different way, or they attack out of jealousy and spite. It is understandable and I am not blaming anybody for this behavior. I know I have made my share of mistakes and there have been many situations that I could have dealt with in a much better way. I am definitely not perfect, but once you are listened to as you speak out, all of a sudden, your "audience" puts you on a pedestal from which you can only fall down. People put such high expectations on you that you're destined to disappoint them at some point.

Hermine:

In Holland there is a saying: "The highest trees catch the most wind." I have seen you dealing with the consequences of those negative wordings and I remember the first time when this happened it amazed me that you didn't go out and defend yourself with a clear statement on your behalf. Instead, you left it with the remark that you were taught not to add any energy to it. You said to me: "I hope my actions will speak for themselves, you know. I hope that those who know me or get to know me will look inside their hearts and make their own judgments. I'll leave it at that." It took me a long time to grasp the deeper meaning of it all, and only when I grew older, did I see how true that was in the long run.

I am not saying you can never defend yourself. But if you're dealing with people whom you don't see face to face, it quickly gets out of hand. If your opinion is asked in a matter, of course you can answer and stand up, but in the other case the judgment is already out there and what you have to say isn't of interest to the people who are phrasing it. Their opinion is fixed and you only do more harm trying to put things in a different light. It takes a lot to stay calm and forgiving, but, in the end, it is part of the journey you are on. These things are also part of your own lesson and you need to look at that aspect as well.

Many people who were also involved and knew me kept saying they wanted to help me out and were willing to put statements out that would correct the picture painted. There have been times that I wanted to write down my side of the story, but my family, my elders, the people at Nanish Shontie all said: "No, you will feed the negative energy and it will accumulate as it gets more and more twisted. Let your actions speak for themselves. Try and be the example you are talking about and do not react." It was very,

very hard, as some people whom I had known for a long time had already chosen to believe what was said on the internet about me and it hurt me deep inside. It also affected my whole family and Nanish Shontie in a big way and we lost a lot of good support.

On the other hand, many people stood by me over all those years, which gives me a feeling of gratitude and humbleness. I sought to incorporate the challenges, see them as lessons I had to go through in order to grow. It's part of my path. Besides, it is not just about my personal feelings in the matter. I tried to keep the bigger picture and everything involved in mind. At the same time I realized that I too, have a limited view. I prayed and asked for support and understanding in the matter and had to trust what Creation was putting me through. There is no way around that.

I have come to understand you can never please everybody. There will always be positive and negative responses to what you are saying or doing, as much as you strive for the most healing way for all.

Basically, you can judge me all you want. That is up to you and totally okay. As this book proceeds and you are reading this, you can look at the information I am sharing. This information comes from what the elders passed on to me and from all the things I have experienced in life. The information itself is neutral and you can use it in a positive and in a negative way. It is up to you.

Done Things Differently

Lately people have asked me more frequently if, looking back at my life, I would have done things differently.

When I imagine myself going back in time and being able to change things, of course I can find things that happened where I unintentionally ended up hurting someone or where I wasn't in a good place and caused harm in a certain situation. I have regretted the pain and disappointment

I caused and would gladly have avoided it. As you live life though, you make mistakes and from those mistakes you learn: that is just how it is and supposed to be. At the time, I wasn't yet capable of doing it differently. Sometimes in life, you come to a crossroads where you have to choose a direction, so it could also have turned out differently according to the choice you made. It is only human to wonder how your life would have been, but I prefer to think that all those choices and learning moments have made me to what I am right now at this moment in time.

My journey has been my journey and it was important that I learned all those lessons. I look at them as gifts that helped me to develop and grow. To answer the question: "No, I wouldn't change anything, as all things that occurred and happened are all part of me. I accept that Creation had a reason for those experiences for me to go through to become more complete."

I have mentioned it before and naturally it also applies to me as well: immaturity, ignorance or stubbornness might cause you to act in a particular way. But sometimes, you aren't yet ready to listen. In my way of thinking, it takes what it takes to finally learn and make a change. Spirit will give you stronger lessons, will hit you on the head, then kick you in the butt to make you aware and look at yourself.

Yes, there are times you wish you'd learn faster and listen better. You get impatient with your own failings, but impatience doesn't lead you anywhere. You have to accept your mistakes, look at them and keep trying to change for the future. Once again, it's a fine line where you have to take care and not blame yourself for them. If you call them failures, you create a negative energy. If you embrace your mistakes and see them as opportunities to learn and grow from, they stay in a positive connotation.

There are times when we actually know better and yet choose out of fear or laziness not to break a habit. We seem caught in that behavior. As I said earlier, we humans are concerned about staying in our comfort zone and prefer to stay there. Even if a situation isn't easy, we'd rather not change because the unknown is scary and uncertain. Fear gets in the way of the necessary change. It is a psychological phenomenon I observed while working with addicted youth at the treatment center in Oregon, yet you encounter this process in ordinary situations, too, with less immediate destructive patterns but nevertheless habitual ones that every human being has to deal with. We hesitate to leave our comfort zone and refuse to take responsibility for our actions. Another negative spiral is where we blame everything and everybody else except ourselves.

Another aspect to take in account, assuming I would have done things differently, is that it would have affected the people around me in a different way just as much. You can't just change your own part as it is part of the whole, and literally everything would have been taken in another direction. Sometimes you go through a hurtful situation because this is also part of the lesson of another person around you. It could well be that you are part of the learning for the other person as well as for yourself. This can apply to whole groups of people or in a larger context to all life on Mother Earth.

You play your small part on the big stage of life. There is no changing the past; you can only learn from the past by reflecting on it and putting it into perspective. Important is that you don't beat yourself up over your mistakes. Forgive yourself and the others involved and continue on.

Dreams and Visions

When a Native person had a strong dream or a vision of some kind, we used to go to a trusted spiritual person to ask for advice.

The spiritual person would pray about it for whatever time was needed and come back to you with an interpretation of the message. He or she had distance to the vision, was not as connected to it as the one who had had the vision or dream. This is very important. Also, there are no real rules that you can apply here. Like explanations in books... they are helpful but they lack the overview and the context, and also the wisdom and experience of a spiritual person who is strongly embedded in the community.

Human beings sometimes have a tendency to take things too literally. When people have some kind of dream or a vision, they claim: "I know what this means, I know what this is about!" And yet, we just want it to be a certain way, we have expectations that lead us astray. I have an example from my own life.

When I was about 25 years old and still living in Nevada, I had a dream that kept coming back to me, over and over for a few weeks. In the dream, I saw a house being built on a hill just outside Elko, where in real life there were only hills and desert. I saw exactly how it was built, the colors, the material and how big it would be. Every time, I got a sense of knowing it inside too. I had a sense that once this house was finished, this would also be the time for me to cross over. The first time I had the dream, I didn't think much of it. When it came back the second time. I started to get a little worried and told Sky about it, whom I was together with already. We both thought: "Well, that's an unusual place to have a house built anyway, so let's not put too much thought into it." The dream kept returning a few more times and then stopped.

About half a year later, we drove into Elko to get some groceries. We drove by the place right at the border of town where in the dream the house was being built. We couldn't believe our eyes, because where the area had been barren, desert shrub before, we now saw real construction going on: heavy machinery leveled the ground, making the foundation for a house! As time went by, they used the colors I had seen in my dream, and the size turned out to be similar: a two-story house with a certain kind of roof, just like in my dream. I have to admit I did feel a little uneasy, but I knew that what you see or feel in a dream doesn't literally have to come true. But I put energy into it: "Maybe something is going to happen to me... Maybe I'll get into an accident or maybe some kind of fight..." My health was very good back then, but we had lost family to violence and were often treated badly by racists, so this was an option to consider. I was a little worried, but didn't freak out. Sky told me: "Just be extra careful and aware with whatever you are doing. This could be a warning." The house got built and nothing happened to me physically. But spiritually, quite a few things changed within me. I had been going to a certain kind of Native American ceremony for a few years and had started to become more and more uncomfortable with it. These ceremonies used to be performed in the traditional way and I had seen powerful things happen, but over time elements of the Christian church had been added and it had become a mixture. I started to back off and eventually stopped going. Then I realized what the dream had meant: a spiritual death I was going through. It was a sign that one path was ending but another doorway was opening. Sky told me: "You know, this dream was showing you ahead of time that you were supposed to close something in your life. It was time to finish a certain chapter and embark on new journey." She was right and it was also what had happened.

I was told when I grew up: all those visions and prophecies are basically guiding us and it doesn't mean that things are going to happen exactly the way they were dreamt. Dreams can help us in our decision-making. But the danger of our own personal interpretations lies in the projection of our fears and insecurities and in our hopes, desires and expectations.

In our indigenous communities, we try not to interpret our dreams and visions ourselves. If there is no spiritual person around, you need to be really careful with your own interpretations. You need to sort of look at yourself from a distance, put yourself in a state where you disconnect yourself from your personal issues, desires, fears and so on. Then really sit with it, pray over it.... and then you can come to a conscious awareness of what the dream or vision was trying to tell you.

Nowadays there seems to be a real hype with people claiming they had important insights from the spirit world or got messages from the other side. Have a humble heart when it comes to these matters. Be aware you are not perfect and that your emotional baggage can blur your insights. When we have an encounter of a spiritual nature, the totality of our baggage affects the outcome and how we interpret the experience. We need to be careful before coming to conclusions. We perceive experiences through logic, through what science tells us how nature works, through what we have been told at school or by our parents, and these glasses will color things.

Nevertheless, you can practice entering situations without having expectations, with an open mind and a neutral heart. The moment you start thinking about experiences while they are happening, you start analyzing and putting things into categories. Then you have stopped the experience you were having. Instead, allow the experience to unfold. Once it has ended -- and you will know when it has -- you can think about it and put it into a concept you are familiar with.

Crossing Over and Concepts on Death

What I am about to share is just my personal belief. It doesn't represent any tribe as such and certainly doesn't cover the belief system of all Native American tribes. I grew up around people with different tribal backgrounds and also my parents each came from a different tribe. I was always told to listen to many ways with interest and an open mind before building my own opinion. After going through the process of hearing many versions and being taught by many teachers, you go with what feels right in your heart and what makes sense to you.

One of the things they were saying was that most Native people consider death merely a transition into another form, into another way of life. The common way of thinking that Native people share is the concept of life as a journey. You start off being a spiritual being in the spirit world. You come into a human body and learn your lessons in the best way you can, then you cross over to the other side where you wait to start all over again, until you have truly completed the ongoing cycle of life.

I grew up hearing white people say: „Ooh, you Indians don't seem to have a fear of death." Many white people see it as the end, and therefore it is something they fear. For us, it's going into another stage with another purpose. It is not a complete ending, it goes on into something else. That is why we like to speak of "crossing over," as you travel to another realm while leaving your body behind.

Our spirit chooses the body exactly fit for the lessons we are meant to learn and which serves our needs most. The purpose of that body is what is in our best interest to grow and learn to be in better balance within ourselves and with the flow of life. Once we are born into a body, we spend our lives in the best way we can. Along the way, it is up to us what choices we make. Do we listen to our hearts? Do we allow ourselves to be guided by Nature and Spirit or do we choose to listen more to our mind? How well do we learn to flow with life? How well-balanced do we live our lives? Do we live our life purpose to the fullest? Human beings can choose in any situation how to deal with it and respond to it. We either make our life harder or easier with those choices. All kinds of lessons are put before us every day and they all happen for a reason. There are no coincidences. It just depends on how we respond to what happens and how it affects us. Even the smallest thing has a reason and purpose.

Again, as human beings we have a habit: we like to be comfortable. Often when something occurs in our life, we choose not to leave the comfort zone. Even though we know it would be good or healthy for us, we'd rather stay where we are and resist the change. Change is uncomfortable to us. Life will present us with stronger and even hurtful lessons like illness, loss and pain, so we finally turn things around and learn the specific lesson that was there all along. The spirits in the meantime are trying to give us messages and hints to make us look again at the matter. Spirits are in truth our helpers, just as much as our own spirit is guiding us constantly. Gentle messages can turn into powerful warnings and wake-up calls. When the trauma we are experiencing is fierce, there is a good chance we are willing to make a change. The necessary changes can be in our behavior, but just as much as in our emotional perception and attitudes, our way of thinking and in our spiritual understanding and growth. That is a very important aspect: teachings have their effects on all levels.

As we go through our lives, changing and adapting and learning things along our journey, we will reach the moment where our life ends. Our body tells us that it is time to make the final crossing and go back to the spirit world. If we haven't completed the journey of life in total balance yet, we will have to come back again. If you have found true balance and true peace within yourself –- we also call this being in harmony with all Creation –- and when you have really learned what you were supposed to learn, my people believe you go to the place where your ancestors are waiting for you and welcome you. The animals, the birds, insects, and all other life will greet you. Great harmony exists between all living things, the way it is meant to be on Mother Earth as well, like a kind of "paradise." Sometimes, this place is referred to as the "eternal hunting grounds." It is similar to Mother Earth. It is like there are two worlds next to each other with a veil between them.

Yet if you have not found that true balance, you will be reborn in another body and will have another opportunity to finish this bit. We believe that many of us have been here many times before. I was taught we are all spirits in human form. We are being reborn and sent again to finish learning lessons from the past.

When you are ready to cross over, whatever is close to your heart is where your spirit will be headed. Your reality in your present life will become your reality in your afterlife, so to speak. For a better understanding: I was taught that our hearts and our minds are powerful. They can create. If you take a lot of people who think in a certain way, this becomes a creation of its own. If you have a lot of people believing in a certain concept -- whether heaven, hell or nirvana -- their joined energies combine this creative power. If a belief system that has existed for over a thousand years is accepted as the truth all around you and tells you that there is Heaven, Hell and Judgment Day, then that is what your reality will be. In Native tradition, there is no such concept. Essentially this explains why we do not have fear in the face of death. During our lives we weren't threatened with: "If you do these bad things you're going to get punished and end up in hell." We just know we will come back at another time in another body until we get it worked out.

From all the teachings I ever heard I liked that in our way it is not about making you afraid but about following your heart and finding balance within yourself. When you cross over, your spirit is drawn to what your heart believes in and how you have lived your life.

We believe that life and death are part of a circle. Crossing over is really a continuation of our journey. It is not the end. You leave your body behind and your spirit travels to the other side of the veil. You only change form and your spirit carries the experiences and lessons you have gathered throughout your life. All the things that have affected you in your life, all the things you have learned and experienced have had an emotional impact on you. The deeper these emotions go and the stronger you have felt them, the more they are imprinted on your spirit, as part of you. Through the lessons you have and haven't learned, you take along all those imprints of energy to the Spirit world. If you have fulfilled everything you needed to and you are in total balance within yourself and with Creation, you will stay in the other dimension.

Different burial customs exist amongst the tribes in the US. Some tribes took care of the bodies by burying them in a cave. Others put the corpses in a canoe up in a tree. Others used arbors just a little off the ground, wrapping the dead in buffalo hide. Some tribes cremated the bodies. Traveling to the Spirit world takes time -- you don't hop over from one minute until the next -- and so we like to give our people some tools or food for the journey. I have heard that those traditions were common amongst tribal people in Europe, too.

Most Native people have a so-called death song. It isn't as bad as it sounds when you see it in context: as death is a transition, this song is there to help you with the crossing over. As you sing, you ask Creation to help you or the person you are singing it for to make it a good journey, to let the person know there are a lot of people who love and care for them, and that it is time for the spirit to let go. To us, it is actually a very positive song. When my mother crossed over in 1985 after she had been very sick for two years, I sang our ancient Shoshone death song while sitting at her bed to accompany her spirit during the time she went to the ancestors.

For the first three days after a person has crossed over, we can do our mourning, talk about the person, call his or her name. This is a so-called human mourning, because the spirits do not mourn. For us humans, it is a departure. We will miss the person, we feel sad, and this needs to be expressed. On the fourth day, this phase is finished and we stop calling their name. It is a day of closing and of celebration. We honor what the person has contributed; we honor all the good and all the qualities in the person. For a whole year we do not say the person's name. Then we come back together again and have the one-year ceremony: a joyful feasting to celebrate and honor them. From then onwards, the name can be spoken again, but always in a cheerful and good way.

There is reason why we stop speaking the name for a whole year. Especially if we had strong feelings for the deceased, there is a lot of power in our thoughts and emotions. So, if we keep talking about the person in a mournful way and calling their name in grief, we keep the spirit of the person from completing their journey because they constantly feel this pull back to where we are. It doesn't mean you can't feel sad or miss the person, but by not calling their name, you avoid getting too deep into grief or falling into misery, as the name energizes that; it is directly linked to the human form and carries the image of the person. So, you enable the spirit to cross over fully and peacefully to the other side.

Corbin Harney and the Dog Soldiers

When the time came for Corbin Harney to get ready to leave this world, something very special happened. To me, it was an incredible sign of his powerful connection to the Spirit world.

We had been very close and I carry him in my heart to this day. He was my main guiding elder and example and I had enormous respect for him. My own health issues prevented me from traveling, as I was slowly recovering from heart surgery. It saddened my heart, but I couldn't physically be present at his funeral wake. Instead, our son Red Wolf went over to be with him during his last days to represent our family, together with Santiago, another close friend who had been working with Corbin for many years.

Corbin was staying at a vineyard in Northern California where good friends had taken him in. Aside from his Healing Center, Poo Ha Bah, he didn't really have a place where he lived permanently. Although Corbin loved being at Nanish Shontie, the winters in Oregon with all the rain and heavy humidity affected him too much and he preferred to stay where it was warmer. A number of people took turns coming to the vineyard and sitting beside him, so he was never alone. It happened to be that Red Wolf was by his side when his time was up. As I had taught him the song belonging to our tribe, Red Wolf started to sing during the time Corbin was crossing.

Santiago, who was outside, heard the song and, realizing what was happening, he gathered the others. Together they witnessed a huge fog of clouds suddenly appearing on the horizon, where there had been only clear sky before. It came closer and closer and just as it was near the house, the fog bank suddenly stopped and started changing shape. It turned into horses with warriors sitting astride them. Santiago immediately recognized them as so-called Dog Soldiers[23], which, for the Shoshone Nation, were the protectors of the people. He knew that they had come to take Corbin's spirit back with them. The Dog Soldiers and the horses were moving in a very agitated and lively manner. They waited until Corbin's spirit came, then turned around and left. It was an amazingly moving and powerful moment of awe for all, where time stood still and the unity of Creation was present. When Santiago told me about this afterwards, it showed me how strongly Corbin was connected to Spirit and how much he was honored and respected.

On my journey through life, I have experienced situations where I have been on the edge of crossing over a few times, even halfway already. I remember one time when I felt I was about to cross over, I saw myself transforming in a little eagle plume, floating around in a kind of grey darkness. At first there was nothing else in that space, just total emptiness. All of a sudden, I saw a massive eagle coming in. With the back of his tail, he was collecting eagle plume feathers. I realized that every one of those feathers was another spirit that had crossed over, just like me. I knew we were heading to where the ancestors were. Then the eagle shook its body and I fell out again: with a jolt of lightning, I was back inside my own body. I knew then that it wasn't my time yet and regained consciousness.

---

23 Dog Soldiers – originally Dog Men, until the American army introduced the word "soldier" in the 1800's. They would actively defend Native people when they were chased from their homelands and massacred by the thousands. In those days, the existing Dog Men formed into Bands that vowed to fight back against the intruding white people and sacrifice their own lives to defend the tribe. They became a strong force that the white army had to deal with for decades. A dog is incredibly loyal and protective. It is the only animal close to humans willing to sacrifice its own life to save the human family it is with.

Being One

Twice I reached an enlightened state in my life, but both times I chose not to stay in it totally. It became more like an opening to see what it could be like if I were in that state all the time and what to aim for in my life. I felt I needed to learn other things to complete it. The first time I experienced it, I was still very young. I was suddenly fully aware of everything around me. The trees, all the animals, the insects, the stones, every bit of life, I could see and sense the completeness of it. With my eyes closed, I knew what was out there in every direction, exactly where it was and what it looked like, how all of life interacted. I was aware of everything around me and my environment was completely aware of me. That's when I knew what true oneness is. It became totally clear there is no separation, that everything truly is one, coming from one source, just in different forms. Sensing and seeing the web of life -- it was an incredible awareness! With it, there was an overwhelming feeling of being at peace. Everything is exactly at the right place at the right time, it's all good and beautiful.

I realized if I made the right choices and did the right things according to what my path was about, I would be able to be in that state more often or all the time.

Once you reach the ultimate state of total flow, you have a choice: you can decide to stay as a teacher, as an example for others or you can cross over and complete your final journey. Being a child though, I wasn't yet ready for it and inside I knew right away I had to finish other things and become more aware on a human level. So, I flipped back into the "normal" state. I was lucky to feel this twice in my life. But each time, I knew it wasn't right to take the opportunity to cross over because there was still unfinished business for me.

If you choose to stay as a teacher, you need to accommodate the energy you are carrying. People notice this immense energy and can have strong reactions to it, because it makes them aware of how they are living their lives. The strong, radiating power can be threatening to their way of thinking, to their concepts and value systems, which most people aren't willing to change. Good teachers are gentle and careful with their own energy, dampen it a little to not overwhelm anybody, yet they challenge and stir to get a message across and to open people's hearts.

Ceremonies help us to understand what this state of oneness could be like. We feel a special kind of connection afterwards to Nature and Spirit; we feel this energy around us and within us. Sometimes you have incredible spiritual experiences that can stay with you for hours. But the actual ceremony is only a tool, it doesn't really create the shift itself. It can show us more or less where we could be going. Be aware of your thoughts, your feelings, your words, your actions. That is when you are -- so to speak -- in ceremony 24/7. Ceremonies help us on our path, they help us heal, they help us connect, and they remind us what it could be like.

Anybody could reach such a connected state, but most people don't want to. They prefer to just live an ordinary life that they are happy and satisfied with and not think much about it. Some do want some spiritual experiences but choose not to go all the way. They are happy with going to sweat lodges and doing other ceremonies, but don't feel the need to reach anything else. It isn't their path. This is all good and meant to be.

My path does lead this way and it means being humble enough to be a good example, having the right heart and truly living a life of service. When you practice this on a daily basis, you strive to be a kind of "walking ceremony" for others. As I mentioned, a ceremony is a tool to let you see what you could reach if you wanted to.

If you meet a person who has reached that state and has decided to stay as a teacher, you know it instantly. You feel their radiance; you recognize their peacefulness, their goodness. You just feel this is a really good person.

They are not in there with their ego, they are not outspoken about it and live their life in service to all life.

We call people who have reached that enlightened state or are in the process of reaching that state "spiritual people," they truly walk a spiritual path every day and in every situation.

Retiring and Making Peace

I have come to a point in my life where I have to face the fact that my energies are dwindling. My health has forced me to quit doing a lot of things and, unfortunately, I am limited in what I can take on. A lot of my energy goes into just getting through the day and the night in a good way. There is the physical side with pain and discomfort, where I am struggling hard to keep going and an emotional tiredness, where I don't feel the desire to continue with what I was doing before.

Yet another layer goes even deeper: it's a happy and contented form of tiredness. All my life I have given and given of myself. I have reached the point where I feel it's okay to relax more with life and I don't have to be at the forefront of everything. I can look back on all I have accomplished and also at the things that didn't work out so well. It doesn't matter, because I truly tried my best, which gives me satisfaction nevertheless. At my age, you recognize you won't be around forever, or that even a hundred years wouldn't be enough to finish things and fit in all the plans you still have. It makes you humble and helps you to take a step back.

With Nanish Shontie I was successful in manifesting my vision, getting it built, going and paid for, but I ultimately had to face that it went in another direction than I had anticipated. Yet I have my fulfillment from it and look back without bitterness or anger. I focus on what I can contribute that fits with my current possibilities. I still like to help Mother Earth whenever I can and am looking forward to working with people with open hearts. It's like Creation has handed me a gift: "You have done your part. Take care of yourself and accept the help offered. You can stop stressing yourself."

In all my talks, I have said this and it reflects what I was taught by my elders: "Creation is always out to teach you a lesson from whatever situation you are in." You can blame others and see it all as having nothing to do with you, or you can look at what you can learn from it. A change in your way of thinking that is connected to passion and heartfelt desires will need especially strong teachings. Your ego wants to hold on and says it's unfair. You resist the experience you live through. You doubt and wonder "why" all the time. You have to go through those phases of ignoring, of blaming, of licking your wounds, but then you realize that you can actually thank those who have hurt you for helping you learn something about yourself. In the end, it is about your personal spiritual growth and development. This was part of my lesson. I was forced to look at my own perceptions and expectations. When I reached that point, I understood I am ready to what you can call "retire." Although I don't really like the word retirement -- in the sense that you never really retire from a spiritual path -- it does show that you enter a different phase in your life, where you are no longer so actively involved. You pull back from certain tasks and responsibilities. It's less on the front line: less doing and more being

My path was always one of healing and love, so my choice on how to continue with my life is based on that.

I am ready for peace in my heart. Asking the question: "What would make me happy?" leads to the essence of what I have been looking for all my life: finding a tribal setting to live in a balanced and happy way. Only now I no longer feel the need to fight for it or to create it myself and am no longer pushing for it to happen. I don't have to prove myself with the big wants and needs anymore. It has gotten simpler, coming down to where to put my energy within my limits and possibilities. I am excited, though, which doorways will open and what Creation still has in store for me.

During our active adult lives, it is important to strive for things, have dreams and visions, feel the need to create and contribute. In my talks and workshops, I shared my personal path and experiences. I hope people have benefitted from my struggles and the insights that came with them. You don't reach that point of peace within without going through all those steps of learning and growing, stumbling and getting up on your feet again. In return, the sharing helped me to become clear on things, so it was a two-way street.

There were times when I was stubborn. Though I knew about the principle of our lessons becoming stronger each time, I chose not to make necessary changes. Sometimes it is easier to talk about something than to really implement it in your own personal life. As they say: you gotta walk your talk! Some of those things reach so incredibly deep and are connected to wounds that go back to childhood or maybe even earlier, if you believe in that. That is just life's journey. Some lessons are tough, some are easy. Looking back, I am always amazed how Nature and Spirit are present to guide and support us all the time. I realize more and more how life is a gift, and as I grow older, I am deeply thankful for all the experiences I have had.

Suffering and Healing

We actually cause a lot of suffering ourselves. As we keep ignoring the nudges for change, the lessons become stronger and we end up being sick or having problems. Although we thought we were escaping from it, we created our own suffering.

Native Americans also see another aspect in this. As you suffer, you can come to great insights and make incredibly transformative changes. The suffering that comes with the illness, the trauma, the accident or whatever you are encountering in your life makes it possible to truly understand and grasp something as you go deep within to survive the process. A lot of people have had the experience that when they get really sick with a fever, they have a powerful dream or vision. This is due to the fact that the normal daily reality isn't occupying you and you go into an altered state of reality. I have seen people who were bitten by an animal who went through pain and discomfort but came out of it with new knowledge and insight, sometimes through being in a trance-like state, almost delirious. Of course, this depends where that particular person is at that moment in their life and what their belief system and upbringing were like. A lot of people say: "I had a dream due to fever and that doesn't mean anything to me." If you believe it's as an illusion, that's what it becomes, but if you recognize and honor it, you can get messages from Nature or Spirit.

Native Americans have used this principle the other way round, too. When we go into certain ceremonies like a sweat lodge or a vision quest, it is like we are saying: "I am willing to go through suffering as I hope to get guidance for my life." Suffering is a way of showing the spirit world that we are serious about growing on our spiritual path.

With the practice of ceremonies, we also train ourselves to become open to those other realities we normally block off in our daily lives. This practice enables us to switch more quickly from one state to another, and makes us more consciously aware that the other reality is present all the time. Your daily consciousness fades out and the suffering brings you into a deeper state of communication with Spirit and Nature. It blocks mind's control and the ongoing noise in the head and helps you focus on the connection you are aiming to make. You open up because it makes you vulnerable and takes away the layers of control and emotional blockages. So, in the end, the suffering helps us!

A ceremony supports us in focusing on what we truly want in our lives. You reach an altered state with the help of the ceremony and often through group effort. Sun dances and sweat lodges are gatherings with bigger groups of people and go on for longer periods of time, or even days.

The vision quest is something you perform on your own, though the elders prepare you beforehand and wait for you when you come back. In tribal settings, the community greets you on your return. The experience of the quest itself though, is that you are on your own and are stripped of all the physical comforts you have in your daily life. Usually with no clothes, food or water, you stay quiet at a certain spot for four days. It is like being put out there in nature in a primary state, as naked as you were born, maybe just a blanket or a buffalo hide for the night and some spiritual objects. You enter into a meditative state where you connect with Nature and Spirit on a very deep level.

In the Native way, we don't have the concept of reward, not in the sense that you feel you deserve something in return. You are willing to suffer and sacrifice something in the hope of gaining insight and growth, but mostly you offer of yourself and you are granted whatever the spirits feel you are ready for. It has nothing to do with your expectations or a need for a certain reward in a certain form.

A misconception is that some people think that the more you suffer, the more you gain spiritually. It isn't something you do on purpose. Sometimes it can turn out you need to suffer greatly in order to make another step on your spiritual path, but not always. When I do a sweat lodge, the first thing that comes to mind is that it is about healing. We aim to heal our spiritual connection to the Mother Earth. It is not true that the hotter the stones are and the more you suffer inside the lodge, the better the outcome. I am familiar that so-called "warrior sweats" exist, but I wasn't taught in this way and am firmly against that. Although sometimes the stones might be extremely hot and you do experience the heat strongly, which can make you suffer and lead to healing, it's different from your ego proving that you're able to withstand as much heat as possible. You miss the whole point when you claim that the more you suffer, the better it is. The suffering is always in connection with the healing aspect.

For some people, it is enough just to experience one round in the sweat, depending on what their physical and mental state is. For some people, it would be dangerous to go on a vision quest without water for four days. It depends on your upbringing, experience, and what state you are in. It is the same with facing the cold. I am used to going outside with just a t-shirt on no matter what the weather is. I have practice that my whole life. If you have never done that, it is a huge step to even go out without warm clothing for a little bit. You gradually learn. All of us have to take steps to reach a certain level. Whatever you do, it takes practice. With the practice, what appears to be suffering for a lot of people actually isn't anymore. I can handle the cold without suffering because I have learned to embrace it, just as much as I embrace the heat in the sweat lodge. So, the suffering has turned into something healing and I can actually enjoy it. Enjoying life is a major concept we as indigenous people have. We are meant to experience joy and happiness on Mother Earth!

We can make use of many of the old ways and ancestral knowledge to help ourselves in a more balanced way that is also less destructive for our planet. Part of what I share in my talks, workshops and in the book is about spreading that information and hoping it will be implanted again. My belief is all life will benefit when we reconnect to Nature and Spirit. It gives us strength and faith; it dissolves fears and insecurities. We grow and are able to walk more gently upon Mother Earth. I understand that evolution, which took place gradually over thousands of years, partly in the same pace and partly at different speeds, brought us to this point in time, but has been going in one direction for too long and is off balance. A lot of human creations were initially for positive reasons. They were developed to make life easier and physically less challenging. We created comfort through houses with showers and technical devices, cars and airplanes, central heating and electricity, etc. You could perceive this as just for comfort, but I think the main evolutionary purpose behind these developments was to help us enjoy life more, to have more time on our hands for other things and less for hard work to survive. I am not against progress and see there is a reason for it. At the same time, these developments have caused pollution and abuse of resources, which had and still has devastating effects on our planet. Due to our human weaknesses, we started using technology for less positive purposes and ended up abusing it to the point where a few people and companies decide and control with short-time benefits in mind only, without thinking with their hearts or looking ahead into the future.

Nowadays we are connected globally as humans, thanks to telephones, computers and means of transportation. In my perception as a Native person, I see the necessity of understanding that we are connected to everything around us, whether mountains, deserts, forests, oceans, animals, insects, rocks or plants. It is a concept that all indigenous peoples on the Mother Earth have in common. We say: "Everything is connected and everything possesses Life."

We can turn things around if we start thinking differently and start applying some of the old principles and concepts again. It is a matter of approach and intent as to how we use technology and scientific knowledge. If you look at modern medicine, you can witness incredible progress in accomplishing high-standard operations and helping people survive illnesses which were once deadly. But we shouldn't lose sight of the origins of why people get sick and how our own responsibility is connected to our healing. If we just put it in the hands of others, we skip important lessons. It is really about why and how we do the things we do. Everything can basically be utilized in a good or in a negative way. Our way of thinking and our level of awareness discern what is good and what is bad. This leads to making choices out of a combination of head and heart, wisdom and compassion, keeping in mind how something will affect future generations and how it impacts all life on Earth. What we need is enough people waking up to using technology in a supportive way for the benefit of all involved. If we are able to understand working with Nature and Spirit, we are actually connecting ourselves again to the source. You can approach what is about to be created with the thought in the back of your mind: "How does this flow with life? Does this feel good on all levels?" If you do that, you help restore balance and work together with Nature and Spirit.

Black Swan Story

Hermine:

We are sitting by the Pacific Ocean and the sun is shining. Mala is sharing stories and thoughts and I am taping.

At one point, I happen to look up and see a black swan flying over our heads, coming from the ocean and flying east. It is just one swan. A black swan is a very rare sighting. We both exclaim: "Wow, you hardly ever see those!" and wonder what this sign could mean.

Three days later on my flight back to Europe, I come across the phrase "the black-swan-effect" in a book[24] and it dawns on me what the Black Swan represented: an unforeseen event that could change everything, make things go in a totally different direction. It refers to the fact that black swans are rarely seen, are a rare species. But only because they are rare doesn't mean they don't exist. It is just that whenever we look at a situation and are trying to make a prediction that we like to bar those "black swans" as a possibility.

---

24 "Resilience in times of extremes" by Gregg Braden, page 177: The black swan or unforeseen event. Nassim Taleb, author of "The impact of the highly improbable" used this phrase for the first time in 2007 in his book in terms of predicting economics and cash flow. Since then this is a common wording.

On the day of the Black Swan's sighting, I had started to feel sick in the morning. Right after my morning prayers out in the garden, I was practicing Qi Gong and took in the energy of a yew tree. I knew it had a poisonous touch to it but something made me take a bit of that energy in anyway. Fifteen minutes later, an irritating cough started that got worse by the hour. All day and the following night, I kept thinking the sickness was related to what the tree had been telling me, namely that it was actually helping me to get something out of my system that needed clearing. My sickness stayed longer than a day though. It manifested as a real flu with all the symptoms: high fever, high pulse, extreme tiredness, body aches, no appetite and a lot of coughing. I was so sick and miserable that I wasn't able to sleep or hardly drink anything. Another horrible night with all kinds of paranoia went by and I was finally taken to an Urgent Care Center where they gave me some medicine that helped. I had to learn to be resilient and find my inner strengths and resources that I could fall back upon. I was humbled by the experience, learning that these things could also happen to me, as I was a person who always claimed not to get the flu. I always thought that by claiming this, I was putting out my faith in my own body and my abilities to stay healthy. Now I learned the hard way that of course it could also happen to me, but, in the end, that I could also have faith in the powers of resilience, rebooting, recovering and recuperation. I had resources within myself and could also call upon help from outside.

The whole trip had already been peculiar up to that point. Because I had failed to get an online ESTA visa for the US before getting on the trans- Atlantic flight, I was refused boarding, though it would only have taken me 15 minutes to fill out the form. I was forced to stay over for an extra night in Amsterdam. 24 hours later I arrived in Portland, Oregon, but unfortunately the flight to Eugene, my final destination, was cancelled and I had to take a shuttle bus. My suitcase had also disappeared in Portland and it took another 24 hours before it was retraced and delivered to my address. Since all the recording equipment was in there, we weren't able to get much work done for the book yet.

A week later, I was dealing with the symptoms of that heavy flu and was in no physical condition to travel home on Sunday. The doctor at the Urgent Care Center recommended I stay in bed for the next several days and explicitly told me not to fly. We tried to postpone my scheduled trip for a few days, but there was absolutely no flight available from Eugene to Seattle the next few days, so it was evident I had to somehow make it on the original flight as planned. I had to get well in one night, make sure my fever was gone and give a healthy enough impression to the flight attendants. I managed all that, though the night before had been rough and I hadn't slept much in the past 48 hours. It is amazing how things can appear to be against you and yet all of a sudden you find those resources in yourself to work through things. The universe was helping me in mysterious ways. I was no longer worried by that point. I just allowed myself to flow with it all and take things as they come. Although I was hardly coughing anymore, I was still only able to close my eyes for an hour, and yet strangely enough was doing ok. We had another delay that forced me to run all the way across Schiphol airport in Amsterdam to reach my plane to Vienna, the last leg of the journey. I made it five (!) minutes before takeoff. Again, my suitcase didn't come through but was delivered later that evening.

Looking back, I understand the sighting of the black swan as a reminder that things sometimes happen in unforeseen ways. The trip evolved around unexpected experiences and the black swan had appeared symbolically in the sky. We really never know how life will unfold. Be ready to expect the unexpected!

Health and Medicine Ways

When I was young, I was very much against any kind of Western medicine. Both my parents had told me when you are very adamant about something, Nature and Spirit are going to teach you a lesson. The cancer I got while living in Nevada was a major lesson that made me look twice. The cancer grew so fast that no Native medicine and no other alternative medicine seemed to help as it was caused by the nuclear radiation in the groundwater in the area. In those years, there were many cases like me with thyroid tumors. I had to go ahead with the operation and woke up without a thyroid, so I was forced to rely on Western medicine for the rest of my life. On the one hand, the operation saved my life and on the other hand, I was stuck to taking those pills. When I was younger, I thought that I would never need anything but Native and natural medicine.

When my other health issues appeared, I was much more careful with my judgment. I would pray about my situation and find myself guided toward a certain medicine or form of help.

Sometimes a Western doctor would offer me a possible solution and I would take the chance, always checking inside if I was responding positively. Sometimes it didn't feel right and I didn't continue with it. Somebody would offer a homeopathy treatment or suggest a herbal prescription that felt okay and I would try it out for a while. Of course, I had to make changes in my diet and habits along the way as well, which was tough on me at times as I was stubborn and thought I didn't need those changes. My diabetes really turned in a positive direction when I started being careful with sugar and soda pops. Certain herbs or other measures that I took for a while stopped working or were no longer strong enough, so I would search for something else. Sometimes only Western medicine helped, and at some point I needed heart surgery.

During all those processes, I always worked on myself on a spiritual level, not only through prayers and ceremonies, but also with the energy within myself, visualizing healing. Again, it is about what works for you and trying to flow with it. Western and Native Medicine can complement each other.

I have really tried to be open to whatever is offered to me and to not be judgmental about it beforehand. You know what they say about love: if you really want to experience true love, it doesn't matter what age, what sex or what color, you have to open your heart for when loves comes to your doorstep. You embrace it in whatever form it comes. The same applies to medicine. The heart "knows" everything and "sees" everything within you; it can weigh what is good for you and what is appropriate for you to try.

My Personal Purpose

When I am asked what I see was my purpose in life and if I fulfilled it, I have many thoughts on the subject. Especially now that I am older and physically less capable, I reflect on it.

On the one hand, there is the prophecy that my parents shared with me that I was supposed to follow. On the other hand, there is the path I chose. The way I understand it: different levels of purposes are lined up that you can act upon. Each one of us is born with more than one gift.

I was able to create Nanish Shontie, which flowed as a result of having lived in a tribal setting in my early youth and at Meta Tantay. I managed to get it up and going in a more organized way than the spontaneous scramble of Meta Tantay, which had made me so happy. It was part a wish and part my purpose.

Through my talks and travels, I reached people from all walks of life, Native and non-Native alike. Some organizations I worked with or set up have been successful in their goals, and as a counselor I was able to help both individuals and groups in the US as well as in Europe. All this has made me content and happy and fulfilled a personal purpose.

As far as my prophecy goes and my purpose as a healer and Medicine person working for the benefit of Mother Earth, human beings and all life, I didn't go all the way. The prophecy said I was to follow the Medicine Path and would take over from my father and others in these matters. I was supposed to speak up for my people, I was going to have a very rough life with many heavy experiences and I would come close to crossing over seven times. When I was younger, I helped my father mostly when he performed healings or worked on people. When the occasion asked for it, I did do some healings on my own, but not very often. Both my parents told me I could reach an even higher level than my father, and he was already incredibly powerful working with energy. When I no longer lived around my father, I pretty much stopped doing any personal Medicine work. My contribution consisted of doing social and cultural support work for my people. The power foreseen in me with my healing gift I have deliberately kept at a distance. My greatest fear in life has always been that I wouldn't be able to control the power inside me and I might end up hurting someone in a bad and irreversible way.

As a young person, I witnessed a lot of Native people using alcohol and drugs, which turned into a vicious cycle of shame, depression and violent behavior. It made me so sad to see that happening. At the same time, I witnessed Native people returning to their traditional ways, which often looked promising but also went astray quite often as they gained power and then used it for selfish reasons or abused it to hurt people when they were angry or spiteful. I really didn't want to become that kind of person.

I have met Medicine people who were still so caught up in their own problems and human faults like ego, anger or jealousy that their Medicine suffered from it. They ended up hurting people, not only those who came to seek help but things also backfired on their family and even on themselves. I had my father as an example and I witnessed the two sides in him many times. He wasn't always in control of his own emotions and at times his anger lashed out. On the other hand, he helped many people with his incredible knowledge and powerful Medicine or simply through his words.

I didn't aim for the big power either, although a lot of people always emphasized I should take on that task, since I carried the healing energy in a natural way and was taught through my upbringing how to focus it. I honestly never had a great desire to become a Medicine Man nor to become a spiritual leader. A part of me just wanted a simpler life than what was being offered to me. I was okay being of service; that fulfilled me and made me happy. That was all I wanted.

To have not used my healing capacities in the way everybody expected has always been a point of friction in my life. I have often been asked: "Why don't you use your gift, Mala?" I always figured I wasn't ready for it and still had to become better at being gentle and capable of controlling my emotions. Isn't that funny? My siblings thought I was trying to be too good and gave me the nickname "goody-two-shoes," yet I still thought I was being selfish on too many occasions. My parents and many elders had put their hopes in me. They saw this different spirit in me and encouraged it whenever they could. Things just came a lot easier to me. A number of times I had Indian friends say: "Why is it that all these animals always come up to you? Why is it that you have all these visions and dreams? Why is it that the spirits show themselves so easily to you? Here I go and pray at sweats all the time and go for vision-quests and nothing appears!" My father used to tell me:

"Stop dragging your heels all the time!" He meant it not only literally but to the extent that I was always trying to delay any process of learning, and he called me "the reluctant apprentice."

For many years, I was in a helper-function for other Medicine people and there were opportunities enough where I could have gone into the next phase, but I kept avoiding and refusing it, which kept me from developing my gift. I purposely chose not to gain any more power, though I have felt the strong presence of energy inside of me ever since I was a child. I knew what it was about and sometimes it would just overcome me, but I withdrew from it and even blocked it from building up inside of me.

The Medicine Path is a huge responsibility and not to be taken lightly. I realized it was a path of no return. Once you go there, there is no turning back: it's a 100% commitment. You can't undo knowledge; you have the responsibility to use it in a good way. It would have changed my life totally and it wouldn't have been within the ordinary norm of a job bringing in some money for the family, and I had a deep sense of longing for that ordinary family life. Just like with anything else, you train your Medicine to get better at it, but at the same time it means you have to be more responsible for your actions, your words, your feelings and even your thoughts. As a consequence, this means you need to be aware of what you are thinking, saying or doing 24/7.

Another aspect if you follow this path: you are obliged to listen to what the elders ask you to do, whatever is needed for the community. Sometimes this brings you into difficult and sensitive situations that can have consequences further down the road. You might end up hurting one person in order to save others. Sometimes you need to choose between two options that are both not nice and not very healing, but you have to listen to what is being asked of you. If a situation occurred that would be harmful for the community as a whole, it could be that you'd be asked to use your Medicine power for the benefit of the community. The Elders Councils prayed over those issues for days and a decision was never taken lightly. I really wasn't keen on being put in that position, having witnessed my father in that role. It's almost like being in a war. You try and avoid being stuck in a fight, but sometimes there is no other option than to defend yourself against an aggressor. If a situation was going to be excessively hurtful for the community, the elders could decide to fight back and go to war. As a Medicine person, you give your life in service to your people.

Remember, if you choose the Medicine Path, this means that all you do and say has much greater impact on everything around you than from a person who doesn't know about the usage of this power and energy. It is clear that we sometimes hurt another person involuntarily or even on purpose and later regret that and are remorseful about it. Those are minor things and belong to life. When Medicine is involved, the energies and the impact are deeper and longer lasting. Not necessarily on a physical level, but they can show on a deep spiritual level. I didn't want to mess with that. With the Medicine way you deliberately step into another realm and take on the quality of that part of Nature and Spirit. Like my father: he had a strong connection to the thunder, the lightning and the rain and those qualities became a part of him and worked through him as he directed with his mind and heart energy. You are one with that part of nature. Wherever my father came, people noticed that the rains would come. They'd say: "Oh, Rolling Thunder is bringing rain," but it wasn't so much that he brought the rain - the clouds just came to greet him because he had such a close relationship them!

It almost happened a few times that I ended up hurting people, and especially those close to my heart I felt strong about protecting from any harm caused by Medicine power used in the wrong way. I wasn't willing to take the risk and instead gave in to the fear.

It is something else to be capable of controlling or suppressing your anger than to not have this anger inside of you at all. Corbin Harney was my big example here. Whenever there was a situation around him that people didn't handle very well or where he got disappointed, he wouldn't be upset or angry. He wasn't hiding his temper. It just wasn't in his way of thinking. He'd say: "O well, that is how it happened. Let us find out what we can do to change it for the better." You could feel he really meant it and wasn't faking. I wanted to get to that point in my life too.

At one point, I realized it was okay for me to leave it and come back in another life to finish that part. I gained an acceptance inside of me that I wouldn't walk the Medicine Way fully and was fine with it.

It is hard to explain, especially for people unfamiliar with the language of spirit, but the spirits can also get really upset with you if they see you aren't using the gift you were born with properly. Up to the point where they actually strip you of that gift and take it away. That in itself is a dangerous process for you as a person. In their way of reasoning, it comes down to: here you are with an incredible gift from Creation that you are supposed to utilize for the greater good and you leave it barren and unused? Then they literally rip it out of you. As the gift is so strongly connected to your own spirit, this process can hurt you deeply. The gift is usually passed on to somebody else in such a case. It can also be that the spirits are patient with you and hope you'll come back to it someday, but it will have consequences for you on some level, like you'll get a lot of health problems to deal with.

I have paid a price for my choice. Spirit has tried to get me back on that path many times, urging me to look at things. I made changes but the big chunk I always left out. Whether right or wrong, I have to live with the consequences. It could well be that that is one of the reasons why my life has been hard and filled with so many challenges. Through sickness, accidents, sorrow and pain, I was forced to make changes again and again. What can I say? I am ready to take responsibility for what I did and didn't do, am trying to move forward in the best way I can for whatever time is left for me.

The prophecy of my purpose foretold that I would have a rough life, but I think on top of that this is what happened to me. I have loaded more health problems on myself because of my refusal to use my Medicine power. I had to pay a price for that choice. I accept that.

> *Hermine:*
>
> *You tell people again and again to have faith in the Creator and to try and find their purpose in life, overcome and embrace their fears and insecurities, and yet in your particular case you haven't totally put that into practice yourself.*
>
> *You seemed to say: "I am not worthy of the gift you gave me and I can't trust myself enough to be able to use it in a good way."*

Like I said, it was because of my fear. And it is exactly the reason why I so often talked to others about this: I recognize the pattern. We say in our language: "walk your talk." It is true I haven't totally walked my talk. I am definitely not perfect and I too, am here to learn. I guess I was pretty strict in my judgment of my own progress in that direction. I do not allow myself to make a mistake. One time I hurt somebody physically in a fight because I was angry. Immediately afterwards I had to throw up. I was literally sick of myself. I didn't want to hurt anybody ever: it is something that has been with me since I was a child. Some say I am in denial, some say it is a waste of my talent. There is truth in all that but I have chosen it consciously. You can perceive it as a lack of courage, but for me it just didn't fit my personality. And in that sense, I don't regret it because I am who I am.

My path was and is to follow the Ways of Nature and Spirit. I listened to those voices and trusted them. I have always strongly believed in those ways and lived my life accordingly. That gave me healing energy in a natural way wherever it was needed.

There were moments that I had this enormous sense of conscious awareness out of the blue, when I was able to see and feel things and be totally one with everything around me. It is a creative source of immensely strong healing energy that is so beautiful and stronger than anything else. Yet I preferred to leave out the spectacular healings.

Looking back on my life, I can say I have chosen to work with positive and simple energies that make people feel good and help the Mother Earth and all Life. What I have tried to do is create harmony and be a good human and caretaker. I knew if I focused on positive energies like love, joy, gratitude and caretaking, it would create healing in the long run.

Healing is a word that you can use in many ways. When somebody is sick, that person seeks healing and goes to a doctor or a Medicine person. In my understanding, healing can just as much be understood in the sense that we try and create something good for the future generations and for Mother Earth. It can be saving a forest or the whales in the ocean or bringing about clean air to breathe in a city.

In my travels and talks, I reached people on a heart level and helped them connect again to Nature and Spirit. It is not so much a healing that I perform for an individual but enabling people in a much broader sense to find peace within through reconnection. I have had a lot of positive resonance and responses over the years, which still fills me with gratitude and joy.

Over time, I got convinced the biggest change we humans need to make is in our way of thinking. I have talked about pollution of the mind. If greed, egoism, jealousy, and such dominate our thinking, the outcome will be negative. This will ultimately create a polluted world. Consequently, if our way of thinking transforms, we can turn things around and create something positive. Our mind is the starting point and the essence is the connection to the heart energy. Many people claim: "This is the way the world works and how it'll always be." But I know it can be otherwise and the world can function differently. I have chosen to go out and talk to people who are interested in a spiritual way of thinking. Creation opened a doorway for me to become a speaker on behalf of Mother Earth. I was lucky because I got to meet people from all over and I simply love to talk. Once I get started, I get into a certain flow and can't stop, which my translators always had to put up with, hahaha!

In Native American culture, walking the Red Road is about being of service to Creation, to the people and the future generations. There are times you really sacrifice parts of yourself. It is constantly asking yourself: "Where can I be of service? What is asked for and needed? Can I give? Can I share my food if somebody is hungry or can I myself go without food so the other person can be fed?" My path basically is one of servitude. Yes, it is about finding balance and personally I do go out on a limb, but it just comes naturally. I don't have to think twice about it. As long as it feels good, it is fine and I can deal with the consequences.

Of course, you have to watch and mind yourself too, but you are not first in line. I look at the greater picture and am aware I'm a small part of that whole piece; in that sense as a person I'm not so important. This kind of behavior is rooted in the tribal way of thinking. The tribe always takes the whole into account, whether people, animals, or trees. A lot of people do it the other way around. They take care of themselves first and then look out for others. This becomes a habit and they no longer care about others, Mother Earth or the future generations. For me that doesn't feel right inside.

The concept of willingness to sacrifice something of yourself for the greater good is the basis of the Red Road. It is not something I question; it fills me with gratitude to be part of the circle of life. Everything in creation abides this law: life comes and goes, you give and you receive, that is how it is. When you give of yourself, whether on a physical level in a giveaway, on an emotional level through caring for and listening to others, or on a spiritual level by praying or focusing your energy in a certain direction, you do this freely from the heart without expecting anything in return. It is not about reward. You do it because it makes you happy and because you feel your action creates something good and positive. That's all there is to it.

It sounds simple but it is also an area where we struggle; we have weaknesses and are in need of reassurance, praise, and recognition. When that mechanism begins to go off-balance, there is a danger of your ego wanting more reward in some form, like money, status and success, and it is hardly ever enough. You have to watch that closely and constantly reassess your attitude. Once a system tips towards gaining power, there is a tendency to more easily get imbalanced.

That is why it is important to show gratitude and appreciation. We have to let others know that we don't take their gifts for granted. If you get a "thank you" without expecting it, it fills your human heart with joy. All the traditions based on the ways of the earth or the ways of spirit have something in common. You don't put yourself first. You think of other people, of the community as a whole, of the effects of your actions.

Christianity also has the principles of helping others and thinking of others before you think of yourself. Though I have experienced very negative actions from Christian people against myself as a Native person when they see themselves and their faith as being better than everybody and everything else, I have also met Christians who did a lot of good. They weren't trying to convince or convert me and went according to the essence of the original teachings, which basically means: to live a good and positive life, filled with love and joy. Over time, I realized it was the people themselves who misinterpreted their religion and fell into a self-made concept of what they thought being a Christian meant. You can observe this behavior everywhere and in any faith.

I once heard somebody say: "If you stay connected with the earth, your heart stays soft!" That special connection has gotten lost for many people over time all over the Mother Earth, and explains a lot of the wrongdoings and abuses. It is the lost connection from our heart to the world. I strongly believe that if we turn back to the path of the heart, things will change for the better for all beings on our planet. Inside me, there is great hope and faith.

EPILOGUE

Over the past few months, my health condition has grown very serious. I seek help from Western doctors and their medication but I also still make use of my ancestral knowledge and the spiritual ways. Just the other day, friends did a small ceremony for me with some drumming. It felt good, regardless how much or how little it helps. All I do is say: "Hey, try and stay as positive as you can." I am not giving up, but I also watch the symptoms worsening. My kidneys are no longer working properly, there is too much fluid around my heart and in the rest of my body. I'm dizzy a lot of the time, nauseous as well and have lost my appetite. The struggles are hard. Sometimes I feel I can hardly make it through the day, let alone the night, which is tough, as I don't sleep a lot.

I know that if I start to give in, get negative about it and want to fight it or start to dwell on it, I will go downhill really fast. I feel one condition leading to another; all the medications affecting each other.

If you ask me: "Is life still worthwhile?" "Yes, it is!" I embrace the journey, welcome all of it. Every day is a blessing! Life is such a gift.

In spite of all the physical hardship, my spirit is getting stronger and clearer on certain things. It almost feels like my body and spirit are separating from each other. They are still working together, but there is no longer a unity. The body is sort of hanging in there, but my spirit is telling me: "I am good and strong. I will continue being next to your body and support it where I can." I can see my body is collapsing on itself little by little while my spirit seems to be more focused and more positive. It's interesting to observe.

When there are still moments that we as spiritual beings are able to grow from, there is healing, and so life's journey continues and develops.

Looking back, I am deeply grateful for the many incredible experiences I have had, the many good people I have met, all of it.

At the end of your life, even if you have physical struggles, you need to remember your whole life's journey. If you only look at the discomforts of getting older, you tend to forget what all has been given to you. It's good to keep the whole picture in mind, have an overview and put things into perspective. It all connects to what your life has been about.

At the end of this book, I want to express my thanks to the Creator and my ancestors for the journey I have been on in this lifetime. It has been mostly wonderful with many hills and valleys and with some hard struggles. It's been a path with the indigenous Red Road and western world side by side. Many times, I had to learn the hard way, and yet often I could listen with my heart.

I was given the opportunity to help many people and a few have felt hurt by an action of mine that wasn't in balance. Sometimes you wish you could go back and undo something, but in the end, you have to live in the present and change your way of thinking to walk in a more healing way in the future.

An elder once told me that to have true balance in your life means accepting everything with true love: loving all things equally. When you can truly do this, no matter how you feel or what is going on around you, each day is beautiful. I am really grateful to have been born into the life I have been traveling in. It has been and continues to be full of adventures.

As I now journey through the sunset of my life, my eyes and heart are more open than ever before. It is truly an incredible world full of opportunities that we live in. The beauty and sacredness of life is becoming even clearer to me. I cherish it in my heart and feel blessed by all that was given to me.

WORDS OF GRATITUDE

F irst, I would like to thank those who have been directly supportive in the creation of this book.

Jennifer Aulie has been involved from the beginning of our project and has helped with genuine interest, critical advice, humor and the necessary practical aid to ensure and encourage our endeavor.

Bob Sewana, Mikki and Cecilia Dreijer, my niece Rhonda Morning Star Pope Flores and my son Michael Thunder Eagle all offered their hospitality and homes for Hermine and I to work on the book, taping, interviewing and writing.

A special thanks goes to Eleanor Kedney Schaffer who has accompanied me on many travels and given valuable tips for the publishing of the book.

So many people have supported me on my journeys around the globe. I cannot name them all, but still would like to mention a few specifically. I feel honored to have worked with the different Wilderness groups both in the US and in Germany and Austria, Europe. I want to thank Anna and Belinda, Elke, Marieke and Lutgard, Kai, Willi Fragosa, Anne and Robert, Eva Ulmer Janes, Anne from Breda, Bruno and Lies, Anne and Paul, Karen, Uta, Mipp, Bernd and Gert, Anna, Ulli and Wilfried, Eric, Joep and Topo, amongst others. Some helped financially; some gave support on a mental and emotional level, some organized workshops or talks. A CD with some of the Camp songs was made and a short video was filmed, others did fundraising for me. All help was greatly appreciated!

Besides those named above, my thanks also goes to the many friends who aren't listed but have touched my heart, each in their own specific way.

My gratitude goes to the many Native and non-Native people I met while living in Nevada (Meta Tantay) and working in Oregon (Nanitch Sahallie), through whom I experienced valuable lessons that in the end all added to how my life turned out.

I thank the people at Nanish Shontie who supported all those years of traveling, giving workshops and talks, thus spreading our vision of reconnecting to Nature and Spirit, the true message of this book, its foundational fabric.

Honest and heartfelt thanks to my closest family, who have stood by me through good and hard times and given me encouragement on my life's journey. I especially name Sky, my wife of 44 years, who sometimes kicked me in the butt when I needed it, but always had a gentle and loving hand for me.

A very special thanks also goes to Hermine Schuring. Aside from sharing many life experiences, this book would not have happened without her strength of heart.

My heart goes out to all the elders who have shared the ancestral knowledge with me and have been my example for leading a life in service. I honor them deeply and hope I have done justice in passing on their words and actions in written form, though this is uncommon in our oral indigenous tradition.

In the end, I give my deepest thanks to the teachings of the Red Road and to Creation for the many blessings of life, and to Mother Earth, the greatest teacher of all.

Mala Spotted Eagle Pope

ACKNOWLEDGEMENTS

Thank you, Mala Spotted Eagle. Through you I have learned to pray. I witnessed you while praying -- at sunrise, before eating, before traveling, when we sat in a talking circle, when difficult situations arose, for others, for the Mother Earth and, much less, also for yourself.

When I was younger, "praying" in my understanding was characterized by the institution of the church with its history of abuse, pressure and violence to force people to believe in their God. Getting to know a Native American who had a conversation with Creation and Mother Earth let me perceive praying in a new light. Having come this far, I realize how happiness and gratitude spread from this attitude and how my heart was content and smiling more. To have a conversation with Nature and Spirit became part of my everyday reality. When you pray with all your heart, without making it a plea or a demand but honestly asking for support and insight, it has so much strength and creative power.

Thanks to the indigenous way of thinking and perceiving, I learned to understand life in a much broader sense, finding connection to source and peace within.

I express my deepest gratitude to Christina Müller who did a wonderful job editing the book. Quite a large task, considering my non-mother-tongue English, and aiming for a book which reads as if you were hearing Mala speak. She took this on with great enthusiasm and positive energy, not realizing how much work it would turn out to be, and stayed with it all the way. Her sense of humor made the editing process so much easier on me!

Eleanor Kedney also gave valuable tips for correcting some wording, whilst putting emphasis on details of spelling and rules of grammar.

I have learned a lot from both of these women along the way!

I also thank Elke Loepthien for her positive response on my request to set up a crowdfunding page in order to finance the publishing of the book.

And thanks to my photographer friend Mascha Verkooijen, who did an excellent job of creating the cover photo.

I give thanks to the team at BookBaby, who helped with the graphic design and the final steps towards printing and publishing the book.

I would like to express special thanks to my children, Dennic, Benjamin (1993) and Eden, who each in their own way accompanied me on several journeys through Native American country and understand how close my heart is to the indigenous Way of Life.

I also thank my partner Thomas, whom I got to know through a Native American human rights organization in Vienna (AKIN), and who trusted -- without making a big fuss over it -- that I would finish this book project.

Hermine Schuring

AFTERWORD

It is with sorrow in my heart that I have to add this piece of writing shortly before the book is going to the publisher.

Mala Spotted Eagle crossed over on the 17th of May 2019.

Three days before he made his transition, he told me he was happy to see that so many people were interested in the book and had already made pre-orders on the crowd funding page.

He timed his moment to leave the earth plane perfectly: after the heavy struggles of the last months he went with ease on a rare blue full moon in May, called "Flower Moon" by the Native people, representing new life in full abundance, visible in the fresh green of trees, fragrance of rosebushes in the air and young birds spreading their fluffy feathered wings for the first time.

Mala,

You were named "the Strong One" and your strong spirit carried you through a life full of amazing moments, powerful lessons and impressive experiences. It was a life of service: for Mother Earth, for your people, for other caretakers, for your family, for all beings.

You had a remarkable ride and you touched many people with your gentleness, your open and happy heart, your patience for every being in most every situation. You welcomed every bit

*of life, singing songs at sunrise, drumming at ceremonies, doing
fun card games, relishing good food, going to the movies, simply
enjoying life and company, just as much as sitting outside alone
in the moonlight on your porch, always aware of signs of Nature
and Spirit, or playing and communicating with animals. When
disappointments occurred -- whether through unfair accusations,
emotional hurt and rejection, or when struggling with health
issues -- you withdrew a little but always managed to stay
positive. Even in your darkest moments in those last months,
suffering pain and extreme discomfort, you aimed to stay friendly
until your time was up, surprising those around you with your
kindness, making sure you didn't take things out on anybody.
You remained at service to those who asked for advice and still
shared the Native wisdom and knowledge whenever called upon.
A true example, a true elder, a man with a large and loving heart,
whose message was to embrace all of life, literally all of it, and
to embrace it with love.*

*The burdens and limitations of the body are left behind and
now you fly with your powerful Spotted Eagle wings, roaming
through the spirit realm and rejoicing with the ancestors. Your
spirit is free and happy! You have fulfilled your life purpose.*

*Rather than "Goodbye," people say: "Until we meet again"
in the Native tradition. Although we will not meet again in this
lifetime, I feel very much connected to your energy. I am full of
joy for the beautiful journey you had here, and very grateful that
I got to be a part of it.*

Abeshai,
Hermine

SUNRISE POEM

Sunrise

My friend who is Shoshone
tells me the most important thing
is to welcome the morning sun.
Each thing in nature does.
Ground squirrels face east,
paws together for minutes.
The birds sing to the morning.
Even the wind breezes across the desert.
He takes his hand drum out of its bag,
and I learn gratefulness,
a tree that's been cold all night
warms in the sun when no one watches,
a young sunflower turns to the light all day.

By Eleanor Kedney
(Originally published in Snapdragon: A Journal of Art
& Healing)

QUESTIONS & ANSWERS

The expression "Mother Earth" refers not only to the planet but encompasses everything that is here, everything we create, all of evolution. It is all one. Do you think Mother Earth can handle the pollution and the climate change that is happening?

You mention the example often that you have a tree in its most natural state and you have things made of wood, like tables, chairs and houses. They carry the spirit of that tree and yet have gotten further away from the wood in its original state. The same applies to oil turned into plastic or concrete, or all kinds of chemical-based stuff. Does she allow us to develop this in order for us to learn certain lessons?

I was taught that the more you change the form away from the original, the more you change the energy, and the original spirit is thus more difficult to reach and to deal with. You can compare this with people: when a person grows up close to nature, it's easy for them to stay in touch, to communicate and feel Spirit in Nature. When you live a hectic city-life, you aren't taught how to approach nature and spirit, your energy is different and your connection grows weaker and weaker. Everything about you changes: your way of thinking, your actions, your awareness, everything.

Creation gives us the ability to make choices while going through changes, while evolving. Creation itself doesn't allow or forbid, it simply gives us opportunities. It is up to us what we choose, wise or not. Those choices have an impact on Mother Earth and on all.

I believe Mother Earth, as any mother, would want to have a strong and positive connection to her children. She wants us to be happy. She wants to nourish us, take care of us and naturally all life on and within the earth.

One aspect indigenous people all over the planet have always shared is that they seek to stay connected to the Mother Earth. Thus whenever they made a choice, they also looked at the impact it would have on the earth and all its life forms when creating something primarily for the benefit of human beings. In most cases, the inventions along the path of evolution were made to make life more comfortable for human beings, beginning with the wheel and the cart, to cars, showers and machines that work for us. Those inventions aren't necessarily bad, but they were made for people and their progress and comfort, not for the rest of life on the Mother Earth.

There are lots of examples where inventions ended up doing things that nobody had anticipated that had huge consequences and weren't thought through all the way. When people start to think in short-term frames rather than the time ahead, this can become dangerous and knock things out of balance, especially when the purpose is greed and power.

To me all these things have to do with the way of thinking. This has become polluted in itself, and then you end up creating things that pollute, creating things that are further and further away from their natural starting point. These products take long periods of time to degrade and release many toxins that in turn destroy the soil, the water and the air. It is a very negative cycle we have embarked upon.

Indigenous peoples, on the other hand, are taught to think seven generations ahead and think as caretakers for all life, not just for humans.

Let's throw in another thought. We need lessons to grow. Could it be that to keep getting those lessons, we are always changing, on the move, searching, creating? This part of human nature that is

restless, looking for what is beyond, paradoxically throws things
out of balance to come to a new balance?

Again, we have the choice how we grow: do we choose to learn the hard way and take detours or do we choose to learn gently? If a person is in a balanced state, his or her sensitivity is on a much higher level regarding everything that involves creation. So, you are also more sensitive to subtle teachings. You can always learn from most anything in Nature by just looking at it, being quiet, waiting.

Could it be that this whole journey with all the negative effects
that have come from industrialization, the abuse of our resources
and all the pollution are now creating a major climate change
that is needed for us to learn to make biodegradable plastic
bottles or move to green technology, for instance?

Once the choice was taken to go in that direction, it was necessary to bring it back into balance. We chose to learn the hard way. We could have chosen a very different evolution all along.

One of the things I often hear white people say when we talk about America before and after Columbus is that they claim they had a much more advanced society than we did. That isn't true. We were very advanced in certain areas, some tribes in the area of agriculture, for instance, other tribes in spiritual ways, etc.

And you can also look at it this way: what and why is it that a society looks for inventions? You could say it comes out of necessity. There is this sarcastic saying that "war is the mother of invention." I don't like it but there is a lot of truth to it. In North America, we did have some wars amongst tribes, but far fewer then over in Europe. We had more space for everybody and less need for invention.

To take this further: do you agree with the statement that since we are all part of Mother Earth, all part of Creation, that all these separate developments that have been going on for so long on the various continents were meant to meet at some point in history? Was it meant to be that invaders from across the ocean came to your homeland and had those devastating effects on the indigenous Native tribes and their cultures?

Well, honestly, I have asked that question many times myself.

Overall... I totally agree with the Way of Life of the indigenous peoples in North America, but there were some tribes that had negative habits or parts in their culture like slavery or hard punishments. These aspects could have gone in the same direction as in Europe and in other parts of the world. If we had been left alone without interference from outsiders, maybe this would have developed that way, who knows?

I have a lot of different thoughts about this whole issue. Why was it necessary for the Native people and the white people to meet? What did they have to learn from each other? Are there lessons for both of them?

As we were people who lived so close to Earth and Spirit, why did this have to happen to us? I have asked many elders for answers. A lot admit they don't really know. A common answer is that the white brother and sister went so far out of balance that Creator had to send them over to a place where this balance still existed. By wiping out the culture and civilization and causing so much destruction, they will have to face that and change it. I am not sure if that is all there is to it, because that still leaves the question: why us? What is our part in it, what did we need to learn?

I read somewhere that a Shoshone elder once said: "The white man doesn't know yet, but he has come to learn from us. Do not begrudge his presence here."[25]

And I ask myself if maybe this is a collective lesson humanity needed to learn?

Yes, it is a matter of getting into balance as a whole. We all have an effect on each other. This is true on a small scale just as much as from a collective perspective. If you take one person, they have many qualities: weaknesses, stronger points, beauty and difficult, darker sides. Nature seeks balance within to suit that particular being in the best way. Collectively, the same process is going on: any system strives for balance. It doesn't always happen peacefully. It just happens the way it happens.

If you embrace the concept of reincarnation, you may have been an indigenous person living in the jungle of South America or Africa, a woman living in China or a man living in Germany in another lifetime. We get to experience life from different positions and angles and can draw a much larger picture going back and forth in history.

If we realize it is not about being Native or non-Native, European, African or Asian, but really about our humanness and the condition of our hearts, we are all developing into the prophesized Rainbow people, the tribe of many colors. Since we have been going through all those cycles in different times, places and roles, in the end it comes down to living out our true nature.

---

25 *"Voices in Stones, Life Lessons from the Native Way" by Kent Nerburn*

Nowadays we can connect worldwide in ways that we never experienced before, and knowledge can surface that is recognized anew by more people than ever before.

The work at Nanish Shontie tapped into what you just said. We stated in our brochure and website the importance of both reconnecting to the old ways yet also incorporating them in our modern world. How can we live in today's world with a more positive way of thinking, and feeling re-connected to Nature and Spirit? We don't want to go back to the old days. We live in the now and there is a lot of good in it. We invited everybody with an open heart and open mind to come as long as they were respectful towards our ways. We aimed to work together because that will bring back balance.

I once heard an Indian guy say something really neat: "You know, it's not about dark fry-bread or light fry-bread.[26] We are just all fry-bread!" That is definitely a Native way of putting it.

There is a concept in psychology that calls victims and perpetrators, those who do the deed and those who suffer from this deed are part of the same problem. Actually, they cannot function without each other, and confirm each other's existence. They create a circle by co-existing and "needing" each other. According to this way of thinking, part of the healing is thus to step out of the victim role and stop belonging to that symbiotic system. The perpetrator no

---

26 Navajo frybread originated 144 years ago, when the United States forced Indians living in Arizona to make the 300-mile journey known as the "Long Walk" and relocate to New Mexico onto land that couldn't easily support their traditional staples of vegetables and beans. To prevent the indigenous populations from starving, the government gave them canned goods and white flour, processed sugar and lard—the makings of frybread. Frybread is revered by many as a symbol of Native pride and unity. The food's conflicting status—representing both perseverance and pain—reflects these same elements in Native American history. "Frybread is the story of our survival," says Sherman Alexie, director of the award-winning film *Smoke Signals*.

longer has a target to direct his or her energy towards and the harmful system dissolves.

Didn't Corbin Harney say this again and again? "We have to work together. There is no time for claiming "only for Native" or "not for white people.""

Corbin Harney was one of the most openhearted people I ever met. He said: "We have to get beyond our differences so that we can stand as one, act as one and be as one."

But we also have to see that in America a lot of healing still needs to be done. Many white Americans deny what has happened to our people and have no idea about the numbers, the enormity of the atrocities and the denial of our rights that still exists today. When you compare it to what has happened to the black people, you can see that a lot has been done there. Slavery is openly admitted to and written down in history books; it is spoken about publicly and the white people have apologized for it. Through this mechanism, a lot of healing has taken place, though I agree that it still needs more acknowledgement. Racism towards colored people still exists on many levels. Native people are waiting for such acknowledgment and rewriting of history books. There hasn't really been any major official recognition. Some mayors and other officials have made a few minor statements, and President Obama also made some efforts in that direction, more than any other president so far. Even if an apology was spoken, it was often hollow and there were no changes in the law and on a governmental level. Under President Trump, many decisions are unfortunately going backwards again.

Nevertheless, I prefer to have faith in the possibility of change for the better, and try to do my share to support and connect people just as Corbin Harney envisioned.

Let's talk about the concept of time in reference to balance. Humans like to have balance within a week or a year or at least

in a life-time, but since the concept of time is not present in the
spirit world, that really doesn't apply and shows our limited
perception. There are much bigger circles at stake here.

Exactly. I have always emphasized that spirits don't care about time.
It's just going to take as long as it takes. There were things that took a good
portion of my life before I was able to understand as something finally fell
into place. I was told spirits have a very different concept of time than we
do. Time doesn't count for Mother Earth, either.

I have heard stories of people who are able to really go into the spirit
world and come back. These stories speak about moving forwards and
backwards through time or covering large distances in our present time-
frame. They bring understanding for evolution and transformation in a
wider sense.

As Native people, you like to speak of the effects your behavior
has on the next seven generations. To my understanding, this
goes in both directions: we can also grasp those seven generations
in our own past.

Whatever we as a human family have done through all our life cycles,
we ended up here at this time. We have made choices again and again and
all those choices had a certain impact on life on the Mother Earth. They
have had consequences we live with now, not just for humans, but also for
all life forms.

I was taught that it is not so much what you do but more about *how* you
do things. Do you think of the next seven generations? Have you learned
from what happened in the past for better and for worse? If we make use
of all our creative possibilities in a good way and with a responsibility
towards all life for the coming generations, whether that goes for plastic,

cars, electricity or computers, then that is a positive thing. If we tie in the knowledge of the ancestors, there is a strong and positive foundation.

Maybe over time we can change those things that so far have had a negative impact on the Mother Earth and Life in all forms. We might find ways to turn harmful things like plastic or aluminum into something less harmful and more in balance. There are so many initiatives already going in that direction, like cars that do not pollute so much or different forms of renewable energies. The sad thing I am witnessing though, is that in many cases big corporations or even governments are hindering or even blocking such initiatives. I think when people start to speak up and say: "We no longer accept your need to control our lives," things could shift. But many times, the governments and those in power do not allow such initiatives of free will and independent thinking. They are afraid of losing their power, and hold on to it by suppressing anything new that challenges how they want to handle it.

Those who dare to speak up are on the front line and are sometimes sacrificed for the greater goal. Those in power do not realize that by suppressing these voices, they are actually adding to the energy that wants to naturally rise and change, to evolve. So, over time it repeats and now there are more people than ever involved who no longer accept how things are done. This process is continuing and, little by little, things are changing!

This belief has kept our people going through the ages, and I am happy to witness a positive revival of our culture. We were on the losing side for so many generations and for so long. It didn't look very positive for us as Native Americans, but we kept praying and having faith, and things are turning around for us.

When people have big plans, inventions or visions to create
something, they need focus to direct that energy to manifest what
they want. Yet while focusing, you often lose the bigger picture,
the wider view. Only later the awareness comes that something

along the way was forgotten, overlooked. In retrospect, one can say that something great was accomplished, but a price was paid, sacrifices were made. Here our human judgment comes in, where we justify and have opinions about whether something is a success and a "good" thing or whether what has been created is a "bad" thing.

Where do we draw the line? How do we define balance? What is appropriate in our judgments? How do we know if we are handling something in the best interest of all involved?

My answer is that we do not decide ourselves, but allow ourselves to be guided by Nature and Spirit. I know I'm repeating myself but this is what it comes down to: really listening carefully before acting and using your power. I am able to use my power to make rain, even if Mother Earth is not in need of it and it could actually be harmful to her. She is not able to prevent it from happening; she cannot stop it when power is used in such a way. This happens all the time on a bigger scale too with pollution and the abuse of resources. In the end though, Mother Earth will respond to it naturally as it gets further and further out of balance. She does things in her own way and in her own time.

There is a difference in how Mother Nature and the Spirit world help us. Nature is a neutral energy. There is no good or bad in this energy, it just is. Nature teaches us by example how things flow naturally, how things work together in harmony, how life moves in circles. This is about natural interaction; there is harmony even when one life needs another life to survive. The spirit world is more interactive with us humans. Spirits know how we function, what gifts lie within us, what our purpose in life is. They try and help us utilize those gifts and live according to our purpose. So both help us and guide us, but each with a different approach.

We have all aspects of nature in us: for example, the gentle flowing of a river, the song of a bird, the first morning sun rays, but also a powerful storm brewing, a volcano outburst. We can look at the volcano and see the damage it does, but afterwards fertile soil comes out of this mixture of ash and humus; renewal takes place. We must see that volcanoes only erupt once in a while and not on a regular basis. Sometimes a strong clearing is needed in order for something new to blossom. Yet we as humans shouldn't use that as a common way of handling situations. We can also reflect on how water smooths the surface of rocks over time and thereby changes their structure. They are different kinds of transformation. It is up to us how we relate to such teachings and implement them in our daily lives. Again, nature itself doesn't judge.

If you look at certain animals in nature, you see they kill to survive. If you look more closely, you realize the mountain lion goes for those animals that are already older or weak or sick. In this way it helps to create balance. They have a way of sensing; they can smell the old and sick ones. That is how balance is kept in a healthy way.

Humans make choices to act in a certain way that should be based on the knowledge present at that moment, that place, that situation. I make such choice from what feels right for me, with my background and cultural and upbringing that influence me. I prefer to follow the path that feels right for my heart. No matter what path we choose, we have to recognize we have an effect on Mother Earth and the life that is here. We are here to be caretakers with awareness and responsibility.

Human awareness evolved over time and needs to be developed as we go along. Part of life is to find our true nature that really fits us as a person, the part that belongs to us.

It is not about going back to the earlier days when everything was so-called 'better.' It is about living in today's world and being aware of our responsibility. Although we live in challenging times, it is also very exciting to live right now. We can witness people all over the planet with different life-styles, in different settings, in different circumstances. Some still live the rural way they did for thousands of years, some live in cities with the most modern technology supporting them, others are somewhere in between. It is all good and there is no need to be judgmental about it. What matters is: "Does your way of life fit you? Does it nourish you on all levels? Do you feel connected to your way of life? Does it make your heart happy?"

Mala Spotted Eagle Pope (1952-2019) grew up in Nevada in a traditional Native American household and is of Western Shoshone and Cherokee ancestry. He lived out in the desert for ten years, where he helped to oversee the Indian Camp Meta Tantay. He then worked as a drug- and alcohol counselor and committed himself to building Nanish-Shontie, a Native American-guided community in Oregon. Already an activist on behalf of environmental and Native issues in his younger years, he later started accompanying elders on their speaking tours. Over time, he was asked to do talks and workshops himself, going on extended trips through the USA and in Europe to help build bridges between cultures and peoples.

Hermine Schuring (1961), born in the Netherlands, has been living in Vienna, Austria for over 25 years. She runs her own physical therapy and energy work practice, and is a mother of two children. Traveling through the United States for two months in 1993, the harsh and troubled living conditions of Native Americans had a great impact on her. Fascinated by the people's unwavering resilience, she became drawn to their spiritual Way of Life. She met Mala Spotted Eagle in 1995 when he first came to Europe, and started supporting him on his speaking tours in Austria and the Netherlands, helping to spread his message by serving as an assistant and translator. A foundation was laid for a deep and special friendship that grew stronger over time –- regardless the geographic distance -- and has led to the writing of this book.